♦♦♦♦♦

ON JUSTICE

◆ ◆ ◆ ◆ ◆

L. E. GOODMAN

On Justice

AN ESSAY IN
JEWISH PHILOSOPHY

Yale University Press

New Haven and London

Set in Galliard Roman type by Marathon Typography Service, Inc., Durham, North Carolina. Printed in the United States of America by BookCrafters, Inc., Chelsea, Michigan.

Library of Congress Cataloging-in-Publication Data

Goodman, Lenn Evan, 1944–
    On justice : an essay in Jewish philosophy / L. E. Goodman.
        p.   cm.
    Includes bibliographical references and indexes.
    ISBN 0-300-04943-9
    1. Justice (Jewish theology)   2. Justice (Philosophy)   3. Philosophy, Jewish.
4. Justice—Biblical teaching.   I. Title.
BM645.J8G66   1991
181'.06—dc20   90-28896
                                                                CIP

The paper in this book meets the guidelines for permanence and durability of the Committee on Production Guidelines for Book Longevity of the Council on Library Resources.

                1   3   5   7   9   10   8   6   4   2

◆ ◆ ◆ ◆ ◆

CONTENTS

Contents

This book presents a theory of justice based on the concept of deserts. Unlike many familiar contract theories of justice, it does not assume that justice is an arbitrary convention. Rather, it derives its conception of what is just and unjust from a recognition of value in the beings to whom and by whom justice is to be done. I call the theory an ontological one because it finds its warrant in the very natures of beings themselves—in the claims they make for space, for life and expression of their characters, for recognition of their subjecthood. The argument is rooted in the assumption that being itself is a value and that the expressions of being warrant claims and establish deserts. In setting out my case, I seek to inform the argument not only from the traditional philosophic discussions of political, moral, and metaphysical issues in the West (and even a few from the East) but also from a sustained dialogue with the Jewish sources that have so enriched our ideas about justice, human and divine. Until very recently, one who wrote about such issues from the perspective of a secularized and sometimes deracinated Christianity was said to write as a philosopher. Others were expected to identify their distinctive cultural outlooks, and their work was expected to be descriptive if it addressed a universal audience, or parochial if it adopted a normative stance.

Fortunately, this is beginning to change. The new sensitivity to cultural diversity and to the richness that traditional cultures can bring to a genuinely cosmopolitan intellectual discourse has begun to allow scholars and thinkers who critically appropriate the materials of their own heritage, for the first time perhaps since the Hellenistic age, to address an ecumenical community in their own distinctive voices. Poets, novelists, directors, composers, choreographers, and all others concerned with the concrete expression of universal human ideals have felt the sea change, which spreads by now from Afghanistan and Ulan Bator to Fiji and Pago Pago but probably began with the black pride movement of the 1960s and its demand to reclaim a distinctive identity for Afro-Americans.

Argument itself is only as effective as the limits of its cultural horizon allow it to be. A typology that fails of comprehensiveness by dismissing or ignoring live options, options kept alive by an intellectual discourse beyond the cultural horizon of the would-be philosopher, is damagingly parochial, regardless of the aura of universality that an abstract idiom may impart. A discourse that has proceeded for centuries within a seemingly self-contained cultural and linguistic tradition like that of classical India or China may be *more* universal than many of our most abstract and sometimes rather scholastic discussions. It becomes so by virtue of the issues it addresses and the conceptual openness of its participants, stimulated, perhaps, by foreign ideas, or by internal dialectics that pose the radical questions which keep philosophy critically alive and growing.

The recent work of Alasdair MacIntyre has shown that just as philosophic theses become and remain philosophic only in the living context of argument, so philosophic arguments themselves attain full stature only within the context of a living tradition. It is here that philosophers draw their conceptions of what is and what is not problematic and thus define the broadest contours of their thinking. "What the Enlightenment made us for the most part blind to and what we now need to recover," MacIntyre argues, "is a conception of rational inquiry as embodied in a tradition, a conception according to which the standards of rational justification themselves emerge from and are part of a history in which they are vindicated by the way in which they transcend the limitations and provide remedies for the defects of their predecessors within the history of that same tradition."[1] First among the desiderata of contextualized philosophical inquiries into the moral, social, and political reasonings embedded in "tradition-constituted" inquiries, beyond those he himself has studied in detail, MacIntyre lists the need for an examination of the philosophic claims arising in the Judaic normative tradition (10–11). It is to such a discourse that I hope this book will make its contribution.

Epistemologists are coming increasingly to understand that the standards by which we judge rationality are many and complex. Increasingly, those standards are seen to be value standards, which diverse individuals in various cultural frameworks can respect or weight in divergent ways. Given the complexity of human experience and of the world which transcends that experience, it should not be surprising that a variety of constructions can be put upon what we know. The diversity of philosophical opinions, which Skeptics saw as the golden key to the triumph of ignorance, and which many philosophers since the Renaissance have seen as a scandal to the ambitions of reason, need be no more scandalous or problematic than the diversity of poetic, painted, or sculptural images in which artistic sensibilities seek to capture some aspect of truth out of the diversity and immensity before us. The real test of any construction is its fit to the experience it seeks to represent. For normative claims, this means above all that the real test is the practical application *in living* of any construct that ventures to propose advice about our ways of life. With this in mind, I say that a variety of reasoned accounts of nature, beauty, truth, or obligation, given the freedom to articulate their claims and to grow and develop in the nursery of their own cultural milieu, can contribute, in spite of their diversity, and indeed *through* their diversity, to a universally relevant human discourse or conversation.

No tradition is culture-tight or logic-tight. There is always the possibility of radical questioning from within and the challenge of imported knowledge from without. Stoicism would never have grown to the brilliant ethical, logical, and theological edifice it became had it not been for the constant badgering of Skeptics and Epicureans. Nor would Stoicism have arisen in the Greek world without the influx from the Middle East of ideas about moral responsibility, universal human dignity, divine providence, and the interconnectedness of all things—ideas that were largely unprecedented or previously undeveloped in Greek thought. The interaction and interpenetration of traditions allows and indeed demands critical testing of key assumptions and thus militates against any natural tendency of thought to come to rest in complacency, parochialism, scholasticism, or dogmatism. To foster such critical stimulation without lysing the values that sustain the integrity of distinctive traditions is in my view the vitally necessary task of comparative philosophical study.

Jewish thought has been stimulated from many quarters—from Greek philosophy, Islamic philosophy and *kalâm*, Renaissance humanism, the sciences, and many other sources. In no cultural or religious tradition can we equate originality with insularity or the illusion of incommensurability.

Preface

◆

The great Jewish thinkers have always known how to translate the significances they saw around them into the language of their hearers. This is true not just for Philo and his creative receptivity to Greek modes of argument and exposition, or for Maimonides and his ability to learn from and respond to the achievement of Islamic philosophers, scientists, and theologians. It can be traced back to the cosmopolitan milieu of early rabbinic thought, the Mediterranean world of the poets and prophets of ancient Israel, and even to the Mosaic rejection and appropriation, critical adaptation and redefinition of Egyptian, Canaanite, Babylonian, and Midianite laws and customs, myths, methods, and symbols.

The method I have adopted here is to work philosophically toward a conceptual solution of specific problems about justice, seeking to enrich and guide the philosophic inquiry with the resources of Western and Jewish philosophy and then to confront the solutions proposed both with their philosophic alternatives and with their counterparts from the Jewish canon, the biblical and rabbinic articulations of values and ideas which validate the Judaic authenticity of the conclusions commended philosophically. In provoking such a dialogue between the sources and the resources of philosophic thought, there will inevitably be some selectivity. Not every argument will raise the questions that seem most relevant, and not every text will lend itself to germane reflection. But the intent has been to inform exegesis with philosophy, and philosophy with the outcomes of exegesis. Rather than the impasse of a hermeneutic circle, I hope that the result is to cast some light on philosophic issues from an angle insufficiently relied on, and to show in turn how the sources speak to issues of universal human concern.

To discuss human deserts in isolation from any question about general deserts, or from questions of a larger pattern of justice beyond the one we seek in human relations, seems to me to involve an unnatural compartmentalization that would ultimately play false to human experience. It does no good to leave out of account questions about justice in history or nature, or cosmic questions about our expectations from God or the fairness of life, if we are only to revert to them obliquely, as so many do who dismiss these questions in positivistic terms but then fall back on the problem of evil as the trump argument against theism. So my scheme has been to conjoin questions about what we are to expect from one another and questions about what we deserve from life itself and from God. To maintain the unity of this discourse is to maintain the dialogue by which human value notions have informed and continue to inform our idea of the divine. That dialogue, in my view, has always and legitimately been a two-way conversation: The idea of the divine, even as we refine it, contributes to our understanding of values in general and of human justice in particular.

The first of my six chapters is definitional. It begins in seeking an understanding of the nature of justice by addressing the question of fairness in exchanges. Reaching beyond simple commercial transactions to the more fundamental relations among persons, I argue that the deserts of human subjecthood underlie all such relations and provide the necessary groundings which theories of contract and consent alone cannot provide. I take my text from Maimonides, who is dissatisfied, as the Torah is, with the idea that justice, considered as a virtue, can be adequately understood in terms of the mere execution of our formal obligations—let alone exaction of our formal entitlements.

Far from being mere ornaments of more basic and more primitive relations, such values as kindness, courtesy, consideration, trust, civility, and understanding are presupposed even in the most elemental exchanges. It is here, in the recognition of the primacy of the moral over the conventional, the personal over the impersonal, the existential over the merely stipulative, that I lay the foundation of my general theory of deserts, which derives the entitlements of all things from their being and scales legitimated deserts to the equilibrated resultant of all claims. I argue from the goodness of being itself, the superiority of something over nothing, and the desirability of maximizing the realization of all things. I argue also from the absence of anything other than being on which any claim could be founded. For there is not anything other than being. Each being makes its claims in an environment, and all claims deserve to be honored, to the extent that they do not infringe on higher or equivalent claims. But the claims of persons have a special standing, both because all moral agents are subject to the demands persons make and because the claims of persons can be reconciled by conscious intent, generating the possibility of a community as the natural framework in which deserts are recognized.

Community, I argue, is antecedent in time and in legitimacy to formal normative claims; these rest upon it and cannot without circularity be used to warrant it. Spinoza's response to Hobbes and Machiavelli and his alternative to the Lockean approach are crucial here. Analyzed with the aid of Mendelssohn's subtle exegesis, that approach guides us to an alternative to the conventionalism that grew from the thinking of Epicurus and the Sophists and still dominates much of political and social thinking in the West. In this context, I argue that equity does not found but rests upon desert.

Preface

Earned desert is only one component of a subject's deserts; one does not need to earn once over the right to what one has earned.

The Torah's provisions for the needs of the poor, the stranger, the helpless, and the dispossessed show us, as Hermann Cohen argued, that beyond the biblical concern for replacing lawlessness with law lies a higher and more demanding concern with guiding civility toward fellowship. As Maimonides shows, such a concern is not merely a supererogatory interest of the Law but a constitutive aim in the Torah's project of seeking our moral betterment. Citing the key biblical and rabbinic texts, I argue that the Torah's interest here is not utopian but practical. For the legislation does not presuppose a transformed human nature, although it does seek to aid us in attaining a moral transformation in ourselves, not merely as individuals but as a community.

The second chapter seeks to discover the moral foundations of punishment. Can punishment be just if it curtails the interests of beings? Can a theory that holds all deserts to be positive, since they are expressions of the very being of things, warrant punishing wrongful acts? Or is punishment simply a melancholy necessity of diminishing some human deserts for the sake of others? On the contrary, and in keeping with the Maimonidean admonition that there is no true compassion but only a fatuous cruelty in attempting simply to abolish punishment, I argue that punishment responds to an affront against civil trust and represents a scaling back of social amenity closer to a level demonstrated to be appropriate by specific acts.

Utilitarian theories of deterrence and idealistic programs of reform lack the restraints and recognitions of desert (including residual desert) that a properly retributive account of punishment affords. But, in keeping with the systematic usage of the biblical text, retributive punishment must be sharply distinguished from the expressive or destructive passions of vengeance and war. There is no benefit to be gained and indeed only dire harm to be reaped from the confusion of retributive punishment with vindictiveness. One strength of the theory offered here, I believe, is that it successfully removes from the idea of punishment the vindictive sting that in the minds of many advocates and detractors is organic to the very concept of retribution.

In the third chapter I raise the question whether human life is somehow lacking in a way that makes it more an imposition than a gift. Does justice demand that we be recompensed for the life we lead? Taking up the deontological and teleological conceptualizations of moral obligation, I show that both exclude any claim upon extrinsic rewards. Yet both, explicitly if paradoxically, insist on unbounded rewards, recompense far beyond the confines of nature. The internal inconsistency of the two traditionally opposed standpoints, as I see it, reflects the artificial self-impoverishment that arises from their polarization and their resultant abstracting away from one another's partial if overstated truths. To remedy the needless thinning of moral discourse in both reductive teleological and strictly deontological moral theories, I call upon the more holistic thinking articulated in the biblical vignettes of the good life and explicit advice of the talmudic and later rabbis. These aid in the recapturing of the idea of obligation as blessing and blessing as obligation.

The Torah's distinctive claims in behalf of the goodness of this life are highlighted by the comparison of the biblical eudaimonism and the allied conceptions of Plato, Aristotle, and Cicero, with the polarized alternatives represented by the Stoics and Kant on the one hand and the Epicureans and Utilitarians on the other. Biblical eudaimonism, developed graphically in the prophetic, poetic tableaux of the good life and instituted through the symbols and practices that seek to establish the good life, does not divorce the moral life from the simple goods of human happiness, or seek to define that happiness without reference to the moral virtues or the open-ended spiritual quest. The impact of the argument is to demonstrate the irrelevance to the concerns of justice of claims upon a transtemporal reward. The real reward of good living is found in the living itself.

The fourth chapter asks directly whether life is fair. Each of us, I think, has always got the sense of some unfinished business that we carry about to be settled with God, and this chapter seeks to sort out the reasons for that sense of lack or grievance and to raise the question of our entitlements from God or life itself. My answer is framed in terms of an appreciation of the grace involved in existentiation, but also in terms of the dynamic of being, which allows room for error and even for excessive claims but visits the consequences of all claims upon those that make them—metaphysically, through the self-definition implied in any action, and causally, through the natural impacts over time of any act or choice upon the doer.

History, psychology, and individual experience are called to witness as the arenas in which each individual may seek confirmation or disconfirmation of the dynamics outlined here, dynamics which are a central theme of the Mosaic view of destiny and human experience, what the Torah calls the laws of life. While no individual can answer in another's behalf the question "Is life fair?" I show in this chapter that the answer to such a question depends ultimately on the possibility of meaningful actions within life, and the affirmation which the chapter makes is based upon the reality of that possibility.

The fifth chapter addresses the Jewish conception of the messianic age. For it is through the messianic idea that Jewish thinkers traditionally voice their conception of the values adequate to justify and bind together into a unified and meaningful sequence the actions and sufferings of history. I locate the significance of the Jewish messianic idea neither in the programs of social or economic reform that reductive accounts take to be its ultimate meaning nor in the apocalyptic subversion of nature which has been seen as portending its ultimately revolutionary significance. Rather, drawing on the biblical, rabbinic, and classical philosophic sources of Judaism, I find the Jewish concept of the messianic age to intend the transformation of our moral nature. The messianic age, as the authentic and responsible Jewish sources portray it, represents the fulfillment of the objectives of the Torah, when Israel attains the character held forth by the Torah and the nations of the world, inspired by Israel's example, learn to live in peace and harmony. The transformation requires no departure from the order of nature, and the rabbinic sages caution against such expectations. But the universal moral change that the idea of such an age does involve originates in no more (but no less) miraculous a movement than the inward transformation of every human heart.

The final chapter addresses the question of an afterlife, in which alone many believe that the only real justice can be found. I argue that such a conception is not only foreign to the central outlook of the Torah, but even antithetical to it. The demand for an afterlife involves a denial of the adequacy of God's creation and a rejection of the biblical claim that the good life is possible for us here and now, through allegiance to the precepts and practices of the Torah. I argue against the notions of reincarnation and eternal punishment and urge, in keeping with themes suggested biblically and rabbinically and developed by philosophers from Halevi and Maimonides to Spinoza and beyond, that we understand immortality in terms of the dimensions of transcendence open to us in this world. The book concludes with a brief anatomy of some of these dimensions, sketching some of the activities that open them to us within this human life.

The overall theme of the book, argued in some detail in what follows, is that the being or power or *conatus* of each individual that exists makes a claim that is validated if it is not countered by some other claim; the being or project or power of each person makes a claim that no other moral subject can ignore. Joined together in community, the claims of persons enhance rather than undermining one another and provide a basis for the progressive amelioration of the human condition. The possibility of such amelioration is what gives meaning to our lives and allows us to make the judgment that existence is a gift and that life itself is fair and worthwhile. It is upon our existential interdependence for the furtherance of our human personhood that we found our natural communities. It is upon such communities in turn that we found our formal, societal institutions and all our social customs, understandings, and conventions. The goal of all such institutions is the optimal recognition of all deserts; this function delineates the scope and boundaries of their legitimacy.

It is my pleasant duty to acknowledge David Patterson, who first encouraged me to execute my plan to write *On Justice*. Although it is meant to be read as an independent work, the book takes up where my earlier study, *Monotheism*, left off. *Monotheism* represented the text of the Baumgardt Lectures I gave at Oxford as the first winner of the American Philosophical Association's Baumgardt Memorial Fellowship. *On Justice* carries forward an argument that I began in the Littman Lectures, delivered at Oxford on the invitation of Dr. Patterson, the founding President of the Oxford Centre for Post Graduate Hebrew Studies. I also express my thanks for the care and concern of the anonymous readers who read this book for Yale and made valuable suggestions about its penultimate draft. As for my own advisory scholars, they need not remain anonymous. David Novak and Menachem Kellner read the text and candidly shared with me the fruits of their wisdom and learning, as they have done so often in the past. Jonathan Westphal and Kenneth Kipnis read good chunks of it and gave me detailed and concrete suggestions about my treatment of Rawls in particular. Thanks are due also to my colleagues, family, and friends, who gave many helpful suggestions as I worked; and, as always, to the people of Hawaii, among whom I have been privileged to live and work as a philosopher since 1969. My wife, Madeleine, took time from her own professional duties to read the whole manuscript more than once, offering warm encouragement and valuable suggestions. And my mother read the final version carefully and appreciatively, making regular comments on each section she completed. I thank her and my father, who read over her shoulder and now can savor the completed whole. The Yale editors, Charles Grench and Caroline Murphy, have shown an accustomed professionalism, which stunningly combines appreciation of broad themes with meticulous attention to detail. Special thanks to F. Glenn Avantaggio and Terrence Dunford for their care and industry in helping me prepare the indexes and to Daniel Glatzer and James A. Stroble for assisting me in checking the citations. This book is dedicated in friendship to David Novak, scholar, thinker, and leader.

LENN E. GOODMAN

Honolulu, 1991

CHAPTER ONE

Toward a Theory of Justice

Consider the logic of exchange. Exchange relations, as anthropologists like to call them, form the basis of trade, but also of much gift giving, hospitality, family, and even international relations. The logic of exchange is often thought to be central to the institution of punishment and to the legitimacy of the state. For criminals are said to pay a debt when they are punished, and loyalty to the state and its laws is said to be owed in return for benefits accrued. What makes an exchange fair or unfair, a relationship just or unjust?

The syntax is one of symmetry. We look for balance — physical, fiscal, actuarial. Reciprocity lies at the heart of fairness. Yet there is more to reciprocity than mere equivalences, and more to justice than reciprocity. Clearly our fictions about the "repayment" a convict makes portray a bit too graphically a rather more complex reality. And the delicate dynamics of understandings and undertakings that make for justice or injustice in a family or a friendship are not to be mistaken for mere sales or swaps. Even a sale, to be fair, involves more than the exchange of goods of equivalent worth. To begin with, it should be voluntary. And a government can hardly claim to be just if it lacks the consent of the governed. But I shall argue that even consent is not always necessary and is by no means sufficient as a guarantee of justice.

The theory of justice I shall propose is ontological. It rests on what I shall call a general theory of deserts. Founding justice on the natures of the beings to whom or by whom justice is done, it seeks to avoid many of the difficulties of theories which assume that justice is a matter of convention. The paradigm for my theory and the project for its practice are embedded in the Mosaic Law. I take my text from near the end of Maimonides' *Guide*, where the Rambam, developing a suggestion made by Aristotle, distinguishes the moral virtue of justice (*tzedakah*) from the mere doing of justice, the fulfilling of one's formal obligations:

> The word *tzedakah* derives from *tzedek*, which means fairness. Fairness is imparting what is due to any possessor of a right and giving to every being according to its deserts. But the books of the prophets do not call it *tzedakah* in the ultimate sense merely to fulfill your obligations toward others. For if you pay a worker his wages or repay a debt, that is not called *tzedakah*. Duties you assume toward others that distinguish and enhance your character, like mending the hurts of all who are injured—these are what are called out as the virtue of justice. That is why it says (Deuteronomy 24:13) of returning a pawned item to the poor: "This will be *tzedakah* for you." For when you live a life of moral excellence you are doing justice to your own rational soul, giving it *its* due.[1]

THE BASIS OF EXCHANGE

The structure of exchange is one of equality, but not merely of equality. I give you this in exchange for that. If we agree, we both must find what we receive in the exchange, or from its taking place, more valuable to us than what we give. Otherwise we would act without a motive. If one of us does not agree, there is no exchange; there may even be reason to believe that one of us has been robbed or cheated. What did we deserve? The equivalent, surely, of what we gave. Yet both of us desired and in a sense received more than what we gave. For we did not simply exchange identical items. There was a diversity of goods and needs, so each of us could receive more than he gave up. What you gave is worth more to me than what I gave. But if scarcity is the basis of this worth, how can exchange be fair?

If I hold a gun to your head and take your wallet, I have given nothing yet received your money. In a perverse sense I have given *more* than I received—spared your life and gotten only your wallet. Hostages when ransomed are given back their freedom. What could be more valuable to them than that? This is what Cicero calls *beneficium latronum*, the bounty of thieves, "who take credit for bestowing life on those they did not kill."[2] Kidnappers impose the conditions in which such exchanges seem advantageous. But exchange, to be fair, must be free. The problem is that all actual exchanges seem to take place in a context of constraint. If I could get what I want without payment—for the asking, say—or for a lower price, it is argued that I would hardly be willing to offer what you ask. A withholding of goods or services from sale below your price is critical in the setting of that price. Even necessities I badly need I cannot secure in the market without force or fraud if I do not meet your terms, or someone's.

The freest exchange, then, seems to involve an element of coercion, your holding back until your price is met or the market tested to see if your price will hold. As people like to say, each party's freedom depends on the other's constraint. What you sell is given under conditions of constraint, although there has been no active deception or positive coercion; and the degree of effective constraint is limited by the accessibility of alternative sources of supply. For you do not simply trade with me but trade from a position of freedom and security to withhold your goods, forcing me either to meet the market or not buy at all. If there is equity here, it is in the reciprocity of my power and that of others to withhold our goods too, if we can. All of us in a sense must value what we get more than what we give if exchange is to occur, but any of us might gladly have paid less or nothing had we not been constrained, in part by conditions we impose on one another.

I say "*might* gladly have paid" and "*in a sense* must value" because this familiar sort of talk presumes shrewd dealers eager to buy cheap and sell dear. Enter charity or social motives into the equation and the character of what is balanced alters strikingly. Suppose philanthropy or fellow feeling, curiosity, custom, love, ambition, or simply generosity or surplus move me not to seek all I can obtain with minimal outlay. In such conditions I may give freely what I perceive you need, not hold back or drive a hard bargain. Such a stance is often called irrational. But is it? One contention of this book is that without the virtue of justice, in the special sense that Maimonides assigns it, the barest practice of equity becomes unworkable.

THE IDEA OF COMMUNITY

In families parents provide for their children, or are expected to do so, on the basis of need and capability. Spouses likewise. Members of tribes and clans often share food or labor and engage in elaborate exchanges of capital—consumable (for example, cattle) and non-consumable or nominal (land, the stone money of Yap, works of art)—following patterns[3] that are highly regulated and clearly comprehensible by reference to the standards that govern them but more or less unintelligible in terms of maximizing economic gain by ego. In some exchanges reciprocity is structural or attitudinal rather than material. There is a symmetry, perhaps, but not always a material proportionality, still less an equal barter. Friends, family members, tribal comrades are not expected to return the material equivalent of what they receive but to live up to certain roles. Only metaphorically is this called repayment. Where expectations are disappointed and benefits are withheld, rarely are the sanctions equilibrated to the immediate material losses. Rather, shame and ostracism, symbolic or actual restraint of access to the community whose unseen sinews have been jangled, are the familiar responses, answering not to the loss of goods but to the abrogation of roles. When Plato puts into the mouth of the laws the argument that one owes allegiance to the state, to the point of death, in gratitude for benefits received (*Crito* 50e), he is, as the laws' analogy of paternity makes clear, describing the special structure of a role, not the balance sheet of a transaction.

In punishment and reward, as in trade, there is again a question of equivalences. Naively, and on the model of trade, this means reversal of positions: One should be "done by" as one has "done by" others—the slayer shall be slain, the mutilator mutilated, the benefactor benefited. The return may be notional—the public benefactor is praised or honored, the malefactor disgraced. Sometimes the symbols take on the autonomy we call poetic justice, as in the satisfaction of seeing a schemer hoist with his own petard. But it may be brutally literal and concrete, or expressionistic —as in some canons of "rational" justice where the rapist is castrated,[4] the thief's hand or the slanderer's tongue cut off—

> The advertising quack who bothers with tales of countless cures
> His teeth, I've enacted, shall all be extracted by terrified amateurs.

The power of symbolic sentencing[5] lies in the imagination; its presumed efficacy is exemplary, hence deterrent. Since deterrence is thought to depend on the saliency of an image, it seems to put a premium on *disproportion*: the thief stole not a hand but a loaf of bread or purse of coins. There is a similar premium on disproportion with exemplary rewards, the glittering prizes of another age contrived to instill emulous zeal and carelessness of death—one's own or that of others.

WHAT IS RATIONALITY IN EXCHANGE?

Draconian laws and feudal boons show the same imbalance as the maxim of shrewd trade: Valuing tranquillity above the general desert, some states place pomp, or the display of terror in keeping the peace, above the deserts of a populace who stand to be harried or pilloried or saddled with the price of splendid public benefactions. The analogy with trade is telling. For we are used to the principle that justice itself requires mercy; we have largely given up open boasting about excesses in the penal system and find means of concealing the weightiest public extravagances, even while subtly advertising them. But in commerce we remain rather open in our admiration of excess under the name of savings or profit. Perhaps we are too readily convinced by Mandeville's bees that avarice will serve the common good. For plainly a society based on concupiscence is unwholesome. Its consummation is an ethos founded on friendlessness. Would-be followers of Spencer or Marx are wrong to imagine that from civil oppression or economic exploitation (even national self-exploitation) the improvement of the race or the happiness of a people can emerge. Social inequity produces only complacency in its intended beneficiaries, anger in its victims, and disharmony in society at large.[6] The recent and still unfolding events in Eastern Europe and in China show that it yields instability as well—that is, that it is self-undermining.

Adam Smith and Karl Marx concur in treating economic gain as the constitutive yardstick of social progress. To the liberal it seems self-evident that to augment wealth in a free market is to augment welfare: Wealth becomes power to secure the objects of desire, and a free market allows free choice of those objects. Public health and safety, and even the interests of the environment, are all too easily immolated on this altar. To the Communist, also, the appropriation of wealth by labor is not merely the symbol but the means of overcoming all alienation: "The proletariat will use its political supremacy to wrest by degrees all capital from the bourgeoisie, to centralize all instruments of production in the hands of the state, i.e., of the proletariat organized as the ruling class, and to increase the total of productive forces as rapidly as possible. Of course, in the beginning this cannot be effected except by means of despotic inroads" (*Communist Manifesto* II). The temporary compromise of principle—ultimately a betrayal of the humanistic values in whose name revolution was called forth —becomes a permanent institution in Communist societies, principally because the socio-economic goals of revolution, assimilated to its political goals, are made permanent and absolute arbiters of value. No mere concern for human rights or dignities can withstand so imperious an aim. Humane values are expected to blossom once economic goals are achieved. But the dominance of the economic leaves little room for their definition and no room for their sanctity. Since economic relations are assumed to be foundational, all moral, metaphysical, social malaise is taken as merely symptomatic of an unsound economic system and expected to vanish once that system has been put down. It became necessary for an Adam Schaff to be expelled from the Party for the heresy that some forms of alienation might survive even when economic exploitation was overcome. "Hunger and want," he wrote, "are not the only widespread social causes of unhappiness. . . . The deprivation of freedom is as strong an incentive to revolt."[7]

Plainly, to adopt a strictly economic test of social progress precludes the ultimacy of higher goals, without whose achievement economic welfare is itself an empty gain. The Western nations, in the aftermath of the moral slumbers of our adolescent growth spurt, the Industrial Revolution, have begun to recollect that adequate social, moral, political, intellectual, and environmental relations are part of what must be computed in the bottom line. The dignity of the family and the sanctity of friendship are prime examples of the values that economic yardsticks cannot measure but must be measured by. Indeed Aristotle saw in disinterested friendship a crucial test of virtue; and in that fellowship which diffuses the social bond that friendship renders intimate, he saw not merely a paradigm for society but its very foundation. For fellowship in general and friendship in particular offer goods distinguishable from (not necessarily opposed to) the gains that acquisitive thinking equates with rationality. When Marx, in the *Communist Manifesto*, castigated bourgeois marriage as prostitution he overlooked the sources from which disgust with prostitution springs. Despite the Marxian myth, they are clearly not mercantile. The argument that would make them so is circular, presupposing the very proprieties it seeks to account for. Rather, the revulsion is moral. It stems from the same unnamed source as Marx's anger at the alienation of labor: the moral roots that ground the zeal of the ancient prophets of Israel and are clearly discernible in the Mosaic Torah.

The Torah aims at the construction—the constitution—not only of a society (*Gesellschaft*) but of a community (*Gemeinschaft*). Its central, thematic interpersonal law is that of fellowship—*love thy fellow*—from which all the rest are said to be derived, not that they are reducible to it or deducible from it, but in the sense that they are its applications—its interpretations, as Hillel put it. The term *re'akha*[8] does not mean 'thy neighbor'. Rather, it means 'thy fellow,' but the regard it evokes is not restricted to Israelites. As Maimonides notes (*Mishneh Torah*, Laws of Ethics, 6.4, 55a), the stranger is clearly and explicitly included among those one is enjoined to love. Indeed, Hermann Cohen's recognition of the parallel structure of the commandments to love the stranger and to love our fellows shows us that the commandment to love our fellows is generalized from the commandment to love the stranger—and paradigmatically, to love the Egyptian.[9] Observe the sequence:

> Thou shalt not disdain the Egyptian, for thou wast a stranger in his land (Deuteronomy 23:8)

> Thou shalt not persecute the stranger, for ye know the heart of the stranger, since ye were strangers in the land of Egypt (Exodus 23:9)

> Thou shalt not vex or wrong the stranger, for you were strangers in the land of Egypt; nor shall ye vex any widow or orphan (Exodus 22:20–21)

> Thou shalt not distort the justice due to the stranger, or to the fatherless; nor take the widow's clothes as pawn, but shalt remember that thou wast a slave in Egypt (Deuteronomy 24:17–18; cf. 27:19)

> You shall love the stranger, for ye were strangers in the land of Egypt (Deuteronomy 10:19)

> Thou shalt love thy fellow as thyself (Leviticus 19:18).

The movement is pedagogic, not historical but moral: from immediacy to universality, but also from analogy to principle, to application. The widest formulation states the moral law in universal terms but embeds it, at the very point of its generalization, in a concrete moral code:

> You shall be holy, for I the Lord thy God am holy. Each of you shall revere his father and his mother, and ye shall keep my sabbaths. . . . And when ye reap the harvest of your land thou shalt not reap fully to the edges of thy field or gather the gleanings of thy harvest, or pick thy vineyard bare, or gather its fallen fruit, but leave them for the poor and for the stranger. I am the Lord. You shall not steal or cheat or deceive one another, or swear falsely by My name . . . nor exploit thy fellow so as to despoil him. A worker's wage shall not stay with thee overnight. Thou shalt not curse the deaf or place a stumbling block before the blind. . . . You shall not render an unfair judgment, showing deference to the little or honoring the great, but shalt judge thy fellow in justice. Thou shalt not go about with calumnies among thy people nor stand by idly when thy fellow's blood is shed. . . . Do not hate thy brother in thy heart but reprove thy comrade and do not commit a sin because of him. Do not take vengeance or bear a grudge against any of your people, but love thy fellow as thyself. I am the Lord. (Leviticus 19:2–18)

Maimonides teaches, again with Cohen his disciple, that love of the stranger is predicated on the love of God. Clearly the love of strangers is the prime test of morality, since strangers are by definition the least of all humanity connected to ourselves by any overt or explicit social bond, and the most dependent on the categorical requirements of the moral law, which are emphatically referred to God's authority—*I am the Lord*—and underscored by the direct assertion, cited by the Rambam, that God *loveth the stranger* (Deuteronomy 10:18). The Law is teaching *re'ut*, fellowship—a mutuality of concern extended to strangers as the paradigm, in Cohen's terms, of the fellow man. It stands in sharp contrast to the formal reciprocity of market relations as conventionally understood, whereby the first person seeks to maximize his gains, minimize those of the second, and ignore the interests of the third. As members of a community, others become second selves, their interests integrated. I meets thou, in Buber's language, and there emerges a still more remarkable term, we.

KATZYA AND ALEXANDER

A telling illustration of the social ideal that lies behind the Mosaic Law is contained in the rabbinic story of a fanciful meeting between Alexander the Great and the legendary King Katzya, ruler of a fabular land beyond "the dark mountain." The visiting Alexander bypassed Katzya's gold and silver but wished to see "your customs, your behavior, and how you administer justice." The conqueror then watched while King Katzya heard a case between the buyer and seller of a field in which hidden treasure had been found. Each disclaimed the treasure, not having bargained for it in the sale. After hearing their briefs, the king found that one man had a son and the other a daughter. He arranged their betrothal to one another and bestowed the trove on them. Alexander, laughing, was asked how he would have ruled on such a case in his own land. "I would have executed both of them and confiscated the treasure." So King Katzya set out a meal all of gold. When Alexander objected that he did not eat gold, the king exclaimed, with an imprecation: "Why then do you love it so?" He then asked whether the sun shone and the rain fell in Alexander's country and whether there were livestock there. On hearing that there were, he exclaimed, again with an imprecation, "Why then it is only by the desert of those cattle that you survive!"[10]

Some comments on the story: Alexander desires to observe customs and behavior, the ethos of the people as well as the justice of their king. The case he witnesses provides all three. For the "claimants" have gone to court to avoid acquiring what is not theirs by right. Such a claim bespeaks the level of popular morality in King Katzya's land. There is a nexus, moreover, between the king's justice and the social ethos, as in Plato's model of social reform: It is because the people live under just and humane institutions that they acquire habits of generosity which in turn allow the law to adopt a rather relaxed stance toward the protection of property and an optimistic outlook toward the forming of new families. King Katzya can presume the prospective bride and bridegroom suited to one another because he observes the virtue of their fathers. He infers the want of merit in Alexander's people from the palpable avarice and life-denying mores of their king, whose values must reflect those of his subjects, as theirs reflect his. The norms of King Katzya's realm are not required by the Torah, yet they are not alien to its aims. His kingdom is utopian, lying beyond a mysterious mountain and into the meta-geography of legend. But it represents the ideal the Torah pursues, the theme that orients its social legislation.

The gold in the story is not irrelevant. Prosperity is a natural consequence of an unselfish social ethos. Nor is it irrelevant that Katzya speaks as Alexander's political equal and moral superior. As Plato urged (*Republic* IV 422), the just society will be strong, autonomous, self-reliant in war and peace. But "Alexander," a tyrant on the Roman model, judges as though gold rather than life were cardinal—hence his being given gold to eat, contrasted with the life-promoting judgment of the king. King Katzya does not state that rainfall and sunshine are consequences of moral desert. Rain falls and the sun shines on the worthy and worthless alike. But, echoing Jonah (4:11), the king allows himself the inference that if nature is bountiful in the land this Alexander rules it cannot be for the sake of its human inhabitants. Their actions show that they do not deserve natural bounty and cannot profit from it. The desert that would justify such bounty in the divine economy, if not found in the moral merit of human beings, must lie in the mere claim to existence made by every creature. In other words, it must belong to beasts—hence the imprecation.

DESERT AND CONSENT

In any exchange there are at least two sets of subjective expectations. Interposed between the two in the biblical system of ethics is a third, objective notion, that of desert (*zekhut*). When justice is reduced to subjective equity, consent becomes the sole determinant of fairness. There is in general no better measure accessible to us of the subjective worth of a good or the subjective desirability of an exchange than the participants' consent to it. But consent, although a necessary condition of fairness in many contexts, is not a necessary condition of justice in every context and is never a sufficient condition of fairness.

SOME LIMITATIONS OF CONSENT

Consent is not a necessary condition of justice. For a minor, a mental incompetent, a person in a coma, unborn, missing or presumed dead, may be treated justly or unjustly without reference to personal consent. Virtual consent is a fiction: We do not know what a non-competent or absent subject would have wanted in the most crucial contexts where such notions are employed, since the person affected generally has not experienced the circumstances about which decisions must be made. Even the virtual consent that liberal theorists rely upon as the foundation of all laws seems not to be a universally necessary condition of justice. For courts can do justice even to those who would never consent, say, to the rule of the majority or the institution of penal laws. Dissent is not sufficient to render all laws unjust.

Consent, moreover, is not a sufficient condition of justice. A whole society might consent implicitly (by acquiescence) or explicitly (by regularly repeated solemn oaths, Nuremberg rallies, Hate weeks, ceremonies of cannibalistic rededication and "renewal") to live under all sorts of conditions which they themselves and others recognize to be unjust. They might choose such conditions, work, fight, and die for them—for an unsafe and unhealthful environment, for example. The phenomenon is not so alien to history that its mention should seem surprising or so unfamiliar that the equation of consent with justice should seem obvious.

Many propositions gain consent although they are unfair. In pursuit of fame or wealth, we might accept inordinate risks, disproportionate to the potential gains; and some risks are too great to warrant any gain. Many buyers might be found for dollar tickets in a lottery with unfair odds. Their decisions are not in every case irrational. Some might have good reason to gamble at high odds for high stakes, despite the disproportion. But the game would remain unfair, inherently, although consent was given without duress or deception. Curiously, the more tickets sold without the prize being augmented, the more unfair the game becomes. Popular sovereignty does not determine justice here. Free consent does not obviate questions about whether an arrangement is exploitative, destructive, or corrupt. Even in a lottery with honest odds it seems unjust to allow bettors to stake their entire fortunes. Acrobats have long ago rebelled against the expectation that they test their skills without a net. But amateur and professional football players, for example, continue to take large risks. Can we say that no choice they may make is unfair to themselves or others as long as it is informed and uncoerced? Or must we disqualify as irrational all materially harmful choices made by demolition derby drivers, stunt artists, or auto racers? Can we call it fair to sell carcinogenic addictive drugs to adults, provided only that they have been warned of the risks and are not coerced into buying? Generally adults are deemed to consent rationally if they know what they are about and might choose otherwise. Second guessing another's standards is illiberal. But many choices meet the liberal criteria which do seem to wrong the chooser.

Young athletes were not told in the 1970s that in America nine out of ten varsity football players each year sustained an injury, that one hundred thousand high-school and college students annually were injured seriously in school sports, or that fourteen in a typical year were injured fatally. By the late 1980s the high-school injuries improved to one in three; but 11 percent of the injuries were major and over 16 percent were moderate, requiring from eight to twenty-one days' exclusion from the sport.[11] Yet even when fully informed, many student athletes would doubtless heed peers and parents, the lure of scholarships, the éclat of athletic prowess, and the distant chance of wealth and glory as professional athletes. Legally most have no capability of rational choice when they first embark on this course. But their aspirations and spirits are high; even as adults, fully informed and capable of choice, many choose a risk which others might not deem rational but which they themselves would not think it rational to pass by. The same is true with volunteering for hazardous service or answering Achilles' dilemma of a long dull life or a short brilliant one. No formulaic, mechanical calculus will reveal the outcome of rational choice in such situations. Some choosers are more generous with their little store of strengths than others are. It would seem incongruous to claim a priori that no one is ever too generous, more generous than one has any right to be.

We look for consent as a pragmatic mark of fairness. Behind that consent there must be some objective equity.[12] In a regular market, an index of equity is readily found by comparing one transaction with the rest; the subjective worth assigned a good by others is an objectifying benchmark. But we cannot assume that every price paid in a market is the price that ought to have been paid. A market, after all, is a statistical summation submerging quite a range of variation, and a mean is an abstraction ignoring all sorts of motives and conditions. A free market is a marvelous device, capable of elaborate and complex adjustments to its imbalances. It can put persons who might never be prepared to recognize their equality in more generalized or intimate relationships on an equal footing. That is the beauty of an impersonal mechanism—and its danger. Oversupply can make a market into a highly effective moral tutor, putting former exploiters in the position of their erstwhile victims and teaching a primary moral lesson. For moral recognition is founded, in experiential terms, on the reciprocity of roles. But, like experience at large, the market is rarely a kindly teacher. It can show us our interdependence and so allow the awakening of moral interest and recognition. But it does not itself accord that recognition. No one can claim that markets, with all their delicacy of response (whether their behavior is compared with that of engines or that of crowds), take a personal regard for the individual interests that create them.

In conditions of scarcity, sharp dealing can operate as a tacit conspiracy in restraint of trade to maintain high prices by withholding goods of limited availability. In other conditions, similar dealing can drive down prices and foster not only efficiency but invidious and destructive labor and production practices; diminished standards of quality, product safety, and reliability; and pockets or great satchels of unfree conditions—all of this demanded even if not directly acknowledged in the dynamics of the free market itself. Scarcity is not a rare, exceptional, or recent phenomenon. All market goods exist in limited supply, and often demand exceeds supply. Some would-be buyers of necessary goods may be priced out of a market and others gouged or made accomplices in injustices ranging from the maintenance of unsafe and unhealthful working situations to the destructive or dehumanized exploitation of labor to the pollution of the environment and the irreversible extinction of its resources, econiches, and potentials.

This being so, additional standards of worth beyond a simple, consensual market price are relevant in the evaluation of fair exchange—in spite of the fallibility of human judgment and the dangers of partiality in the setting of external standards. History has demonstrated rather clearly that neither a free market nor a controlled economy is a sufficient guarantee of fairness. A free market offers a powerful mode of distribution, but provision to all of minimal levels of all necessary goods, in conditions of dignity, safety, liberty, and health, is not what it was designed for.[13] Even a relatively free market may need assistance from more socially conscious, responsible, and responsive agencies. As for so-called planned economies, their now familiar shortchanging of expectations is both a consequence and a cause of their neglect of subjective deserts. A symptom of their characteristic unresponsiveness to the wishes that free markets treat as canonical is the notional dismissal of distribution activities as non-productive. But their now all but universally recognized systematic perpetuation of shortages in the interest of an increasingly remote and fictive future or of rather abstract or grandiose social aims also indicates that recognition of the broader dimensions of human desert is not generally what they were planned to achieve, even when the rhetoric of their revolutions appeals, as an irritant and goad to action, to the sight or memory of festering injustices.

The impact of market forces may be catastrophic upon some—as in the situation of justified concern to Marx, where the price of labor falls or is driven below the level of subsistence, or where interest rates drive farmers off their land and the hard-pressed farmer, as in Steinbeck, asks the process server, who is only doing a job, who it is he is supposed to shoot. History has taught us that locating ownership, government, labor, and management all in the State, the Party, or the hypostatic People does not alleviate such impersonality but may exacerbate it by violating the liberties markets articulate. Yet markets serve only a subset of human interests and may skew the order and weighting of the values they serve. When the Torah interfered with the free market to the extent of legislating that no land may be alienated permanently, or restricting the "right" of an Israelite to sell himself permanently into slavery, or requiring that the wages of a day laborer not be held overnight and a millstone or a coat not be taken in pledge, the law was placing limitations on the legitimacy of consent, as if to say that some choices are so unfair objectively that they ought not to be sanctioned even if those who make them exercise the full resources of human will and understanding in consenting to them.[14] All codes of contract law "interfere" in this way, and we can gauge such codes by the values in behalf of which they seek to limit consent.

THE CONSENT OF THE GOVERNED

We like to say that government is by the consent of the governed. But when and how does that consent occur? Alexander Bickel contributes to demythologizing the notion by speaking of a "process of consent,"[15] dethroning any unique event upon which a contract theory of justice might be predicated. Instead we have the suggestion of an ongoing activity of

cooperation and integration which is the political life of a society. Even
such activity is a measure of vitality, an index of justice, but not inter-
changeable with it.[16] The Torah (Deuteronomy 29) has all Israelites consent in behalf of their descendants. Plainly, then, that consent is symbolic.
But what does it symbolize—this contract between an unseen God whose
demands are not negotiable and a people whose generations will never
meet at one time and place to offer their joint consent to any given set of
terms? Clearly the law whose terms are not negotiable and whose author is
the Sovereign and Judge of all the earth is the law of justice, the only law to
which it can be said before even hearing it, "We will obey, and we will
hear" (Exodus 24:7). Not only the rabbis (Midrash Tanḥuma, Nitzavim 8,
ed. Buber 25b; Exodus Rabbah XXVIII 6; cf. *Mishnah Pesaḥim* 10:5) but
the text itself (Deuteronomy 29:13–14) tells us that every generation must
regard itself as a party to this primal consent. But how is such agreement
articulated?

The Epicurean doctrine, arising out of the theory of the Sophists, is
that justice is a convention, an artificial arrangement among men: "Justice
is not anything in itself, apart from human relations in a particular time
and place, mutually undertaking not to harm or be harmed. Natural justice
is a compact of mutual advantage to restrict the parties from harming or
being harmed by one another. For all living things which have not been
able to make contracts not to harm or be harmed by one another, there is
no justice or injustice. The same holds true of those peoples who have
been unable or unwilling to make compacts not to harm or be harmed."
These sentences (*Kyriae Doxai* 33, 31, 32) are ancestral to the Hobbesian
contract account of justice both in their formalism—the thesis that there
is no law or obligation beyond what is explicitly agreed—and in their
negative definition of the aims of justice—to secure the participants against
harm from one another, not to secure one another's aid in common
projects.[17] This ancient compact theory appeals to a kind of reductionism.
Surely, it is argued, there is no right or wrong in nature; the only obligations are those we undertake. The difficulty with the theory is in how it can
assume such undertakings to take place. If all duties arise by convention
and have no moral force beyond what the participants *create* by agreement,
there is no obligation to abide by such agreements. Appeal to a prior (and
more mythic) agreement to abide by our agreements once they are agreed
would only push the issue back, opening the way to an infinite regress and
exposing the circularity more clearly: Why *ought* one to abide by such an
undertaking? With such thoughts in mind, Spinoza argues that compacts

are binding only to the extent that the interests motivating them continue
to be served by them:

> The pledging of faith to any man, where one has but verbally promised
> to do this or that, which one might rightfully leave undone or *vice versa*
> remains so long valid as the will of him that gave his word remains un-
> changed. For whoever has the power to break his word has given up his
> rights not at all in reality but only nominally. Thus, if he who is by the Law
> of nature his own judge determines—rightly or wrongly (for to err is
> human)—that from some pledging of faith more loss than benefit follows,
> then he determines by his own judgment that that pledge ought to be dis-
> solved, and by natural Law he does dissolve it.[18]

The language may differ, but the concept is that of the Declaration of
Independence. Does Spinoza here advocate bad faith?[19] The reference, explicitly, is to arbitrary conventions, compacts which it is not *intrinsically*
wrong to break. The argument addresses Hobbes and others who suppose
that all systems of justice are conventional but then attempt to give them
some force beyond convention. As Mendelssohn wrote, in what amounts
at once to a subtle gloss of Spinoza and a critique of Hobbes: "If men are
not bound by nature to any duty, they do not have a duty to keep their
contracts. If there is, in the state of nature, no binding obligation other
than that based upon fear and powerlessness, contracts will remain valid
only as long as they are supported by fear and powerlessness. . . . But if
contracts are to remain valid, man must by nature, without contracts and
agreements, lack the ability to act against a compact into which he has
voluntarily entered."[20] We human beings have obligations toward one another even apart from any formal undertakings we may make. Consider
our obligations to our mates and offspring and, in general, the social nature of our species. For there is no humanity prior to community.

What this means is that the primal consent on which all our agreements
are predicated cannot be of the explicit kind. The social contract must be
metaphorical, and the object of the metaphor is our existential interdependence. The reference is not to an explicit undertaking but to that level
of community which we cannot help but share in. Thus, in the biblical
case, the covenant in which the people of Israel bind themselves expresses
not only consent but the engagement of every member of the nation in the
fate of the whole. It is for this reason that the explicit articulation of the
covenant dwells upon the consequences to the nation of disaffection and
on the shared experience of tribulations (Deuteronomy 29:15–27). Com-

mon history and destiny complement the immediacy of the common situation (vv. 9–11) in constituting a community. They are not merely determinants but constituents in a communal identity and thereby foci of an allegiance which becomes individual to the extent that common projects can command appropriation by those whom experience invites to share them. We are bound together by bonds of obligation, not simply because we have promised to pretend we are, nor even because it is convenient to bind ourselves to rules, but because the promises we make to one another can and should have the attainment of the good (for ourselves, for one another, for the human species, its posterity, and nature at large) as their objects. Such promises, with such goals, cannot be broken without violation of the sacred values in behalf of which they are made.

Thus behind Plato's myth of an implied contract stands the more powerful image of the laws as parents and educators. For the laws demand allegiance even from those who cannot freely consent to their sentence: children, prisoners like Socrates. They protect even non-citizens and mediate the transition to freedom and maturity, regulate and oversee the status even of those with no notion of their authority. Laws claim allegiance as the articulate institutions of a community to which one has obligations beyond those even tacitly acknowledged. Nominally Plato argues that acceptance of their benefits binds us to accept their sentence. But concretely what this means is that laws are the condition of human community and so belong to the natural necessities of human life. In rabbinic parlance the same necessity is expressed in saying that it is an obligation for all descendants of Noah to establish courts and magistrates—that is, the civil and civilizing conditions of law.[21]

We are all born into a social condition, a structure of roles and dependencies that is flexible but unescapable. As a result, we are potent through trust; impotent, even mad, through anomie. The moral requirements of our condition are the foundation of all interpersonal rights and duties. In this sense, justice is the spelling out of the moral logic of our condition —what we are bound to recognize and accept as a result of our existential and social situation, what we are and how we live.[22] Our conventions and agreements merely articulate the structure of interdependencies with clarity; they highlight and refine its symmetries and rhythms. Enchanted by the articulateness of such tacit or explicit recognitions of interdependence, conventionalists mistake them for the fabric of society. For they do bear the visible color and pattern by which societies differ. But conventionalists often overlook the warp on which this visible weft is woven: the universal human requirements for survival, welfare, dignity. Underlying our formal institutions are the natural human institutions that sustain social identity over time, place, and culture: the tribe, family, and nation. These institutions are natural in that membership in them does not rest on consent or agreement in the first instance, or even the second or third, but only in the last and least exercised cases of the stressing or breaking of their bonds. We are members of our families, nations, and yes, tribes, in the first instance by birth, and in secondary ones by language and by our odysseys as dependent, later interdependent social beings. On a tertiary level, that large component of our identity which is social defines itself through our participation in the past, present, and future fortunes of these groups of ours. Facets of our social roles do come into question, since we are rational and irrational, questioning and querulous beings. But such questioning, in practical terms, is a drop in the ocean of our customary behavior. Formal institutions are invoked, modified, or created when a need is felt to recognize or state more clearly or more fairly, in formal terms, the rights and wrongs of relationships otherwise taken for granted or enforced in informal, often unformalizable ways.

I mention this not to glorify the group at the expense of the individual[23] or to exalt an organic conception of the state. On the contrary, I do not think a formal institution like the state can be organic.[24] It would be foolish, moreover, to suppose that institutions designed to safeguard the equilibrium of human relations would inevitably fail to do so, or prove inevitably less effective than the ambiguous, often tacit relations they seek to regulate. I mention the priority of the informal to the formal in human obligations solely to show that it is in the exigencies of human need and well-being that all social obligations—formal and informal—acquire their moral force, not in the fictive skyhook of an act of consent which hangs in turn upon a convention that we must abide by our conventions.

VIRTUAL CONSENT

Rawls has argued that the critical test of justice is a rational willingness to consent to an arrangement without knowing one's own potential role in it.[25] This resolves the image of consent analytically to its core while preserving the fictive moment of consent as a regulative idea, like that of the children's cake-cutting rule—you cut and I'll choose. The verisimilitude of the analysis rests on our ready recognition of the elements of consent, but the normative appeal derives from insistence on the freedom and rationality of choices made in the fictive original position. A "veil of ignorance" objectifies the position morally by ensuring the interchangeability of roles. The notion of virtual consent is thus used as a touchstone of justice; and the outcome of the test as Rawls applies it is recognition of the lexical priority of liberty over all material goods and the injustice of any inequalities that are not advantageous to the parties they favor least. For, it is argued, rational choosers would not assign genuinely invidious roles if they were as likely as others to draw such lots, and they would sooner part with any potential material gain than give up their freedom to choose the arrangements they will live under.

Empirically, freedom to choose is never absolute, and history is as much the story of freedoms compromised as of liberty sought. Rawls abstracts away from the constraints of material necessity by assuming that in the "original position" all the resources of a potential society remain unclaimed and no liberties have yet been infringed. The abstract generosity of the scheme comes back to haunt him when he allows for justifiable inequalities based on social contributions. For the theory does not entail an answer to the question of social differentials beyond the insistence, whose motivation on the part of the original choosers is somewhat problematic, that the least advantaged must benefit from any inequity. We are not told how much the rational chooser would expect to benefit from a disadvantaged role, or whether rational choosers might differ on this question.[26]

Rawls obscures the possibility that liberty might have a cost in other goods. He exempts the value of liberty—but not its price—from the veil of ignorance, allowing it to shine through to the original choosers. But how would those who know nothing of their own values and have no experience of the testing of liberty against rival urgings and exigencies understand liberty? By what standards and with what reservations would sacrifices in behalf of liberty be recognized and rewarded? On one level we can say that the primacy of liberty is an analytic matter in decision theory, the choice of the power to make choices. But if Rawls' argument for the lexical priority of liberty resolves to the formal priority of the power of choice to the exercise of choices, it tells us nothing of the primacy of any particular *kind* of liberty—political, social, economic—or of the contents, boundaries, and relations of such kinds.[27] It seems to tell us something about a sacred or transcendent value like the one we call liberty only because of the rhetorical associations we supply to the abstract language of the argument. But such values and their historical connotations and interpretations are morally unknown within the veil of ignorance.

Empirically speaking, it is not clear what self-interested choosers would prefer. Some might make equality rather than liberty their paramount value; others might reject the project of maximizing equality. Some individuals are more concerned with honor or glory than with either formal liberties or tangible goods. And many say that they would rather suffer a bad government of their own than a fairer government of foreigners. We act and choose not only under the constraint of material exigencies but also under the influence of our own notions and values and our diverse, changing, and conflicting ideas even of liberty itself.[28] We may differ in the steepness of the social slope we will tolerate or prefer and in the degree of personal or social risk we choose in grasping for a brass or golden ring. We compromise our rights—not always out of desperation but often out of ideals or eagerness for gains, some authentic, some illusory.

Is the rational person one who would or would not consent to live in a society where murder was a capital crime, not knowing whether he would be a murderer? The matter remains in doubt. Convicted murderers disagree about capital punishment, much as lawmakers, jurists, theologians, journalists, the kin of victims, and the general public do from one place and time to another. Appeals to rationality do not settle such disputes but merely shift them to focus on the content of rationality. If we could make the choice of a society without knowing which sex we would belong to, most of us would probably opt for some sort of gender equity. But what sort? Some prefer a system in which the sexes are treated in accordance with their "natures"; others say that sex should make no more difference than eye color.[29] Some demand a clear-cut role differentiation (whether in style or in a division of nurturance from sustenance or in some other polarity), and others might choose pluralism. This last, perhaps, is the response a veil of ignorance might predispose us to expect. But many regard all significant departures from their own conceptions as inherently unjust. Justice in the eyes of some is represented by the notion that even in marriage there should be no distinctions of gender, men being as free to marry men as they are to marry women, and vice versa. Others believe a society is unjust if low-cost child care is available, because it encourages women to work outside the home. Such differences cannot be resolved by Rawls' model, since it debars the fictive chooser from any knowledge of his or her subsequent role and values. But there are comparable differences about most social issues;[30] typically, about what constitutes advantageous or disadvantageous treatment of children. Of those who maintain diverse views, there are doubtless some who would accept in principle any position in the diverse societies they project.

But curiously few would accept just any position in the model societies projected by others.

I would not be a poor man in Galton's model state. But advocates of such a state, who hold on principle that the proper role for the poor and weak is to languish economically and die out genetically, can certainly be found. The women's pledge at Oneida was to forgo both choice of mate and hope of posterity if they were deemed by "God's true representative" unfit to reproduce.[31] I have read a defense of the transcendent spirituality of suttee as the ultimate expression of a wife's devotion. The author's glowing colors clearly enunciate his faith that, had he been born a woman, he would have regarded suttee as a lofty fulfillment of his destiny. Garrett Hardin and his followers advocate a new morality with a warmth that betokens their consent to have died of starvation had destiny made them members of those societies and underclasses which would be pruned and lopped away from the human tree by the policies of genocide they have bruited.[32] Many martyrs have thanked God for the order which makes possible and necessary their immolation. Mishima testified by seppuku to his absolute unwillingness to live in a society where seppuku had become all but irrelevant.

Does rationality preclude all such preferences, or is it possible for different individuals to interpret rationality and self-interest in diverse terms? If rationality rules out such disagreements, then rationality violates the veil of ignorance. But if rationality allows such differences to persist, then Rawls' model fails to yield the substantive conclusions he expects from it: Centrally, it does not resolve the proposed rivalry between liberty and other values or demonstrate that the rational would not risk gross disadvantage for the sake of grand opportunity if the potential gains were high enough or widespread enough. Some, if truly free to choose without constraint, might deem it rational to allow no inequalities at all, or only inequalities more generously compensated than Rawls' rational chooser would deem feasible. But others, if not constrained by a stifling interpretation of rationality itself, might prefer to take their chances on glory in a society where glory was very rare and achieved only at an enormous cost in human liberties. For who can say that no one would prefer life at Athens in the time of Aeschylus or Socrates to some egalitarian but undistinguished and now forgotten commune?

Flesh and blood choosers assign material contents to their choices; they *construe* advantage and *use* their freedoms, spend them in a way, even exhaust or alienate them, sometimes irretrievably—not just because human choices are limited in scope or power but because it is in our nature to commit ourselves, sometimes totally or irrevocably, to what we desire or believe in. Few of us are wise enough to anticipate the outcome of all our choices; and, even given certain knowledge of those outcomes, few could guarantee their power to choose again more wisely than at first. The empiric chooser, then, cannot guarantee a Rawlsian outcome, although some empiric choosers, in particular historical circumstances, have struggled to define and preserve such an outcome.

Rawls does not intend his model as an empirical description of the behavior of actual choosers.[33] Rather, the surrogate authors of rational choice in his argument serve as a regulative fiction: They tell us not what flesh and blood humans *do* choose, but what ideally rational beings *would* choose. Rawls avoids falsifiability by relying on the veil of ignorance. The predilections of mere empiric choosers are irrelevant to the truth of his claims. But because the prospective choosers in the original position do not know what their own values will be after birth into the society they consent to live in, Rawls faces a dilemma: If such choosers genuinely know nothing of their own values, they will be unable to specify the character of the society they plan, even to the extent of reserving certain liberties or specifying their nature. Lacking access to the values and insights that might inform such a choice, they do not know whether honor or fame or some wholly unknown value would prove more important to them than liberty, or whether they would be wise in preferring liberty to material goods or other intangibles. Rawls can argue that in a condition of ignorance the most prudent choice is to preserve the power of making choices. But only one who knew the value of choice would know whether this is so. A chooser who did give preference to liberty might find that social factors deemed less significant rendered his freedom of choice an empty sham once the veil of ignorance was lifted. If rational choices are corrigible in this way, then abstract rationality is insufficient to inform wise choices.

To avoid such an outcome, Rawls must fortify his idea of rationality. Not only an egoism but a substantive interpretation of egoism must be imported into the notion of rationality to yield the desired results.[34] By building into the idea of rationality culture-bound values about the paramountcy of personal choice, Rawls makes the desired outcome predictable. The imported values are familiar enough and widely enough taken for granted to be all but transparent against the background of the idea of rationality. But they are far from universal or self-evident. They are interpretations of rationality. Without them or some alternative interpretations in their place, no substantive determinations could be made as to the constitution of a new society. But with them Rawls' model loses its heuristic value and becomes only an illustration (rather than a demonstration) of his theory. The rational chooser has become an exemplar of Rawls' ideal, and the *would* that predicts his choices is firmly announced to be a *should*. Thus the argument becomes circular. It no longer *shows* that rational choosers would plan as Rawls predicts, because it has invested the conception of rationality it uses with that very outcome.

It is difficult at times to see just which horn of this dilemma Rawls prefers to be impaled on. To the extent that the surrogate choosers are Rawls' ideal men, we know how they would behave: We form a notion of their choices by reading out of his ideal of rationality the values, preferences, and priorities that have been implanted there. But if that is what it does, Rawls' argument becomes equivocal by gaining assent to a rather formal notion of rationality and then shifting to a far more material notion that projects material preferences to interpret the idea of self-interest in a specific way. Whereas, to the extent that genuine ignorance and neutrality about values are preserved, the exercise of any real choice remains impossible.

Understandably, Rawls seems prone at times to want to have it both ways: The abstract, fictive chooser, in his cocoon of ignorance, knows nothing of his own preferences or tastes—yet judges both freedom and advantage, his own and that of others. The liberty he preserves is for that very reason a formal thing, the option to keep his options open, not to exercise them. But even such a choice requires values, as much as does the choice between risk and safety, individualistic versus communitarian institutions, or long-term versus short-term gratifications. The purely notional chooser of Rawls' abstract model, if that model is kept rigorous, cannot choose at all. Rawls makes his choice *for* him by supplying a basis of choice. In itself, then, the hypothesis of initial ignorance combined with rationality, even if they cohere with one another, does not adequately determine the two outcomes Rawls expects: the primacy of liberty or the protection of the least advantaged.

Rawls' account of justice resolves the myth of a historical contract more clearly than do most of the old exemplars of the contractarian tradition. In spite of its idealization of the abstract chooser, though, it does not wholly dissolve the assumption that justice is what we agree to, for it relies on that assumption in appealing to virtual consent. Aristotle's having a theory of human nature and a material, well-grounded conception of human well-being and happiness is of substantial benefit to him here. For, whereas Rawls knows that slavery is wrong, his theory of justice makes it difficult for him to say why, and he must fall back upon the problematic assertion that slavery is just not the sort of life that a free and rational chooser would ever choose to risk. But Aristotle, who does not believe that slavery is always wrong, can specify quite clearly the grounds on which *we* can hold slavery wrong categorically: the fact that it excludes the possibility of a human being's attaining the full realization of his or her humanity.

Surely justice is more than a matter of finding (or defining) what a real or even ideally rational group will accept. Once we know what all of us desire, it remains to be seen what each of us deserves. The insufficiency of consent, actual or virtual, as a criterion of justice points to the need for objective as well as (and beyond) subjective standards of fairness. We can see this need dialectically from Rawls' own premises: If freedom and rationality are to aid us in making choices, they call upon objective reference beyond their own claims to competence. For it cannot be sufficient in determining what I ought to desire to know that I have desires. What *seems* worth choosing or what seems an inevitable dichotomy among "live options" must be made relative to the realities of what *is* worth choosing and what *are* inevitable alternatives for choice. Rationality that is not corrigible but self-justifying is no criterion, and freedom that is not contextual but abstract is of no practical use. Consent, then, as a criterion of justice, requires definition partly in objective terms, in terms of real possibilities and real worth or merit in things, persons, or relations. Fairness cannot be constructed solely out of a rational surrogate's abstract agreement to a proposition, and justice cannot be construed from the virtual consent of a regulative placeholder to the terms of a proposed system.

AN OBJECTIVE THEORY OF DESERTS

The logic of exchange is of varied form. We have the precise equilibration of subjective satisfactions that characterizes sharp dealing and the calculated disproportionality of deterrence and reward, the relaxed expectation of generosity and the heightened expectation of that form of personal aid which awaits a vastly disproportionate return in loyalty or commitment or exacts a disproportionate penalty when its role expectations are unfulfilled. We have the contractual requirement of a meeting of minds and the existential involvement of a person in a family, community, or nation, establishing bonds of obligation which are termed contractual only metaphorically yet cannot be violated without grave injury. Where among these can we find the objectivity of justice?

FORMAL AND MATERIAL DESERTS

Aristotle attaches a clear syntax to the intuition that justice is somehow mathematical, associating distributive justice with geometric proportion and rectification with the arithmetic. Distributive justice allocates goods or ills, such as honors and awards, according to desert; rectification seeks a balance of goods and costs, as in suit for civil damages. But Aristotle does not expect a great deal from the abstract models. Criticizing a simplistic equation of justice with reciprocity that he finds in Pythagorean thinking, he points out that mere reciprocity does not discriminate social roles—the jailer or executioner from the kidnapper or murderer. Nor does it discriminate intentions—murder from manslaughter, negligent from innocent injury or death. Still, the formal scheme retains its curious attractiveness for Aristotle, as for us, and calls forth from him a generalized recognition that "this sort of justice does hold men together . . . it is by exchange that they hold together." Some kind of equivalency underlies human association —the return of good for good, symbolized in the temples of the Graces, and of ill for ill, without which men would "think their position mere slavery" (*Nicomachaean Ethics* V 5, 1132b–33a).

Formal symmetries structure our exchange relations and provide an abstract framework against which concrete social arrangements can be criticized, conceptual nubs or fulcrums against which our arrangements can be rubbed dialectically or pressed rhetorically and so tested and improved. Geometrically we know that two days' work is worth twice the wages of one, other things being equal (1131a). But geometry does not tell us what wage anyone should earn—whether two workers should be paid at the same rate or whether either has been paid adequately. Arithmetic may equilibrate objective worths or subjective satisfactions, but it cannot announce when it is unjust to participate in a given exchange and when it is unjust not to. In such material determinations, the notion of desert asserts its primacy.

The idea of equality is perhaps a little misleading here, for it seems to set all deserts at unity. Still it tells us nothing of material deserts—no more than any other purely formal notion, such as that of hierarchy. Henry Higgins may treat a duchess the same as a parlor maid or vice versa. But for either to be treated as she deserves requires some practical recognition of a baseline of entitlement. Justice posits deserts—some equal, some unequal, some based on need, some on merit, and some existential, like the right to be told the truth. You deserve to enjoy the fruits of your labor unmolested. You do not (lest there be an infinite regress) need to earn, besides your pay, the right to non-interference from others who have not shared in the labor, capital, and social costs of production. This desert is yours simply, existentially, prior to any contract or convention which may formalize, specify, and regularize its terms. It is primary, like the right by which conventions, compacts, and agreements themselves are entered into and their fulfillment rightfully expected when their conditions are being met. Otherwise there is a vicious regress and there are no deserts at all. For we cannot anchor deserts in conventions and then turn around and seek to ground conventions in deserts.

Your desert of the proceeds of your labor is not something that another can confer, so it is not something that another can legitimately withhold. Equal work deserves equal pay *because* our existential deserts are equal; you may merit an added increment for your years of faithful service. But existentially we all deserve to be treated decently, afforded a safe and wholesome work environment, and paid a living wage, regardless who we are. These are corollaries of the maxim which selfishness negates—interpretations of "love thy fellow as thyself." That is, they are primary dicta of morality. But they are also constitutive in the groundwork of all our dealings. Just as contracts presuppose community, all formal undertakings presuppose a context of communication and accommodation. Our social positions do not determine our deserts in the first instance but morally speaking are founded on them. The basis of community is only metaphorically called agreement or consent. Its real nature is the pragmatic recognition of human dignities and needs, the social articulation of the very identities that are the primal basis of our claims. Paradigmatically, there is no dealing without trust. And courtesy, which may seem a mere ornament masking something far more elemental in our dealings, pertains in fact to the deeper level on which the more tangible transaction is grounded. For all notions of worth are parasitic upon the idea of desert, and all exchanges and transactions rest on the affirmation and confirmation of desert: One cannot say that any exchange is fair unless its parties and all affected others have been treated as they deserve.

Since desert is equal or is presumed equal with respect to many goods in many transactions, the weighting factors that can differentiate concrete deserts often drop out of the equation, and desert itself tends to fall out of account, leaving only the relative worth of goods or ills to be equilibrated.

Equality comes to mean that one man's dollar is worth as much as any other's, and we are lulled in the illusion that deserts have little bearing on our practical lives (except, perhaps, with regard to punishment). We may come to think of all relations as market-contractual. But clearly such goods as life, health, and dignity are not to be bought and sold. Our existential entitlement to these is not proportional to anything; it is grounded in our very being as subjects.

Some goods must be apportioned by standards incommensurate with the seemingly universal coin of the marketplace. In distributing honors, equity itself must look to a host of criteria: Dignity belongs to every human being, but respect does not rightly belong to whoever can bid for it and is not due equally to all, saintly and vicious alike. We may agree that human beings are equal absolutely in their desert of basic rights yet disagree about the extent and nature of their equality in authority, say, to rule. All of us deserve equally to be heard in our own defense. But not all of us equally deserve a Nobel Prize; and those who do, for work in chemistry or physics, may not deserve much deference at all as humanitarians or epistemologists. The radical democracy Plato speaks of, where citizenship is a sufficient criterion of authority and rulers, like our jury members, are chosen by lot,[35] is unpalatable to most advocates of democracy. Unless we wish to equate democracy (as some revolutionists do) with the rule of force, we must devise some rules about rights; and, in so doing, we inevitably interpret and compromise equality for the sake of equity. If we are to be equal absolutely in our right to vote, there must be an inequality by which we are obliged in certain contexts to obey the officer at the polls. Merely to speak of equality without establishing some basis of desert—in merit, capability, office, seniority, need, or the purely existential claims of personhood—is to speak at a level of abstraction that leaves open the most crucial issues about justice and injustice. An anatomy of justice ought to establish the order of priority and optimal relationships among equalities and inequalities. Above all, it ought to discover the material as distinguished from the formal basis of deserts.[36]

One benefit of the notion of equality in this regard, once we have cleared away the suggestion that it levels all deserts, is that it brings us back to the foundation of deserts by its reference to those respects in which all of us stand on the same ground. For both the formalized deserts of our social and civil roles and the underlying deserts of our personhood are expressions of the same fact. That fact is our being, which is both common and unique; indeed, our uniqueness is one feature we have in common. It undergirds our most primitive claims, the deserts I call existential. Marx grasped the shirttail of this idea when he sought an existential basis for deserts beyond the merely formal equity of the marketplace.[37] But it was an ancient idea, albeit dressed in new words. And Marx failed to discover the ontic basis of deserts or to differentiate those deserts and uncover their individual anatomies and complexities, perhaps in part because he lost sight of the crucial differences between the economic and the moral in his eagerness to ground the moral in the seemingly more solid stuff of economics.[38] I say that the formal system of our earned deserts and even of our civil rights rests upon more basic claims—ultimately, on the claims we make, as all beings do, to existence and the expression of our natures. These claims, I maintain, have a prima facie validity and can be qualified only by claims of comparable magnitude. If *A* makes a coherent claim that is uncontested, it is legitimated. For this claim is not merely a request but an expression of being. It speaks in its own favor; and, if nothing speaks against it, it is established. Its validity can be impugned or its scope delimited only by counterclaims. But in nature counterclaims to the demands of finite beings are made constantly and from all quarters. The real desert of a being is the resultant of its claims in juxtaposition with these others.

Value, I assume, is intrinsic in all being, not merely in subjects or in objects of desire. Value, in fact, is identical with the being of things, dynamically considered—that is, with regard for their projects and potentials. It follows that justice amounts to giving beings their deserts and that deserts are the claims of beings, their positive self-affirmations, as scaled against those of all other beings. Every being makes claims on its environment. Bodies, minimally, claim space, but they also claim the affirmation of their specific characters. This is what Anaximander called the injustice of things toward one another. He meant their aggression; the equilibrium of nature he called justice.[39] Just what is legitimate for a being to claim, I argue, varies with the nature of the being. Generalized this becomes whatever it can compass. That seems to be what Spinoza meant by equating right with power. He cannot mean that I deserve all that I can get or grasp by hook or by crook. Rather, I am entitled at least prima facie to any good pertinent to my nature. The legitimacy of claims made by other beings is what renders my entitlement only prima facie. As a rational being I can claim infinite terrain of many kinds. But also as a rational being I must acknowledge other deserts and confine my claims accordingly, reserving those which are infinite for the universal realms of the sciences and arts, the pure domains of mind and spirit. I must ground my positive claims in an appreciation of my capabilities and limitations.

From here we can see why it is that our formal entitlements, civil or contractual, rest upon the informal structures of community: For these in turn rest ultimately on our existential deserts, which community alone can recognize and foster. It is not the case that we have property to protect and therefore enter into contracts, whence arise the niceties of moral consideration. On the contrary, we are persons and need property to sustain our projects as persons, but the systems we erect to second our projects are the creatures of our claims as persons and have no higher authority or deeper basis. All our formal undertakings must be held to the moral purposes for which they were set forth and in which alone they have their warrant. Here we see the true referent of the reciprocities social theorists delineate. For here we see the living heart of society, which is no mere static balance or formal equipoise but a material and dynamic engagement. It is not enough for deserts to be equilibrated; they must also be recognized, that is, treated as positive.

It is because your deserts are positive and material, and not merely formal, that I cannot compensate you for destroying your property by destroying something of my own. In civil and criminal law, as in commercial transactions, we focus typically on formal equivalences, not seeking to assay a character or a relationship holistically. We say this damage has that cost, this service has that worth, this crime (perhaps with specified mitigating or aggravating circumstances) merits this or that response. In court even the idea of merit is constricted to cover only specified (and, it is hoped, operationally definable) areas of concern. A general determination of merit and desert is far too open-ended to allow ready and reliable estimation—and far too liable to bias and abuse. But, in law, as in trade, every judgment is a specification, with the aid of formal rules, of some logically prior claim to material deserts.

By *deserts* I mean much the same as what is often meant—and what I mean—in speaking of rights. In this I follow the usage of the Rambam. I find the term deserts useful since it lacks the immediate connotations of absoluteness that rhetoric commonly attaches to the idea of rights. Not all deserts are trumps. Prima facie deserts may conflict, and the task of morals centrally and of government peripherally (in critical areas where morals or mores are insufficient) is to work out those conflicts optimally. Through this process objective or legitimate deserts are sought, or perhaps approximated, from an appraisal of interests. The idea that deserts require mutual accommodation is certainly not far from the Mosaic tradition. It is eloquently voiced in the Talmudic maxim that Jerusalem was destroyed because its people insisted on their rights according to the Torah (*Baba Metzia* 30b). Accommodation requires generosity and fellowship. These are the principal means by which the Torah seeks to optimize the realization of human claims. Hence Maimonides' emphasis on the virtue of justice as distinguished from the bare practice of justice. But the virtues that sustain justice do not detract from but add to personal fulfillment. Hence his thesis that they distinguish and enhance our character.

Evidently the concept of rights is not explicitly articulated in the Torah for much the same reason that the technical concept of citizenship is absent there: because the project of the Torah extends beyond the formal level. Biblical law is as interested in civil guarantees of rights, such as those afforded by its rules of evidence, as it is in communal relations, such as those fostered by the rules of aid on the highway. But the Torah does not focus narrowly on civil rights, as do the great declarations of the eighteenth century. Rather, it creates what is in a sense a far more ambitious and still unrealized program in the communal area, beyond and beneath its juridical concerns at the level of rights. Modern rights can be absolute in part because they are minimal, secular declensions of that fuller program which contains both minimal, absolute rights and open-ended, but therefore necessarily relative entitlements among broader deserts.

Every person has certain positive deserts. And, as with equality, it is fruitful to make a set of somewhat arbitrary presumptions about these. We may presume, for example, that any human being is redeemable or has some degree of merit (based not on individual observation but solely in deference to the fact of humanity). We typically presume some measure of honor, trustworthiness, intelligence, gentleness. Such presumptions are corrigible, but we resist giving them up, even in the teeth of impressive evidence against them in particular cases. For we presume an inalienability in human worth of a special kind that does not enter into the ordinary calculus of exchanges and is therefore called dignity.[40] Our presumption of dignity sometimes resolves to a prejudice in behalf of humanity at large. Yet it is not an arbitrary prejudice. We cling to it as a saving grace of *our* humanity, and behind this partly a priori presumption lies a fact which the ascription of dignity serves to safeguard as a necessary margin of defense (*seyag*): the actual sanctity of the human person, variable in some of its dimensions, uniform in others, but coextensive with the reality of the being to whom it belongs.

The ultimate existential claims of human beings are never simply over-ridden by rival claims. Obviously they are not overruled by the claims of lesser beings. But neither can they be challenged by rivals of equal or greater ontic stature, since such beings are called upon to recognize rational subjecthood in others. Consciousness not only existentiates itself in its social milieu but also calls upon other subjects to accord the recognition that consciousness alone can give. Morally this cannot be withheld. The claims of personhood upon personhood, then, in a sense are absolute, but they are not for that reason infinite. They are limited by one another, by human nature, and even by the existential claims of lesser beings, when these do not impair (they may indeed augment) the highest claims of personhood. Human survival and well-being may supervene as against many such lesser interests, but they do not require and hence morally cannot demand the suppression of all, even if it were rational and prudent for them to do so. We must defer to one another's existential claims and recognize the intrinsic (not merely instrumental) merit in the claims of lesser beings.

It is often, rather arbitrarily, assumed that any bearer of rights is also a bearer of duties. But this infant has never worked, has made no promises or undertakings, formed no alliances, contracted no obligations, tacit or express—yet it has positive deserts. Obligations are owed it, by its parents and by anyone who comes upon it, should it be lost or abandoned, not only to refrain from harming it but actively to help it. When grown, the child may have an obligation to reciprocate the aid received—by showing appreciation or by contributing to the human community which has sustained it. But the claim that it has obligations now, as it lies in its basket, or else has no entitlements, is a mere aftertrace of the contractual image taken too literally—urged, perhaps, by the somewhat adversarial assumption that the only real obligations are those we choose to lay upon ourselves. Generations unborn have a desert, as environmentalists rightly urge, to receive a world no less habitable than ours. Those generations make a claim on us even though they can do nothing to benefit us materially, have made no promises to us, and will never be able to show us their gratitude or disappointment in our choices. Rights do confer correlative duties, but only in a structure of interdependencies, a community. And individual deserts underlie communal claims just as communal bonds underlie formal obligations. Thus the nature and basis of reciprocities must be demonstrated and legitimated contextually rather than inserted a priori into the definition of 'rights', an artifact of our familiar rhetorical bartering and dialectical bantering with that term.

Non-rational beings for the most part do not acquire obligations to-ward their benefactors—certainly not moral obligations or duties "commensurate" with benefits received. Yet they are entitled to proper treatment. Even an insect is not to be tormented at a child's whim. Helpless beings of all kinds have deserts, even when they can never fulfill correlative duties. In saying that rights are equal to powers I mean that deserts are proportioned to claims, not (as Hobbes might have it) that authority is limited by effective destructiveness, or even by usefulness. Serious and unpleasant paradoxes result, in theory and in practice, from the presumption that rights *must* involve reciprocity—not least, a willingness to ignore the rights of the incapable, ineffectual, or even unpromising. I find it a grotesque and damaging reduction of humanity to seek to evaluate a person's worth in terms of "usefulness to society." Yet equally serious problems arise from the opposing illusion, that opportunities never confer obligations. Curiously enough, that presumption, too, is fed by the contractarian myth. For shirkers often complain that they "never asked for" benefits conferred, meaning that they never agreed to the price or penalty now expected or exacted. Their thinking affords no basis for anticipating the role expectations laid upon them by engagements too subtle for casual thinking to apprehend and commitments which their theories (if they plead theories) were often designed to ignore.

The idea of deserts that I am advocating argues for broad social efforts in behalf of human capabilities. Among other entitlements, it supports the idea of universal, publicly funded education, to the full extent of the recipients' talents and capabilities. But it does not balk at the idea, say, of universal service as a means of funding those entitlements. Such service does not lean upon but rather breathes life into the image of a social contract. For entitlements are neither a bottomless pit, as tax rebels fear, nor an ever normal pot, as welfare advocates may hope. The same community that sustains them is sustained by them.

In espousing an ontological theory of deserts I am seeking a reintegration of the notions of claims, interests, and benefits with those of rights, deserts, and duties. The primacy of human dignity, for example, is a direct consequence of an adequate understanding of the kind of beings we are. And, in general, the approach I am advocating seeks to integrate morals with ontology on the basis of respect for being in all its phases, in all its interests or claims. Bentham was suspicious of the notion of rights as a fictional hypostatization of claims.[41] He thought it more honest to speak openly of claims if claims were meant; and I agree. But I equate prima facie rights with claims, and I equate legitimate rights with claims founded in the deserts of every being in relation to the interests of all others. Here is a basis for a naturalism as to the rightful treatment of all beings which is neither reductionistic nor equivocal: It does not place the higher claims of subjects or persons on all fours with lesser ones, nor does it equivocate by stretching the term 'rights' over radically diverse levels of ontic entitlement.

The naturalism of deserts is not a denial of transcendence. Every being claims for itself a possible perfection transcending its empiric givenness; every act presupposes transcendence in pursuing a goal not given in empiric immediacy. But our ontic theory is a naturalism in that it finds value in the being of things—recognizing the identities of things, as Spinoza did, in their *conatus*, understanding each being in terms of its project. This idea is as old as Aristotle and remains foundational in the existentialists. It is only the artificial severing of the realms of value and being that has tended to deny us access to the ontic foundations of any moral claim.

Does our assigning existential deserts to all beings perpetrate a naturalistic fallacy? I can reply only that if beings do not have deserts, I do not know what does. The purity of the *ought* has been kept too pristine if it becomes impossible to say that A deserves x; and it seems to me self-evident that any truths about A's deserts must be grounded in the nature of A's being. I find value in the being of all things. If desert is not equivalent to the reality (or "power") of beings, I do not know what it can be. There *is* nothing else. If there is no value in the existence of this tree and of all other things, then nothing is of value at all. I see here no opening for an open-question method.

The discovery of value in the reality of things does not equate desirability with facticity. The distinction of what is the case from what ought to be is crucial to all moral discourse, both practical and critical. But the *is* that is criticized or rejected is not the reality of legitimated goals, projects which realize the natures of things in a community of maximal regard for all claims. On the contrary, what is rejected or objected to in facticity are those facts or factors which negate or exclude the maximal realization of existential projects. We reject vice, viciousness, whatever is destructive of self or other—not what affirms reality but what denies it. Our naturalism makes no Panglossian claim that all facts are desirable; we do not find it shocking that fulfillment for some beings is destruction for others. In identifying reality with perfection and locating goodness in the reality of things, we seek maximal realization of reality in the maximal recognition of existential claims. But we need hardly regard all claims as sound or viable.

Closely examined, the affirmation that justice is the resultant of all claims made within an environment has no Spencerian implications either. Founded in the prima facie legitimation of all claims, justice requires their maximal recognition, not their subjugation. It does not demand passivity to the supervenient forces of viruses or pests. For their claims to our bodies are countered by the more ambitious claims our bodies make. But neither does it allow wanton exploitation of lower forms—wanton meaning, for example, destruction of their econiches when they pose no threat to us.[42] Of course lesser beings can overwhelm higher ones, although being is power and desert. For not every power is defensive, just as not every power is destructive. And it is the nature of powers neither to govern all domains nor to be fully actual at all times. Wisdom is a higher power than destructiveness, because wisdom can create community where mere aggressiveness can assert itself only frontally. But even wisdom in the human case is fallible. And (since we are animals) we cannot avoid the frontal mode of self-affirmation. It is a condition of our existence. We may (because we must) exploit lower beings—plants and animals. But we may not exploit one another, treating persons as means to the exclusion of their own ends, rejecting their deserts. For their claims hold by the same rule that legitimates ours.

These findings are relevant to the claims of libertarians and "ragged" individualists. Our recognition of the primacy of existential over earned desert, of earned desert over vested interest, and of vested over merely asserted interest in the hierarchy of moral claims shows us that the market, despite its many and wonderful capabilities, may not be adequate to ensure fairness. From the notion of consent alone we learn that no human transaction can be isolated from its context of needs, dignities, roles, suppositions, and entailments.[43] Markets themselves presume the existence of a community, of bonds of trust and understanding, courtesy, and other varieties of moral regard, although that fact does not seem to preclude market forces from negating many of these values. Even laws, which are designed to protect deserts, cannot reach the core of the identity that underlies their authority. This can be done only through human fellowship—that is, through community.

In speaking of community I do not wish to speak romantically. A community is not a mystic, unaccountable body but a group joined together by shared interests and common concerns. Such interests and concerns accompany all human relationships. They are ignored only through an act of abstraction, an impersonality that lies at the root of much human evil.

Mutuality, by contrast, is articulated and intensified through human language and by numerous informal and formal institutions. That formal institutions presuppose informal ones whereas informal institutions rest on the existential givens of our human situation does not, I emphasize, render the informal, communally defined structures unconditionally "superior" to societal, formally defined social arrangements. Formal institutions often reform, regulate, and correct the excesses and deficiencies of unrecorded, non-explicit, or non-specific structures. Paradigmatically, laws regulate the structure of marriage; constitutions articulate the structure of a state, through which a nation of individuals may exercise their capability of self-governance in a regulated fashion. The task of building a community is relevant to the concerns of justice because a community is the primal sphere of interactions intimate enough in character and global enough in scope to afford a locus for the recognition of existential claims. But the establishment of a community is a necessary, not a sufficient condition of material justice. Even in formal terms we do not want merely a state but a just state. In the same way we do not want merely a community but a good community—one not only capable of moral action but effective in its exercise, and founded on individual respect and mutual concern. That the Torah seeks to maximize such concern is obvious from the language it employs to specify the kind of love it deems appropriate in the community at large: "Love thy fellow *as thyself*."

IS THE GOOD COMMUNITY A UTOPIAN IDEAL?

The obvious charge against such a project (for the word *torah* etymologically connotes a project, and the rule of fellowship defines the social backbone of that project as the placement of human relations on a footing of moral community) is that it is impractical. This charge, already suggested in the mythic setting of King Katzya's realm, is clearly articulated in Bentham's thesis that the ultimate utopianism is reliance upon human generosity: "Every system of management which has disinterestedness pretended or real for its foundation is rotten at the root, susceptible of momentary prosperity at the outset, but sure to perish in the long run. That principle of action is most to be depended upon whose influence is most constant, most uniform, most lasting and most general among mankind. Personal interest is that principle and a system of economy built on any other foundation is built upon quicksand."[44]

Can a society be founded on the basis of moral regard? In view of the priority of community to society, and of deserts to laws, we must ask if a

society can be built on any other footing. Surely Bentham, of all philosophers, knew that human character is malleable and that the conception of
self-interest is open to many and diverse interpretations.[45] Yet Bentham's
generalized critique presumes human character to be static and follows the
Sophists in assuming an inevitably invidious tendency, capable in the mass
of regarding the interests of others only when they are mechanically united
to the narrow interests of the atomic ego. But history, as Ibn Khaldûn is
perhaps most thorough to point out, is full of examples of effectively and
enduringly extended conceptions of the self.[46] Indeed, there would be no
story to tell—no history, no historian, and no politics—were this not so.

The project of the Torah is to establish an *ethically* extended self as the
foundation of a reformed society. As Maimonides puts it, glossing the
Nineteenth Psalm, The Law of the Lord, being perfect, perfecteth the
soul.[47] But, examining the biblical laws, we find that the Torah is not utopian in the sense of presupposing the universal change in human nature
that it seeks. Rather, it builds, and builds upon, an ethnic consciousness,
and creates reformative institutions legislatively, influencing character by
regulating behavior, so that character, as it emerges, will regulate behavior
in turn. Thus the Torah does not merely command particular actions or
omissions on pain of punishment or with promise of reward. It presumes
on history and on a modicum of human sociability—but not on affability
or any of the other virtues it seeks to instill.

Spinoza, using the word utopia, argues that utopias are fantasies because they presuppose the radical transformation of human nature
(*Tractatus Politicus* I 1). This idea is anticipated by Epicurus' advice against
efforts to change society, since human mores (based on the pursuit of
pleasure and the fear of pain) are fundamentally unalterable; political
efforts will lead only to frustration or worse—zealotry. The theme, ultimately based in the Sophists' appeals to "realistic" recognition of the
penchants of human nature, is developed into a grand structure of per-
suasive presumption in Voltaire. Bentham does not deploy a rigorous
definition of utopianism as reliance on the reforms one proposes to bring
about. He simply presumes the now "commensensical" view that transformation of human character, whether radical or gradual, is impractical
on a social scale. This is a variant on the view suggested by Thrasymachus
and argued by Plato's brothers, Glaucon and Adeimantus, as devil's
advocates in the *Republic* (II, 359–68), namely, that anyone who refrains
from taking advantage of his fellows will be choosing disadvantage for
himself. As long as individuals are capable of recognizing their self-

interest, will not invidious standards and exploitative behavior inevitably prevail?

The objection rests on three misapprehensions: (*i*) it perpetuates the romantic myth that morals belong purely to personal conscience and are not a matter of social ethos; (*ii*) it identifies rational self-interest with sordid selfishness, promoting a perspectival and paradoxical view of interests, by which all claims diminish in legitimacy as they recede from any atomic ego; and (*iii*) it perceives no palpable benefit in the establishment of community. Indeed, it treats the interests of others as necessarily in conflict with one's own. It assumes that recognition of my deserts can be enhanced only by diminishing yours.

But (*i*) the Torah does not naively impose upon individuals an obligation to perform unwonted or unwanted acts of supererogation as expressive feats of saintliness. It is not a product of that Hellenistic *Weltanschauung* which sets the individual against society and lets the spectators wager whether the lone gladiator called to unequal combat will struggle against the odds like the Stoic Herakles or retreat in quest of untroubled repose to an Epicurean garden. The Torah does not propound homiletic maxims for an individual but legislates for a nation. *Baba Bathra* (89a) makes clear how deeply Jewish Law grounds itself in prevailing social custom as its foundation and fulcrum:

> How is it indicated that we may not give level measure where the practice is to give a heaped measure and vice versa? The text declares, "A perfect measure" (Deuteronomy 25:15). And how is it indicated that if the seller says, "I will give level measure," where the practice is to give a heaped measure, "and reduce the price," or "I will give a heaped measure," where the practice is to give level measure, "and increase the price," he is not allowed to do so? The text declares, "A perfect and just measure." How is it indicated that we may not give exact weight where the practice is to give overweight and *vice versa*? The text declares, "A perfect weight." And how is it indicated that if the seller says, "I will give exact weight," where the practice is to give overweight, "and reduce the price" or "I will give overweight," where the practice is to give exact weight, "and increase the price," he is not allowed to do so? The text declares, "A perfect and just weight."

The Sages reason that the Torah seeks to forestall that mercantile motive which would give extra but charge disproportionately, or give less and discount disproportionately. That is why the Torah specifies (without redundancy) "a perfect and just measure" and does not omit to add "a perfect and just weight"—lest one be tempted to apply the rule to volume measure only. The law demands precise measurement, the frequent cleaning of standards—twice weekly for commercial measures, according to Rabban Simeon ben Gamaliel, weekly for weights, and after each weighing for scales. Yet the Law does not forbid but expects generosity. Rabban Simeon mandates 5–10 percent augmented measure, but without charge (Baba Bathra V 11). This is a matter of yielding the margin, giving the benefit of the doubt, promoting generosity and communal spirit. The Law does forbid specious boons. It demands adherence to local custom regarding full or heaping measure so as to prevent deceptive practice—sharp dealing. But there is no ordinance of exemplary extravagance. Rather the Torah anticipates conformity to prevailing practices. The changes it seeks in social mores are achieved not before but through the implementation of the Law—through the growth of prosperity, trust, generosity, and friendly relations—not by the heroic endeavors or expressive postures of isolated individuals. Thus the notion that the Law is utopian in placing upon the individual an unreasonable burden of unilateral altruism is unfounded.[48]

(*ii*) Morally as well as prudentially I cannot achieve my interest at others' cost: morally, because we do not attain self-perfection as parasites or vipers; prudentially, because exploitation is inimical to the cooperation we all require. By oppressing or exacting unfair advantage from others I am alienating their trust and strength and so undermining the basis of the relationships I might have forged with them toward creative or productive accomplishment. In so doing I also undermine my own effectiveness. That is a prudential problem, although it has obvious moral impact as well. But consider the moral issue alone: I am diminished in stature by selfishness. Hillel makes the point when he argues, "If I am for myself alone, what am I?" Self-diminution is not rationality. There is no law of nature corresponding to Boffin's "Crunch or be crunched!" I cannot give due regard to my own interests by overriding those of others. The Golden Rule does not demand self-sacrifice in the sense of self-exploitation. Indeed it cannot; for it predicates the love of fellows on the love of self. But when it commands the avoidance of sharp dealing or asperity, it does not regard as a sacrifice my recognition of obligations to assist others. Rather, this is a virtue that enhances one's character.

(*iii*) Experience does not bear out the assumption that generosity is impractical even in commercial relations. Trust is requisite in all human affairs. Its presence is productive and humanizing. On the broadest level, the incorporation of more charitable, thoughtful, considerate, or concerned motives into the practical ethos aids the common good and its constituent interests. The recent history of industrial and agricultural labor in Eastern Europe and the Soviet Union shows clearly that even hunger and want remain unsettled issues on the human agenda until the seemingly impalpable issues of freedom, dignity, and fellowship have been squarely addressed. But the evidence for the practicality of the ethical is far more widespread. Impersonality has the efficiency of a machine—replaceable parts, formally reciprocal relations among expendable terms. But the anomie which is its byproduct is destructive. Where impersonality is paramount, persons come to hate their work, despise their neighbors, frustrate their social nature, and so generate a social system that damages its members and runs rockily, not smoothly. Arson, vandalism, sabotage, waste, pilferage, malicious mischief and juvenile crime, alcohol and drug abuse, promiscuous, demeaning, and self-denigratory sexual relations, and suicide—neglect and abuse of persons, processes, and things—are among the symptoms.[49]

The efficacy of a community is organic rather than mechanical. The interactions are not merely reactive and functional, but responsive and personal, based on concerns that go beyond the confines of a mere transaction. Fear as well as love may create such bonds—fear of penury, of a hostile force, or of isolation itself. But love creates more lasting bonds, because these can withstand prosperity as well as adversity and risk.[50] The responsiveness of a well-integrated community, its powers of collaborative effort, and the willingness of its members to make personal sacrifices in behalf of a common good render it far more efficient and productive than any strictly legalistic or formal system can be. Here we see in terms of social utility rather than purely personal integrity why it is good and not merely a matter of convention for us to keep faith with one another. Spinoza can thus argue prudentially:

> Many things outside ourselves are useful to us and therefore to be sought. Of these none can be made out to be more helpful than those that fit squarely with our own nature. For if two individuals having just the same nature, for example, join forces, they form a new individual twice as powerful as either was alone. To man, then, nothing is more useful than man. Nothing, I say, more beneficial in preserving men's being, can be wished for than for all men so to come together as to form one body and one mind, as it were, so as to strive all together to preserve their being and seek for themselves the common good of all. From this it follows that men who are ruled by reason, that is, who seek what is beneficial to them under reason's guidance, desire nothing for themselves which they do not covet for the rest of mankind but are just, trustworthy and honorable.[51]

The saving of societies presided over by legalistic structures has come time and again from the capability of their members to pull together in a crisis to form a community of communities along the lines of preexisting bonds of fellowship—as happened in the United States and in Britain during World War II. The efficiency of the communal type of bond is demonstrated repeatedly in the experience of the early kibbutz, the resiliency of the family, and in every case of communal interaction where the intimacy of communal relations is not subverted by rapacity or perverted by the (generally emotional) type of exploitation which plagues all kinds of intimate human relations and is parasitic upon the emotive energies that support communal regard. Community is in general more efficient than society in integrating human energies; and, as I have intimated, community lies at the root of societal efficacy as well as societal legitimacy. So plainly it is not the case that a utopian (meaning unworkable) demand has been made when a claim is put forth that human relations should be founded less exclusively on the precise quid pro quo of particular transactions and more on considerations of general and individual desert—in which, of course, earned desert will necessarily remain constitutive.

NATURAL DESERTS AND THE MOSAIC LAW

That the Torah adopts a project of maximizing the recognition of deserts is shown most clearly, perhaps, in one ordinance of the laws of war: "When thou besiegest a city for many days in warfare, so as to capture it, thou shalt not destroy its trees by wielding axe against them. Thou mayest eat of them but not cut them down. For is a tree of the field a man to fall away before thee into a stronghold? Only a tree that thou knowest is not a food tree mayest thou destroy and fell to build siegeworks against the city that maketh war against thee, until its fall" (Deuteronomy 20:19–20). The rhetorical question "Is a tree of the field a man?" demands to know how a tree became an enemy and pleads the trees' powerlessness to withdraw. The passage plainly implies that trees have a desert. Their fruit may be eaten, and they may be cut down for their wood if they are not food trees. But the land is not to be made desolate. Beyond prudential concern for the welfare of the victors and the vanquished, even besiegers must consider the welfare of the trees—a fortiori, beings that make higher claims. Thus it was on the text of this passage that the Rabbis founded their global prohibition *bal tashḥit*, thou shalt not destroy.

The claim in behalf of the deserts of all beings is moral. Thus the rhetoric of the scriptural claim in behalf of the land (Leviticus 26:34–35, 43; 2

Chronicles 36:21). Rhetoric is the bastion of deserts only obliquely recognized by imagination. Personification—as with Balaam's ass and, negatively, with the besieged trees—gives voice to what I have called virtual subjecthood, assigning to creatures the empathy of personality.[52] The Mosaic concern that the ox not be muzzled in threshing (Deuteronomy 25:4), the ass not be yoked with the ox (Deuteronomy 22:10), all domestic animals be included in the Sabbath rest (Exodus 23:12 and 20:10) and in the land's sabbatical provender (Leviticus 25:6–7); the Talmudic provision that the Sabbath may be violated to rescue an animal (Shabbat 128b); the Midrashic projection into the sensibilities of living things (Exodus Rabbah II 2, where Moses expects that his strayed lamb must be tired); even the requirement that animals be fed before their owners eat (Berakhot 40a, citing Deuteronomy 11:15) and the general prohibition against acquiring any animal one cannot properly feed (Jerusalem Talmud, Yevamot 14d)— all argue that the concern biblically articulated and rabbinically elaborated is moral, directed to the deserts of animals and humans, not merely prudential. It is because the foundational desert is existential that it is regarded biblically as God-given.

The relativity of existence in the diversity of natures renders natural deserts relative as well. There is a price in human suffering or need which renders appropriate the sacrifice of animals' prima facie deserts. But there is also a limit to the claims humans may make upon the environment, a limit set by the absolute requirements of other species, over and above the positive moral claim placed upon subject by subject. As beings approach consciousness they enter the penumbra of protection for their deserts as quasi-subjects. But even with snails, slugs, or roaches there is a relative desert, based on the existential claims *they* make—not to be made needlessly to suffer, for example—and the desert of species, as unique exemplars of reality, not to be expunged. If the deserts of species are in one respect like those of artworks, in another, they are like those of an individual human being—defeasible only in the utmost exigencies, under the rule of pestilence, where existential claims may be forfeit. A basis for the parallel is Mishnaic, in the argument of Sanhedrin (4.5) that each human individual has the uniqueness of a people, a kind, a world.

The text argues for the sanctity of the human individual, but it *assumes* the irreplaceability of species. When an artisan works, the Mishnah argues, each exemplar from the mold is alike, but when the Holy One, blessed be He, creates human beings, each individual is unique. That is why to slay or save a person is to destroy or save a world. Our uniqueness, as Shmuel

Sambursky used to point out, is not the embarrassment for the Talmud that it was for Greek thinkers in the Platonic tradition. Rather, that uniqueness, which rests in its highest phases on the fact of subjecthood, is the mark of our inestimable worth as persons. Our primal existential deserts are due no greater or lesser weighting than those of other persons and may not be bargained away, since to forfeit them would be to forfeit the irreplaceable subject that we are. Here, in the givens of our being, not in any compact or theory of what we might find rational, lies the inalienability of our fundamental deserts—our freedom to consent or withhold consent, our right not to be tortured or toyed with, even when we merit punishment. Freedom is the classic case. It is ours not as our possessions may be ours to dispose of as we like. We lack the right and others lack the power to alienate it from us, not merely because it might be imprudent or inexpedient to do so (for there are conditions, we all know, in which prudence or expediency might seem to counsel otherwise), but because to alienate freedom would violate our being as subjects, strike at the root of all our deserts, negate our personhood.

Freedom is crucial, not merely as a higher order right—like the wish for further wishes in a fairy tale—but because it expresses our identity even more intimately than the will, with which it is closely bound. Freedom lies so close to the core of our identity that it is held sacred, not merely useful; it is valued as life itself or even above life. But freedom is not the only existential datum of the human condition that is not to be compromised even by consent. So in many ways are our bodies and our minds. Human dignity can be violated not only by assault or suicide but by drug abuse and some forms of asceticism and sexuality. Our sexuality is as integral to our claims and vulnerabilities as is liberty of choice or spiritual panache. It is for this reason that rape is so heinous a crime; and prostitution similarly degrades those who debase sexuality to a commodity of impersonal exchange.

In all human relations there is the potential for interactions based on violence and violation, on civil respect, and on dignity and community. Clearly an object of the Mosaic Law is to humanize life by substituting civil and societal relations for hostile, violent or suspicious, exploitative ones, and to mitigate the civil forms by strengthening their communal backbone. The prominent images of contract, covenant, and consent in biblical legislation underscore rather than competing with the foundational role of community: Israel becomes a community through history, not through covenant. And the covenant itself (which is between Israel and

God, not among the Israelites) rests on (and thus cannot create) the free-dom of the covenantors to accept God's law. Even those unborn at the original epiphany can still stand in the place of its original recipients inso-far as they discover truth and justice in the ancient message. For they re-ceive it not as subjects of a formal undertaking in which they had no part but as members of a community which preserves the memory and expands the meaning of that epiphany as the core task of a communal mission sustained across the generations.

The life of the Law is through community, through generosity, consid-eration, recognition of personhood in self and others. Refusal of such rec-ognition is morally unsustainable and pragmatically unwise. Wherever a societal nexus displaces (rather than refining) a communal one (as in at-tempts to place marriage on a strictly contractual basis) there is tragedy in the air,[53] much as tragedy is in the air when violence, suspicion, hostility, and exploitation displace bare formal ties. In a society like ours, where mercantile, juridical, and political interests and experiences have taught us to value and overvalue impersonality in our institutions, the programmatic thrust of the Torah in behalf of community is a matter of moment. The Torah's thrust toward the maintenance and enlargement of the sphere of respect and concern rather than of interest and advantage as bases of human motivation is critical—especially in our economic and political relations, where impersonality has its strongest hold. It is crucial in these areas to recall that in any calculation of worth, desert lies at the root.

Biblical legislation, the locus of an alternative paradigm to that of pure civility, restricts market contractual relations in numerous ways, from the reservation of the gleanings and the corners of the field for the poor to the prohibition of land ownership by priests and the ordination of a fallow period for the land.[54] The nisus of the Law tends to deflate the notion of the omnisufficiency of economic welfare—for example, in the demand that even when we grow prosperous we should present ourselves at regular intervals before a God who expects more of us than mere prosperity and who will not accept "the hire of a whore or the price of a dog." Through-out, the theme is uniform: the replacement of lawless violence (*ḥamas*) with uniform legal ordinances (*ḥukkim u-mishpatim*) and the vitalizing of civil relations with communal bonds of respect and concern (*reʿut*), whose model is friendship, reverence—ultimately love—founded in the recogni-tion of universal existential desert and the human potential for human perfection.

CHAPTER TWO

Punishment

In an ontological theory, real deserts are positive, since they are coequal with the being and power of actual entities. To say that some being deserves ill is to urge that reality should be diminished—a paradox by our account. Yet plainly not every project deserves to be fostered. Some actors should be curtailed in their claims, and not merely for what they are doing to the deserts of others but also for what they *have* done. Justice is concerned with punishment, and punishment addresses not only what might be done but always and essentially what has been done. Does it involve an intentional diminution of deserts? I will argue that it does not, that punishment must and can be distinguished from vindictiveness. "Blood vengeance," Cohen writes, "as the primitive form of the notion of law, was an impediment and contradiction to the more developed stages of culture, in which there was a judicial organization. The three Cities of Refuge were established to maintain justice against blood vengeance. However the altar's protection of the murderer was abolished."[1] Can we construct a rational theory of punishment to make clear why and how it is just to punish wrongdoers? Again I take my text from the Rambam (*Guide* III 35): "There is no more fatuous fool than those who claim that the abrogation of all punishment would be a kindness to mankind. It would be the most barbarous cruelty to men in fact and the ruin of civil order. What is compassionate is what God commanded: 'Establish judges and magistrates in all your precincts' (Deuteronomy 16:18)."

THE LOGIC OF PUNISHMENT

Ordinarily it is in the context of particular actions that we speak of punishment and reward. A rapist has been apprehended and there is agitation for his punishment, concern that it will be too lenient or, by arduous defense work, evaded altogether. A poor man has found and returned a wallet full of cash. Many would say he deserves a reward that is in some measure proportioned to the value restored or the temptation overcome. Sears Roebuck was found to have stinted in rewarding the employee who conceived Snap-on Tools and proposed them to the firm through the company suggestion box. The court awarded him one million dollars, ruling that the corporation's nominal douceur did not respect the value of the concept. Similarly, it is expected that punishments be proportioned to the gravity of crimes. Penal laws set down parameters of due proportion for larceny, fraud, grand theft, murder, arson, extortion, assault, kidnapping—all based on what is taken to be the objective seriousness of the crime. Maimonides emphasizes that intentions and the frequency, ease, and attractiveness of an offense are also factors in the setting of penalties (*Guide* III 41). But the relative status of the offender and victim, the day of the week or season of the year are not determinative.[2]

The idea that wrongdoing merits punishment has roots historical, psychological, and social in the desire for vengeance on those who have harmed interests one holds dear.[3] If the harm was undeserved, the call for reprisal readily gains support. A penalty unexacted is an injustice, and to reward a malefactor is a perversion, a flouting of justice, much as a benefit unrewarded is an injustice. But rewards are not generally statutory. They are usually assimilated to the laws of contract, like some year-end bonuses, or left to private or public discretion or social convention, like gratuities, medals, and prizes for achievement. It is because punishments curtail interests that no just civil society allows their imposition except by law. The maintenance of formal equity and the presumptive deserts it protects are deemed too sensitive to be left to any agency not directly and constitutively answerable to the articulated authority of the society itself.[4] Strict rules of evidence and procedure aim to ensure that no rights are overridden. The resulting bias against punishment is canonical biblically. It does not arise from softheartedness or even from judges' willingness to set themselves in the place of the accused. Rather, the proceduralism and presumption of innocence familiar in the liberal and humane tradition protect and mark positive ontic deserts.[5]

In secularized legislative schemes, where the biblical heritage is often tacit, the procedures that guard presumed innocence are often hung from the unsteady hook of historical or virtual consent. Thus the paradox arises that inalienable rights like the right to a jury trial and the immunity against self-incrimination can be waived, and there is a need for vigilance against a slide from the waiving of rights to their dissolution, as in the public confessional of the show trial. We associate the *lex talionis*, blood feuds, and clan indemnities with societies that lack adequate civil means of enforcing uniform laws. But punishment on private initiative and retaliation against the kin and associates of offenders or dissenters persists in totalitarian societies. For the ends that are to be enforced in such a state far exceed what is rationalized in its laws or attainable by civil authority. Hence the association of terror with totalitarianism and the usurpation of powers that gives the police state its name and infamy: The civil and civilizing presumptions of legal order are sacrificed to "the social good" or "public safety," since they seem mere weightless abstractions beside the concrete gains purchased or pursued at their cost. Totalitarianism incites zealotry as its secular arm, and terrorism becomes its characteristic tool—a sign not of strength but of weakness.

The rejection of private punishment is the birth of civility, and in a way of the state itself. We can see some reflection of the sea change in the traditions of Jewish law about the outburst of Phineas, a paradigm of the zealous urge toward private punishment of a public offense. The outburst was problematic to Moses and not accepted as a norm of Mosaic law.[6] Nor can any civil system countenance its like. But members of a civil society will pass judgment on the success of the state in its retributive capacity. So the risk continually recurs that individuals will act or judge with a *parti pris*, reflecting not objective deserts but a sense of injury or pride, propriety or decorum. Projecting such emotions onto the work of punishment returns it to the realm of vengeance, crossing a subtle boundary which it is the task of justice not only to defend but also to define.

THE PROBLEM OF LEGITIMATING PUNISHMENT

Restitution is not punishment. It may affect the author of a crime very little, and it does not eliminate even the crudest incentives for crime until the likelihood of apprehension is perfect. To counteract criminal incentives is the province of deterrence, controlling dangerous persons and giving pause to prospective wrongdoers. Yet deterrence touches the lives of many who entertain no criminal intentions and modifies the ethos of a community in many unwanted ways. Nor does it necessarily make a criminal a better person. From the viewpoint of reform, punishment is expected to enhance the character—penitentially, therapeutically, even educationally. Yet no legal system has ever successfully disentangled the ameliorative aspects of reformation from its invidious, moralistic accretions. Retribution is sterile without reformation and useless without deterrence. But deterrence and reform, as rationales of punishment, rely upon retribution, despite any disdain we may feel for its seeming primitiveness. As Kant explains:

> Judicial punishment can never be used merely as a means to promote some other good for the criminal himself or for civil society, but instead it must in all cases be imposed on him only on the ground that he has committed a crime. For a human being can never be manipulated merely as a means to the purposes of someone else and can never be confused with objects of the law of things. His intrinsic personhood protects him against such treatment, even though he may indeed be condemned to lose his civil personality. He must first be found to be deserving of punishment before any consideration is given to the utility of this punishment for himself or for his fellow citizens. The law concerning punishment is a categorical imperative, and woe to him who rummages in the winding passages of a theory of happiness for some advantage to be gained by releasing the criminal from punishment or reducing the amount of it in keeping with the Pharisaic motto: 'It is better that one man should die than that the whole people should perish.' If legal justice perishes, then it is no longer worthwhile for men to remain alive on this earth.

Even to commute sentences, say, in return for submission to medical experimentation is unacceptable: "justice ceases to be justice if it can be bought for a price."[7]

We may blanch at hearing retribution called a categorical imperative because we think of retribution as vindictive and prefer to talk of rights rather than duties, imagining that all public actions should be forward-looking toward some good—as are deterrence and reform. Yet there is sense in Kant's notion that legitimate punishment accords the criminal the dignity of a subject because it treats him as a free agent, accountable for his own choice of ends. It is a moving moment in the film *A Gathering of Old Men* when a young man comes forward to "own" his crime rather than cower in denial to let another bear the blame. What is unescapable in Kant's claims is that without reference to retribution there would be no basis for the determination that only the guilty should be deprived of freedoms or other possibilities—rather than, say, those deemed *likely* to commit crimes—or even prospective victims whose freedom of movement should be curtailed. For it is always harder to apprehend criminals than to cage a docile civil population.

But what is retribution? Is it returning harm for harm, repayment of a debt? The confusion of punishment with vengeance under the name of debt fosters the illusion that a penalty has not been paid until the "debtor" has suffered harm—a manifest incoherence if deserts are legitimated claims. Besides, I cannot collect a real debt by burning your barn. The commercial imagery does not help but merely conceals. Society rarely reaps a return from the exaction of punishment and is often more affronted than damaged by a crime. This is suggested in calling crimes offenses rather than inroads. For society and its laws are abstractions, patterns, norms, ideas. One can attack or rob, injure or insult a person, but one can only violate, respect, or ignore a norm. The premise of retribution is that crime involves a violation of the norms, dignity, and composure of society, quite apart from the harm to particular interests. The state's monopoly of juridical, legislative, and coercive authority transposes the nisus of the offense from its immediate victim to the body politic. Thus, in a recent case, the state prosecuted a rape victim for agreeing in a civil settlement to withhold testimony in the parallel criminal case: The criminal offense was not simply against that one victim, and the decision to withhold testimony, obstructing prosecution, was not hers alone to make. When government takes on the retributive role, it is insisting that at times the public affront is paramount.

To isolate retribution from the excesses and arbitrarinesses of vengeance demands some measure of impersonality. Punishment must be directed not at the criminal but at the crime. Is this a distinction without a difference? It is if the impact on the punished is not differentiated, as it should be. An avenger acts out of anger; the state, seeking retribution, out of a particular conception of justice. The idea of retribution, then, can moderate punishment. Vengeance, as a passion, will rarely do that. And even when passion slackens, it will hardly relent just where justice—let alone mercy—would require. So there is good reason to distinguish retribution from vengeance and to prefer it. Distinctive problems remain with retribution: Crucially, it does not restore what is lost, impaired, or destroyed by crime. Yet in virtually all human groups, retribution does seem a fitting response to offenses, and we must ask why.

Confining attention for a moment to the injured interests of the most immediate victim of a crime, we can say that when punishment asks for more (or less) than restitution, this may be because restitution is not possible or not relevant to the concerns that punishment addresses. For not every crime involves a taking, and not every loss is restorable. Besides loss of life, consider the *risk* of death inflicted by a drunken driver, violations of privacy, or destruction of peace of mind. Even in burglary what is violated is distinct from what is taken. Retributive punishment is more concerned with the former. Is punishment, then, a ritual undoing of wrongs that cannot be undone? Perhaps ritual is meant to mediate the imponderable gap between the physical and the moral, much as language mediates the seeming incommensurability between idea and act. If ritual belongs to the symbolic dimension of behavior, clearly there is much of ritual in punishment. For punishments are meant to convey a message and to efface a wrong. The first task can be done only by symbolic means, and the second seems to rely on symbolism where praxis alone is inadequate—for no penalty can be said to efface a wrong except stipulatively.

To regard punishment as ritual may seem to make it mystical and harder rather than easier to justify as rational. But it can help explain some of the features of punishment—why penal laws are rather precise and standardized, for example. Symbolism, after all, is not to be equated with barbarism. Punishments are ritual in nature, I would argue, for the same reason that laws in general are ritual, and with the same utility that language is symbolic. For they specify and schematize what is in itself immeasurable. Punishments may be flexible or rigid, harsh or mild; their membership in the genus of rituals does not establish their modalities. What all penal schemes have in common is that they are constitutive symbolic systems. Their organization defines a hierarchy of values—not to punctuate a contract but to demarcate priorities—specifically, inviolabilities, lifting the boundaries of personhood out of inchoate incommensurability and setting them in an articulate order. The assumption is not that injury or affront can be measured but that crucial communal relationships will lack the articulation society requires in them unless formal public measures are assigned to the values they enshrine, in those extreme but crucial cases where their violation demands that they be pragmatically weighted and expressively reaffirmed. Thus it is characteristic of punishment that it is not applied where there is "no harm done"—where restitution, say, is sufficient to restore a prior equilibrium. Rather, punishment is employed (as distinct from civil remedy, complementing or even supplanting it) where at least part of the harm done cannot be undone—where human dignity or some related value has been violated by an agent who ought to have done better. It is for this reason that punishment is inevitably backward-looking.

Pragmatically, of course, punishment is not symbolism alone. It is an interference with the affairs and projects of a moral subject, and its measure is set not merely by the significance assigned to past acts but by the intent of altering future behavior. Yet the notion that punishment is a melancholy necessity for societies (in their present imperfect state), aiming to wrong wrongdoers and so combat crime, involves a dangerous admission, couched in the language of benevolence. It allows that penal laws are necessary and useful while conceding that the necessity is a wicked and ugly one. Ideally, perhaps, punishment will be replaced with some kindlier response. The danger is this: If punishment is always an evil, it becomes difficult to see how its practice can be controlled. All purely deterrent rationales of punishment and indeed all rationales that see punishment solely as an instrument of social policy suffer from the same defect. Only if some good can be found in punishment, in whatever makes it right, can punishment find its limits within itself—in the measure of its rightness or the determinate good it serves. Otherwise it remains inherently immoderate, measured only by the undefined reach of social policy—law and order in their broadest and potentially most excessive applications.

CRIME AND TELISHMENT

Utilitarians argue that the value of punishment arises in its potential for reducing pain—that is, its capacity to prevent crime. In some ways this justifies too little; in others, too much. Punishment is notoriously inefficient in preventing crime. Its impact has never in history been great enough to eliminate recidivism. Enhanced likelihoods of detection and apprehension, successful prosecution, and significant sentencing do curtail the incidence of many crimes; "specific" deterrence is won through incarceration, especially of career criminals. Anomalously, "general" deterrence affects individuals in inverse relation to their likelihood to commit a crime. It has the least effect on those toward whom it is most crucially aimed. Crimes of passion or obsession; crimes of abject want or desperation;[8] crimes of "principle" or "dispassion" like political terrorism, sabotage, and espionage; crimes of calculated risk like major robberies and arsons; crimes by persons in positions of influence or security—all are resistant to the Benthamite calculus of potential losses and gains. No realistically attainable probability of arrest, conviction, and full serving of a sentence seems able to produce an impression sufficient to render crime a negligible factor in social planning. Indeed, for some categories of crime, heightened "deterrence" may only heighten the seriousness of offenses by raising the stakes and heightening the desperateness of lawbreakers.

Crucially for my argument, deterrence legitimates too much. Even assuming the efficacy of deterrence within some acceptable tolerances, ignoring the inefficiencies of our penal institutions and setting aside their role as centers of criminal activity and colleges of criminal skills and attitudes, we confront a moral problem: It is conceivable that we might find execution of sentence upon the innocent no less effective a deterrent to crime than punishment of the guilty. Should we find that adding innocent victims to the numbers of those sentenced improves the overall crime statistics, a strict Benthamite calculus would leave us little choice but to hang, scourge, torture as many likely victims as we could lay hands on, regardless of their innocence, until our object was achieved, the crime rates fell, and it was demonstrated that there was now a social utility in calling a halt. Morally such a policy is insupportable. It is inconsistent with just punishment, and few would defend it. Yet its legitimacy follows from the assumption that punishment finds sufficient legitimation in deterrence.

Defending and adjusting the Utilitarian account of punishment, Rawls has argued that the force of the retributive idea attaches properly but solely to singling out a particular individual for punishment, not to the justification of the institution, which rests, he claims, wholly on Utilitarian grounds.[9] In his endeavor to segregate the particular from the general aspects of legitimation, Rawls strikes a rich vein of inquiry, but he does not follow up on this important step with a developed account of the symbiosis of deterrence and retribution in penal theory. The development would not be easy in the framework he sets out. For to justify an institution is to justify each act it mandates, and to justify any application of a rule is to justify the rule. When Rawls concedes that retribution tells us whom to punish but not how, he eliminates the retributive proportioning of punishment to crime and leaves only deterrence to moderate sentencing. But deterrence is not regulated decisively by justice. It has its own concerns to prosecute.

Rawls dismisses the claim that Utilitarianism would condemn the innocent. Utilitarians, he urges, would never willingly "hang an innocent man." He quotes Bentham himself in support. But my concern is not what Utilitarians would do, but what their theory demands. If there is one common and empiric measure of good and evil (and it is the hallmark of Utilitarianism to claim that there is), then it is easy to conceive situations in which justice is compromisable for some "greater good" or avoidance of some greater evil than relaxation of its standards. Utilitarianism affords no basis for Rawls' strict lexical ordering of values. That was the classic difficulty on which Mill's Utilitarianism foundered when he appealed to knowledgeable enjoyment rather than pleasure alone as arbiter of the dispute between poetry and pushpin. It remains the central difficulty with Utilitarianism, if justice (or any other good) is to be uncompromisable—or compromisable only in the direction of mercy.

Inflicting disabilities upon non-wrongdoers for social ends, Rawls urges, is not punishment at all. He prefers to call it "telishment." Such an institution he argues, would be unworkable—unwieldy, too difficult to keep secret (he presumes that the innocence of victims must be kept secret), too subject to abuse. But punishment, too, is unwieldy and subject to abuse. And we have a difficulty in convincing the public of the guilt of the convicted and the innocence of the exonerated that exactly parallels the difficulty in keeping secret the innocence of the telished. Given the inefficiency of all communication and the problems of institutional credibility, it can hardly be claimed that telishment is necessarily more unworkable technically than punishment. On the Utilitarian account it would not at all be difficult to make a moral case that telishment as a policy should be substituted for (rather than merely supplemented by) punishment in certain social circumstances. That is just the weakness of reliance on deterrence as the sole legitimation of punishment. In Utilitarian terms it is a contingent matter, depending on the empirical question of social benefits and disabilities, whether those guilty of crimes should be punished and social benefactors rewarded, or vice versa.

Imagine a society whose people are very susceptible to suggestion, more so than to the claims of rational argument—a society not wholly unlike our own. Suppose that in that society persons are inclined to be violently hostile on slight provocation. And suppose it were found empirically that such violence could be restrained by keeping the populace cowed —through media messages that sap self-confidence, through browbeating in school and at public recreational activities, and through a systematic program of randomly applied, undeserved benefits and disabilities. The program would not have to be kept secret. It might be found more effective if its purposes and methods were well known. On Utilitarian grounds such a program would be legitimated if it had the desired impact—a measurable effect on crime rates, say, in such categories as robbery, burglary, and aggravated assault. It might even be legitimated in people's minds through the awareness of its effectiveness and accepted as a necessary evil, as we accept the release of the guilty in order to preserve our procedural protections. It would not be necessary for the program to be *highly* effective. Even if it were only marginally effective (as compared with some practicable alternatives, and perhaps less costly than others), it would be justified on Utilitarian considerations. And if excessive or bizarre penalties heightened the impact, they too would be justified. So would either excessive or deficient rewards. Utilitarians of high moral principle and good upbringing may abhor this outcome. But their philosophy is not the equal of their principles of practice and does not articulate the values bespoken by their upbringing. It contains no dictum by which such institutions as telishment can be declared unjust. If they afford a desired benefit at a cost acceptable to the majority, then they are justified in Utilitarian terms automatically —indeed, tautologously.

The evidence of many kinds of tyranny suggests that our illustration is not entirely fanciful. But the real question is not the verisimilitude of the example but what it reveals about deterrence. The case is conceivable; and Utilitarianism, recognizing no values beyond those of social preference, affords no grounds by which expedient measures can be dismissed, provided they are feasible technically and accepted popularly. It is not possible for a Utilitarian to object on Utilitarian grounds that an institution is intrinsically unfair. Only if it proves ineffectual or counterproductive can its use be discredited. But evidence to that effect will always be corrigible, so it will always be possible to argue that in some circumstances telishment may prove marginally effective. There is no vocabulary to express the objection that an expedient policy might be dishonest, dishonorable, or unjust. There are only the two realms—the politic and the impolitic.

No matter how outrageous a policy might seem to the sensibilities of an age, based on the perceived situation *then*—even rounding up just under half the populace and butchering them without any immediate pretext— that policy might become a desired (hence desirable) goal tomorrow. It could not be ruled immoral a priori. The example is extreme but not beyond imagining a world that has seen Hitler's genocide against the Jews, Pol Pot in Cambodia, Mao in China, Stalin in Russia, the Turks in Armenia, or others in Pakistan, Bangladesh, Sri Lanka, East Timor, Assam, Ethiopia, Somalia, Eritrea, and Chad—to mention only some examples within the century not yet ended. We must reckon with the fact that what people will accept or advocate as social policy is to some undetermined extent an open question. And the openness of that question undermines the claim that a

Utilitarian legitimation, say of telishment, could never lead to its implementation. Mass murder has been proposed and is being practiced today on a national scale as a matter of policy in more than one place. Garrett Hardin and others advocate starvation of entire peoples and are welcomed as serious and progressive ethicists for the radical expediency of their proposals.[10]

Telishment, like torture or brainwashing, intentionally violates human dignity and integrity. That is reason enough for rejecting it, without extrinsic justification. But human dignity is not a natural, measurable quantity, like crime rates or self-reported satisfaction—the sorts of variable that Utilitarianism renders canonical. Utilitarianism can respond to the unpopularity of draconian measures if they become unpopular. But popularity can also be wooed and swayed, and opposition can be suppressed. Utilitarianism, taken strictly at its word, can offer no objection but must await the popular verdict. As citizens or advocates, Utilitarians may favor or oppose any policy that pleases or irritates their fancy. But as theorists they cannot declare any policy unjust or wrong apart from what the balance of the populace may think of it. Later in this book I shall argue that unjust policies tend to undermine the societies that tolerate them. Even those who do not expect to find themselves singled out as victims might hold such policies in repugnance, sensing that they are imprudent or seeing that they are unjust. But the broad consent of a nation to injustice in the name of perceived interests is not so foreign to history that we can readily assume national consent (or advocacy) to coincide with justice. And the process of historic retribution is not so swift that we can afford to delay our judgment that an institution is unjust until history has proved it unworkable. Indeed, if such delays were necessary, no social criticism could be made of any institution until after it had righted itself or found enough rope to execute upon itself the sentence folded in the maxim of its marching orders.

The essence of prophetic morality was to detect and denounce social injustice before its damnable character had fully run its course. Warnings of historic judgment were pronounced before the time for moral reversal (*teshuvah*) had passed. Many institutions (slavery, the Gulag system) have had long lives, although they proved ultimately unworkable. Prophetic criticism insists that moral and historic verdicts will coincide in the end. But morality regards the deserts of all, not merely the politically well articulated or prevalent. It sustains a level of respect for human dignity which only wisdom recognizes to be of the essence of practicality. Its universality renders its perspective long as well as broad. Today's seeming expediency can pave the way to tomorrow's extinction. Those who lack the kind of strength that only an other-regarding ethos can confer might well fall foul of the momentum of history. But one cannot for that reason make "workability" the sufficient criterion of justice. To do so is to risk deferring moral criticism to a time when it can have no helpful bearing on policy, when the long neglected and easily ignored notes of moral unworkability have come due. That injustice tends to undermine itself I believe is true. But that injustice cannot persist because it is "unworkable" and will be found ultimately insupportable I take to be no more than a fond hope.

I emphasize the application of our argument to *policies* of arbitrary telishment and the like. For much is made of the claim that rule Utilitarianism, as distinguished from act Utilitarianism, would never justify the sort of opportunism that allows punishing an innocent man for reasons of state. But our illustrations refer not merely to the secret selection of one victim known to be innocent but also to the publicly acknowledged and potentially accepted policy of "telishing" the innocent at large—the *institution* of telishment and punitive excess. Such policies can be brought under a rule. Rule Utilitarianism does not hold back the bizarre conclusion.

Mill says that equal treatment is "the highest abstract standard of social and distributive justice," and he derives that standard from the greatest happiness principle.[11] But the ideal of equality, as we have seen, is a formal principle that assigns no positive deserts; and the greatest happiness principle does not exclude the violation of one individual's baseline entitlements if sufficient gain to others is to be secured thereby. Only some provision for the sanctity of the life, liberty, privacy, and dignity of the individual can preclude such an outcome. Rule Utilitarianism seeks to mitigate the familiar defects of Utilitarian situationalism. But the old Utilitarian warrants ground its formal guarantees. These latter must be either presumptive, thus appealing surreptitiously to material deserts, or (if still Utilitarian) empirically disconfirmable and so rescindable, "in the public interest."

The metaphysical commitments of rule Utilitarianism are visible even in Mill's notion that the greatest happiness principle somehow entails "perfect impartiality between persons." But clearly it is possible that in some circumstances human pleasure might be maximized through highly inequitable means. For example, some fantastic society might be devised in which a small number of intelligent individuals worked fiendishly or slavishly to keep the vast majority in a continual state of drugged euphoria. Here pleasure might be maximized, but justice would not be served. Indeed, even equality might be preserved, if the custodians could be conditioned or convinced that theirs was an ideal state, so that they too were maximally pleased or pleasured by their sense of power or command, or service to the euphoria of the rest. Then pleasure would be complete, but justice would still be absent.

The illustration is not entirely fanciful, but even if such a state were completely illusory, rule Utilitarians would be hard pressed to explain why they should not work doggedly for as close as possible an approximation to it. Applying the same reasoning to punishment, we return to our central criticism: If it cannot be ruled out that the arbitrary tormenting of the few might enhance the pleasure of the many or diminish their liability to pain all out of proportion to the "necessary" suffering, then rule Utilitarianism finds no refuge in its formalism from the charge that it justifies and mandates our pursuit of such an arrangement.

Utilitarian deterrence justifies injustice precisely to the extent that social utility can be found or imagined to subsist in injustice. This outcome is no more than a consequence of the fact that in Utilitarianism, as Kant put it, everything has a price, nothing a dignity. Kant's charge is more than rhetoric. For the essence of Utilitarianism is the placement of all values on a single scale: None will be incommensurate, but none will be inviolable. Both punishment and mercy will be part of the social calculus. If penal laws are to operate with a view to justice, as distinguished from seeming expediency, then they cannot be framed solely on the basis of deterrence but must constitutively regard retributive considerations as well.

PUNISHING THE GUILTY TO REQUITE THE INNOCENT

Many recent thinkers have recognized the need for joining retributive considerations to their (often largely deterrent) conceptions of punishment. In one instance of this hybrid sort of approach, it is argued that punishing crimes balances a potential loss against the potential gains of criminal activity, supporting the social compact by ensuring that those who uphold it are not worse off through adherence than criminals are through their offenses.[12] The model assumes that criminal activity is intrinsically beneficial to the criminal; non-criminals are somehow deprived or "missing out." Such an assumption can be refuted at two levels of strength. For we can argue that crime is not always beneficial to the perpetrator (or harmful to the intended victim, for that matter) — it need not involve *A*'s loss and *B*'s gain. And we can argue for the stronger claim that crime is never beneficial but always harmful to the perpetrator. One claim employs while the other avoids common notions about what constitutes a benefit or gain.

As to the first, there are many ways criminal schemes may go awry. But the trouble and risk do not generally exempt culprits from punishment.[13] A victim may gain immensely in wisdom or even in wealth through a theft, assault, or kidnapping. He may learn to reorder his life or be forced to abandon an unprofitable business, dangerous neighborhood, or crabbed lifestyle. Such effects have no bearing on guilt or blame. Joseph's rise to greatness in Egypt cannot be credited to his brothers' moral account. Further, not all crimes even aim at gain. Some are irrational or merely vicious. We judge them by their impact and their intentions.

With certain crimes it seems evident that the criminal never gains. Rape is an example. Tasteless and ill-informed accounts have too long suggested that rapists gain sexual gratification at the "expense of" their victims. But sexual experiences are not a commodity, and rape is not an erotic but a violative crime. Typically it uses sexual degradation to exercise hostility. In this respect rape is like mugging, where an excess of violence indicates that terrorization has become an end in itself. Even burglary shows an element of this autonomous thrill of violation. In vandalism destructiveness for its own sake is paramount—the source of Augustine's remorse about his senseless wasting of stolen pears as a youth. An important component of violence is not assignable to pragmatic ends.

According to the model I am criticizing, rapists are punished to ensure that they do not unfairly gain a good, a freedom, that others forgo. It would be unfair *to those others* (!) if rape went unpunished. But rape is not a good. Still less is it a freedom. Behind such assessments lies the notion that rape is somehow a pleasure enjoyed rather than a fixation acted out. The assumption does not square with the phenomena. Whatever is experienced by a rapist seems hardly to contribute to his happiness or well-being. And it is scarcely material penally whether a rapist enjoys the experience, undergoes an orgasm or (as is often the case) does not. The "gain" is a phantom. While acts of violation involve a certain license, in that boundaries are transgressed, mores flouted, dignities degraded, they do not add stature to character, value to experience, or any enhancement to the latitude of liberty. Rape is punished because of its impact (actual or potential) on its victim and its intentions vis-à-vis that victim and human dignity in general. The moral concern is not that a good has been illicitly appropriated which others might have enjoyed. That reckoning feigns a rationality in an act that is irrational formally and materially: formally, in the disproportion assigned in criminal intent to the victim's personhood vis-à-vis an arbitrary motive; materially, in the inversion of the response to legitimate deserts, from recognition to violation.

Apprehending the fundamental irrationality of violative acts brings us to our stronger line of objection. For all crime is ultimately violative, and in an important sense never brings a net gain. The disparity between specious and legitimate rationality observed in the case of rape typifies the irrationality of criminal acts. Their character is to alienate the criminal from others and from himself, since human identity is inherently social and thus implicitly ethical. Taken to its extreme, the dynamic of criminality is not to build up but to destroy the criminal. Only in the subjective scale that weighs others' deserts lightly and one's own passions or caprices heavily does the semblance of a balance appear. But that is by an abstraction that ignores the intertwinedness of interests, the undermining of one's identity in the very act of jeopardizing that of another. The criminal bails into his own bilge and seeks to lighten his craft by cutting sections from its keel.

Such self-destructiveness is pinioned in the psalmist's (92:7–8) vivid image of a patch of grass that seeks to claim more territory than it can hold and hastens its own destruction through overextension. The object of the image is the self-deception of the immoralist calculus. In slighting the interests of others it neglects the ultimate concerns of the self. The point is made by Plato, too, in his celebrated psychoanalysis of the tyrannical soul: In becoming an enemy to others the tyrannous personality looses the bonds of its own integration and becomes alien to itself. Along with regard for others' interests it has destroyed the orienting principle (regard for the Good) which alone can give coherent definition and direction to human identity and desire.

Cicero argues that it matters very little what a thief may acquire by theft; in and through his act he has become a thief.[14] Cicero's liveliest concern here, characteristically, is for the social dimension, name and repute. But his argument bespeaks a deeper, linked concern. Beyond reputation lies the question of what a thief (or prostitute or forger) is to think of himself. Criminals have many strategies of slang and hardened thought, ironic self-deprecation, or romantic self-aggrandizement to cope with or evade such questions of self-identification. All say in effect that one simply does not care. But that is where the greatest loss lies. For property can be recovered or recouped. In ceasing to care about his own ultimate worth and prospect the thief forfeits something far more precious than he can steal, a possibility of integrity founded on the consciousness of rectitude and grounding human projects worthy of respect and collaboration. The boor, as the psalmist puts it, does not know, nor does the fool understand this. What they do not understand, if we spell it out, is that we are by nature both social and moral beings—social in the natural exigency of our existence, the fact that we must live with others; moral in the necessity of our freedom, the fact that we must live with ourselves. The boor and the fool do not understand that we live in the esteem of others and can live adequately only in our self-esteem. Nor do they understand that self-esteem is much harder won than superficially appears, and even harder to deserve.

Christians express the loss criminals undergo in the language of immortality: "What profiteth it a man that he gain the world if he forfeit his immortal soul?" (Matthew 16:25–26). But the language can be misleading. The point at issue morally is not that God will punish a man eternally for some one crime or other. The fear of consequential punishment misses the immanence of retribution and the indissoluble moral nexus between actions and their requital, which is suggested by the rabbinic image drawn from Scripture (Job 37:7) that the signet sign of each man's hand is imprinted on his acts, and on the divine sentence by which they are judged. It is not possible, of course, for a criminal to "gain the world." That, perhaps, is what the criminal ultimately, irrationally, desires. The essence of criminal maxims is their boundlessness—hence their violative character, their relative deprecation or absolute negation of counterclaims. But what is captured most clearly, I think, in the idea of losing an immortal soul through vicious choices is the fact that human dignity, which rests on recognition of one's own and others' deserts, has no profitable exchange. Muḥammad, a merchant by trade, thus derided the vicious for selling their souls cheap.[15] The ingenuous analysts who suppose that criminals must know the worth of what they gain seem too ready to forget the disparity between what the criminal pursues and what he achieves.

The commodity model, resting on a Utilitarian analysis of the social compact, is an eversion of the theory of deterrence. Rather than argue that potential criminals must be motivated by the punishment of actual criminals to regard crime as disadvantageous, it maintains that the law-abiding should be motivated by the punishment of criminals to regard adherence to law as advantageous—a clear case of treating criminals as means and not ends. As in pure deterrence, the theory justifies more than it should: If it seems socially desirable, we may inflict the most grievous penalties to motivate desired behavior; and the question remains, why rule only against criminals? If these consequences are rejected, it must be asked if we are not merely rationalizing our familiar practice. If all and only actual criminals are to be punished, and in due measure to the gravity of their offenses, then both positive deterrence against lawbreaking and negative deterrence in behalf of law observance justify too broadly. Only if it can be said rightly that so-and-so (and he alone) deserves such-and-such a penalty (and neither more nor less) on account of what he has done (not in anticipation of what others might do) are we assured that a punishment is just. And the application of such a framework is the unique strength of the retributive model: Deterrence itself rests on retribution in legitimating punishment, if deterrence is to be just. Yet both deterrence and retribution seem to assume that some harm ought to be done. It was against this assumption that Plato directed his powerful critique of conventional ideas of penal justice.

RETRIBUTION AND DESERTS

How, Plato asks, can justice harm anyone?[16] If penal justice makes the criminal worse, where is the good we expect from justice? In the reasoning of the Sophists punishment *is* an injury, but one man's injury may be society's benefit. Much of the excess and abuse condoned in the name of punishment arises from this perverse concept, which admits that justice may be good for some only by being bad for others. Socratically expressed, the tragic tension or conflict of Sophistic justice becomes a paradox: Justice should leave all that it affects improved—never worse. But this standard seems to justify only reform, never retribution.

A similar outcome is hinted at even in the idea of deterrence. For the object is not simply to render crime disadvantageous but to rectify future behavior. Yet chastisement may have quite the opposite effect. It *may* discipline redemptively. But it may also harden resentment and embitter criminal malice. Prudence argues for moderation, especially when rigor looks counterproductive. But the claims of fairness urge against singling out special cases. It would seem to follow that if severity is ever imprudent it is always unjust. And that would seem to counsel that punishment as we practice it must be abolished altogether.

Much of the muddle of our present penal practice suggests a wavering of societal attention between the conflicting claims of severity in the name of deterrence and mitigation in the name of compassion. But efforts at mitigation can be as counterproductive as severity and may seem to offer condonement. More is at issue here than the falsely linear question of how severe punishments should be—questions about what kinds of punishments are appropriate and what purposes we expect punishment to pursue or achieve. Plato's challenge, raised in the form of a Socratic aporia as to the legitimacy of punishment, thus only seems purely academic. Like all

Socratic questions, it is one of fundamental practicality: We shall not know how to modulate punishments until we understand why anyone should be punished at all.

REFORM AND RETRIBUTION

Plato never proposed abolishing punishment. His point was that the proper practice of justice should make us more just, as the proper practice of music makes us more musical. It is unjust, paradigmatically, to seek to deter crime by means of prefrontal lobotomy. Even some fines might so diminish a human being's effectiveness as to lessen his being. It might well be unjust to remove a person's livelihood or parental role, except to debar a noxious livelihood or put a stop to child abuse. Socratically, *any* diminution of a person's status appears to be an injury, and hence a wrong. Yet if penalties require the offender's improvement, punishment seems to be replaced with a reward.

The dilemma is not quite as perfect as may appear in the abstract. For rehabilitation of the penal type, reformation, penitential efforts at salvation, or modern excursions into behavior modification touch the penumbra of privacy in ways that a free society would never tolerate unless in cases of convicted criminals. Where punishment in general is not consensual, programs of reformation must be voluntary. Unless personally appropriated, they will fail; even when "chosen," say, as alternatives to or options within prison or parole, programs of reform for criminals remain obtrusive and are therefore retrospective in their warrant, although prospective in their aims. Thus they are inevitably retributive, even when not at all retaliatory. Genuinely reformative efforts, then, do not fit the model of rewards, even when they improve the external conditions for former criminals. Any betterment is won at a heavy cost in loss of privacy and liberty. But this consequence, which differentiates penal reform from general self-improvement, entails its own need for limitation. The rehabilitative right of access to another's personhood, for which legitimation is sought on retributive grounds, is not vindictive; but it cannot be absolute even on its own terms and for its own stated purposes. Residual rights remain; and among these, clearly, is the desert of a rational, choosing subject to establish the primary focus and direction of his own intentions. By this standard, brainwashing and other types of mind control are illegitimate in prisons, as elsewhere —even with "consent." We must reckon with the possibility of persons imprisoned or otherwise penalized retaining the resolve to live and die as criminals. One can attempt to influence. To browbeat is usually counterproductive. To deflect personhood by force, fraud, or psychic manipulation may not be impractical but is clearly immoral.

Reform, then, like deterrence, requires modulation and limitation lest its edifying aims be swallowed up in the implications of its means. The proper limits, paradoxical as it may seem, can be derived, as with deterrence, only on the retributive account. For only on that account can it be determined whether and when a criminal has been treated as he deserves —what efforts at reform must be offered, to whom and how, when they are completed, and when such efforts are invasive or excessive.

Can our theory of deserts contribute anything of value here? Our penal codes have not yet found the optimal modalities. Having abandoned corporal punishment in the name of humaneness, we now operate a system of incarceration that is in many ways less humane. Clearly one measure of a society's success is the degree to which partial exclusion from its full range of activities is an effective deterrent to crime. In a well-conducted state the severest penalty is exile, just as in a well-integrated community the severest chastisement is ostracism. Such standards are utopian for times when many criminals are so alienated that they regard exile as escape and some states are so tyrannous that exile is a privilege rather than a penalty. We generally do seek the rehabilitation and reintegration of offenders, so the issue of supervision is probably the most crucial and sorely neglected dimension of our penal process. Philo pictures the Biblical Cities of Refuge as designed to address this concern. The Levites, he argues, will decisively influence the cities they administer—not by prying catechisms or sententious lectures but in socialization to a new ethos, a kind of therapy for the guilty soul in its new environment.[17] Clearly this model is a saner one than the plan of prisons in which criminals create the ethos to which even the guards become assimilated.

We find, at any rate, that reform can be penal without becoming a vindictive penance and that punishment can be reformative without becoming a reward. To build institutions that pursue these possibilities—impose punishments without wronging those whom they punish—remains a prime desideratum of our age. That leaves us still with the question how any disability can be warranted.

DIMINUTION OF DESERTS

Our answer is that punishment is not a denial of extant deserts but a scaling back in the recognition of deserts demonstrated to have been impaired. In all communities we make claims upon one another and so erect a

superstructure of enhanced and presumptive dignities. Civil communities
are distinguished by the formalization of such assumptions, allowing their
extension on a far wider scale than bonds of friendship, clan, or family. The
enhanced, accrued, or presumed deserts created by society, however, are
not absolute. We make them existential insofar as we appropriate the conditions of civility into our identities, but when we violate them we lose
them. Their benefits are privileges, although within the civil context they
are entitled rights. They are conferred and thus may be withdrawn—not
arbitrarily but for cause. We may lose the right to their free exercise, but
only by our actions.

Nature always speaks *for* interests, never simpliciter against them. And
morality cannot do otherwise: It is founded on the recognition of deserts
and can never justify their flouting. But the social recognition of deserts
may require downward adjustment of specific claims when it is demonstrated that some component of recognition has been founded on unwar-
rantable assumptions. Clearly there is a diminution in desert corresponding to any objective declension in the standing of a being. We do not treat
a corpse as a person. A criminal, as long as the category of humanity can be
applied, retains the deserts of a moral subject. But not all deserts are inalienable in this way. Some may be tarnished or diminished; others, lost.
To imagine otherwise is to adopt a static essentialism that would judge
without reference to particularity, choices, or actions. If deserts are existential, then surely they are individual. If existence is dynamic, deserts cannot
be static.

Further, to assume that all deserts reside intrinsically, impassively, and
inalienably in each subject is to adopt an atomism that masks the communal character of all being.[18] For the being of each thing is not only what it
claims for itself but what its universe allows, invites, or requires it to be.
The notion of desert has primal reference to the atomicity of each entity;
but only at the secondary level, where projects are undertaken and higher
order claims are made, does individuality acquire its elaborated moral
significance and operative force. Whether we speak of the community of
electrons and protons in an atom or of the community of cells in the
porifera, the symbiosis of trees or grass, the commensalism of lions and
hyenas, or the community of nations, purely individual deserts are a mere
baseline, often a conceptual limit given significance pragmatically by communal endeavor. Naturally, supremely naturally, all deserts depend on what
we are, and something of them survives as long as we are something. But,
for that very reason, all depend as well on what we do. Our actions in the

concert of our social environs can make us more, or less, or critically other, than we have been. We acquire or lose deserts according to our standing in the order of being and—crucially—according to the extent that we have fostered, maintained, or forfeited the desert of collaboration, through which we have enlarged our claims by expanding our identity from its atomic base, linking it with the identities of others.

A being, then, can undermine itself—in three ways: by contradicting the laws of its own nature, by running counter to the interests of others on whom its interest depends, and (combining these) by degrading its own nature *through* disrespect for other beings' interests, undermining the moral basis for certain higher order claims upon their confidence. The typical concern of our criminal procedures is with the last.

Diminution of desert does not always depend on conscious awareness and choice. Desert is not, as we might have supposed, coextensive with moral responsibility. One organism may aggress against another, or a species may compete directly or indirectly with the interest of another in some resource, quite without awareness of that fact. The relative deserts of the claimants are proportioned to the ontic magnitude of their claims and limited by all counterclaims. But affirmative claims can be undercut by the prospective or actual dependency of one claimant on another—immediately for existence or growth, or mediately for higher realization. Conscious knowledge and moral projection aid in making good higher order claims, but their curtailment, by choice or by nature, does not assuage the impact of their absence. In living, growth, and evolution all players act with their own uncompensated handicaps of finitude, whether natural or self-induced. We are accountable not only for what we know and are capable of achieving but also for what we neglect to know and do, and even for what we cannot know and have no way of doing. We play in earnest and "for keeps." Only so can knowledge, awareness, moral recognition, and other capabilities become sufficiently advantageous that development can be measured in their terms. Consciousness becomes a yardstick of evolution; and the yardstick of consciousness is conscience. For it is only where knowledge is valuable that consciousness can evolve, and only where claims of conscience can be articulated that consciousness imparts the full claims of subjecthood. Desert, then, can be curtailed, and such curtailments demarcate the character of the being that bears them, as its antitype, the negative imprint or impress of its failure on all that a being is, can be, or might have been.

Moral agents capable of recognizing the deserts of others because they have an integrated and projective view of their environment establish communities of trust through which greater claims are made in behalf of each participant than any could make alone. Such claims are jeopardized, diminished, or forfeit when good faith is broken. Thus words are believed in virtue of a tacit compact to truth telling—not a contract but a constantly negotiated mutual understanding. When truth is compromised or violated, credence is diminished or dissolved—and should be. A counterlie is not the fit response. Skepticism followed by disbelief is natural and appropriate. Here we see the basis of an answer to the frequent canards against Kant on the question of lying: Kant argues that any "intentional untruth in the expression of one's thoughts" robs the liar of human dignity. To deprive another of truth is to repudiate one's standing as a moral personality engaged in the exchange of ideas.[19] The Kantian presumptive right to be told the truth thus rests on the claims of civility and may be weakened or dissolved where the bonds of civility are frayed or rejected. The terrorist or assassin has no particular entitlement to be told the whereabouts of his quarry, having loosed himself from the bonds of civility which ground the rights and expectations of free interchange in ordinary human communities. That Kant himself sees this implication is clear from his inference in the *Groundwork* that one who lies will simply not be believed, and that in a society where false promises were the rule, "no one would believe he was being promised anything, but would laugh at utterances of this kind as empty shams."[20] Again with exploitation: We have seen that all human exchanges rest upon a humanizing bond of mutual recognition. Abuse of such bonds is a reneging on claims of trust or courtesy which are constitutive to the relation. Diminished normative claims are to be expected as a result.

It is where criticism, including self-criticism, is possible and useful that the moral categories have become most ramified and elaborate. Expressed in the tones of pleasure or displeasure, our articulate moral categories are structured to accord approbation (praise, honor, or reward) to those who grant recognition as we believe is due and disapprobation (blame, shame, or punishment) to those who fail to do so. When the failure has an overt impact and a maxim judged repugnant to the maintenance of community, crimes are identified and punishments are mandated. The principle in its barest form: like to like, tit for tat. The primitive injunction of associative, emotive logic gains a primitive articulacy through personification: dressed up as a goddess to denote the wisdom of a societal proceeding, blindfolded for impartiality, and made quantitative by the placement of a balance in her hand. But what the icon stands for and what the shibboleth *measure for measure* voices is the proportioning of recognition withheld to recognition forfeit.

Retribution, as distinct from vengeance, then, is not the tailoring of a criminal's desert to meet his denial of desert in a victim, adding injury to injury. It is the tailoring of the social scope afforded to desert to fit more snugly to its actual proportions. The generous presumptions that make civil society possible are partially defeated. In response they are withdrawn in due measure and kind. Privilege conferred is cut back to adjust for trust betrayed and so renounced. The response is mandated by the fundamental requirement of morality that recognition follow the contours of desert. It would be irresponsible to persist in the extension of unmerited trust. Reform will hope and plan for the return of the powers that made trust reasonable, and mercy will restrain severity, respecting the haven of such powers in the past. But justice commands the formal, societal institution to look beyond conventions of civility and take cognizance of the now demonstrated fact.

RETRIBUTIVE PROPORTION

Punishments constructed on this model and confined to what it authorizes will not convey amorphous hostility, ennui, or anger—emotions typical of the criminal. Rather, if properly devised, they will articulate just what sort of privileges the criminal has presumed upon and forfeited. The ritual specificity of punishment is not confined to symbolizing authority as violence but may speak with conviction and dispassion, with all the clarity of language and social structure. What precisely will it say? To the victims of an embezzler the immediate concern is restitution. Society at large wants protection from like offenses. But what is interesting for us is that society may demand that the embezzler be removed from certain positions of trust even if he can promise truthfully that the offense will not recur. Even if he posts a bond to indemnify any future losses, the demand can still be made, perhaps mitigated by concern for the embezzler's livelihood or the welfare of his family. The penal response says in effect that the embezzler has confuted some measure of the trust placed in him and is now to be treated as unworthy of such trust, in certain respects and with certain limitations and provisos. It would be excessive to regard him as unworthy of any sort of trust ever again. Likewise for the drunk driver. Retribution carries with it strict limitations by reference to the character of the offense. For the magnitude and type of punishment aims to reflect the magnitude and type of trust broken.

A thief, perhaps, has made no promise not to steal. Yet society has an obligation to uphold the assumptions the thief has violated. And society alone can assign the significances of each offense and withdraw social amenity in due measure. Government, then, as the formal, institutional organ of society at large, acquires an obligation not only to deter the thief and seek his reform but also visibly to withdraw some portion of the general social support against which the maxim of his actions has offended, bringing the thief and others face to face with the moral consequence of a loss of tacit trust. His liberty to impose upon civil trust is restricted according to his diminished desert. But he is not made the victim of a compensatory theft.

Civil crimes always involve a breach of trust. Their gravity is a product of the magnitude of the injury sustained and the sanctity of the trust violated—whether of family members, business associates, passersby on the streets of a city, or riders in an elevator, who repose a simple yet sacred trust in one another. No undertaking is needed for such trust to be understood and extended, and no license is needed for it to be withdrawn when violated palpably. There is a weighty refutation of presumed desert when the behavior of a human being excludes so fundamental a presumption as that by which we assume of one another that the frisson of violation will not be held more precious than the sanctity of recognition. When such perverse valuations result in action and are therefore matters not of speculation but of unrefuted fact, our norms require a corresponding withdrawal of the liberties made possible by the violated trust. To imprison an ax murderer or sniper is not to deprive him of some right but to diminish the privileges he would have enjoyed on the basis of a presumption of desert which his actions have belied.

The moral authority behind the notion that criminals should be treated "as" they have treated others, we now recognize, is not a demand for vengeance. Nietzsche was misleading in holding vengeance to be the foundation of morals, and so are those who seek to reform our penal codes by reinstating vengeance under the name of retribution *or* by purging them of retribution mistaken for vindictiveness. It is never right to diminish deserts. But it is necessary and appropriate that social privilege, born of trust and sustained by the civil security and collaborative efficiency which trust makes possible, be curtailed when actively violated, cut back to a more empiric level of recognition than our general reverence for human dignity leads us to propose and our reliance upon one another leads us to expect as civil standards.

Complete loss of desert would be tantamount to non-existence. The wasting of desert so badly that society is loath to suffer an offender to walk the earth is rare. Usually there is at least the chance of starting afresh, and one of the functions of punishment generally is the ritual restoration of desert. By treating offenders in a limited way and for a limited time in accordance with a formal recognition of their loss of desert, we exercise and express societal displeasure and can reextend the customary presumptions upon which civil life is founded. We may look for the signs of moral reformation, but we may not conduct an inquisition into the restoration of positive desert beyond the scope of societally mandated, retributive requirements.

Claims in behalf of reform presume corrigibility. The determination of incorrigibility is thus a severe judgment implying the futility of further efforts at rehabilitation. Fortunately for the criminal, other factors confer protection. These include mercy, mitigating circumstances, reverence for human life, and respect for the human image and sensibility. These last two are our sole absolute guarantors against maiming and torture. Few criminals exhaust the entire reserve of credits that society accords. Even when mercy is spent, the dignity of the human image persists, even in those who have defiled it; and the sanctity of human sensibility persists even in those who have shown it no deference. That is why we may not rape or castrate rapists or bugger child molesters and can never legitimate torture, mutilation, or the exposure of corpses. Acts done in the name of punishment but without the strict, ritual particularity of penal retribution are not acts of justice at all but expressionistic acts of violence—expression for the sake of expression and its emotive release. Where punishment, as an expressive and pragmatic act, articulates the moral bonds of a community in formal terms, acts of injury and terrorism, even of state terrorism, express unmeasured and often diffuse or misdirected passions. Retribution, properly conceived, is the antithesis and alternative of such acts, never their vehicle.

Fortunately again, no human agency is competent to determine absolute incorrigibility with certainty. Yet there are cases that indicate incorrigibility so strongly as to make efforts at reform seem impractical or imprudent. It is hard to doubt in the age of Mansons, Specks, Gacys, Eichmanns, and their ilk that members of our species may by their own choices so diminish their claims upon common humanity as to be worthy of no more deference than is due the generalized human image and sensibility. Operatively, a sniper in a tower is a pestilence to be removed. Moral deference toward his deserts becomes feasible only once he is disarmed. Can it be said that he remains a pestilence, having once become one, even after being disarmed? What are his deserts at that point?

Merely to have a theory of deserts is not to resolve thorny questions about capital punishment. These turn on residual deserts in particular cases and types of cases.[21] But I see no paradox in saying that a criminal's personal deserts, as distinct from those of the human frame, may be forfeit globally. He may deserve to die. True, existential claims are still being made as long as the murderer takes a breath, sips water, or eats a meal. But his claim upon the sanctity of human life may be lost through acts which make him operatively a pestilence. He may be bottled away to end his days in isolation from human tact. But society has no obligation to sustain him, except for the comfort of its own sensibilities, and the state has no right to impose him upon its constituents or its neighbors. The withdrawal of social amenity can be extreme in extreme cases. A society provides sidewalks, roads and parks; these clearly can be taken back. The cases are rare when complete excision (whether by capital punishment or by life imprisonment) will be legitimate, since these involve near total loss of the deserts of subjecthood. But such cases can arise. As Maimonides argues, irreparable loss reaches an extreme with murder: "A property owner might be indulgent and forgive. But a murderer, because of the enormity of his offense, is in no way to be condoned; no indemnity is to be accepted from him. . . . For none among all the crimes of man is more grievous" (*Guide* III 41; cf. *Code* XIV, Sanhedrin 20.4; XI, Rotzeaḥ, 1.4).

Social utility might seem to demand that every malefactor be expunged under the rule of pestilence. But even the incorrigible are defended by the principle of proportionality implicit in the rule of retribution. They cannot be treated as pestilential creatures, even if they are without potential for moral growth, unless their crime merits it. Before a judge can pass any sentence he needs a semantics of punishment to supplement the logic of punishment derivable from the notions of retribution, deterrence, and reform. And the authors of penal codes, in encoding such a semantics, must be cautious to ensure that the penal significances they assign do not become excessively associative or expressionistic. Only the rule of retribution can define the character and extent of punishment, by looking back to the character and sanctity of the bonds a criminal has violated and to the maxim of his actions in so doing. The claim of retribution is not to injure but to curtail spurious claims in a particular case and to a particular degree. Retribution, by contrast with vengeance, is neither a lashing out nor, as the etymology suggests, a giving back of injuries given, but a *taking* back by society of what was its own—civil presumptions now defeated and social privileges accorded in a measure shown now to be unwarranted.

PUNISHMENT VERSUS VENGEANCE

We find that we must integrate the diverse claims of retribution, deterrence, and reform. None will stand alone. Social utility will justify deterrence but must be held in check by considerations of retribution and reform. The hope of reform itself requires moderation, lest it justify invasive, ultimately violent acts against individual integrity. The requirement of reform is spoken for by the existential desert of every human being but qualified by the demands of retribution and deterrence and by any limitations in an offender's corrigibility. Retribution is a response to diminutions of moral (in the last analysis, ontic) standing which some voluntary acts bring upon us. Prerogatives accrued through social standing in a community are integral to the functioning of that community and serve as unquestionable data in normal considerations of desert. For that very reason they may be forfeit through violation of the bonds of trust on which they rest.

The appraisal in which the proceeds of crime are always of short weight relates to the standing of the criminal in the order of being. It does not exempt social agencies from their penal responsibilities. But the moral calculus to which social agencies must respond is concerned with the expression of deserts in actions. The ontic response cleaves to intentions as well and is far more immediate: It is a logical and causal consequence of our choices. Divine requital, it can be said, operates on both levels—through social responses and through the responses of identity. Society is part of nature, not the whole; and the large entirety of nature does not await its verdict. The inertial recalcitrance of character affords some respite or reprieve from the immediacy of logic—an opportunity for penitence before an act of theft makes a man a thief. But changes in ontic status resulting from confirmed choices appropriated into the identity of the chooser cling closer than a nimbus or a shirt of Nessus. For they are, in fact, matters of identity, and in the close adhesion of identity to act, as in the seamless causal fabric of nature, we can see the constancy of the act of God.

BIBLICAL VENGEANCE

The term vengeance (*nekama* and its derived forms) occurs some seventy times in the Hebrew Bible, often twice in the same passage, for the word is a strong one. Twice it occurs in Genesis for the protection of Cain, once in Proverbs anent spite and jealousy, twice in Exodus (21:20–21) as to restitution for a slain servant, non-retributively. Vengefulness is ascribed to Edom, the Philistines, or other foes in Psalms and Ezekiel. In military harangues, the rhetoric of bloody vengeance is invoked in Numbers 31:1–3, Joshua 10:13, and 1 Samuel 14:24, 18:25. A military context is evoked as well in Esther 8:13 and Psalm 149:7. Vengeance, then, is part of the repertoire and rhetoric of military passion, a character flaw in the spiteful, a vice of Israel's enemies for which God shall punish them (Ezekiel 25). It is the tragic passion of Samson, bereft in Gaza, exhorting himself to strike out against his tormentors (Judges 15:7, 16:28). In all its remaining occurrences, some forty-five in all, vengeance belongs to God. What then is the Torah's theology of vengeance?

If we apply the Maimonidean analysis of the biblical conception of God,[22] it will be clear, since God is affected by no passions, that vengeance as assigned to God can have no emotive animus. The vengeance reserved to God, then, is not the human passion eager to inflict pain for pain, injury for injury, in more than equal measure. Rather it is the metaphoric name given by the text (much as God's exclusivity is called jealousy) to the ultimate or intimate accountability that we call natural and the Torah calls divine. Just as *Avot*, by synecdoche, calls God a seeing eye and a hearing ear, referring to accountability,[23] so in the Torah the impact of our actions is located under the rubric of vengeance and recompense, referring to the dynamic of moral and natural consequences that enhance or diminish our deserts on a moral plane and set the stage for accountability on a causal plane. Vengeance and recompense, from this point of view, are called acts of God to express their universality, their justice, and their ineluctability. The incumbency of being at large, the agent's own being and that of all who interact with him, exacts a heavier and more perfect consequence than any human agency can be authorized to exact—and pays a richer and more transcendent recompense than any human agency can afford.

The notion I have put forward, that diminution of civil prerogatives is the moral responsibility of the criminal, is comprised within the manifold significances of the biblical conception of accountability voiced in the proposition that every man shall bear his own sin (Deuteronomy 24:16, Numbers 16:22). That punishment does not involve societal negation of real deserts but rather a societal response to the demonstration of diminished desert is suggested by the words ascribed to God: "Mine are vengeance and recompense" (Deuteronomy 32:35). God assigns beings their positive deserts in bestowing existence and metes out the consequences by which deserts are diminished or enhanced, as with all the laws of nature, through the dynamics of being itself. My thesis is not that God imparts negative deserts in the same sense that God imparts existence (positive desert) but that God imparts natures capable, by their own actions, of enhancing or truncating their own capabilities for action, of sullying the waters they drink from, diminishing their own characters, and reducing their own degrees of freedom—in short, of diminishing their own deserts. Beings, as Ibn Ṭufayl puts it, are capable of begriming or even corroding the mirrors in which they reflect the image of the divine Perfection.[24]

WAR AGAINST CRIME?

Vengeance, then, is not a virtue in man or a passion in God and is not the moral basis of the retribution that underlies penal laws. As a human passion, it will be spoken of biblically when the extreme limits of military savagery are described or exhorted in the heat of battle and struggle for survival. But in such military contexts, when we speak of deterrence or even punishment, we are speaking in a wholly different sense from that employed penally. Military deterrence is monitory or interdictive, whereas penal deterrence is exemplary and at least in part retrospective, reapportioning civilly conferred deserts. Military retribution bears an animus of intent to destroy an enemy's destructive power. It therefore tends to the global or unrestricted and is emotive rather than expressive, violative rather than articulative of civil standards. It is moved by spite or fury, not measured by sensitivity to diminished and residual deserts. Its context is the absence or breakdown of civil standards.

Mitzvot against vengeance and bearing a grudge are conjoined with the central social commandment, *Love thy fellow as thyself.* Vengeance is the antithesis of that love, and its rejection is equally a corollary of God's sovereignty, for the verse ends, "I am the Lord" (Leviticus 19:18.)[25] We are given many penal laws and institutions, but we are globally forbidden to exact vengeance. Militarily perhaps, spite in some form is essential—the desire to destroy, whether aggressive, defensive, or vindictive. But in punishment proper—morally warranted, just punishment—there is no rancor, although anger may be aroused in the heat of pursuit and destructive impulses may grow from frustration when the impact of crime is not contained. Civil society punishes crime but does not wage war against it, except in the case of organized crime, which it rightly sees as a threat to the existence of civil order rather than a simple affront to civility. The civil goal is to contain, subdue, and judge criminals. Society does not seek to destroy or diminish them more than their own acts have done. Vengeance, then, has no place among the norms of a civil society.

JUDGMENT, HUMAN AND DIVINE

The practical impact of the theory proposed here is the confinement of human retribution to the withdrawal of social amenity—the phased retrenchment of civil privileges, always reserving the dignities due humanity itself but removing specific presumptions of social trust on which civil profit rests, for a period, to an extent, and in a manner proportioned to the gravity of each offense and appropriate to its nature. We do not and should not merely protect ourselves from criminals and seek their rehabilitation. We do and should diminish their opportunities to benefit from the bonds of trust they have offended. We may imprison offenders, isolating them from the full measure of effectual social contacts. But criminal acts cannot justify the horrors of the familiar prison pecking order, sexual abuse, filth, brutality, or diminished health care. We may isolate but not mutilate—for we may not negate desert. We may not even isolate where isolation would be tantamount to mutilation or psychic injury of intact deserts.

There are cases of overreaching so egregious that self-stultifying destructiveness overbalances the stock of positive deserts and an individual effectively destroys himself as a moral agent. Hitler was such a person. So were those in Russia, Cambodia, and Africa who denied food relief to their starving countrymen because they placed political aims above human need. So are those who vent some private anger as snipers against a civil populace, or serial killers, or the terrorists who transform private injury or public grievance into a vendetta against humanity. I do not think we need have much compunction about invoking a doctrine of just war against such creatures if we cannot bottle them away from the human tact they have betrayed, but we must guard carefully in any warfare lest the dialectic of combat bring civility down on all fours with its adversary. For warfare embitters the lives of innocents and brings combatants morally to eat at the same trough. With a Hitler, as with Deborah's rallying cry against Sisera, the elimination of a viper under the rule of pestilence becomes a moral imperative. But so long as civility is intact it is not necessary for societies to declare war on every felon or mobilize the full force of human passion and destructive ingenuity to wipe out the destroyers and undermine the very basis of their survival. In most cases it is possible to contain the actions of the violent, restrain their social effectiveness, thoroughly cut off their capability to terrorize and destroy, and then adjust their civil standing to accord with their deserts.

The principal practical feature of my account of retribution is its lack of animus. Legitimate punishment does not seek to "get even," to make the culprit suffer or "pay," to harm or injure, but only to respond socially to the curtailment of desert. In common cases that means not global loss of moral standing but diminution of social trust. In Jewish norms the problematic standing of the extreme case appears in the readiness of the biblical constitution to identify specific crimes as capital—coupled with strict evidentiary and procedural standards that curb this final resort. The death penalty is not abolished, for it is recognized that overt actions (never those against property) may refute the restraining presumptions. Yet capital punishment is restrained, in recognition of the extreme difficulty of judging human agents quite as severely as their acts may demand.

The theory I have been developing does debar the use of cruelty, at all stages and phases of the penal process and to all degrees. Cruelty is infliction of pain, harm, or degradation for its own sake, treating the suffering of others as a good. Spinoza defines it by its intentions: the desire to do ill to one whom we pity. He gives savagery as its synonym and explains that hate can arise from pity through our loathing of the misery of an unfortunate—who thus becomes a prospective victim.[26] Cruelty must be distinguished from punishment, for punishment is appropriately founded not in an emotion but in a scaling of actions to deserts, and I would deny that human deserts ever sink so low as to wipe out the residual deserts of the human sensibility or the respect due the human image.

Historically the animus against criminals is the passion aroused by the battle for civility and against the harm and pain they inflict, the hot breath of defense and pursuit cooled into wrath in surveying the destruction they have done. It is not surprising that such passions exist, since crime and its horrors are by no means contained as yet. But the notion of punishment as an alternative to passion is as ancient as the idea of law. Penal law as an institution is a moral containment of both crime and the passions it arouses. It places the criminal and the state, his accuser, on the footing of a moral judgment normally reserved. But the criminal is not to be permitted to engage his captors. Deterrence, reform, and the rolling back of social privileges are the only legitimate penal responses. All other purposes, whether intended or (like the dehumanizing conditions of most modern prisons) wholly accidental to the primary intention, exceed the scope of penal legitimacy and are in urgent need of speedy extirpation. So much for the practical impact of our theory.

As for the speculative impact, it rests in our effort to unsnarl a long-vexing tangle of confusions about the justification of punishment and extends into the realm of natural theology, assigning a fitting meaning to the biblical images of divine vengeance and recompense. Here, too, the animus is removed. The God who is absolute perfection harbors no passions and certainly no spite. So no passional meaning can be found for the divine vengeance reserved to God. The meaning I have suggested, conformable to our theory of deserts, is borne within the notion of an inexorable moral law by which each being acquires a desert commensurate with its own (tenable) claims. Here God acts not against our interests but through our very choices, in the dynamic of their consequences. Our humanity wins us a presumptive but revisable status in civil society. The impact of our choices on our characters and, through character, on our interest falls with the constancy of any natural law and is thus aptly and legitimately referred to biblically as an act of God. The conformance of desert to the actions, maxims, and policies adopted by each agent is a matter of identity. Human punishment is not the execution but the recognition of that consequence.

CHAPTER THREE

Recompense

A dissatisfaction natural to all consciously striving beings may lead us to suppose that there is some undistributed remainder of requital which nature allots inadequately. We ask whether life is fair, whether God can be expected to right things. My answer about the fairness of life will be an affirmation voiced in a few lines from a poem by my mother:

> It is enough,
> This air bubble,
> This melting jewel,
> This human life.[1]

But like the philosopher who asked how the goose got into the bottle before he would undertake to get it out, I must also inquire about the way the question arises.

Shared raillery or cynicism can raise the question, but the premise is often to dismiss the goods of life by taking for granted what nature affords and asking what God has to add—as though grace were not found within nature. God is treated mythically, churlishly, and inconsistently—blamed for the supposed inadequacies of nature, conceived as his act, and blamed again for not intervening in ways that would undercut the very meaning of that act. Any actual interventions could be apprehended by us only as natural events and would thus be added to the body of occurrences whose mere naturalness leaves them always open to the demand for supernatural supplementation. The citizens of Chelm wonder why God provides the sun in the daytime, when there is plenty of light, but only the moon and stars at night, when light is needed most.

The myth of God as a paradoxical host, an absentee landlord or negligent gardener,[2] like most myths, owes something to displacement. It is not simply that we mistake the table setting for the dinner we were left to prepare, nor simply that we fail to see the garden for the profusion of wildflowers and weeds in God's intricate and indulgent plot. A projective problem lies closer to the bone: A sense of irritation at the puzzling behavior of our host stirs thoughts of our parents and their deaths, anxieties about what they did, or might have done, to us or for us. The drama of the myth, its sense of foreboding—the silence of the garden, the emptiness of the chair at the table's head—echo with our inner misgivings. The negativity becomes a property of the absent or silent god, a source of resentment even (or especially) when God's existence is denied.

Many who dismiss the question "Is life fair?" go on to answer it in tone or act or inference. I think the question is askable. My concerns do not dismiss it as a pseudo-question but caution against the rhetorical and question-begging innuendos that familiarly accompany it—above all the assumption that answers about the fairness of life or adequacy of nature must begin where life ends or nature gives way. What I hope to do in this chapter is demonstrate the impertinence of the quest for recompense outside the logic and dynamic of our acts themselves. Then in the next chapter I shall attempt to evaluate that logic and dynamic, in which I have already suggested our acts find their most perfect requital. I develop my position via a critique of two contrasted ethical stances. Both, I argue, are deficient and better viewed as complementary than as self-sufficing alternatives. A third position, synthesizing some of their strengths, is characteristic of the classic moral sources and can be studied in the moral approach of the Torah. With the help of the Torah's distinctive mode of visualizing the good life, I believe it will be possible to overcome the expectation that the reward of good actions is extrinsic to their logic and dynamic.

DEONTOLOGICAL AND TELEOLOGICAL ETHICS

When we ask why a given course should be taken and hear that this choice should be made because it is right, the further question can be raised, "What makes it right?" On the deontological account we are told that there is a special moral realm, a nest of imperatives distinguished by their paramountcy. Their content derives from their own logic—that is, from the transcendent perfection of the moral ideal itself. To reject them is (incoherently) to reject the very idea of value, as to deny truth is to deny the very basis of all claims. The rival, teleological account typically appeals not to a transcendent ideal embedded in the logic of right action but to our mid-range goals. Acts are right because of the goods they bring in tow and wrong if they result not in goods but in ills. Deontology appeals to duty and teleology to happiness, but both claim a warrant of rationality: teleology, in the adjustment of means to ends; deontology, in the seeming omni-sufficiency of rightness.

THE DIALECTIC OF TELEOLOGY AND DEONTOLOGY

Part of the greatness of Socrates in the eyes of Plato was his detection of an inner appeal to ultimate value in all acts and choices. At the heart of Socrates' aporetic method Plato discovered an awareness of transcendent ideals. Every valuation that denied or even fell short of the ultimate union of all values seemed to that degree to undercut its own claim to worth. Even spurious claims always appealed openly or surreptitiously to some glimmer of the good. It was on this fact that Socrates founded his faith in the inner incoherence of all false claims. He thus gave rigor to ethics by demonstrating the inconsistency of all efforts to call wrong right or make the worse case appear better. Kant perfected the Socratic method when he spelled out the formal contradiction within every specious maxim. With the same analytic genius that allowed him to conceive of nebulae as galaxies, where other cosmologists saw only dust or mist or murky stars, Kant made the aporetic, anti-sophistical sophistry of Socrates apodeictic, teasing out and rendering explicit the tacit, operative imperatives in which the illogic of bastard maxims is concealed. The Kantian critique thus systematically exposes the contradiction in assuming that one can make a principle of bettering one's lot by suicide, securing one's estate by undermining the security of property, seeking peace through plans of war, or humane ends by means of terrorism.

But strict deontology goes beyond this. It is founded in insistence on the moral irrelevance of the consequences of our actions. The Stoics, for example, made a point of arguing that outcomes, being ultimately beyond our control, are morally indifferent to the sage. Some qualified this view, when pressed with the objection that surely it is better to be a healthy and prosperous than a persecuted or tortured sage. But the admission played havoc with Stoic consistency, because it allowed external factors, alleged goods extrinsic to the question of moral choice, to exercise a determinative role in morals. That would make morals dependent on something other than virtue. And it degraded the moral good to the level of externals, admitting in effect, as Kant argued, that human dignity or integrity were commensurate with such outcomes as pleasure and pain or wealth and poverty —and putting a price on the highest goods.

Despite its rigor—perhaps in part because of the implied threat of its claim to rigor—Socrates' transformation of ethics into a mode of reasoning and argument tends to be dismissed by the simple expedient of its recognition only under the character of its genus (the discovery of critical reasoning), ignoring the focused and pointed urgency of its species: the fact that it is moral discourse, first of all the disciplines, that is rendered scientific. Historical recency does not permit the relegation of Kant to archaeology. And the philosopher's clarity precludes underrepresentation of what he is about in the concise and vividly explicit context of *The Groundwork of the Metaphysic of Morals*. So dismissal takes another route, that of reduction. Mill argues that Kant's seeming rigor arises not in logic but in a surreptitious appeal to the benefits of adherence to the moral law:

> This remarkable man . . . lay[s] down a universal first principle as the origin and ground of moral obligation; it is this:—'So act, that the rule on which thou actest would admit of being adopted as a law by all rational beings.' But when he begins to deduce from this precept any of the actual duties of morality, he fails almost grotesquely, to show that there would be any contradiction, any logical (not to say physical) impossibility, in the adoption by all rational beings of the most outrageously immoral rules of conduct. All he shows is that the *consequences* of their universal adoption would be such as no one would choose to incur.[3]

Mill's reduction rests on a misrepresentation, but it exploits an opening which Kant's purism does not readily close. For the appeal to the logic of the good—as Plato and later Leibniz recognized—is not simply an appeal to formal principles. It is an appeal to the material conception of the Good. Such an appeal is suspect from the empiricist side of Kant's own philosophy; but it also smacks of—it is of the essence of—teleology. How can Kant flesh out the requirements of the moral law without reference to concrete goods? The slide to consequentialism is braked only by invoking the centrality of intentions. For without the primacy of intentions as determinants of moral worth, consequences surely would be seen to govern. To Mill reliance on intentions seems absurd. Actions, he argues, not motives, are what count in ethics. For only actions cause benefit or harm, happiness or misery. Any notions of good intentions, virtue or vice, must be parasitic upon these.

Thoughts of moral autonomy yield the opposite conclusion: An action does not even enter the moral sphere insofar as it was determined externally. We are free only to the extent that we are the authors of our intentions and that they are the product of no external thing. Only the moral law itself, Kant argues, can provide us with an intention so pure. But if choices are not to be judged by their effects, how can they be made? Deontologists who seemed prepared to justify all rightful choices to the world now appear simply to identify a given course (or virtue itself) as right, without explanation. When teleologists step in with a demand for justifications, their inquiries sound refreshingly down-to-earth. They at least can ground prescriptions in appeals to advantage, specifiable in some socially recognized, personally intuited, or naturalistically validated standard or measure of benefit. Yet here, too, there seems to be a need for supplementation. As a seeker of goals, the teleologist finds rationality in an action insofar it serves some suitable end. But if a universe of values or choices is to be justified, some must be justified as ends in themselves. Their value will derive from standards of worth which teleology unaided does not supply.

Rationality takes satisfaction in the notion that this action was justified as a means to that one; and that one, as an end in itself. If nothing is of intrinsic worth, then no activity can be justified. The rationalism of teleology might seem able to satisfy itself in the mere recognition of means-end relations (as causal rationalism might seem able to satisfy itself in mere discovery of causal relations). But just as some fact must be self-explanatory if anything ultimately is to be explained, so some act or goal must be an end in itself, if any are to be justified as means to ends.[4] If all rationales point beyond themselves, none will be anchored. In that case, as Aristotle argued at the outset of his *Nicomachaean Ethics*, all activity would be vain or futile—meaningless, as we might say. If life is adequately described as a mere pursuit of means, there is no basis for talk of justification and no ground for preferring one theory of ethical choice over any other.

No category of discourse can legitimate its own use. So one cannot argue in behalf of explanations, truth, or any other locus of intrinsic value by pointing out that our language presupposes them. Even a Kant could not validate moral and causal notions simply by pointing to their constant use in social intercourse or in science. For this may establish nothing beyond the prevalence of a prejudice or a form of cant. Yet one can argue dialectically against those who reject fundamental notions while employing them and who use the very categories they reject in the arguments by which they reject them. Should one confront an interlocutor who holds it to be true that there is no truth or who urges the value of abandoning all values, the refutation comes within the claim itself. Ecclesiastes offers such a *tu quoque* refutation of one who claims that every goal is valueless and every pursuit pointless.[5] For Kohelet stalks just such an adversary within himself. The global condemnation that melancholy proposes rests on a capability of comparing worthwhile goals and valuable pursuits with others which are not. The absurdist mood thus rests on and pushes off from the contradictory of what it seeks to prove. As a result, it refutes and ultimately even psychologically dislodges itself: We must assume that there are meaningful actions (ends of activity or worthwhile goals) if we are to use the idea of goals at all.

It follows that the rationalism of teleology is no mere arbitrary perspective to be adopted or laid aside at will. For goal orientation is implicit in the logic of action just as commitment to truth is implicit in speech. Every act entails a valuation, and every valuation presupposes some goal of intrinsic worth. If teleology is to offer justifications and voice discontent with the seeming positivism of the deontologists' blanket "It is your duty," it must do more than simply refer means to means and thus to unexamined ends. In the same inquiring spirit that seeks for justifications beyond the claim of right and duty, it must seek grounded ends as well. To justify all acts as means is tantamount to masking ends with means and making life a pursuit of unexamined goals, the scurrying of a dog after its own tail, too engrossed to scrutinize what it is chasing. So the same rationalism that prompts the teleologist to seek a goal for duty leads the deontologist in turn to demand a basis for the claim that what is pursued is good.

A hypothetical imperative, I argue, presupposes a categorical one, if the hypothetical is adopted. One cannot *act* upon the maxim that x is desirable relative to an object y without presuming that y is desirable and that some goal z is desirable simpliciter. To adopt a maxim is not merely to act in accordance with it, nor is it merely to entertain it, as one might entertain a hypothesis about apples and health. Rather it is in a practical way to acknowledge derivative value here, by reference to intrinsic value elsewhere. If I eat this apple on the presumption that to eat is worthwhile, in itself or as a means to some end I have adopted and deemed sufficient to justify a choice, then I have committed myself in a limited but unmistakable way. Indeed I commit myself deontologically when I presume the rightness of doing what I take to be prudent or desirable. It is sterile to talk of right and wrong without reference to the goals we actually pursue. But in the same way it proves idle to invoke the notion of goals without taking cognizance of the requirement implicit in such notions that some goals will be intrinsically desirable—thus choiceworthy in themselves—without reference to or dependence on another thing (though not necessarily in isolation from all other things). If all goals are valuable insofar as they serve life, then we must say so; and if life means more than mere survival, we must acknowledge what more it means and how values like honor, dignity, or truth serve life or are served in it or through it.

DEONTOLOGY, TELEOLOGY, AND NATURALISM

Perhaps the longstanding dispute between teleological and deontological ethics reflects a tendency of the adversaries to pick up the same stick at opposite ends. Teleologists seek a common denominator among motives. Deontologists single out the motives that would render a choice praiseworthy. Yet even here an unacknowledged interdependence of deontology and teleology is evident. For teleologists give interests a higher claim than that of interest alone when they call their fulfillment moral. And the praise cited by deontologists has no purchase without pride—that is, without some conception, some *higher* conception of interest.

By invoking the standard of praise deontologists in a way prejudge the issue between themselves and the teleologists. For praise is employed in a specific sort of social context. What we praise is what we think needs encouragement. What we censure is what we hope by words to put a stop to. Typically, we praise what is hard for the doer and beneficial to others. We dispraise what is seemingly attractive to the doer but harmful to others' interests. We rarely praise self-serving, even when we think it prudent or justifiable. Yet the trend is not uniform: We also give advice and issue warnings, and these can praise benefits or decry risks. Deontologists seek to isolate such counsel as prudential or discount it as paternalistic. But advice has no less to do with morals than has altruism. It is as normative as censure, reproof, or approbation, even when it appeals to prudence.

Our ontic theory of deserts shows that it is arbitrary to isolate the self as the one locus of interest not subject to moral concern. The categorical command is that we treat humanity in ourselves *or* in others as an end and never merely as a means. Similarly, the Stoic equation of happiness with virtue suggests that the self is to be cultivated, as Socrates urged—even though the thrust of most moral suasions is not toward praise of self-regarding acts. The emphasis on altruism in moral discourse, then, must be read as an artifact of context, of our attempts to offset a bias, rather than as the distinctive mark of morality.

Kant disagrees. Of the maxims of heteronomy he writes:

> The principle of *personal happiness* is, however, the most objectionable, not merely because it is false and because its pretense that well-being always adjusts itself to well-doing is contradicted by experience; nor merely because it contributes nothing whatever towards establishing morality, since making a man happy is quite different from making him good and making him prudent or astute in seeking his advantage quite different from making him virtuous; but because it bases morality on sensuous motives which rather undermine it and totally destroy its sublimity, inasmuch as the motives of virtue are put in the same class as those of vice and we are instructed only to become better at calculation, the specific difference between virtue and vice being completely wiped out.[6]

The confusion of morality with any form of self-interest is the most pernicious, to Kant's mind, of all defections from sound principle, because it coddles and promotes self-flattering delusions that he does best by his fellow who does best by himself and he does best by himself who finds himself most satisfied with his own doings.[7] But, as Mill says, any philosophy can be abused. The hypocritical use of the idea of enlightened self-interest no more proves it spurious than does the hypocritical use of the idea of virtue. The notion of egoism is a red herring. As I have argued already and as Mill explains (*Utilitarianism* III), our social nature can foster the assimilation of individual interests and feelings to those of a group. Teleologists may spread their nets of identity and interest too narrowly or too widely, but that does not discredit teleology itself.

What does weaken teleology is any tendency to treat goals reductionistically. Since teleological ethicists paint the moral life as a quest for personal or group reward, the adequacy of their moral vision will be limited by the adequacy of their conception of the goals worth striving for. If naturalism, for example, leads one to the belief that one ought to do what one thinks best and pursue what one desires, and if that is right by definition, then one desire is as good as any other. There is no basis to prefer or reject any choice. It is arbitrary on these terms to interject any principle of hierarchy to govern among disparate interests—even the seemingly innocuous rule that any preference may be pursued that does not infringe on the choices of others. For such a principle of equity, as we have seen, is not grounded without the assignment of positive, material deserts.

On a strictly reductive naturalistic account, moreover, no room is afforded for moral growth. If one ought to seek the goals one does seek, one may change one's goals, but the change is always arbitrary, never for the better or the worse. One might change one's "values" or one's tastes, but would not as a result become a better or a worse person, morally impoverished or enriched.

Yet narrowness, as Mill's critique suggests, is not confined to teleologists. Deontologists, for their part, may inject a dose of moralism into morals. Their standards for praise or blame can be priggish, and their interest in rules can degenerate into formalism. To be effective, morals must be embedded in the thick of life. If we drive a wedge between the kind of praise we give a noble act and the kind we give a musician or an athlete for a fine performance we are saying in effect that some part of human excellence can be allowed to drop from the large complex of strengths that together perfect the human condition. The deontologists' hard distinction, then, between right and good or between wrong and harm appears to exaggerate and distort social usage. It makes a canon of the conventional disparity of interests between individuals and their communities and conscientiously ignores, as a moral distraction, the fruitful ground of the complementarity of those interests. As a result, an artifact of language is enlarged, rigidified, and set in thought-constraining Gothic type. The living distinction of right from good traverses a continuum and could not function in life unless it did. Notions of right and wrong, when invoked in living contexts, will have at their backs some ideas of benefit or harm to give authority to their pleas — as I point to the damage the neighbor's dog has done in my garden, or the harm it might have caused to passersby or to itself, if I hope to be taken seriously in urging that the dog ought to have been tied up. But notions of good or harm will similarly rely on the idea of right, if they are not to remain vacuous.

Both deontology and teleology classically appeal to nature. Teleologists are naturalists by inclination and typically use naturalism to move, say, from psychological to ethical hedonism.[8] Deontologists appeal to natural languages and moral usage for support of the claim that what is praised or blamed is not pursuit of self-interest but devotion to duty or obligation. Both schematizations, then, tend to restrict the conception of the good. Deontology takes as its canon a range of discourse circumscribed by the desire to avoid obvious self-serving and by a rhetoric that seeks to enlist others in common projects;[9] teleology frequently applies reductive notions of biology. A difference about the relevance of biology is a hallmark of the disagreement. To teleologists historically it is relevant to morals that animals pursue pleasure and avoid pain, seek to procreate their kind and protect their young, that species evolve and that more complex and adaptive forms emerge from others which are less so.[10] Such considerations serve as paradigms for the notion of interest. For the teleologist seeks the object of all rational pursuit in a readily identifiable good beyond or beneath all decadence, pretense, or artifice. Given a name, that good is advantage. But the notion is not as readily defined in empiric terms as easy phrases about needful pleasures or necessities of survival might lead us to suppose.

If sensations are to be judged good beyond the purely sensuous goodness of the sensum itself and the effusive expression of its enjoyment, there must be some standard or criterion of judgment in whose terms that claim is made. Similarly, if sensations are to be ordered, as in the Utilitarian preference for the pleasure of the many or Mill's preference of poetry to pushpin, there must be some standard external to the mere sensation. Hedonism by itself, as Epicurus understood, affords no such standard, since it acknowledges no moral datum beyond the varieties and degrees of sensations.[11] The degrees may seem to offer a criterion of choice, but the varieties may well be incommensurate with one another, and even the degrees cannot be ordered without some rule of precedence—not merely maximizing and not merely linear—if the dicta of physiology and perception are to be heeded. The same is true of that broader and more formal system of moral evasions which makes value the "object of any interest." Unsupplemented it offers no criterion for discriminating or establishing priorities among subjective interests or opinions about them. It is for this reason, I suspect, that hedonism and relativism tend to decay into pragmatism.

But pragmatism, once again, possesses no criterion of moral judgment. Its bankruptcy in this regard is trenchantly summed up in Orwell's Juvenalian satire of the "Efficiency Ritual" at Toots Commercial College in his 1933 novel, *The Clergyman's Daughter*: "'What is the secret of success?' 'The secret of success is efficiency.' 'What is the test of efficiency?' 'The test of efficiency is success.'"[12] The catechistic circle is completed when pragmatism fuses efficiency with success. Can empiric data break the circle? We say little about advantage by defining it as the goal empirically pursued by all living beings; living beings pursue many goals. Empirically speaking we must say that what some pursue de facto is their own extinction. Even to define what most beings generally pursue as their advantage does not help. If living beings prove to be on a collision course, an empiric definition of advantage would make it impossible to say so.

The fact is that a notion of desirability is embedded in the very concept of advantage that teleologists use. Without this they might just as well conclude that one should pursue what animals avoid and avoid what they pursue. When teleology *assumes* that what animals pursue normally is what is good for them, an extra-teleological standard is invoked. Similarly with human choices: The person of taste or wholesome judgment, sound sentiments or uncorrupted appetites, is assumed to know what is worthwhile and thus by his actions to guide us to it. Teleology does not define that goal so much as cite instances of its pursuit. Can the goal of biology be empirically described? The prominence of evolution renders such a project dubious.

Although interested in evolution since the times of Epicurus,[13] ethical teleologists have not given much weight to it in accounting for animal behavior. The tendency is to assume that pleasure is the best available guide to animal interests. But species survival rests on the capability of animals to discriminate cases where that is not so. Paradigmatically, animals defend their young. The notion that species interests can be equated with any mechanical principle—maximization of pleasure, biomass, or numbers—is refuted by ecological discoveries of species interdependency. Overgrazing, overpopulation, overexploitation of a parasite's host can lead to extinction. The mechanist expansionist model of advantage is refuted again by the observation that the goal of plant and animal life is not merely to reproduce but also to flourish—developing, expressing, and elaborating a distinctive character.

Every instance of sexual reproduction involves a differentiation of identity between parent and offspring and a transference of interest from parent to offspring. In the language of my first chapter this means the creation of a community of interest and the extension of that interest across the generations. Ideas of transferred or extended interest are somewhat alien to the atomistic model of identity and the hedonistic model of choice. But transgenerational communities of interest are a prominent fact of nature. In the evolution of sexual reproduction they involve a preference for qualitative over quantitative development. For sexually reproducing organisms are not merely multiplying when they reproduce; they are being fruitful in a broader sense. Sexual reproduction focuses the *quantitative* brunt of selection pressure at the gamete level, where biological investment is still small. It thus allows and promotes progressively heightened parental investment in offspring. Further, sexual reproduction evolves as an evolutionary strategy. Unlike budding or other vegetative modes, it does not merely proliferate biomass but enhances variability and thus enhances adaptability and fosters qualitative efflorescence. So it is no accident that the more advanced species are the sexually reproducing ones.

Biological individuation (hence death as we know it) emerges *pari passu* with sexuality, since sexual reproduction requires discrete parents and discreteness of parents from their young.[14] And consciousness emerges with individuation and the demand for a clear division between specious and emergent advantage.[15] Strategies evolve in pursuit of that difference. Thus thought is relevant before it evolves. The senses distinguish what is beneficial from what only seems so, and consciousness advances in the same direction, defining itself and its goals even as it emerges. Through abstraction it even generates the idea of duty.

Teleological modelers of ethical choice tend to assume that interest for animal species is fixed in "survival" or "procreation"—at best in "differential procreation."[16] But it seems necessary to recognize the Bergsonian truth that species pursue an open-ended goal, fruitfulness in directions never fully specified by what has gone before. What animals pursue universally is neither pleasure nor survival nor even perpetuation of their kind, but a goal which, like the rainbow, symbol of God's covenant with nature, always retires beyond their reach. Only the reach of evolution is not fixed. Part of God's covenant with nature is that creatures are never left without a goal beyond their grasp or without a grasp to reach out further—lest striving become trivialized, static, or empty. The common denominator of all goal-directed behavior, then, on the most empiric possible account, can never be defined in sensuously reductive terms. It can only be alluded to as an infinitely receding pure or highest good. We see the incompleteness of familiar teleologies now perhaps resolved more clearly, as a product of their reductionism. The common goal of all living beings can only be described as open-ended—a fortiori in the human case, where creativity rests with the individual and not only with the species.

Interest cannot be equated with some empirical or physical event, the maximization of a specific sensation or family of sensations. For all sensations can be simulated, and all events can be misjudged. No sensation or event carries the guarantee of being worth the price we pay for it. And no single strand of the good is whole enough, unless twisted into the thread of life, to form a fiber in the fabric of happiness. If happiness that is objective and lasting is defined as the adequate goal of rational endeavor, then, it is clear that happiness can be discovered only in the integration of numerous worthwhile values in a proper pattern or system of life for the individual and for an entire society or universe. Fulfillment of the social and moral dimensions of human character is constitutive in this totum. So are spiritual and intellectual fulfillment. A teleology that neglects these is impoverished of the potentials that consciousness and culture open up.

Deontologists sharply distinguish animal volition from ethical choice. In Kant, where deontology is perfected, virtue stands proudly aloof from interest. But even in the Stoics, whose ethical naturalism, pantheistic materialism, and paradoxical determinism render their system problematic to Kant, the "primary division" between advantage and disadvantage, which underlies all animal choice, is introduced not as a groundwork for morals but as a backdrop against which distinctively moral concerns differentiate themselves: *Honeste facta*, moral action, is cut off from the general realm of reputed goods, and moral maturity brings the recognition that the supposed goods of self-interest are opposite to what lies above them (*superiori contrarium*). Since there cannot be two ultimate criteria of choice (*ne quis sequi existimet ut duo sint ultima bonorum*) they must be dismissed as morally negligible (*inaestimabile*). Only what is praiseworthy is choiceworthy, and only moral virtue is praiseworthy.[17] Here value is not reduced to self-interest but developed from it by enlargement of the self. The assumption of the full panoply of our roles and their attendant duties in society and nature raises the human spirit to a stature that surveys all seeming conflicts with a divine detachment and recognizes the paltriness of all that we might previously have called interest.[18] Nature itself is no mere congeries of lifeless atoms but a living, breathing, organically interactive (sym-pathetic) plenum. True interest is virtue in much the same way that nature, while retaining its physicality, is ultimately redefined as spirit (*pneuma*). Stoic naturalism, then, is the opposite of reductive. Only what is distinctively human and humanizing is held to be of real value to us. Even those goods which Aristotle could treat as necessary means to higher ends are dismissed as mere externals and, in that sense, not only irrelevancies but distractions. In Christianity these will become temptations to be renounced or things of the flesh to be transcended. In Kant, appeal to their desirability will be treated as a subversion of moral purity and the undermining of all real freedom.

COMPLEMENTARY VANISHING POINTS

Deontologists put great store by freedom—Stoic self-reliance, resolution, and integrity, not swayed from the path of virtue by threats or inducements—and Kantian autonomy, which acts solely out of reverence for the moral law. Purity of intention—the candor and disinterest that the

Stoics inherit from the Cynics, and the sincerity of the "holy will" which Kant learns of from the Pietists[19]—becomes not only a necessary condition of moral action but also, in a way, perforce, a sufficient condition, since all mere objects are disparaged. Autonomy becomes almost a criterion of action, as freedom was among the Cynics before the birth of Stoicism and would become again in Nietzsche and the Existentialists after Kant. Freedom is so critical to the moral realm that deontologists assign it an almost mystical character. In Stoicism the absolute freedom of righteous intention is a striking exception to the otherwise universal externality of *heimarmene*, the one point at which individuals in the monistic plenum appropriate their own identity and actually become themselves, by placing themselves in perfect harmony with nature and its pervasive *pneuma*. In Kant again, necessity pervades nature, now through the omnicompetence of our own explanatory categories. The Stoics' psychologized nature has been internalized or reinternalized into the psyche from which it sprang, and *sympatheia* has been Newtonianized and logicized under the categories of inherence, causality, and community—as action, reaction, and interaction. But freedom is preserved, still a surd, unaccommodated to the categories of nature. Nature is the realm of external determinations, conceded to fate or destiny—again read as causality. Freedom survives (as in the Stoics) within the inner citadel,[20] despite its empiric extinction, its smothering by the refusal to allow that motives, values, objects of choice may yet belong to the moral self when they are freely appropriated, since we are continuously the authors not only of the law but also of ourselves.

All ethicists must draw a line between long- and short-range interests. All must discriminate between the boulevards that open to a social totality, humanity, or nature at large and the alleyways that allow passage only to the particular concerns of the atomic self or a narrow collectivity. All should distinguish higher interests—spiritual, moral, and aesthetic dimensions of value—as well as sustaining the foundational interests which are the cynosure of reductive teleologies. But many moralists are misled about the nature of these distinctions. Observing that progress from short- to long-range goals demands gradual detachment from the immediacy of gratification, that progress from narrow to more universal objects requires a subduing of selfishness, and that spiritual, moral, even aesthetic growth places sensuous values in positions subordinate to those it cultivates, they have presumed that ideals are necessarily in competition with the earthly ends that serve them. The perfection of morality is therefore thought to lie in perfect disinterest. Its goals, far from being objects of desire, become abstractions. Asceticism is only one outcome of such false dichotomies. The deontologists' idea that freedom and moral standards are unnatural is another. We recall Kant's "light winged dove" and his warning that the thinning air of abstraction does not betoken that winged flight in a vacuum would be the freest and highest of all.[21] In pursuit of moral purity Kant himself has been taken in. His strictures against heteronomy would empty the moral ideal of its material content—exactly the error he warned against in the case of the metaphysical ideal of purely formal knowledge.

Here we see the mirror image of the vacuity we have already noted in reductive teleologies. These profess to give a naturalistic content to morals by making reference to the matter of experience but fail to ground the values they appeal to. Since they lack a deontic or indeed ontic framework in which to justify their ends, their claims recede in an unending series of unanchored means, diminishing to a vanishing point beyond the horizon of moral relevance. A corresponding and complementary regress eats away at deontology. Lacking the material content that would flesh out their formalism, bare deontic claims recede in the opposite direction, toward another quarter of the horizon of moral irrelevance, their ideals dismissed as empty or impractical.

The illusion that all mere interests diminish in significance as the moral perspective advances rests on a failure to observe that longer aims and broader identities involve larger interests, not ever-smaller ones, receding to a vanishing point. The illusion indeed is one of perspective, symmetrical with the illusion that reduces incautious teleology to egoism. For just as it is not the case that objective interests diminish with their distance from ego, so it is not the case that values lose significance objectively as the field of view grows broader. It is not the case that the whole heavens are small simply because the only human view that can scan them must render small all that is in them. Our discovery of the vastness of the heavens does not diminish the galaxies or even the planets. The ancient prophets of Israel knew that God was infinitely more vast than these—nations, as a drop in a bucket—yet they found cosmic significance in a widow's hunger or a fat man's sloth. The legitimate abstraction in morals is not from interest, or even particularity, but only from bias.

Both Kant and the most sensible Stoics strive to tether their notions of the moral ideal to prevent their escaping altogether like balloons into the thinning atmosphere of moral irrelevance. Thus the Stoic appeal to nature and that of Kant to human dignity. Even the Cynics and Nietzsche give content to their moral ideal through their antipathy to convention; and the

Existentialists, following up another lead in Nietzsche, by appeal to the dynamism and self-creativity of human individuality. In each case the content-giving goal compromises deontology—renders the system teleological in effect. But the idealization of the goal fights shy of a reductive teleology. And in each case reductive naturalists work to cut the tether, arguing the impertinence of all notions of the ideal and assuming that the catalogue of human motives is well known from natural history or psychoanalysis. No moral scrutiny of the sort that Kant (and the Pietists before him) recommends is likely to turn up "a holy will" for the simple reason that in nature no such thing is to be found. Kant himself is all too ready to concede the point. His Christianity and his naturalism come together in agreement here. And the Stoic sage is a rare bird, whose indifference to externals makes it unlikely that he will be found on earth.[22]

In the framework of reductionism, even the attempt to enunciate disinterested principles becomes suspect as a camouflage for unacknowledged goals. Righteousness, called saintliness, is treated as unearthly—magical or fraudulent, if not a form of madness. The disguised or sublimated fear of death, we are warned, breeds repression, fanatic zeal, intolerance, and demagogic pretensions.[23] No one, it is argued, can be expected to be wholly disinterested. Here the elevation of ideals plays into the hands of those whose stated aim is to bring ethics "down to earth." But perhaps what is needed is not the abandonment of ideals but the recognition that practical ideals should not be placed, as the Torah puts it, "in the heavens" or "beyond the sea"—out of touch with what Aristotle called the doable good.[24]

Kant does discover a material content for the moral law in the idea of humanity. He identifies the human being with the rational subject, presuming on our shared moral capability and the tact of our interactions. He ignores the rare extremes where humanity and personhood fail to coincide, and with the indirection of a master prestidigitator he appears to wring the material demands of the categorical imperative from its formal logic. For it comes naturally to say that subjects deserve to be treated as such because that is what they are. But deserts are operative dynamically at all levels of being, as claims, not as implications; they are not confined to the absolute claims of moral subjects.

Materially Kant's appeal is to human deserts. Only the proximity of an Aristotelian essentialism makes his claim sound like an analytic inference, as though the formal imperative of the universal law of nature had yielded up by deduction the material formulations of the end in itself and the universal kingdom of ends. Kant, of all Hume's readers, surely knew that a man's being a man does not unaided imply that he should be treated as a man, as a subject or end, which he takes himself to be, as he would like, or in any other way—no more than a bald sensory datum implies causation by itself, or the bald 'is' of facticity conveys an ought. Deserts reside in beings; they do not arise in the mere universal quantification of a formal norm or in bare species membership. We acknowledge personhood in human beings not because they look like us but because they are (or have been, or might become) moral subjects. It is not the *concept* of personhood that calls forth moral recognition but the reality of personhood—that is, the ontic claims made by a being capable of consciousness and choice. Robert Burns' poem remains perhaps the pithiest exegesis of the kingdom of ends.[25] But what makes it so is not its being founded in a tautology: "A man's a man for a' that" voices a moral precept only by shifting the word 'man' to a much richer sense at its second than at its first appearance.

The Stoics, like Kant, cover the formalism of their pure appeal to duty by importing the content of virtue from external sources—from their own enriched concept of nature, to begin with. Stoic nature is enlivened by its equation with providence and further moralized by the overcoming of the Sophists' dichotomy between nature and art. As a citizen of nature, Stoic man bears not merely Cynic immunities but positive obligations. Yet the opening up of the Cynic idea of cosmopolitanism to a new positive meaning, while humanizing and universalizing Greek ethics, presents a danger as well. For as Stoicism draws upon nature, including social nature, for more and more material detail, its obligations become increasingly conventionalized. The hardy individualism and iconoclasm of the early Stoics shifts into conformity. The same pattern can be observed in Kant's endeavor to overcome formalism, and in the dialectic of Confucianism with Taoism: The dourness of seeming to value only duty for its own sake is mitigated by humanism, and abstract principles are given material content by communalism, familism, even nature mysticism. For duty itself would have no concrete meaning beyond the arbitrariness of authority unless it contained reference to some material conception. To act *solely* out of reverence for the moral law is to rob that law of all that makes it worthy of reverence. To avoid such emptiness, Stoic duty is assimilated to Roman duty; Kantian duty, to Prussian duty; Confucian duty, to Chinese filial obligation. The philosophic system fills itself from the cultural ethos and traditional code—in the extreme, losing its character as an *ethical* system altogether. For culture, like nature, abhors a vacuum.

EXTRINSIC REWARDS

Superficially the theories of deontology and teleology seem to exhaust the possibilities for justification. For if a choice is to be justified at all, it can be only by reference to its intrinsic choiceworthiness or by reference to the choiceworthiness of some beneficial consequence. The former type of appeal is characteristic of deontology; the latter, of teleology. But here I see complementarity rather than incompatibility, suggesting the value of an effort to reconcile the two theories, if it is possible to capture what is sound in each of them. For surely the truth in the idea that human dignity is not to be bought and sold is neither exhausted nor even approximated in the theory that good intentions are the sole and sufficient locus of moral worth. And the truth in the idea that virtue is of value because it perfects human life as human is not captured in the notion that all virtues can be "cashed out" in empiric coin. The notion of interest that ethicists typically contrast with duty or right is impoverished by abstraction so as to exclude much that is necessary to orient the idea. And the idea of right that theorists contrast with interest is denuded of those references to benefit that flesh out our workaday notions by which a right course is deemed right, that is, worth pursuing. The artificiality of the resultant contrasts is manifest from their familiar context—the rhetorical, pedagogical, or polemical exaggeration of the claims of right or duty, benefit or expedience against one another. This is not the practical moral context, where we must essay an integration of all values relevant to choice.

That a synthesis can be found is suggested by considerations of logic and language. For no truth can be isolated from all others. When deontologists call certain choices right in themselves, they use a kind of license, abstracting from a tacitly understood body of consequences and assumptions, as logicians do when they speak of certain propositions as a priori and hold that they are true without reference to any other state of affairs —ignoring momentarily large systems of formal and informal assumptions without which such presumptively "isolated" propositions would have no meaning.[26] Deontology abstracts not from all goods but from a particular range of goods held to be disruptive of sound moral judgment. When teleologists, by contrast, speak of the value presuppositions "implicit" in any categorical imperative, they address the connections of one element of our judgment with the rest, as scientists do when they demand that every element in the factual and theoretic web be made coherent with the rest, that there be no abstraction from the interconnectedness of nature—

recognizing all the while that without abstraction (and thus notional departure from perfect holism) we would have no conception of discrete
identities or principles and thus no possibility of integrating them. We
speak of the right as irreducible in contexts where we wish to emphasize
that the right is not for sale. We speak of its organic relation to the good
(and canonize the relation as analytic) when we address the value of right
actions. But when we argue for the exclusive truth of either model we are
not demonstrating some profound truth about the right and the good but
only illustrating the protean flexibility of our language.

The question of rewards may catalyze a synthesis of the deontological
and teleological, for it finds the traditional polar opposites on common
ground. Both imply that rightful choices require no reward. If a course of
action is advantageous, that is its justification; no further incentive is
needed. Bentham, to be sure, uses rewards to promote public utility. But
such inducements belong to social hydraulics, not to moral necessity. They
align our energies in service of a common goal, but they demand no more
incentive than this goal itself affords. Indeed, that is the standard of their
rationality. Again, it is tautologous to say that we ought to do what is
right. So once we know that a given course is right it should be self-
evident, on the deontological account, that this is the course to be taken.
In these terms one can readily understand Socrates' amazement at the notion of a person's knowing what is right and yet not doing it. The deontological turn may contribute to the sense that moral choices lack incentive.
But a committed deontology can express no need to seek rewards beyond
the actions it commends. It praises them on the sole and sufficient grounds
that they are right. In either case, then, no further warrant is needed. A
right choice is justified either by its advantage or by its intrinsic rightness
and does not need to be justified further.

DISCLAIMING A REWARD

Kant, with the advantage of his historical position, could see the damage done to deontology once Stoics attempted to qualify their position
with the admission that some things "indifferent" might yet be desirable.[27]
So he restored the purist position: Rewards do not morally enhance
choiceworthiness. For deontologists who maintain, as the Stoics did, that
testing of our mettle is the object of existence, it seems clear that rewards
extrinsic to our choices would distort the authenticity of our situation and
undermine the very purpose of life.

In a non-reductive teleology the self-sufficiency of right action is self-evident. For every wise and proper action is a constituent of the good life. Each contains sufficient worth within itself and needs no more to render it worthwhile. The eudaimonist can truthfully say at any moment that if he died now he would die happy, although not all his projects are completed. No extrinsic reward is needed. As for the reductive teleologist, again the notion of reward is foreign logically. It would seem odd for an egoist to expect rewards for pursuing private aims. But even the social hedonist has no moral claim. In doing well he has only pursued interest as he construes it. Someone might wish to encourage or discourage him, but no one is under an obligation to do so. A socially sensitive society might institute sanctions to encourage valued behavior and discourage nuisance, but in so doing it is only pursuing its own goals, not meting out deserts. For by the nominalistic account of a strict reductionist no act is intrinsically praise-worthy but only more or less prudent or imprudent. There is nothing intrinsically good in pursuing the societal carrot or avoiding the societal stick. These might be interchanged, should perceived social interests alter—as often happens, say, in population policy, when governments attempt to influence reproductive choices, now for expansion, now for limitation. Even the moralism of such campaigns is to be accounted as just another device. Social policy may seek to reinforce a course of action; but, unaided by objective values, it can speak for none. Rewards are deserved only in the sense that they are called for by the social scheme. There will be no reason beyond the economy of manipulation why reinforcement should be proportioned to the magnitude of the goal pursued—or even why it should be positive. If disproportion proves effective, it is in that degree advisable. If irritation or frustration seem productive, they are to that degree to be promoted. But no policy can be called good except in the question-begging sense that it stimulates responses deemed socially beneficial.

Teleology of all sorts seeks the justifications of actions in their ends —whether in pleasure, in social utility, or in the construction of human life and personality. Actions that fail to find such justification are unsuccessful or irrational in those terms. It is hardly appropriate to reward the irrational and usually imprudent to create incentives for failure. Effort, of course, may be rewarded, but a teleologist would be hard pressed to claim that efforts *as such* should be rewarded, since efforts as such have sufficient justification in their likelihood of success.

On neither the deontological nor the teleological account, then, does right action require a reward independent of its content and consequences or the nisus of its intent. If, as Kant argues, the moral maxim is a categorical imperative, to whose rightness all other considerations are irrelevant, it is foolish to demand a reward for acting out of reverence to it. If a choice is morally adequate it needs no addition. If it is not, no independent response can make it so. Similarly with teleological claims: If the right is the advantageous, it is unnecessary to add to its advantage to render it worthy of choice. Any incentives offered or sanctions instituted cannot be called deserved except in the purely stipulative sense that they seem motivationally apt in enlisting private energies toward common goals. The notion that a reward is due for meritorious action, then, is inconsistent with purely teleological ethics, just as it is inconsistent with purely deontological ethics. Even in broaching the subject of reward deontologists begin to talk like teleologists; and teleologists, raising the issue of deserts, like deontologists. Nevertheless, classic moralists of both schools have endeavored to supplement their claims by the added notion that the right is worthy of reward and somehow insufficient without it. Like the suitors of some fairy tale princess, they arrive proclaiming that they seek no more than the joy of their beloved's hand, yet none seems inclined to depart before being promised a moiety of the kingdom.

RECLAIMING A REWARD

Both deontologists and teleologists claim to find part of the reward they seek within the logic and dynamic of the course they recommend. For deontologists say that virtue is its own reward. And hedonists since Epicurus have proposed that the pursuit of personal pleasure will bring peace of mind, satisfaction, security, mastery of the fear of death, even social harmony—as an outcome of detachment and toleration. The same consequentialists who tell us that there is no intrinsic good and that all valuations are subjective, socially relative, and mutable praise certain concrete goods—peace or promise keeping—for their benefits to trade or art, or human trust, or pleasure—as though it were established that trade or trust or even pleasure are objectively worthwhile. Yet surely it is strange to offer pleasure, trust, or the flowering of the arts as rewards of virtue unless one knows that peace or pleasure, say, count as goods—and has reckoned with the contexts where neither does.

But the desire to find or promise a reward is not easily silenced, and hedonists are rarely content with internally generated rewards. They traditionally complain against the gods or fate or nature for not requiting human actions, deeming it a grave injustice and a powerful argument against theism that rain falls and the sun shines on the just and unjust alike and forgetting their own definitions of justice as a convention, right action as the pursuit of pleasure, and happiness as its attainment.[28] Rarely is it asked why those who pursue pleasure should be rewarded or whether any who do not should be punished for the omission.

Are deontologists interested in rewards? It was the absurdity of congratulating anyone for the singleminded pursuit of personal or group advantage that led Kant to insist upon the distinction of the moral from the prudential. Since the very logic of morality demands disinterest, rewards would be a detriment. Yet Kant argued that right action deserves recognition, that virtue unrequited has been slighted, and that innocence made to suffer has been wronged. The scales of justice afford the fulcrum by which human expectation vaults to the reality of God. Where others find God in the grace of his works, Kant springs from unrequited righteousness to the postulation of its remedy. Without a transcendental reward, moral goodness would be irrational and insupportable:

> Morality constitutes a system in itself. Happiness does not, except insofar as it is distributed in exact proportion to morality. But this is possible only in the intelligible world under a wise Author and Ruler. Such a Ruler, together with life in a world, which we must regard as a future world, reason finds itself constrained to assume; otherwise it would have to regard the moral laws as empty figments of the brain. For without this postulate the necessary consequence which reason itself connects with these laws could not follow.[29]

According to Lewis White Beck, Kant "transcended" the doctrine that "without a God and a future world . . . the glorious Ideas of morality are indeed objects of approval and admiration but not springs [*Triebfeder*] of purpose and of action," never to recur to it.[30] Clearly, under the influence of Mendelssohn, Kant did modify his conception of the afterlife.[31] But in his later doctrine, too, the need for an extrinsic reward still dictates the constitution of reality:

> The achievement of the highest good in the world is the necessary object of a will determinable by the moral law. . . . But complete fitness of the will to the moral law is holiness, which is a perfection of which no rational being in the world of sense is at any time capable. But since it is required as practically necessary, it can be found only in an endless progress to that complete fitness; on principles of pure practical reason, it is necessary to assume such a practical progress as the real object of our will.

This infinite progress is possible, however, only under the presupposition of an infinitely enduring existence and personality of the same rational being; this is called the immortality of the soul. Thus the highest good is practically possible only on the supposition of the immortality of the soul, and the latter, as inseparably bound to the moral law, is a postulate of pure practical reason. . . .

The same law must also lead us to affirm the possibility of the second element of the highest good, i.e., happiness proportional to that morality; it must do so just as disinterestedly as heretofore, by a purely impartial reason. This it can do on the supposition of the existence of a cause adequate to this effect, i.e., it must postulate the existence of God as necessarily belonging to the possibility of the highest good (the object of our will which is necessarily connected with the moral legislation of pure reason).[32]

Kant derives a practical impossibility from the command to pursue perfection by omitting one small qualification, which Plato had been careful to include: "so far as humanly possible." The dimensions of perfectibility which transcend the confines of the individual body (and hence of personality as well) are attained spiritually, intellectually, communally, and through our social, cultural, and generational advances. To expect absolute transcendence of individuality while we are individuated is not to articulate any true demand of the moral law but merely to overlook the dimensions of partial and relative transcendence open to us and to press the inveterate yearning for transcendence to the point of incoherency.

Kant's motives here are tangled. Without a cosmological or ontological argument, God's justice becomes a moral postulate: Since morality is categorical, our future use of the concept of God is to be anchored there. But how? Surely morality, being categorical, is rational without a paymaster. The contradiction between the purity of morality and the demand for transtemporal requital reflects the scintillation of Kant's viewpoint from the purity of disinterest to the interestedness of discontent. For a philosopher of the Enlightenment transcendental accountability was the linchpin of religion and morality. A man was a bounder who did not expect an eternal accounting. Yet realism for Kant demands the recognition that nature does not meet our wishes, even in their most elevated, moral form. The demands of deontology are therefore taken no further than to moralize the notion of requital: God does not interfere in nature; yet he does intervene outside its boundaries to right its balances, as one might arrange the cards in winning order after a lost game of solitaire. Kant's God restores the moral equilibrium much as Newton's God restores the dynamic equilibrium of nature. But to invoke God to set nature right is to undermine the elegance of God's scheme, which had been Newton's theme. Similarly, God's moral intervention, setting up a transtemporal game of asymptotic approaches to perfection, undermines the authenticity and earnestness of existence, which had been Kant's theme when he spoke of freedom, not happiness, as the inner principle of the world.[33]

Kant was not the first to link the thought of God to the idea of reward or to suggest that without transcendent requital morality would be irrational.[34] Yet it speaks little good of God, whom we know only as the Creator of nature, to regard this world as so botched a job that the impersonality which conditions its existentiation requires it to be replaced (by God, of course) with another, radically unlike it. I sense here an ancient and traditional bad faith about the world. It turns its back on cosmology and moves a step closer to treating God as a wish—the wish that everything, despite all that cynicism concedes—will turn out all right.

THE NEED FOR A SYNTHESIS

Here, then, we have a curious division of the house. On the one hand are those who claim that right is coextensive with interest, most often as subjectively or relativistically perceived. Such theorists, to be consistent, should find the notions of reward and punishment irrelevant, except for manipulative purposes, since they have abstracted from all questions of merit, duty, or desert, at least in their intention. Yet they hold out personal or social tranquillity as constitutive rewards of the pursuit of pleasure. And, failing to find a satisfactory economy of requitals in nature, they complain that good men are not adequately or consistently rewarded, while the evil are not adequately punished. In so doing they invoke an objective standard of desert distinct from conventions and contracts and demand vindication of our yearnings in accordance with the dictates of a metaphysic of morals for which their moral theory provides no foundation.[35]

Across the aisle we have the deontologists, who hold that we must value the right for its own sake, setting aside all else for moral purposes, even the particular values to which the idea of right inevitably makes reference. In Kant's instance, deontology condemns any attempt to derive right from interest on the ground that when the two diverge, as they must, the specious ethics of teleology will become the apology of appetite. Yet morality may still expect, must expect, a reward outvaluing all the worldly goods risked for its sake. Here heteronomy returns with a vengeance.

With all their talk of afterworlds, the Rabbis were clearly aware of the incongruity of such a position. Antigonos of Socho said: "Be not like servants who serve their master for the sake of receiving a reward, but be like servants who serve their master not for the sake of receiving a reward, and let the awe of Heaven be upon you" (*Avot* 1:3). Philo, echoing the thought of Plato's *Euthyphro*, argued in the same vein: "They who give, hoping to receive a requital such as praise or honor . . . are in reality making a bargain."[36] The Rabbis were not content to substitute an otherworldly for a worldly reward. Their motto, based on Deuteronomy 11:13, was to act out of love. One should not say, "I will study the Torah in order that I may . . . acquire a reward in the world to come" (*Sifre* 41.28). Bahya, Kant's predecessor in the philosophical explication of the ethics of Pietism, cited as ancient wisdom the precept, "If you wish to discover whether your motive is pure, test yourself in two ways: whether you expect recompense from God or anyone else, and whether you would perform the same act in the same way if you were in solitude, unknown to anyone."[37] And Kant's older contemporary, the Baal Shem Tov, who revived Jewish Pietism in the modern age, just as Kant's teachers were modernizing Christian Pietism, was even more explicit: "I don't want Your this world, I don't want Your world to come. I want only You."[38]

Kant holds the palm as the ethical purist par excellence. He completes the Stoics' Augean labors of purging ethics of external motives. His references to the moral necessity of a hereafter are not usually seen as any derogation of his thoroughness in that task—just as the references of hedonist conventionalists to the injustice of life or of God are not seen as flaws in their reductive naturalism. But the issue shows that the deontological and teleological modes, in their purest forms, are not only insufficient but also inconsistent. Deontology declares rewards irrelevant, yet it pursues them even to the point of demanding a God to dispense them. Teleology pursues rewards and declares all else irrelevant, yet it continually regulates its idea of a reward by notions of objective value borrowed from the masses or the philosophic or aesthetic—or ascetic—elite.[39] And while it often avows no interest in rewards unknown empirically, it may rail at the divine or fate, denouncing or threatening to renounce the reality of that which determines all things, unless it can be shown that the righteous or the innocent are rewarded and the wicked or the vicious punished by transcendental sanctions of which we have and can have no tangible evidence in nature. For any lesser recompense would be accessible to the vicissitudes of fortune and would thereby represent an insufficient guarantee.

Recompense

◆

INTRINSIC REWARDS

Perhaps the perspective of the Torah can help here. For, like the classic moral writers—Plato, Aristotle, even Cicero—the Torah escapes the over-subtle analysis that seeks to define good and duty without reference to one another. Much modern moral theory pursues an abstraction, or a pair of abstractions, which (once dissociated) retreat in opposite directions, toward contrary but still mutually referential vanishing points. Theorists who offer the choice of morality or happiness have not understood either. For happiness, on its minimal, subjective side, requires knowledge that one has chosen what is best. And morality is empty without the material prescription of what is best. Thus the Torah's command: Choose the blessing, choose life. This axiom might seem self-evident, but many choose less wisely. The pursuit of pleasure, gain, or satisfaction, the quest for any goal but perfection is ultimately stultifying—a source of frustration to those who do not reach their aim and of ennui to those who do—vanity and striving after wind. Only that activity which is constructive of our humanity—moral, social, spiritual, and intellectual—can meet the criteria of the pursuit of happiness, combining the venturesomeness of an open-ended quest with the satisfactions of continually fulfilled desire. There is no separate, distinctively moral sense of 'good.' Living well is doing well and acting well. Accordingly, it is choosing well.

TOWARD AN INTEGRATED VIEW

Rigidly defined, the two abstract positions are mutually excluding. De-ontology resists corruption of the pure and free will by the appeals of externals—even to the point of denying moral relevance to the necessities of a contented life. Rigorous teleology of the reductively naturalistic type, symmetrically, rejects as mystagoguery all notions of the appeal of duty or right—even to the point of ignoring such imponderables as honor (except as subjective goals) and reaching incomprehension of its own sister tradition of liberal, constitutional guarantism, whose absolute rights and their corresponding duties are opaque to its utilitarian or pragmatic categories. For what has flexibilism to say of *habeas corpus*, or what has Utilitarianism or pragmatism to say of government by emergency decree, or militarism, or the nominal dictatorship of the proletariat, or compulsory sterilization? The questions ring with contemporary relevance, as we observe the eager-ness of liberal democracies to reopen trade with China in the aftermath of Tiananmen Square. But although they might have been asked by a Burke, these questions receive no concrete answer in sheer traditionism à la Lord Devlin, which scrupulously avoids reference to the *content* and moral basis of the traditions in which preservation of human dignities is lodged or sought.

Deontology can be defined, however, as uncompromising dedication to the right as such, without excluding reference to those goods which give the right its value. And teleology can be defined broadly rather than narrowly, recognizing the interdependence of natural beings and the transcendent goal presupposed in the strivings of those beings. Using such definitions, deontology is not sterile, cold, or empty, and teleology does not exclude the goods of justice, kindness, and human growth. When the two perspectives are so defined, they do not diverge but converge in a single vision, with the perspectival differences complementing one another, as in the adequate functioning binocular vision. The deontology that accommodates what is true in teleology does not isolate intrinsic from instrumental values. The teleology that acknowledges the truth of deontology does not subordinate a loftier to a lesser good. The key to a synthesis, if one can be made, is the integration of all goods in a system that recognizes the transcendent character of some goods and so does not seek to reduce all to one least common term but rather measures the lower against the highest good.

Kant knew that eudaimonism is not subject to the criticisms he leveled at reductive systems. For a teleology of human perfection subsumes the moral claims of deontology. But Kant found the synthesis unsatisfactory, in part because it groups what he deemed to be purely moral standards along with other human goods, but also because he did not recognize that the categorical imperative itself—although more articulate and definitive in many of its dictates than most philosophical discussions of happiness—is dependent in the ends-formulation upon those very discussions. Acknowledging a sharp distinction between the counsels of personal happiness and those of perfection, Kant classed the former as empirical and the latter as rational grounds of heteronomy.[40] Yet when eudaimonism represents personal happiness as unattainable except through personal perfection, it seems to me to surmount heteronomy. What could be more one's own than one's perfected self? At the same time eudaimonism seems to me to bridge the Kantian gap between sentiment and rationality. For the moral demands of the higher self are not mere formulae but objects of motivation, striving, aspiration, and desire.

Seeing that eudaimonism was not as vulnerable as other forms of teleol-

ogy to the charge of heteronomy, Kant took a different tack in addressing
the counsels of perfection, arguing that eudaimonism is vacuous, "useless
for discovering in the boundless field of possible reality the maximum reality appropriate to us." The ontological concept of perfection, he argued, is
inevitably circular, unable adequately to define its goal without ultimately
appealing to the morality it was meant to ground. It is superior to theological ethics, because they rest only on notions of arbitrariness and power
when abstracted from the moral idea to which *they* circularly appeal. And
it is superior to intuitionism, because appeals to moral sentiment rest ultimately on sensation, an unreliable counselor in the grave business of morals. But it has no content of its own.[41]

Yet it was Kant who isolated morals from the conceptions of theology
and perfection. It was he again who dismissed the relevance of human
feeling as a guide to moral action by discovering its groundedness in sensation and declaring a holy purgation of sensory emotion in his ethics. The
approach contrasts sharply with his response to the parallel discovery of
the centrality of sensation in his epistemology. Surely if our a priori categories of the understanding allow us to construct conceptualizations from
the materials of sensation, they can also (as the Stoics urged) allow us
morally to rise above mere enslavement to our feelings. As for theology
and the idea of perfection, it seems arbitrary to empty them of moral content when morals has so long nourished and been nourished by our idea of
the divine and our vision of perfection in humanity.

Kant's accusation of circularity against the counsels of perfection is based
on the assumption that perfection is a mystery—as if there were no patterns in experience or thought to give content and direction to such ideas.
It is true that neither divine nor human perfection can be treated as a
closed and determinate notion, since divine perfection is properly construed as infinite and that of humanity as a goal to be defined in the living.
But that peculiarity is an expression of the character of our condition as
creatures in process. Morality cannot be made more determinate than our
ideas of perfection allow, as Aristotle was the first to urge. But we know
our interests (and, projectively, those of others as well), not perfectly but
adequately to have come thus far, to have constituted ourselves as living
beings capable of thought and purpose, self-consciousness, self-criticism,
consideration, and responsibility. We did not achieve this by knowing from
the outset what our ultimate goal would be. Yet, with all our lapses and
confusions, we could not have achieved what good we have gained without
recognizing the good when it was in or near our grasp. Our progress,

then, is better described in Teilhard's terms—as a spiral rather than a circle. For it need not lead back to where it began and does not presuppose its endpoint in its initiation but advances in a direction defined in part by its past trajectory, in part by its present existential state, in part by a perception of the future, seen not exclusively as destiny but also as possibility, by reference to a variety of concrete models of human excellence, and, ultimately, to a concept of absolute Perfection.

Moral discourse, theological dispute, and human self-definition are intertwined. The endeavor to isolate them from one another impoverishes morals as much as it evacuates theology. We know God by morals and morals by God. Like rock climbers who gain altitude in a rift by chimneying between its opposing faces, we improve each discourse by improving the other. The process would be circular only if each discourse were closed and static, giving no purchase to imagination or project to conatus. But in that case our climb would never have begun.

Against the Kantian complaint that vice or viciousness might be harbored in perfectionism, we can only cite Spinoza's fine but crucial line between hypocrisy and humanity.[42] The task of ethical discourse is to help us discern that line, not to simplify it or to underscore it so heavily as to obscure it. Clearly counsels of perfection may be confounded with egotistical maxims that immolate deserts on the altar of misconceived self-interest. But that is the perversion, not the application of our principle, just as the notion of an arbitrary and mercurial divine will is a perversion of the concept of divinity, and the idea that absolute power is capricious is a perversion of the idea of power.[43] The loftier a maxim reaches, the graver and more imminent are the possibilities of its abuse. But there is no more logical connection between egotism and a reflective eudaimonism than there is between any thesis and its caricature.

Eudaimonism does not, of course, reduce the good to an object resolved in the senses or detected by some instrument. But it does identify the good with a real goal. It is a form of naturalism, non-reductionistic and thus not subject to the critique of the naturalistic fallacy—for the same reason that the identification of the good with God and the right with God's will do not fall into the naturalistic fallacy.[44] Moore could rightly object, as the Sophists did long before him, to the identification of the good with any fragment of itself. Where the good has been identified, say, with pleasure, it is always possible to ask, "But is it really good?"—and the very intelligibility of the question shows that no analytic equivalence has been established. But when what is proposed is the whole of the good life, no room is left for the question. That is why Aristotle could argue that happiness is what all men regard as their ultimate goal and could focus in the *Ethics* on the means contributory and the ends constitutive of that goal.

To conceive the good life as a pursuit of human capabilities—for wisdom, kindness, holiness—assures that there will be no reduction of the good to its elements. But as the list expands, the door is closed progressively on Moore's question. It is intelligible to ask, "Is this life good?" of a life of pleasure, wealth, or other prima facie goods. But when a life of actions in accordance with the thoughtful and considerate modes of character is asked about, the question becomes increasingly unaskable: Is a wise man really happy? Is his life really good—if he lives in harmony with his fellows, enjoys and uses the means of securing their well considered interests and his own, in an integrated community founded in mutual respect and strengthened by trust and fellowship, warranted pride in its past and hopes for its future? The more the list expands, the less room remains for the intelligibility of Moore's question. And the growing list evokes a pattern—as past steps in an artistic or scientific progression suggest the directions in which human creativity will discover footholds for its next steps.

When Cephalus in the *Republic* offers a conventional account of duty as promise keeping, debt paying and the like, in answer to the question "What is justice?" it is easy for analysis to generate a conundrum by posing the case of a promise to return a weapon to a friend now in a rage or frenzy. Justice must pursue the good in all ways, not just in literal adherence to a behavioral rule. Kant has serious difficulty with the same conundrum.[45] Humanity, he argues, exerts a claim, possesses a desert to be told the truth. Granting this, and granting the legitimacy of Kant's concerns that if exigency or expediency are allowed to govern there will be no halting the demands of church and state to lie in the public interest or to save our souls, the fact remains that Kant has no better response to the pursuer at the door than silence or prevarication. Pure deontology is as damaged by this silence as reductive teleology is by its willingness to harm the innocent. Kant's problem stems not (as Dewey suspected) from the fact that he has principles but from his tendency to treat each principle as an absolute rather than relate it with the rest in a larger, integrated scheme topped by just one absolute, not "principle" in the abstract, but the Good itself. Kant feared such a hierarchy because he knew how readily all positive values are crushed beneath misguided efforts to serve the absolute, transforming religious ethics into vicious opportunism. But the fear of what can be done and has been done in the name of the Absolute does not obviate the need to subordinate some values (such as truth telling) to others (such as life saving) in the face of the Absolute.

Kant is misled, I have suggested, by the presumption of a more civil state of human relations than a terroristic illustration presupposes. The subjects whom we owe some measure of the truth are linked to us by bonds of civility and acknowledge obligations to respect our privacy and win our trust. But Kant ignores the critical distinction between civil or social man and the bare rational subject of his analysis. He is pinned, accordingly, by an overly behavioral notion of duty. Setting all principles on a par, he forgets his own first principle, respect for subjecthood. For if I owe truth to my fellows, a fortiori do I owe them protection, whereas the truthfulness I owe is predicated on the very bonds of community that tyrants and terrorists violate.

Compare the directness of the rabbis' answer when the same question was put to them, not by analysis but by history: When should one prefer death over disobedience to the Law? Their answer: rather than murder, incest, or idolatry, rather than lead the whole nation into desecration of the Law itself—but not for mere behavioral conformance to a single precept. Their rationale: "It is a law of life" (Yoma 82a–85b; Deuteronomy 30:15, 19-20; 32:47; Proverbs 3:18). The Law contains the criteria of its own elaboration. "The Sabbath may be desecrated for a living infant one day old, but not for a dead King David" (*Tosefta Shabbat* 17.19). The articulation of such lines of priority is a vital responsibility of cultural authority. The Torah's guiding aim in exercising that responsibility is the perfection of life; its principles moderate one another toward that aim.

An overly behavioral thematization of duty expresses the isolation of obligation from its attendant and constituent blessedness. If duty may be shallow or mechanical, virtue will naturally seem to lack a reward. But in a broader perspective right choices will contain within themselves all that they need to justify them, and whatever follows extrinsically is good or ill fortune, not to be judged as fair or unfair recompense unless it is the act of some social agent who ought to have borne a social regard for the recipient. The fulfillment of the Law is its own reward, not because there is abstract merit in the fulfillment of God's wishes (as though God's will might have had just any content), nor because no palpable rewards arise in and through the life of virtue, but because the fulfillment of the Law is the attainment of happiness as promised and prescribed by the Law.

Recompense

◆

The Torah does not expound principles but prescribes obligations, some minimal and others in growth-inviting series. It draws vivid images and promulgates symbolic gestures to foster an atmosphere of fellowship, concern, tact, and forthrightness.[46] From the meaning it gives the past the Torah projects a common futurity and sense of community in the present. Crucially, it projects tableaux of the good life, not as a supernatural compensation for the hardships of upright living but as the natural (thus God-given) consequence and concomitant of such living. Here the moral and prudential—or (less narrowly) the wise and provident—are integrated in a sensibility that can properly be called enlightened.

The Torah breaks down the dichotomy between the right and the good by projecting blessings as obligations and obligations as blessings. It lays out and often insists upon a certain path. But it defines that path as wisdom and praises it for its inherent welcomeness and consequential blessedness (Proverbs 3:16–18). Erich Auerbach has shown how alternating sentence and silence inform biblical narrative with a striking chiaroscuro that brilliantly highlights the facets of character and incident that the text calls into high relief.[47] The same technique is used prescriptively. Lucid and memorable vignettes mark the union of an obligation and its attendant blessedness so strikingly that few readers or hearers can overlook the nexus that unites the two and thus energizes the legal themes and ethical teaching of the Law: "See how good and lovely—brothers dwelling together in concord" (Psalm 133:1). The obligations of peace and brotherhood are not imposed, like the law against murder, by a stern "Thou shalt not . . ." but proposed in a tiny, shining vignette of the life of an integrated community, whose harmony and blessedness will be as sweet whether they blossom within a single family or bud among the nations. The obligation and its blessedness are identical. The famous lines are followed by a less familiar but equally powerful image: "It is like fine oil on the head running down into the beard . . . like the dew of Hermon that comes down on the mountains of Zion. For there the Lord ordained the blessing: life forever." We read not only that the mores the Law prescribes are pleasant or good but that its ways are the ways of sweet fortune (*no'am*) and that all its paths are peace—not peaceful, but peace: They are well-being (*shalom*, the wholeness of well-being in all its dimensions), not just means to happiness. The life of the Law is happiness.

Tableaux built up from such vignettes aid in the articulation of moral truths as legislative norms. The cities of refuge, for example, are founded on the vignette of the unintentional homicide whose ax head flies off its helve. Or, cultivating an ethos rather than instituting a law, the Torah projects a vignette of helping reload an enemy's ass, or admonishing a fellow (rather than suffering in resentful silence). Against vengeance morality it sets out the vignette of Lamech's vindictive boast. Each picture fuses the image of the moral life with that of its inherent blessedness or vividly projects the emptiness and bootlessness of the lawless, thoughtless life. Orienting the scheme: the vision of each man under his own vine and fig tree with none to make him afraid; or the good woman of Proverbs, at once defining an ethos and delineating its reward.

The good life is hard to describe to those who have not seen it. But the Torah images it vividly to a nation of former slaves: "You shall eat and be satisfied and bless the Lord thy God for the good land which He hath given you." Gratefulness is not a payment but the natural expression of contentment, a part of the good life.[48] The Law is not merely ordaining gratitude but defining the good life iconographically. Similarly, the biblical commandments of life and of freedom—"Choose life," "Proclaim liberty throughout the land, to all the inhabitants thereof"—are crucial features of the Law, because love of death and slavery are not wholly alien to human desire. They can be made goals—even ultimate goals. Death, narrowness, avarice, and mean-spiritedness are readily misidentified as power, pride, thrift, and strength. So there is nothing otiose in naming life and its values as the blessing and their alternatives as the curse, nor in filling out the portrait or the landscape in which each is enjoyed or suffered (Deuteronomy 11:26, 30:19). Thus the Torah will not only make rules but define, orient, and integrate values, assign them concrete meanings and bearings, institute practices that touch thought and imagination, hope and expectation. The laws of the festival sacrifices (Deuteronomy 16) give gratitude a focus in the round of human labors, drawn up and pursed together into a significance that celebrates the union of the virtues that the Law defines. Achievements are not merely won or passed through but savored before God.

One law anchors the community by prescribing the context of sexual experience, not in arbitrary fiats, readily caricatured in the specious concept of taboo, but in the brilliant homily of Eve's emergence from Adam's side—man for the first and only time becoming the mother of woman, and so not alien flesh to hers: "Therefore shall a man leave his father and his mother and cleave unto his wife, and they shall become one flesh"

(Genesis 2:24). Like so many of the Torah's moral syllogisms, the inference is a non sequitur in purely formal terms. Slavery in Egypt does not logically entail special consideration for the Egyptians. It acquires such moral force by reference to a moral framework that sympathetically equates another's plight with one's own. So here, man and woman's being of one origin does not by itself imply a man's duty to leave his parents and cleave to his wife. But the derivation of this obligation from that premise evokes a system of moral assumptions underlying the enthymeme: Each person is to emerge into the adult role by disengaging from the matrix of familial support and attaining the responsibility of a carer rather than a mere recipient of care. The boundaries of dignity and privacy which sustain that possibility are outlined with it in a single image. Each of these values is simultaneously an obligation ("Therefore shall a man leave . . . and cleave . . .") and a blessing, an end desirable in itself and for what it makes possible and forestalls.[49]

The first commandment to all living things, "Fruit and multiply," again fuses obligation and reward—merit and bounty—in a single blessing, fleshing out the primal command to creation, that all things should be, actively and expressively, each giving forth of its own God-given nature —the commandment "Let there be light." The fusing of blessing and obligation is achieved through perspective, much as a Renaissance painting bespeaks individuality by presuming an ideal subject. But here the subject is a cosmos in which each *I* has a role. It is here that we most clearly see God in nature, in the regard each being bears toward itself and every other in constituting a community. Such regard acquires a special significance when conscious and considerate. But its analogues are found at every level, and vibrantly, if implicitly, wherever a procreative urge is found.

The interests of ancestors and descendants are fused when the biblical narrative equates the fortunes of the Patriarchs and growth of their spiritual awareness with the founding of the fortunes and insights of all Israel and when the dire or blessed state of Israel in future days of peace and war is made the concern of their ancestors who act and choose today. Consequences are vividly drawn: loss of the nation's grip upon the land in the loosening of the cord of social union among the people and strengthening of their hold through the strengthening of that ethical bond. The fortunes of the entire people in all epochs are shared.

The Sabbath is a paradigm of the fusion of duty and interest that will aid us in overcoming the sharp dichotomy of the right and the good. What begins as a work stoppage becomes a vehicle for the humanization of life, confirming that the *mitzvot* invite aspiration toward perfection of our humanity rather than merely imposing arbitrary disciplines.[50] For the Sabbath symbolizes the act of creation and thus affords occasion for intellectual and spiritual perfection as well as re-creation of the body. It fosters the community of all Israel and of their fellows within the purview of the Law. It even creates a community with the beasts, whose labor is spared but whose requirements are respected on the Sabbath;[51] and it links us, as A. J. Heschel has argued, even with inanimate nature, whose processes and continuities it respects. The commandment is a grave and comprehensive one because its preservation is the preservation of human life and spirit. Aḥad Ha-Am touched more than a simple irony when he wrote: "More than Israel has kept the Sabbath, the Sabbath has kept Israel."[52] Rabbi Jonathan voiced the same theme when he said, "The Sabbath was given to you, not you to the Sabbath" (Yoma 85b). And the idea was vivid in popular consciousness. Hertz wrote, "The Falashas . . . were some generations ago sorely harassed by hired missionaries to name the Savior and Mediator of the Jews. . . . They answered 'The Savior of the Jews is the Sabbath.'"[53] The value of the Sabbath here is symbolic but also constitutive, anchoring a corner of life and helping to give it a fuller sense than mere survival —humanizing life and enriching it, a blessing conveyed by a norm.

The conception of divine obligations as blessings runs throughout the biblical law. It enhances Kant's idea that the pious and holy will treats moral obligations as divine commands. Just as virtue is a means to happiness, the *mitzvot* are acts of grace. That the Torah sees procreation as both an obligation and a blessing is a source not of ambiguity but of instruction. For the Torah does not assume that duties must be unpleasant or unwelcome; it does not consider laws mere sanctioned imperatives. Rather, its goal is to teach the pleasantness and welcomeness of its obligations and so to foster virtue in the way that Aristotle had in mind when he argued that the good take pleasure in virtue and find vicious acts painful and unwelcome. For even sexual activity and the pleasures of the palate become sources of pain, anxiety, and grief to the vicious.

The simple and natural goods of the senses are welcome to appetite, but they are not self-regulating. Culture must paint in the detail. Thus the need for the larger, more integrated picture of the good life: Peace, civil contentment, goods enjoyed in security, the poor provided for, so that want need never mean destitution or desperation.[54] The Torah provides a buffer against hunger and legislates against the alienation of patrimony.[55] But the moral virtues and civil laws enlisted against such ills—holiness and civil righteousness (Leviticus 19:2, Deuteronomy 16:20)—are more than instruments of well-being. They are ends in themselves as well. The Torah associates grain and oil with the subtler but still graphically depicted goods of concord and holiness and shows how just institutions can create the good life it envisions, tailoring that life from the fabric of a progressively reforming human character.[56]

In projecting the endeavor, the Torah plainly obviates the question "What shall we do, which shall we choose, when interest conflicts with right?" When right and interest are properly construed, no such conflict is conceivable. There is no question, "Why ought I to do what is right?" The codifier of the *Mishnah*, R. Judah the Prince, said: "Compute the cost of a *mitzvah* against its benefit and the benefit of a sin against its cost" (*Avot* 2:1). He is confident that every *mitzvah* will involve greater benefit than loss, since he has classified every law under the rubric of its benefit and understands the principles on which all are founded. By the same criteria he can be confident of the divine basis of the Law[57] and can see the lines on which its further development must be guided. Each *mitzvah* fulfilled is a blessing. Thus in *Avot* subsistence (*kemaḥ*) and morals (*derekh eretz*) are made prerequisites of law (*Torah*) and vice versa, and so with wisdom and piety, knowledge and understanding (3:6, 3:20–21). Each is a good in itself and contributes to a larger system of goods. Interest here *is* doing what is right; there is no greater advantage. We lose sight of this truth only when we construct interest too narrowly, constrict the net of our identity too tightly about the atomic personality, or conceive of justice or right too impersonally or abstractly, as something in which we have no stake.

The visions of the Torah seek to correct such narrowness. When Jacob wrestles with an angel, his experience is emblematic of our endeavor to capture one aspect of the Divine on earth. Wrestling in behalf of all his successors, he captures what humanity can discover of the commitment of God to creation and so to the material content of the right *as* the good and the divine investment of the idea of the good with the ideal of righteousness. The bounty of creation and the goodness of nature as the abode of man are not merely evidences of God's power but markers of the direction in which happiness and fulfillment lie. They are proof of the possibility of happiness. For nature, like its Creator, is straightforward, not perverse. Happiness can be enjoyed in simple pleasures, in personal, conjugal, and communal integration, and in the intellectual and spiritual perfection for which nature lays a foundation. Retention of what Jacob captured —apprehension of the beauty and bounty of the doable good—becomes the mission of his descendants, by which they as well as he acquire the name of Israel.

The Torah remains close enough to the theater of choice to recognize that we have no way of defining right except by reference to interest and no adequate way of defining interest except by reference to right. Biblical thought does not artificially seek to avoid reliance on either of these categories out of deference to the other. Nor does it become circular by reducing the conception of each to that of the other. Rather its vignettes draw upon our experience of both prudence and principle to inform both ideas. Being no closed formal system but open to experience, the Torah can instruct us in the integration of the two by making reference to our common experience of either. In so doing it enriches both conceptions; and its vignettes teach, beyond their specific messages, the more general thesis that the happiness which is the reward of virtue is not a recompense for some ungrateful task. Rather, virtue is the habitual making of choices on an individual and on a social level which are conducive to and constitutive in happiness.

Socrates clearly stated the identity of right and interest, properly conceived, when he argued that no one knowingly does wrong (*Gorgias* 475). But this explicit identification became necessary only because the distinction, typically between your right and my good, had been overdrawn by Sophists. Biblically, the identity of right and good was confirmed by a different sort of dialectic. The contrast of nascent prophetic morality with the death cult and slave morality of Egypt and the blood cult and orgiastic savagery of the Fertile Crescent and Canaan, seemed to make it obvious and yet necessary to proclaim a truth spoken silently by nature itself: that life and prosperity, health, freedom, purity, honesty, fellowship, responsibility, kindness, justice, charity, joy, and love are the core of holiness. Where the organs of society have overreached their proper functions of fostering individual growth through promotion of the common interest, or where individuals have become alienated from a community whose advantage is not their own, it is natural and legitimate to separate individual from group interest. But in a nation united by danger and hardship the notion of a conflict between the individual and the community is a more speculative matter.

In Greece articulate professionals found profit in insisting that justice is a mere convention and nature a struggle, that the good is a bone of contention definable only from disparate viewpoints: What might be virtue in a victim would be folly in a victor. Here it became necessary for a Socrates to rediscover the unity of the virtues—that piety is not harebrained or igno-ble, that courage is not stupid, rash, cold, or vain. When politics had shown its insufficiency as arbiter of the public good, it was left to Plato to find higher ground, from which the transcendental unity of all goods could be seen. Arguing dialectically, Socratically, Plato could rediscover that the pur-suit of interest in oblivion of the higher good was a fool's errand.

In the Mosaic context the Socratic reuniting of disparate goods was unneeded, since the Sophistic elenchus had not occurred. It was well known to the later prophets, compelled to restate the Mosaic message, often in a new rhetoric. But the original audience of the Torah did not wholly dissociate themselves from their ancestors or their distant posterity. So it was possible to address them in behalf of a good that was at once transcendent of their individuality yet readily apprehensible. Their sense of community allowed their morality to be informed with projects reaching far beyond the immediate. They could receive a command to become a holy nation, a kingdom not merely of ends but of priests, called to quest for perfection in themselves, in one another, and in humanity at large. The sheer bestowal of the command does not imply that every hearer was wholly good or that the community was perfectly integrated—only that our receptivity made the command intelligible. Hence the dictum of R. Eliezer that at the Red Sea, every handmaid of Israel saw God with an immediacy denied even the most visionary of the prophets.[58] Liberation had made us receptive to the overarching vision that grounds the idea of the good life in the commandments. For these commandments are not reflections of disparate passions projected upon rival deities or adversarial parties but are blessings from the one, all-integrating God. So they do not dissociate virtue from virtue, strength from wisdom, right from happiness —as sophistry will, as tragedy does, as paganism must. No merely beatific vision could equal this practical apprehension of God's presence: the pure intuition of the unity of right and good.

The Torah builds an integrated conception of the good life upon an integrated conception of the good, which its original recipients had not sophistically unlearned. It was natural to speak to this people of long ten-ure in their land, prosperity, peace, and contentment as rewards of the ordinances of the Law. For the life suggested by these images was a natural consequence and constituent of practical adherence to the Law. Indeed that was among the reasons it was enjoined. Happiness as ordained and promised in the Torah is at once the fulfillment of virtue and the fulfillment of desire. No need is recognized to assume that one person's good limits or restrains that of another. For legitimate interests are not served at one's neighbor's cost. Rather, the law founds the attainment of one man's good on the attainment of another's. But the commandments are not merely means to happiness; they are specific instances, causal paradigms, elements, in the good life. None are arbitrary behaviors, mere instruments to win the favor or propitiate the wrath of a capricious God. For the biblical God is not an arbitrary deity but the universal Fount of justice. He will be pleased only with justice and angered only by the assignment of divine reverence to vice and terror rather than to what is holy and just. Thus a corollary to the existential self-expression of God in the first of the Ten Commandments insists that God's name not be applied to ill—that the absolute not be identified with the negative or base, that his name and reverence not be shifted to any vanity or viciousness.[59] Correspondingly, it is in this name that the people of Israel are blessed (Numbers 6:22–27). Only through allegiance to absolute, unique, and infinite Perfection can Israel hold fast the integrated system of values that guides her way of life.

AN OPEN-ENDED GOAL

Peace, national well-being, prosperity, stability, and strength are not extrinsic to justice. Justice is the reign of peace and mutual regard. The same holds with purity, holiness, and all the other virtues of the Law. They are not merely formal or abstract demands but concrete, material goods woven into a fabric that reaches across the discontinuities of personal identity and difference, time and the generations. By the same token, the enjoining of such virtues is not simply utilitarian or prudential. The discovery that the Law serves human purposes does not allow its reduction to the service of those purposes. This again was to be an error of the Sophists—the fallacy of deriving the relativity (and so compromisability) of all values from the recognition that human values are anchored in human needs. Sophists argue that if the rules of law serve human purposes, those purposes might be served better in any given case by other means—specifically, by some more situational maxim. When the situation has been narrowed and particularized sufficiently, the question becomes *whose* interests shall be served— yours or mine, this class or that, the individual or the state, the self or the family? There follow all the *let-us-deal-wisely-with-him*'s, which seek to set up private gods by the murder of the one God but express only alienation and build nothing. The maxim is what Scripture calls "every man doing what is right in his own eyes"—a sharp contrast to the rule of law, which is the rule of principle, not mere uniformity or formal consistency but the rule of well-being, founded in and funded by the integration of otherwise competing interests in a dynamic complementarity. Thus lawlessness—every man judging his own case—is called violence (*ḥamas*); the radically opposite principle is grace and kindness (*ḥesed*)—a product of the rule of law.

The Law is preserved from paring down to a bone of contention or class struggle by attachment of the moral goal to a transcendent reality. The pursuit of justice is to be unswerving,[60] and this uncompromisability marks the nexus of the commandments with the love of God. God is absolute, and his will is therefore absolute. A principle can be compromised, then, only in behalf of a higher principle. With holy things one does not reduce but may only upgrade, and nothing is more holy than justice. One may not simply invent one's own version of the ultimate commandments of the Law, professing to pursue their purpose while ignoring their content. For their purpose *is* their content. They are not merely means to the good life but elements in the definition of it, subject to review only in the light of the ultimate legislative principle and authority, namely God himself, the Author and Principle of perfection.

Revision of the Law, conceived as its refinement (*tikkun*), may be accomplished, then, only by application, at each point, of the entire countervailing weight of the thematic balance of the Law. The bearing of each commandment is subject to interpretation and reinterpretation in keeping with the Torah's global intent. But the substance of the laws is categorical. They cannot be reduced to any of their merely expedient functions. For their larger function is to project for us a progress toward civil, moral, spiritual, and intellectual perfection. The palpable goals we might seize upon or be seized by on the way direct us toward a higher and more comprehensive goal, which will not be consummated before union is achieved with the Absolute Transcendent. Yet each of them, as a constituent in our progress toward perfection, is sacred in its measure; and the standard of its measure is God's perfection, the good itself.

As to reward, then, we find that no stage of life is more properly regarded as recompense than as consequence. And no action is to be weighed more heavily by its consequences than by its intrinsic character as blessed or unholy. If the path is toward perfection, as Maimonides suggests in reading the words of the psalmist—the Lord's Torah, which is perfect, perfects the soul (Psalm 19:8)—then every step and stage along that path is meaningful intrinsically and worthwhile in itself. Each is given meaning by the whole in which it forms a part, and none is an onerous or unrewarded undertaking requiring extrinsic compensation.

Pleasure, fellowship, contentment, wine, grain, fruit, oil, the bounties of concord and life on the land, wisdom, respect, even holiness can be held out by the Law not as premiums but as products of justice. In such a context there is no need to regard pleasure as evil. On the contrary, all wholesome pleasures are set within a moral context.[61] What makes them wholesome is that they are enjoyed in recognition of all due deserts. For Augustine, sexuality seems a gateway to impurity. And the experience of his growth reveals why: At every turning choices must be made—between *eros* and *philia*, loyalty and fulfillment, *eros* and *agape*.[62] Such dichotomies are the precipitate of the all-too-familiar secular mores that *use* persons rather than fostering their development and so demand practical and symbolic commitments of a life-denying kind, choices between eros and marriage, pleasure and progeny. Contrast the biblical integration: the bridegroom must give pleasure and joy to his bride. Even the call to war cannot withstand the primacy of this joy, another blessing in the form of a command: "When a man takes a bride he shall not go out to the service or be charged with any office but shall be free at home for one year and rejoice his wife whom he hath taken (Deuteronomy 24:5)." The obligation, in its sphere, is a kind of moral absolute. Against its primacy, in the long history of the Law in powerfully ascetic and natalist environments, no ascetic impulse or natalist exclusivity can prevail.[63] Canonically articulated, the ethic established in Genesis (2:18, 23, 24) regards sexual pleasure, marital fellowship, and erotic enjoyment as intrinsic goods whose motives, distinguished from, although integrated with, those of procreation, do not require procreative intent or even potential. All the "duties"—of husbands and wives giving and taking pleasure in one another, reproducing, and maintaining (psychic and spiritual as well as physical and hygienic) purity —are positive goods. The need for law and its characteristic tool of specifying and particularizing ritual[64] arises in the need for balancing competing goods (as in Plato's model of the psyche), not in a need for balancing conflicting interests. Thus Mosaic sexuality is not political—or more accurately, its politics is not of the meretricious kind that gives the cynical edge to sly equations of sexuality with politics. Sex is not evil.

Comparably, there is no thought that wealth is evil, but instead the explicit assertion that prosperity stems from God—from allegiance to God's laws of justice. Wealth isolated from other goods is worthless. But integrated among the goods of life, wealth is an instrument of a fulfilled human existence.[65] Asceticism gains no firm foothold here as a legitimate mode of spirituality—no more than hedonism does—because it offers too narrow a conception of the good; its vision is too wan and cheerless for the robust mentality of the Torah. Pleasure need never appear evil as long as it has not been isolated and turned against the other goods of life—consideration, for example.[66]

The question whether virtue is rewarded by God, then, involves forgetting what is meant by good—or, possibly, by God. The real question is whether we are able to perform good actions. And if there is an answer to the question "Is life fair?" it lies in the conformance of our actions to our characters and our characters to our actions. Here, as I shall argue in the next chapter, we find the unswerving agencies of divine judgment. For the capability of acting itself is often a "reward," as a pattern is made easier and more accessible by its institution as a habit or a custom. As Ben Azzai said, "One *mitzvah* furthers the next, and one sin draws another in its train, making a *mitzvah* the recompense of a *mitzvah*, and sin the recompense of sin'" (*Avot* 4:2). Spinoza made the same thesis the final conclusion of his *Ethics*: "Blessedness is not the reward of virtue, but virtue itself; nor do we enjoy it because we restrain our lusts; rather it is because we enjoy it that we are able to restrain them" (V, Prop. 42).[67]

My thesis, then, is that goodness does not require but already contains its reward and that this truth is obvious when goodness and advantage are properly construed. I apply this thesis specifically to the demand that God ought to reward those who act or choose rightly. The plaint in behalf of extrinsic rewards is made, we have seen, even by persons who do not believe in God, as a ground for dismissing the idea of God. It is made even by Kant, despite his insistence that choices adopted for the sake of a reward lack moral worth. But the righteous do not require more from God or nature for their choices than they receive through them, although they may deserve recognition or requital, fellowship, gratitude, respect, admiration, or honor from their moral fellows, who are spectators, beneficiaries, or participants in their goodness. God provides the context and possibility of such recognition. But these come through nature and human tact. To expect more from God than the unfailing action of natural characters and the fallible but for that very reason approachable responses of human personhood is to place God on the level of his creations.

Morality is the recognition of desert, and in a social community desert can be enhanced as well as diminished. Acts of self-sacrifice deserve honor or more tangible returns from their beneficiaries or from others capable of recognizing and requiting them. But whenever a sacrifice is made—of my interests to those of my children, of society's present comfort to the welfare of its posterity, or even of one person's life or many for the sake of dignity or honor, an interest is served, and the service of that interest is all that the sacrifice can be said to deserve from nature. Even if the aim sought is not achieved, the judgment made that the chance of reaching it was worth taking shows that the choice itself was valued—that the effort may have failed but the act, if not in error, still served an interest and was not in vain. Even a "failed" sacrifice may carry transcendental moral triumph in its train or in its essence. It is in this sense that our martyrs are said to die *'al kiddush ha-Shem*, in the sanctification of God's name. The sacrifice of life testifies to the transcendence of values beyond life itself; and, ultimately, to the absolute transcendence, or sanctity, of the ultimate Source of value. Innocence in death offers a comparable if silent testimony through the transcendent, eternally inviolable sanctity of its purity.

If we see our chosen, perhaps lesser sacrifices as unwarranted, it is perhaps because we have not spread the net of our identity widely enough to compass the interests they serve. A sacrifice in behalf of no interest or good is no moral action but an empty gesture. To which it must immediately be added that not every symbolic gesture is empty in this sense of having no significance for the furtherance of the good, of nature or of culture, or the cause of truth. Hence we include idolatry along with murder as a crime which it is better to die than to suffer oneself to commit. Hence too, in part, the inclusion of sexual crimes. For their impact weighs as heavily in the symbolic as in the physical, psychic, and social realms. But if every sacrifice susceptible of moral meaning yields some good, none is without reward and none requires recompense. Each is already requited in nature and recorded *sub specie aeternitatis*, in the divine order.

Kant holds that there are conflicts between principle and interest: Principle must have the advantage morally, although interest may gain the upper hand pragmatically. Such a conflict, as Kant would have it, is the acid test of morality, where morality is detected in isolation from interest because it speaks contrary to it. But why should morality quarrel with interest? One can object legitimately and coherently to the adoption of too narrow or too shallow a base for the estimation of interest. But if interest is not confined reductively but must extend to the perfection of humanity, of nature, of all that is, and, transcendentally, to the expression of the highest and profoundest truths of life made poetry and divine art made life, then no objection can be made to equating the service of morality with the pursuit of interest—bearing constantly in mind, of course, that human perfection includes and requires moral perfection and is not to be achieved by the immolation of any rightful claim on the altar of some vision of perfection.

Only by such an equation can one annul what otherwise becomes a tragic conflict of reason with morality, a typical outcome of Kant's compartmentalization of human discourse. For what grounds have we to prefer morality over prudence, the categorical over the hypothetical imperative, or even the Enlightenment Valhalla over the here and now? Kantian ethics has a moral ideal but no chance of connecting it with practical decisions in the world, unless by importing from the world a set of conventions about decency, dignity, or deserts. By contrast, our demand for the recognition of desert arises from the claims that beings make, entitatively. These claims are substantive, grounded in nature, but open-ended. They do not submerge devotion to principle in the mere formal consistency of a rule, and they do not seek further reward for moral action (or even passion) beyond what the act or suffering itself may bring in train or bear within it.

All reductive teleologies offer limited and limiting notions of human happiness. And Kant, by way of alternative, demands that we put no store in happiness for this life but act solely out of virtue—with a view to deserving happiness in the next. Both systems are inadequate because they are incomplete. To paraphrase Kant's famous remark: Morality without interests is empty, pragmatism without principles is blind. Happiness, to be whole and human, requires the fulfillment of many human capabilities here in this life. It finds infinite and transcendental goals within that very project. In behalf of such goals, all steps taken serve the good, if they are predicated on the due recognition of deserts—and all constitute within themselves worthwhile ends, all intrinsically rewarding.

♦ ♦ ♦ ♦ ♦

CHAPTER FOUR

Do Beings Receive What They Deserve?

Two kinds of justice are apparent if our reasoning up to now is sound: a universal natural justice and a more specific, human justice. Natural justice regards the tenability of any being's claims. Human justice, a subcategory of natural justice—not its antithesis—concerns the conscious recognition of deserts. An important special case is the moral recognition of subjecthood. Because our awareness is finite and corrigible we are responsive to admonition and encouragement, where the hortatory or monitory nisus of moral language finds its pragmatic context. Nature, not being self-conscious, and God, not being finite, are not appropriate subjects of warning or encouragement. Yet it still makes sense to speak of natural justice insofar as we can ask whether beings receive what they deserve. On that basis, we can recognize a justice in the operation of nature at large. Natural justice acts at a mean between the metaphysical justice of existential desert (perfect but impersonal) and human justice (personal but imperfect). Natural justice works slowly compared to logic, which judges instantly, outside time. But it weighs a world of data that human justice, with its abstractive references to particular acts and choices, persons and situations, cannot possibly consider—the claims of viruses and bacteria; strengths and weaknesses of character, blood vessels, or genes; the power of technology and the risks of shortsightedness.

Not being conscious, nature at large knows nothing of referential opacity and hence makes no allowances for ignorance or self-deception. Its only turbidity is that of its complexity. Its inefficiency is no more than its mitigated deference to the complex of all claims. Being non-subjective, hence disinterested, nature at large cannot abstract pragmatically and so can distinguish criminals from saints only by their strengths and weaknesses. Yet it does so decisively, in aggregate and cumulative measure, with far more thorough and telling accountancy than human agency could deploy. It operates not by considering the merit of salient acts in accordance with human standards and social needs but by tallying the impact of each aspect of being and doing against universal standards which human morals only partially reflect.

It is not my intent here to attempt to prove exhaustively the actuality of divine justice in nature. For this is a thesis not to be argued in the abstract but to be studied and gleaned from history and biology, even from physics and astronomy, where we witness the symmetries of equipoise and the asymmetries of emergence. My purpose is the more modest one of indicating the sorts of phenomena in which natural justice is seen and to note some reasons why it can be overlooked. In the preceding chapter I argued that some actions must be intrinsically worthwhile if any are to be rational and that even to designate an act as meaningless we must be capable of calling other actions meaningful. These arguments are dialectical. What they leave to be shown is that there actually are meaningful or worthwhile actions. But my arguments in behalf of natural justice provide the missing thesis as a corollary; for they involve the claim that nature allows successes. Human endeavors and the strivings of beings in general are not systematically frustrated but are given scope for fulfillment.

MORAL, METAPHYSICAL, AND NATURAL JUSTICE

The claims of being, I have argued, express the reality of those beings. Legitimate deserts are claims adjusted to the universal milieu of all conflicting and complementary claims. No being can legitimately claim more of reality than its nature and character permit. All beings seek the limits of their potential and grope[1] to expand those limits. But such seeking is fraught with liability to excess. Even its spoken claims can be unreasonable, thus incoherent, like a prayer for limitlessness. Each living individual must die, if it is to live at all. And the conscious recognition of conscious moral worth, although it is the paramount value of our communal life, cannot be the sole value in existence. When unreasonable claims are pressed, nature has ways of expressing and enforcing its own more global standards of what is reasonable. Nature leaves room for human claims but does not simply serve them.

Part of the conative character of being is that individuals develop their capabilities and enhance their chances of achieving higher goals. But such endeavors need not meet with success. They are endeavors precisely in that countervailing forces may defeat them. Vulgarly, when noble efforts are defeated, it is said that virtue is not rewarded. I call such sayings vulgar because they are unquantified, like the saying broached in Ecclesiastes, "the race is not to the swift" (9:11; cf. 3:16−4:6).[2] The sayings suffer, lose their bite and cogency, through their lack of quantification. Generally the race *is* to the swift. And virtue, properly conceived, is intrinsically rewarding, representing a heightening of ontic status that is conducive to further growth. But the key word is *conducive*. Nothing is guaranteed. Regularities in nature, as Aristotle put it, are "always or for the most part." Virtue must stake its finite claim in a world full of rival, supportive, or indifferent alternatives. Any quality that yields hope of realizing a valid goal is likely to be celebrated as a virtue, and should be, without any imputation of unfairness or tragic irony over the cases where, as finite endeavors will, it fails of its highest aspiration or the goal beyond that aspiration. A virtue wholly guaranteed of its extrinsic success is not a real virtue.

The angels, so the legend goes, witnessing the martyrdom of Akiba and his colleagues, cried out in heaven: "Is this Torah, and is this its reward?" A voice responded: Another word and the world will be turned back to water.[3] The angels here are called "servitors above" (*sarfei maalah*) to emphasize their want of understanding. The answer they receive is no mere ultimatum but a reminder that there need have been nothing; the costs and risks of existence, especially of the highest and noblest kind, are themselves very high. The reward of Torah is the life according to Torah, a life that would be impossible and meaningless without its risks. In homogeneous matter, in water, there is no martyrdom; one part does not rise above the rest. The condition of existence is differentiation, and the price of excellence (not its reward, as in the irony of the angels) is risk. Its rewards are the intrinsic and consequential gains that make it worthy of the name of excellence.

It is by way of their strengths and under constraint of their weaknesses that beings achieve whatever may be theirs. Justice in this sense is rooted in the law of being. Natural justice is the dynamic *expression* of the metaphysical principle of identity, which would remain a static equation but for the fact that beings exist in time and with one another. They realize rather than merely being what they are, and they develop capabilities that enhance their being and their power, not as implications but as expressions of their being. Without the birth of consciousness, and so of conscience, natural justice would have remained a blind battle or unwitting alliance. But with consciousness it becomes in part a process of considerate accommodation and creative cooperation. In the unfolding of the metaphysical as the natural, and of the natural as the moral, we see the wisdom of the ancient idea that God created the world for the values it would contain—the idea Saadiah expressed in saying that God created the world for man and man for the sake of justice.[4] For it is an accepted Aristotelian and prophetic usage to speak of outcomes in terms of purpose or intent.

Justice does not award every being a desert commensurate with its claims—not even those claims that violate no human want. Nature affords a much broader but for that very reason less personable recognition than we accord one another. Each being, by its specific and particular character, receives and achieves what it can. Nature tests claims and allows for adaptation and the cumulation of advantages by experience, evolution, and culture. Indeed nature demands that beings and their kinds *must* grow, by projecting goals as well as pursuing them. But for this very reason, nature also harbors risks. Such a system is to be called just and generous not because it realizes all tendencies and desires (a natural impossibility) but because it affords a theater for the attainment of some potentials, the development of others, and the expression of all that involve real capability. Nature denies much that beings claim. But it is only in nature that making and fulfilling claims is possible.

Human justice makes conscious allowance for objective characters, including deserts. We can step aside, exploit, or offer care, love, and friendship. Nature at large parallels such relations only blindly or gropingly. In natural justice, as in causality, we glimpse the certainty that marks the act of the Divine—but mitigated by its mingling with finitude, its compromise with space, time, and specificity. Human justice is contingent, dependent on moral accommodation. Here we taste the inevitably pleading character of all moral claims. Natural justice as such is not subjective; for that reason it is not considerate. Nature stands aside for no one. We take that fact for granted in our practical affairs yet often feel offended by it when we shift to an evaluative mode.

◆

TWO CONFUSIONS OF NATURAL WITH MORAL JUSTICE

Confusion between natural and human justice takes two main forms: We may apply in the human sphere themes abstracted from the realm of natural justice—"survival of the fittest," say, as though it were a moral principle. Or we may apply our moral notions to the natural realm, demanding that nature at large show sympathy for a plight that has arrested our attention. The first confusion screens many apologetics for injustice, not only of the social Darwinist variety but also as in the Sophists' suasion, "What did you expect? It was only natural," and other appeals to nature as a moral arbiter. Since we are taught by prudence to expect the worst, catchphrases about expectations can cover quite a multitude of sins. The anthropomorphic confusion breathes disappointment with the cosmos, sometimes voiced in the cliche that existence is cruel, an imposition.

To make of competition an apologetic for human violence or violation, even in the mitigated forms of negligence or exploitation, is to read invidious moral standards into the rule of nature, a telling projection in beings who can rise above impersonality. Appeals to the naturalness of violence and exploitation are pseudo-naturalistic; for they balk at a central theme of emergent nature, the rise of moral consciousness. A genuine naturalism does not ignore the higher ontic level represented in the capability for community and responsibility or make normative the limitations of lesser beings. Failure to acknowledge the role for which our nature fits us is made no sounder by the confusion of violence with power. Real power is far more integrating and far more integrated; nature tends to countenance it insofar as it is founded in maximal regard for deserts—through the construction of communities. To overlook the synthetic character of power is radically to misread the laws of nature and the meanings of biological and historical succession and success.[5]

The projection of our moral standards onto nature similarly transposes the categories of personality and impersonality, demanding for being a level of protection appropriate only for what has not yet emerged from its ontic womb into the light of actuality. All beings struggle or flourish for their moment. This is what gives value and authenticity to the universal project in all its parts. Disappointments are inevitable if there is to be a universal drive toward perfection and dissatisfaction with anything less. Our tendency to project human expectations onto nature expresses mythic thinking, our own desire for recognition. But disappointment with the reticence of nature at our entreaties is not just a product of mythicism but an author of it and a bulwark of systematic, emotionally fired ignoring of the actual workings of divine justice in nature. We find the actions of that justice in the acts and tendencies of all beings, securing to them their tenable claims, undermining their untenable ones with remarkable efficacy and compassion, grounding deserts in claims and claims in fact but equating deserts with reality, not with claims.

Nature, as the All displayed explicitly, cannot focus perspectivally, cannot abstract, hence cannot be conscious. Consciousness depends on the abstractive differentiation of subject from object. Nature at large cannot accord personal recognition to its members if it is to be the theater in which personality is achieved. One cannot say simply that nature does not focus. For nature does contain determinate particulars. But nature does not focus on one or a few to the exclusion of the rest. Its "failure" to do so is the condition of its justice: Each being has the same degree of determinacy, the degree requisite for existence. As the Midrash puts it: "The rule with flesh and blood is that one cannot hear clearly when two people cry out at once. But that is not the case with Him who spoke and the world came to be. On the contrary, even when all the denizens of the world come and cry out before Him, He hears their cries clearly, as it is said, 'O Thou who hearest prayer, unto Thee doth all flesh come' (Psalm 65:3)."[6]

If capabilities are dynamically developing tendencies rather than static givens and the full dynamic of a being can be established only in its conative interaction with all others in its social universe, it is not surprising that there should be contingency in the fulfillment of generic potential. No thrust or force operates with absolute efficiency. So it can hardly be expected that adoption of the best or most advisable course will lead invariably to complete achievement of the desired or intended results. The most that can be said is that each being deserves to attain what it seeks insofar as that attainment is compatible with its nature and the maximal realization of all beings. This is the desert that nature recognizes. A being that overreaches contradicts more than a formal principle; it militates against the laws of its own nature and the (social) possibility of its existence. Small wonder that finite rationality combined with infinite aspiration puts itself in jeopardy.

Divine justice as it works in nature is the optimal recognition of all claims. The claims of fire and water, wind and frost, are real and recognized according to their power, even when the elements, the weeds and pests, villains and scourges which may bedevil our existence or that of other creatures are not on the same ontic level with the beings they threaten or torment and do not accord recognition to their claims. A mode of existence may be predicated on blind assertion. The intrinsic (but limited) legitimacy of its claims is what is meant by Job's invocation of the elements. They too will make their claims, the whirlwind and the worm. God's favor and mercy in nature are that they do not win lasting victory to the exclusion of higher ranging possibilities.

JUSTICE AND THE EXPRESSION OF NATURES

It is inconceivable, except through the expression and development, failure or betrayal of their potentials, that beings receive any more or less than they have. But, by abstraction from such givens, infinite alternatives are conceivable. Beyond the existential datum, which expresses what Saadiah calls "encompassing grace"—in glossing the psalmist's dictum "God is good to all"[7]—emergent from that datum, the dynamic of beings expresses their identity, giving it content and so contributing to the project of their kind and of nature at large. No individual can achieve all that is laid open to it. Nature as emergent lacks the perfect fit of the divine creative act apparent in nature considered as a universe of determinate and therefore perfect individuals. But that, we can say, in the full richness of the term, is a mercy.

Not every tendency is aggressive. And, left to their own devices in nature, beings do not pursue even their aggressive tendencies unchecked. There are opportunity and need for self-checking, the potential, the selection gradient, for evolution, physio-chemical or biological. Living beings in particular, because of the ambitious character of their claims, do not advance unchecked. A single cell cannot grow beyond its capacity for heat transfer and chemical transport. Nor can a cell multiply to engulf the world.[8] Long before that endgame, such a population would have depleted the resources necessary to the other members of its food chain. There is a let upon the efficiency of living beings, as upon their chemical forerunners. There is room in the world, as well as need, for growth—not boundless room, but room for more than one sort of thing. The assertion of self does not require (as in a *very* small and limited universe it might) the elimination of other. And the overextension of self does not lead immediately and inexorably to self-destruction. In nature there is, as it were, a slowing down to practical speeds of the immediacy of the divine act, allowing time for adjustment, modification, and, ultimately, for learning. And there is space, affording escape—a first, second, and often many a subsequent chance for error and experiment before the claims of time (of past misjudgment and rival claims) come due. In a sense, then, natural claims are corrigible by natural justice; and such corrigibility, the trial where learning in the proper sense emerges, can itself be regarded as a manifestation of divine grace.

The possibility for the more advanced, adaptable, or integrated (including the ethically adapted or considerate) to emerge unscathed or even enhanced from its encounters — hostile, exploitative, or cooperative — is favor. Natural favor is not a matter of preferences. Nature does not choose favorites arbitrarily, as failed human justice might. Rather, natural justice is founded on two principles: the fragility of all claims in a milieu where rival claims are made and the redundancy of opportunity, which affords room for rectification far beyond what might have seemed appropriate to our proprieties. Nature at large does not view malefactors with the inflamed eyes of injured interest or seek to cast back upon them their disregard for others' claims. Criminals may escape the severest measure of retribution. Yet none of us escapes the logic and consequences of our actions — any more than we might escape our skin. For our identity, beyond the existential datum, is self-made and socially defined. On this level, God's justice, as in the Quranic (50:16) phrase, is closer to us than our jugular.

Accordingly, there is a bias in the tradition whose wisdom I am seeking to recapture. Our bias in behalf of being pleads softly but winningly in favor of letting nature take its course — not because human justice is inadequate, but only because it is not inerrant. The justice we must pursue unrelentingly is not justice *against* any interests (we have seen it cannot be that) but justice in their behalf. We are right, therefore, when we can, to remit the severer sentences of justice in favor of gentler ones, to *define* justice by the demands of mercy, and to abjure any claims of specious expediency in behalf of draconian measures. Not every Jean Valjean must be run to earth. Our confidence that nature's justice is God's and a complement to what humans may do or fail to do sheds a salubrious and forgiving light.

The Talmud reports a dialogue between a Roman officer and R. Eleazar, son of the famous R. Simeon. The Roman had orders to round up thieves in the district. How can you be sure not to capture the innocent, the rabbi asked, while the guilty go free? The officer insisted that the imperial command was that he must capture the guilty. Taking the order at face value, R. Eleazar proposed a scheme: "Go to the tavern at the fourth hour of day. If you see a man dozing with a cup of wine in his hand, ask what he is. If he is a scholar, he has risen early to study; if a day laborer, he must have been up early for work; if he is a night worker, he has been rolling out thin metal. If he is none of these, he is a thief; arrest him." In some irony, Eleazar was charged with executing his plan. Given the premise he adopted from his interlocutor, in a sense he had no choice. Without arresting some of the innocent he would miss some of the guilty. The flaw was in allowing primacy to punishment. Sympathy toward suspects was natural in the circumstances of the day, since Roman officials often used the term 'brigands' as a euphemism for rebels against the state, refusing to acknowledge acts of rebellion as acts of war. "R. Joshua ben Karḥah sent word— 'Vinegar, son of wine! How long will you deliver up the people of our God for slaughter!'" The reply: "I weed the thorns from the vineyard." R. Joshua retorted, "Let the vineyard's owner come and weed out the thorns himself!"[9]

Like preventive detention and presumed guilt, execution of thieves is an inveterate distortion of human justice. R. Joshua does not forget that even actual brigands are God's children, whose lives are forfeit only for the gravest cause and only on the starkest evidence. I doubt he expected God literally to come and weed his vineyard by any means violative of the normal course of nature. Rather, his faith was in a slower and more relenting but in some ways all the more perfect justice than the frenetic human kind can be.

The anecdote has modern echoes in Wisdom's parable of the garden, which Flew subjects to a folkloristic twist by slanting the story to make it *obvious* that there is no gardener and that one who differs is mad. Wisdom focused on the possibility of rational disagreement and relevant evidence, even in the absence of conclusive proof.[10] One popularly circulating version ends with a parishioner telling the vicar, "You should have seen the place when God was taking care of it by himself." Plainly God's standards are not identical to ours if he leaves the "weeds" to be taken care of by us or by each other. But we could hardly manage for ourselves with too fastidious a gardener. Perhaps Roman efficiency in crucifying brigands is not the ultimate model of the pursuit of justice. The parishioner's retort only brings us back to the imagery of Genesis: What would nature have been like had God's part been left undone? Recognition of the complementary roles of God and nature or, specifically, of God and man (cf. Psalm 115:16) is the foundation of all ethics.

JUSTICE AND MERCY, FAVOR AND GRACE

The fragility of claims and redundancy of opportunities are biblically referred to aspects or "attributes" of God, justice and mercy, just as creation and the endowment of specific capabilities are referred to divine grace. Not that divine justice and mercy *are* fragility of claims and redundancy of opportunity; rather, these are characters in nature that can be read as hallmarks of the Absolute and Non-contingent in a realm inseparable from contingency and relativity.

For reasons of social tact and communal regard we do not like to say that a human being stopped in mid-career toward a valued goal did not deserve to reach it. And we hesitate to exonerate malefactors who have blocked the way. Rightly so—as long as we do not mount on our moral umbrage the delusion that nature owes us inviolability. The free course of nature may trap the morally innocent in their struggle with beings of lesser worth. And, with the evident collusion of nature and nature's laws, culprits can evade the measure of accountability human justice might assign. We are indignant at the reprieve of those who have flouted standards we uphold, and indignant again that nature at large does not accord deference to our subjecthood. We press to the conclusion that nature is hostile or cold, indifferent rather than impartial. But we forget, in our disappointment at nature's refusal to call upon us by name, as a human family or community might do, that only in nature do we acquire the individuality and find the community to give us a name. We take our gifts for granted and carp at their conditionality.

Against the background of the obvious disparity between human moral standards and the events of nature and of history, the more perfect fit of identity to action and of character to intention which marks metaphysical justice is readily overlooked. Its omnipresence and invariance camouflage it; while natural justice, its slower and less efficient counterpart, being speckled and spotted enough for us to see and slow enough for us to follow, rouses our impatience. Its disparity with our own standards of accountability seems ironic. But the irony is not a logical one; it expresses only the discrepancy between our moral ideas, which are and ought to be founded on recognition of personhood, and the impersonality of nature at large, whose operations must be grounded in the more general dialectics of deserts as power. To call nature's impersonality a denial of justice seems to me an error. For it leads us a priori to overlook the operations of a system, traditionally discussed in theological terms, whose laws we should know as intimately as possible. Can we naturalize those terms—return them to the experience they reflect—and thus express their sentence in a language that does not violate the very categories from which they arise? We must attempt to do so, if only to avoid circularity. For to attempt to ground our idea of natural justice in theological claims would undercut the foundation of our theology in the experience of nature and history.

When the daughters of Zelophehad tell Moses (Numbers 27:3) that their father "died in his own sin," they are not charging their father with some unstated guilt but acknowledging in the biblical idiom the natural fact of their father's frailty. Like all living beings, he had aggressed in nature. As all living beings must, he had paid the price or repaid the debt which God's justice, through the law of nature, exacts as the condition of existentiation. He had died, and there is no death without some initial overstepping, even if it has no more portentous name than life. The innocent are never pure in the sense the Jains seek, of aggressing in no way against any thing. All beings aggress merely by claiming space; all are liable to retribution and aggression from lesser beings, whose existence and natural functioning are as much to them as ours are to us.

The miracle of creation, setting nature under the attributes of justice *and mercy*, is the space that permits confrontations not always to be no-exit, life-or-death struggles. One claimant or both may escape. That is mercy. There is grace (*ḥen*) in the opportunity for sustenance or survival of anything at all, particularly in the face of a challenge; and favor (*ḥesed*), in the opportunity for the emergence of higher forms from lower and the enhanced chances of survival for the higher forms. Such favor, as we now know, grounds the possibility of evolution. Indeed it defines the direction of evolution and places the mark of specificity on the open-endedness of the conatus. That it is a foundation for other forms of growth as well has long been known.

Moses did not know of evolution in the sense that Darwin or Teilhard did. But he did know that nature allows the escape of an aggressor and the growth, triumphant emergence, and further development of a victim. This was his experience personally and the historic experience of Israel, for whom he spoke. Thus grace and favor, the two components of mercy (in its broad sense as an expression of love), are central in the words through which Moses grasped the tenor of God's governance: "A merciful and gracious God, long suffering and abundant in favor and truth, preserving favor thousandsfold, bearing with wrong, and transgression and overstepping, but by no means effacing them" (Exodus 34:6–7).

Traditionally, justice implies proportion between deserts and what is imparted. The equivalence is more than matched when gifts are freely given in an act of grace. But grace must be unininvidious to be just. Favor, traditionally a regard for particular persons,[11] must be proportioned to desert.

Mercy—that is, compassion or long suffering, in the specific sense of showing grace even where it seems undeserved—must be openly accessible to be just. Thus existentiation, the affording of potential and of opportunities for its fulfillment or enlargement, is an act of grace, since there is no desert apart from being. Survival and evolution are acts of favor. The redundancy of opportunity that allows lesser beings to avoid direct conflict or competition or to escape them unscathed are acts of mercy. And justice is found in the measuring of what each being is allotted according to the limits of its capacity.

All these processes are at work continuously, biologically and even physically, chemically, astronomically, on a cosmic scale. Consequently reflection on what Thoreau calls "vast and cosmogonic themes" in the Jewish tradition has always led to thoughts of divine mercy and justice and their fusion in favor and grace. Isaiah wrote, "Not as a waste did He create it, but He made it to be dwelt in" (45:18). Even as casual beneficiaries of the vast scheme, humans may regard all as existing for our sake. Like all other creatures we are guests. But the vastness and resultant impersonality of the great themes have led many to doubt their harmonies. They are not attuned to human heartstrings, and the recognition of that fact can be a source of sorrow and affront.

The impartiality we see is not easier to bear when we ascribe it to One we love, as we must love what engulfs all perfection. But it is a fact of nature nonetheless—and necessary, since only absolute impartiality to the claims of all could count as justice in the Absolute; only favor proportioned to desert could account as favor from such a being; and only restraint which did not render absolute the advantage of higher over lesser beings could count as grace and mercy—or even wisdom in a universal God. This is what the Sages ask us to see when they call upon us to regard all events—above all (since this is humanly the hardest) those that harm our interests—as truthful and just judgments of God, even to count them as blessings: truthful, in their absolute objectivity, the truth mentioned by Moses along with the mercy of God; blessings, as concomitants of the initial and continual endowment of existence.

The claim that life is unjust because the innocent may suffer, or because the good are not rewarded adequately and the wicked not always punished, reasons wrongly on several grounds. Innocence is not always to be measured by human moral standards, reward and punishment are not paid only in external coin, reprieve is not always unjust, and natural disaster or prosperity need not be read as a judgment but may be quite accidental to moral merit, a concomitant of life in nature. In his Commentary on Job Saadiah laid to rest all credibility in the thought that human sufferings must be punishments for moral wrongdoing. Yet the superstitious association of all suffering with guilt persists, perhaps nearly as widely as the contrary belief that if innocents can suffer nature must be unjustly founded. Neither avowal reckons fully with the authenticity of existence.

Divine justice is not meted out by a marionette-master providence that would negate the very reality of nature. So we cannot read merit in *per accidens* success or desert in *per accidens* prosperity. But our account does not imply that human agency should simply sit back and observe the natural dialectic, fatalistically abstaining from taking part in it, having been assured that the process is just. The justice of nature is a matter of its structural thrust, not its unfailing conscious intention, and that thrust derives its impetus from the wills and energies of all the participants, among whom we are numbered. What our account does mean is that we have no basis for complaint against the general scheme of things when we see a dishonest man in physical vigor, wealth, or reputation or a virtuous man in physical misery, poverty, or disgrace. We know enough of nature to know well that there is no one-to-one connection between such externals and vice or virtue, although vice degrades and its thrust is noxious and although virtue ennobles and its thrust is beneficial.

The bestowal of existence is an act of grace sufficient to warrant real risks. But the dynamic of existence, the continued renewal of existentiation, requires the constant possibility of loss. In concrete terms this means multiple sclerosis, malaria, cancer, bilharzia, glaucoma, sleeping sickness, spina bifida, river blindness, Alzheimer's disease, and leprosy. For many it has meant plague or goiter, death by diabetes, crippling by arthritis or osteoporosis. Existence represents no more than a probability of flourishing. Each person must answer individually whether existence is a boon. No one can answer for another, as if to put prayers of praise into another's mouth—or curses, as Job's wife would when she tells Job to curse God and die. Between her despond and his "The Lord hath given, the Lord hath taken away; blessed be the name of the Lord" lies an apprehension of the preciousness of life's miracle as weighed against its cost. There is merit in yea-saying. But there would be none if acceptance were obvious, automatic, or naive.

In arguing that divine mercy and justice, favor and grace are manifest to us objectively in nature, we recapture a position long occupied by our classic thinkers. From Maimonides we learn that God, being simplex, as an absolute and necessary being must be, has no actual attributes which differentiate divine unity into multiplicity. The human notion of attributes projects upon divinity those characteristics in which we find perfection and differentiates as distinct attributes those facets of nature in which we most readily apprehend the work of Perfection. A prophetic compulsion and poetic necessity license characterizations of the Creator in the categories of his creation without at all warranting the notion that our characterizations somehow define, delimit, analyze, or account for that by which all else is to be explained. Maimonides assigns the *order* of nature to an attribute of wisdom most apprehensible in that aspect of reality which Aristotelian philosophers call intelligible form; he assigns the chance or arbitrary seeming aspect of things to an attribute of will most manifest in what Aristotelian philosophers call matter.[12] Neither of these "attributes" *is* God, and their very distinctness is the mark of *our* finitude, since each is tailored to the categories of our understanding. Preserving these anti-reductionistic provisos, we can assign time and space to divine grace, since the system they bound opens possibilities, affords reprieves, allows coexistence — indeed demands it. But, correspondingly and simultaneously, the givens of finite being and the demands of all things in nature, in thoroughgoing interaction with one another through space and across time, require the limitation of each by all. Justice and mercy are of a piece.

Nature affords an environment to all sorts of things including organisms dependent on and constitutive in ecosystems that offer room for parallel, convergent, and divergent evolution. The limitations of space and resources do not stifle the flourishing of life but allow the modification and enhancement of the milieu in which life may flourish. We have evidence now for the inspired conjecture of our poetic cosmologists that such possibilities were not inevitable. To take just one example: The universe is thought to contain some 10^{11} galaxies, or 10^{22} stars, giving a life span "from Big Bang to Big Crunch" of 59 billion years, long enough to allow the "cooking" of heavy elements in some star systems and thus the evolution of all manner of beings, including conscious selves, whose emergence and self-discovery give heightened meaning to the entire process. With a lesser quantity of matter, sufficient only to the generation of one typical galaxy of 10^{11} stars, the duration "from Big Bang to Big Crunch" is estimated on the order of one year. There would have been no "cooking" of heavy elements, no evolution of life, and no finite thinking beings.[13]

In applying the language of justice, mercy, favor and grace, to the exfoliation of time and space, the provision of matter, its elaboration into elements and living forms, I have in mind this sort of contingency. Many more instances could be given, even failing our present model of cosmic history. Opportunity is afforded for the realization or fulfillment of potential. But the allotment of finite (hence vulnerable) being contains no guarantee that every finite being shall receive all that it grasps for. The demand for immunity to contingency, as Bahya suggests, is among the subtler ploys that human willfulness uses dialectically to dislodge our moorings upon reality.[14] Such guarantees, could they be stated coherently, would be incompatible with a universe of diverse and dynamic actualities. To equate divine justice with the granting of all claims is to pursue a delusion.

THE WORKING OUT OF NATURAL JUSTICE

Aggrieved at the thought that the wicked escape punishment, we easily think of them as wholly evil. But we are too prone to overlook the saving graces that prevent ruin from falling quite as swiftly or irrevocably as poetic imagination might have dreamed. God takes a longer view, allowing the dynamic of action to take effect, or waiting, as Isaiah (30:18) puts it, for a change. If the evil were absolute, such a change would be impossible. Even in approaching absoluteness evil destroys itself, and much earlier it has limited and lost the freedom to transform and reclaim itself. Incensed at the idea of evil unpunished, we incline to overlook the mounting burden that all overstepping lays upon those who aggress. Nothing, as Moses heard, is erased.[15]

ACTION AND CHARACTER

The engraving of acts and choices upon our minds is often imperceptible to us and certainly to the interested but not intimately informed observer. Hence the illusion that we act insulated from accountability. The Psalms discover the illusion implicit in the choices of the immoralist: "The fool hath said in his heart there is no God" (53:2)—for by acting on the assumption that there is no accountability he has failed to reckon with the consequences of his acts, above all and most intimately, upon himself. Each individual seems to act alone, sole arbiter in his own moral world. Yet somehow there emerge Gandhis and Hitlers, Schweitzers and Sacher-Masochs, Einsteins and Sades. The great prophets and historians, psychologists and tragedians have always understood why. For life as an art is not without an artwork: We human beings ourselves are creatures of our imaginations, and imagination is the product of our times and choices. "Times" refers to social circumstances—the past, the future, and the present, in which we act. We limit or enlarge ourselves, and in that sense are formed in God's image. Character is indeed our daimon. And character is formed by acts and attitudes—ours and those of the others we depend upon. That is the whole burden of ethics, insofar as ethics is a science.

Outraged morality will protest at the spectacle of liars, thieves, and cheats enjoying their gains, and at the apparent impunity of murderers, drug sellers, and withholders of famine relief. Such outrage can be useful and relevant, since it may seek the reform of offenders, punishment of offenses, and deterrence of their like. But it may also lose its moral footing and degenerate into a quest for vengeance; or, taking outrage to the communal or societal plane, into acts of terror or warfare. But whether active or passive, rage obscures our vision of the subtler retribution at work in the logic and consequences of an offender's acts, undermining a wrongdoer's effectiveness and that of the society that tolerates wrongdoing.

AGENCY AND ACCOUNTABILITY

As social scientists have long urged but our systems of law have had proper difficulty in recognizing, individual agency is to some degree a fiction. Not that individual choices are mere products of social "forces." To say that would only push into the indefinite past or diffuse into the indeterminate environment the onus of moral responsibility. The truth, I think, is better expressed Spinozistically: We are partly responsible for our own actions, partly passive respondents to the acts of others. We are both actors and objects.[16] Yet we are accountable de facto and responsible de jure for every event we might have altered for the better. Such responsibility may weigh heavily; but like freedom or risk it is part of the price of being. We are held accountable by nature at large not only for what we have done and chosen but for (and through) our limitations of judgment, capability, and moral nerve. It is true that we do not absolutely create ourselves. But natural justice holds us accountable for every measure of the extent to which we fail to create ourselves and rewards us in the measure of our success in just that contest. Mercy defers the strict sentence of immediate accountability; grace enters us in the game; favor is our chance of winning—never without limit.

Morally, accountability belongs to the doer of an act. But all sorts of social agencies of varying complexity—firms, communities, foundations, societies, mobs, tribes, nations, sects—are capable of harmful or beneficial action, recognizing or failing to recognize deserts. So accountability is not confined to private actions. If we act through social agencies, our actions and omissions include the failures of our participation and our acquiescences as well as our private choices and abstentions. An institution, after all, is an instrumentality through which individual acts are magnified or altered. Plainly an individual is not *less* responsible for acts committed with a tool or weapon than for those committed, as it were, bare-handed. Even institutional modifications of intent do not eliminate responsibility: One is responsible to some extent to know the sorts of distortions likely in the effectuation of one's will by the various instrumentalities one employs or is employed by. A firm, an army, a government, a gang are not wholly unknown in this regard. Just as investors must know that financial leverage can work for or against their interests, so all of us as social beings must reckon with the impact of our actions not in isolation but in their social context. And part of what we must know is that such impacts inevitably will affect the lives and fortunes of every member of even a moderately well-integrated corporate body, tellingly. It is because individual choices are constitutive of the acts of a corporate body that corporate accountability can be just.

Even in a nation that is not well integrated—a monarchic tyranny, or the more modern type of democratic tyranny of all against each—the fact of oppression does not obviate but heightens moral responsibility. For the victims themselves are in complicity with what they tolerate, share in, benefit from—especially with oppression on a mass scale, where victims might have articulated themselves into a power of resistance. Surely individuals can be caught in a web of circumstance not of their own devising. Such is the romantic image of all victims of oppression, war, economic hardship, and other vast and faceless "forces." But the image bears within it a tinge of bad faith. It assumes that nothing could be done—nothing, that is, by an individual acting alone. But why was the individual alone? Why did he remain alone if aloneness was the condition of his powerlessness? Isolation is not the natural but the desperate condition of man.

I am bound up with every other human being—with every living and non-living being, in fact—but most intimately with human beings. For every act or omission of mine, every choice, potentially affects everyone now living and is affected (conditioned was Spinoza's word,[17] not in Pavlov's sense but to designate being affected but not wholly and solely externally determined) by every act and choice of all who coexist with me or who have preceded me. Bound up together in causal community, all choosing beings are co-choosers, and accountability on a moral as well as a natural footing can be expected to be shared. The society that breeds criminals, as well as the individual criminals, can be expected to suffer from crime. The notion of the innocent bystander is a convenient (and necessary!) legal abstraction. But rarely in reality can we say that in a society well enough articulated to bring a criminal and a victim into proximity with one another was there no missed opportunity for prevention or detention that might have made this crime less likely.

We require the abstraction, the legal fiction of the innocent bystander for the same reason that we require the abstraction of the criminal act, criminal mind, criminal intent—*mens rea*. Only through such abstractions can we tease out from all natural and moral entanglements those aspects of a concrete situation that are sufficiently assailing to our pragmatic requirements and sensibilities to demand case treatment—penally, or perhaps through the methods of social welfare. In law we restrain ourselves from considering holistic merits and demerits lest casuistic judgment become too freighted with biases, too easily distracted or distorted, its prejudices too readily camouflaged or enlarged, masqueraded under the garb of reason—or too global, and so confounded by uncertainties of relative weighting among the numberless principles which might come into play. Yet our rule-bound proceduralism in the abstractive isolating of cases does not eclipse but only silhouettes the facts in the rather polarized light of the values that law as law must regard as salient.

Nature at large does not so narrow its gaze, not because nature is dead or unresponsive but because nature at large cannot avoid holism. Where juridical institutions institute arbitrary exclusions,[18] nature does not isolate individuals from their milieu. Rather, it operates through the universal causal nexus, where no one is absolutely innocent but there is the opportunity for goodness to exist and emerge—not unscathed always but potentially unbowed or even enlarged. Contemplating the course of natural justice, the psalmist makes explicit the immanence of accountability by calling out the oblivion of the brutish to the subtlety of God's design, which makes the very aggressiveness of the wicked fuel their destruction:

> When the evil are in flower like grass
> And all workers of wrong are in blossom,
> It is that they be destroyed completely. (Psalm 92:8)

The reasoning behind this crucial and repeated thesis[19] is articulated in Proverbs (11:19): "As right pursues life, so one who pursues evil pursues his own death." The Mosaic groundwork of this reasoning lies in the identification of goodness, life, merit, and worth as the objects of right choice—centrally: "Choose life." Evil is the name of the ruinous course. Its nature is exploitation of self and others, disregard of deserts. In the meshing of natural events the impact of evil becomes ruinous not only to the one who chooses it but to the community condoning the perpetuation of such choices: "The integrity of the upright guides them, and the crookedness of the deceitful destroys them. . . . Through the blessedness of the upright a city is raised up; by the mouth of the wicked it is brought low" (Proverbs 11:3, 11). There is no magic *baraka* in the presence of righteous persons or magic miasma in human wickedness. But a city is blessed directly through the goodness of the good and ruined by the acts of treacherous and deceitful inhabitants. Thus: "The Divine judges the righteous, and God pronounces sentence each day" (Psalm 7:12). The temporality belongs to nature, the theater of a judgment that does not act wholly externally.[20]

The delay of divine justice is merely its natural incubation, what the psalm calls the flowering of evil, the time it takes to bear the poisonous fruit by which it destroys itself and all who depend upon it. Thus the wicked are pictured as falling foul of their own snares (Psalm 9:16, 141:10); and the same nets (*pahim*) are envisioned as rained from above by God (Psalm 11:6). For to say that the snares are set by our own actions and spring up by the laws of nature, character, and history is to say that they are set by God, the same fact stated in complementary idioms.

THE SINS OF THE FATHERS

Seemingly paradoxically, the Torah couples God's epiphany as merciful and gracious, long tolerating wrong but not condoning it, with the startling further epithet: "visiting the wrong of fathers upon children and grandchildren, thrice and four times removed."[21] What can we make of accountability borne across generational lines, when the Torah itself is the great original teacher of individual moral responsibility?[22] The first impact of the statement that God visits the sins of ancestors upon subsequent generations is that of a warning directed more to the parents than the offspring, a caution as to the impact of our acts. As cultural beings we perpetuate the impact of our choices and abdications with far greater continuity than would be possible for a solitary species or one that practiced strict intergenerational segregation. The power to transmit experience, not genetically but by tradition—literature, science, art, religion—allows our advance to be cumulative. Without such progress, even our survival would be in question. But the price of progress, even as a possibility, is the possibility of regress, undesirable inheritances, which only the most penetrating criticism can detect and only the most intelligent discipline can extirpate. The crucial limiting factor of all generational growth is the ethos, whose vehicles of expression and transmission are the mores and myths of a community or a society. A cruel family nurses cruel children, not by heredity but by example and image. A cruel society nurtures cruel citizens continually and systematically, through its rituals and institutions. Kindness, holiness, reverence for life or beauty or learning, hatred of sin, or love of wit are transmitted in the same way.

So offspring can be victims to the lapses of their forebears, not only physically but morally. Latercomers suffer or prosper when their degrees of freedom are curtailed or enhanced by the choices of their predecessors. But beyond this primary damage, further choices are made to join, resist, or reject an ethos or an action. Secondary choosers are punished or rewarded in and through the ethos of their forebears and their peers, to which they have joined themselves willfully. Thus Exodus warns not that later generations are punished for the sins of their forebears but that these are *visited* upon them. Leviticus (26:39) makes clear just how: "and those that remain of you shall rot away in their sins in the land of their enemies, and also in their fathers' sins shall they rot away with them." As Saadiah explains, the successors suffer not *for* but *through* the sins of their fathers —inasmuch as they have shared them.[23]

All generations are in causal community with their successors through the effects of forerunners' acts upon posterity. But in a certain sense my actions affect even the past, and those of my successors have an effect (as yet undetermined) upon me. For later choices affect the fulfillment of forebears' projects. Present hopes and fears are rightly expressed in visions of the future, since future generations are manifestly our beneficiaries or victims. But, although the birth of modernity involved its hot denial, they have a responsibility toward us as well, since their choices will affect the fulfillment of some of our loftiest aspirations and will validate or invalidate some of our most basic practical assumptions. We assume that the populace of the year 2500 will not make human life impossible by the year 3000, so we take into account the environment of the year 3000 in our practical decisions, trusting our more immediate successors to do the same. What use are sacrifices in behalf of future generations if they have all become Nazis or otherwise proved unworthy of efforts in their behalf or inaccessible to the goods we have stored up for them materially, morally, or intellectually? If their actions can in this sense affect us, through the fulfillment or desecration of cherished hopes or the confirmation or nullification of fundamental practical presumptions, *they* have a responsibility to us—not merely as our beneficiaries but as co-projectors upon whom we rely and whose collaboration we need.

Culturally future generations shall be in part what we have made them; in part, what they have made themselves. So in part their acts are ours, and we retain a measure of responsibility for them. In part, crucially, the same acts are theirs, as long as they might have lived or chosen otherwise than as they do. Joint agents are jointly accountable; and generally, with human actions, more than one person might have forestalled an outcome. In a firing squad, all who shoot are executioners, and all members of a society are accessories to whatever justice or injustice is accomplished by it. The ethos and institutions in which future generations live are factors that may limit their choices, and in forming these they are co-actors with us. They as well as we are justly punished or rewarded by and through these: they, directly, through their own failings, of imagination or of nerve, or triumphs of mind or spirit; we, indirectly, through the failing or success *in them* of our inchoate dreams.

The responsibility of future generations toward us is not a mortmain, an obligation on their part to do what we would have them do, live as we would have them live—or even to complete our projects, regardless of their content. No human being can impose such obligations on another, violating the condition of autonomy without which there is no morality. Yet the members of future generations, whatever else they may be, are of the stuff our dreams are made of. Their obligations to us stem from a moral imperative on them to continue to fulfill what we have begun insofar as it is worthy of fulfillment, lest nature and our noblest strivings be frustrated. The world would be the less—the projects of literature and culture, civilization at large would be diminished—were it not for the possibility and actuality of future generations' taking up the uncompleted work of the past and making it their own, not merely for its intrinsic value (although never in contravention to what is of real worth) but through a sense of commitment to the work of forebears which filial bonds can prompt and axiological claims can confirm.

We can hope for the fulfillment of our aspirations by the members of distant generations only to the extent that those generations can comprehend and appropriate those hopes. We are punished or rewarded through them, and justly so, insofar as their capacity to comprehend, appropriate, and strive to fulfill our dreams is stunted or enriched, limited or expanded, as a result of our actions or inactions. If our successors are alienated from our hopes by the falseness, limitedness, or inarticulateness of our vision or theirs, then we are punished through them and they with us. If they can grasp what we strove for and fulfill it in ways we might never have imagined, we are rewarded through them and they with us. Such punishment and reward are not without desert, since even the most distant generations are partners, witting or unwitting, in one another's projects.

BIBLICAL PROPHECY AND NATURAL JUSTICE

When a prophet pronounces the doom or blessedness of certain mores or a way of life, his message may be reduced in the minds of hearers and scholarly overhearers to an expression of alienation from the practices or identification with the dreams he censures or praises. His projections of a future or of iridescent alternative futures are reduced to mere conjectures. But we can presume that there is no insight in a prophet's apprehensions, no matter to his morals, only if we know that it is impossible to discern the real dynamic of present tendencies. Prophetic promises and threats, I am suggesting, are not wishes but warnings and invitations. They follow not mere conjecture but a powerful grasp of the thrust of specific mores and a sensitivity to the openings toward (and from) such mores in a particular society. The appropriate questions to ask of prophetic promises and warnings, then, are not about the plausibility of surreal scenarios. For the instrumentalities of prophetic concern are the familiar ones of nature and history—war, famine, poverty, wealth, health, and peace. One should ask of any historic or futuristic vision not about its imagery of judgment, then, but about the adequacy of its comprehension of the natural and moral dynamics it addresses.

In the light of our thinking about natural justice, the biblical oathing ceremonies (Deuteronomy 27:9–28:68; cf. Numbers 5:22) take on a clearer meaning. Rhetorically, they impress upon the multitude the enormity of the covenant and the gravity of any breach of it. But the covenant is not a mere agreement among human beings. It is a system of law and a way of life ordained by God. Thus its warnings acknowledge in grim detail what is understood to be the consequence of evil, as much as to say: Should we choose to violate the laws or reject or neglect fulfillment of their concatenated system, we have, in effect, wished all these consequential disasters upon ourselves.

THE FORMER AND THE LATTER RAIN

Maimonides tells us (*Guide* I 54) that Moses' "seeing God's back" refers to a comprehension of what follows from God, the acts of God, and entails a comprehensive grasp of the laws of nature, in accordance with which the people may be governed. *What* laws of nature are meant, and how did Moses envision their dynamics and make them visible to others who had not shared the intimacy of his revelatory experience? The Torah articulates, to the best of Moses' vision and understanding, the laws relevant to human choosing—the laws, as it is put, of life. The Mosaic message exceeds what is conveyed in the prescriptions of the Torah only to the extent that myth and metaphor, the fleeting but all-orienting poetic and metaphysical glimpse of the Absolute, builds a bridge between God's two utterances, Law and nature. The elements of promise and threat make vivid the significances of our choices. But the nexus between command and promise is the unity of being and value, the mark of God's handiwork in creation, referred to as God's back.

The Mosaic Torah does not speak at length (as Proverbs does) about the teaching of wisdom.[24] For theory in the Torah is rarely speculative. Its central practicality[25] is captured in the Mosaic idiom: "circumcise your hearts" (Deuteronomy 10:16). We must take the impress of wisdom into our choice making (Exodus 13:16, Deuteronomy 6:8, 11:18, 30:13) as if it were a primary mode of feeling. The object is not universal comprehension of great truths but the informing of our actions by those truths. The wisdom sought founds an ethos on practical preference for the collaborative and considerate above the exploitative and mechanical. This is the impulse that quickens all the visionary projections of the Torah's principles in specific social and historic circumstances.

Here, as in the wisdom of Socrates, there is little difference between vice and folly. Consciousness and choice expand the possibilities, and so the deserts, of beings. But they do not ever wholly remove us from the plane of objecthood or prevent us from becoming victims in some regards. For finite subjects are subjects conditioned by their objecthood. It makes only a partial difference whether an agent was unaware of the consequences of his actions, intended them, or did not give them serious thought. Actions bring their consequences in train, and it is through those consequences that natural justice is enacted. Counsel to knowing, choosing agents naturally admonishes them to employ all the wisdom at their command to make their choices congruent with the fulfillment of their being in all its dimensions including the collaborative and the considerate. But the advice bears no guarantee of success. Consciousness renders human claims more extensive, more responsive, more fraught with danger and opportunity—more responsible if they are to hold, at greater risk if they are to give way. If a beaver dam fails, the outcome is like the failure of a human dam, but on a different scale. The failure of a nuclear power plant, a nuclear waste disposal policy, a nuclear arms policy is far weightier. Our claims on our milieu are systematic, and the impact of any failure will be correspondingly systemic.

Let me illustrate biblically. In speaking of corruption the Torah refers repeatedly to pollution. It says that the Israelites will inherit Canaan because abominations have polluted the land. The land is unfit for habitation by the Canaanites as a result of their cruel and obscene idolatrous practices. Yet it remains habitable by Israelites. The telling and lasting impact of the cultural inarticulacy of the Canaanites was not agricultural or even historiographic but moral—not mere overcropping but the persistence of orgiastic cults and life-denying values. The "sins of the fathers" were visited upon their offspring not simply because the sons were innocent victims of their forebears' irresponsibility but because they became participants, morally accountable severally, collectively, and cumulatively for their negligence of the moral criticism that wisdom might have directed against a polluted ethos. Their disinheritance, as the Bible calls it, was a natural consequence.[26]

Twice daily the observant Jew recites the *Shemaʿ*, Deuteronomy 6:4–9, 11:13–21, and Numbers 15:37–41. The first of these three passages is the celebrated affirmation of the unity and uniqueness of the God of Israel, followed by the beautiful and ennobling admonition to love God with all our being, to keep the thought of his commandments constantly before our minds, their mention on our lips, and their practice in our intentions. There follows the all-important commandment to impart them to our children, and then the ordinance of fringed garments, by which we are reminded of all the *mitzvot* through which Israel will be made "a holy nation." Midmost of the three passages, dominating by its length the entire meditative sequence, is the apparent combination of a bribe and a threat, promising good weather, plentiful crops, and economic survival in return for obedience to the law and warning of unfavorable weather, ruin, and genocide in retaliation for disobedience.

The 1917 Jewish Publication Society translation of the passage reads:

And it shall come to pass, if ye shall hearken diligently unto my commandments which I command you this day, to love the Lord your God, and to serve Him with all your heart and with all your soul, that I will give the rain of your land in its season, the former rain and the latter rain, that thou mayest gather in thy corn, and thy wine, and thine oil. And I will give grass in thy fields for thy cattle, and thou shalt eat and be satisfied. Take heed to yourselves, lest your heart be deceived, and ye turn aside, and serve other gods, and worship them; and the anger of the Lord be kindled against you, and He shut up the heaven, so that there shall be no rain, and the ground shall not yield her fruit; and ye perish quickly from off the good land which the Lord giveth you.[27]

The speaker is God, but the words are not set off by the usual preamble, "God spoke unto Moses, saying, speak unto the Israelites. . . ." The admonition occurs, in fact, in the "second discourse of Moses." Yet the intention has seemed clear. "Moses speaks in the name of God," wrote Rabbi Hertz: "Deut. XI, 13–21, contains the promise of reward for the fulfillment of the laws, and of punishment for their transgression." The ancient rabbis agree. In the Talmud, Rabbi Judah, in the name of Rav, cites the passage to show that good weather ("a good year") is a proper object of petitionary prayer.[28] The standard commentaries concur: God is promising a reward of plenty for loyalty and a chastisement of penury, exile, possible destruction, for disloyalty. He will execute His sentence by granting or withholding favorable weather.[29]

Does God bribe and intimidate his faithful[30] while admonishing them to act out of love (Deuteronomy 11:1, 6:5)? This the rabbis deny. Hence the bite of the admonition of Antigonos of Socho: "Be not like servants who serve their master in order to receive a reward but rather like servants who serve their master not for the sake of a reward, and let the awe of Heaven be upon you" (*Avot* 1:3). Antigonos, the first Jewish sage to bear a Greek name, contrasts the unselfish awe of God with the tainted motives of one who slavishly seeks his serf's fare (*pras*) for acts pleasing to God.[31] So the awe of Heaven means that we must choose our actions for their intrinsic worth—value them for their own sakes and not for some repayment or gratuity. What then of the apparent meaning of Deuteronomy 11:13–21? Is it supererogatory to serve God out of love, and will the Law be satisfied with something less than the wholehearted devotion it explicitly demands?

In commenting on Antigonos' words, Hertz reaffirms the tenor of his reading of Deuteronomy: "According to Jewish teaching it is not wrong to hope for God's reward of righteous living."[32] This runs head on against what Antigonos is saying. Hertz apparently saw no harm in regarding religion in the terms he quotes with approval from Wellhausen, as a give-and-take transaction: "Piety is not content to stretch out its hands to the empty air—it must meet an Arm descending from heaven. It needs a reward; not for the reward's sake, but in order to be sure of its own reality; in order to know that there is a communion of God with man and a road by which to reach it." Hertz missed the suggestion of theurgy in Wellhausen's high-flown but ironic vocabulary as to the needs of piety—the idea that piety demands a magic road to God and an effective means of forcing God's will by winning God's pleasure.

Philo, however, articulating what was no doubt a long-standing discomfort with the apparent sense of Deuteronomy, was ready to seek a deeper meaning, with his usual tool of allegory: God is the "perennial fountain of all things good," and the rains here are "the shower of the other virtues . . . delicious and most salubrious, giving immortality as much as or more than nectar."[33] As was his common practice, Philo retained what he took to be the literal meaning of the passage,[34] but grafted to it his naturalistic interpretation, saying of the social virtues: "These are the first blessings which he tells us will fall to the lot of those who follow God and always and everywhere cleave to His commandments and so fasten them to every part of life that no part can go astray into new and unwholesome ways. The second blessing is wealth which necessarily follows peace and settled authority. Now the simple wealth of nature is food and shelter. . . . These, if anyone is willing to eliminate costly and superfluous extravagance, are very easily obtainable."[35]

For Maimonides similarly the implications of a literal reading of this passage—the mutability of God's will, the overtones of divine vindictiveness, and a kind of court traffic in favors—were profoundly disturbing. Thus, he gave the troublesome passage the most radical treatment of any in the canon, arguing from the mentality of the age when the Torah was revealed:

> If you study these ancient beliefs, you will find the accepted view of all people was that worship of the stars is what makes the earth habitable and the land fertile. The scholars and devout and holy men of those days exhorted the people in such terms and taught them that agriculture (upon which human survival depends) can be successful only through worshipping the sun and stars, that if you angered those celestial beings by disobedience, the land would become barren and ruined. . . . Thus they connected their idolatry with agriculture. . . . And the pagan priests, in their homilies

to the people assembled in the temples, drummed it into their heads that it was on account of those rites that rain fell, trees bore fruit, and the land became fertile and capable of sustaining life. . . . They came to promise even more—long life, immunity from illness and injury, and high yields of crops and fruit. . . .

Now since these beliefs were so widely held that they were regarded as certainties and God in His mercy wanted to efface this error from our minds and remove the toil from our bodies of the laborious and useless tasks idolatry had imposed upon us and give us our Law through the instrumentality of Moses, Moses told us, on divine authority, that worship of these stars or idols would cause the rain to be cut off and the earth to be ruined, so that nothing would grow and the fruit would drop from the trees . . . that conditions would be bad, there would be bodily illnesses and shortening of lives; while, if they abandoned such worship and accepted the worship of God, then the rain would fall, the earth would be fertile, conditions would be good, there would be bodily health and long lives—just the opposite of what the pagans preached to the people . . . for the foundation of the Law is the elimination of that view and the obliteration of its effects, as we have explained.[36]

When the Law was revealed to woo humankind away from paganism, including all beliefs that the Divine was partial or in any way to be coerced, the association of worship with sacrifice and of sacrifice with agriculture was too deeply ingrained to be immediately eradicated. Rather, Moses sought to wean the people gradually of their former beliefs—to regulate rather than abolish the sacrificial cult, and to transfer to the Universal God not only the allegiance of the people but their expectation of good weather. For sacrifice, Maimonides explains, was the only notion those people had of worship; and favorable crops were the core of their idea of divine favor.[37]

Thus, by the Rambam's testimony, the passage in which God seems to promise good weather and fine crops in return for obedience represents an economy of Moses, a homily couched in the terms of a pagan age. Does it then have no positive relevance to those demanding individuals who do not believe that the weather is altered by the inclinations of our spiritual allegiance? Doubtless the Rambam was uncomfortable with this conclusion, as was Spinoza, who was left to believe that the sole object of the Law is obedience in a sense close to the one that Wellhausen affirms and Antigonos rejects.[38] But even Maimonides, with his powerful method of seeking a higher significance in biblical passages where the surface meaning is unacceptable, does not seem to find an acceptable alternative to the conclusion he drew.

I think there is an alternative—a Maimonidean one, in fact, in that it is based on the Rambam's method and arises out of the naturalistic reading of providence that he elicits from the Torah. Maimonides at one·point praises "Onkelos" for juggling the syntax of a biblical verse to avoid an unfortunate anthropomorphism. Anthropomorphism, he argues, is a demonstrated falsehood, while the construction of the sentence is open to interpretation. Maimonides betters Onkelos' gloss but admires both his ingenuity and his intention (*Guide* I 28). Here, too, there is a problem of syntax, but far from asking that we twist the natural syntax of the passage I shall simply ask that we read it as written, as a single sentence. In Hebrew and Arabic, when the protasis of a conditional is compound, the beginning of the apodosis is marked by the ending of the string of conjunctions that link the elements of the antecedent clause. Thus I would translate:

> If indeed ye harken to my commandments which I command you this day, to love the Lord your God and serve Him with all your hearts and with all your souls, and I give the rain of your land in due season, the fall rain and the spring rain, and thou gatherest thy grain and thy wine and thine oil, and I give grass in thy field for thy cattle, and thou eatest and art sated, then guard yourselves lest your hearts be gulled and ye turn aside and serve other gods and worship them and the Lord's anger be aroused against you and He shut up the heavens and there be no rain, and the earth not yield up its produce, and ye swiftly perish from the good land which the Lord giveth you.

The conjunctions link the elements within the main clauses, and the absence of a conjunction before *hishamru* ("guard yourselves") signals the beginning of the consequent. The function of *ve-hayah*, traditionally translated 'and it shall come to pass', is to indicate that the entire complex is a single conditional statement, by standing at the beginning as a kind of surrogate verb, leading the reader or hearer to anticipate the consequent, particularly, its main verb, *hishamru*, 'guard yourselves, take care'.

Confirmation of this interpretation is found in a sentence of identical structure expressing a closely related if somewhat simpler thought:

> When the Lord thy God bringeth thee to the land which He promised thy fathers, Abraham, Isaac, and Jacob, to give thee great and goodly cities, which thou didst not build, and houses filled with goods, which thou didst not fill, and cisterns hewn, which thou didst not hew, vineyards and olive

trees, which thou didst not plant, and you eat and are sated, then guard thyself lest thou forget the Lord who brought thee out of the land of Egypt, out of the house of bondage. The Lord shalt thou fear and Him shalt thou serve, by His name shalt thou swear. Ye shall not go after other gods, of the gods of the peoples who surround you, lest the Lord thy God's anger be aroused toward thee and He obliterate thee from the face of the earth. (Deuteronomy 6:10–15)

Once again *ve-hayah* introduces a complex conditional sentence, but *if* is replaced by *when*, since actual entry into the land is contemplated rather than potential good weather followed by bad. Here it is not climatic changeability but the unstriven for benefits of an existing settlement that pose a hidden danger. Yet the message is virtually identical. If we translate 6:12 "then guard thyself . . ." then we should locate the apodosis of the other passage correspondingly at the warning "guard thyself . . ." rather than at "I will give . . .": The *Shemaʿ* passage, too, is a caution against complacency, not a promise of payment or a threat of reprisal.[39]

Historically in the *Shemaʿ* the clauses regarding rain have been placed in the consequent rather than the antecedent, at the expense of the parallel with the earlier passage. This has introduced an unnecessary element of browbeating into Mosaic theology—an aspect made central in some Christian conceptions of Judaism, which follow Paul in contrasting the fleshly sanctions of the "Old Covenant" with the spiritual rewards of the New. Such readings extend from the pages of Christian polemic to most modern biblical commentaries.[40] But in the reading proffered here, on the level of *peshat*, we are no longer being told by Moses that favorable weather follows from divine pleasure at our obedience to the Law. Rather we are admonished that if conditions are good we should guard against complacency and any resultant spiritual or moral laxity.

Why then the talk of divine displeasure in the complex consequent of this intricate clause? Why the mention of God's wrath—the kindling of his nose, if the literalists are given their head? Here again the observation of the Rambam that divine anger is mentioned only in the context of idolatry is borne out. Talk of divine disfavor in the Torah marks conceptual, and, we add, moral distance from God. God's displeasure, then, means not the unfavorable weather but its combination with disloyalty to God and his law. For the aim of the Torah, repeatedly stated in the context of these admonitions (see Deuteronomy 11:21), is to secure the tenure of the Israelites in their land, through their adherence to the Law and allegiance to the God who is its source. When rain falls in due season and crops are good, such adherence may seem unnecessary. We may slacken our commitment to the conditions of justice and mutual aid which are the nerve of the system projected by the Law. When unfavorable conditions recur, we will then be an easy prey to adversity.

Thus there are reward and retribution in the passage—but not as an extrinsic result of divine pleasure and displeasure. Rather the outcome is organic to our choices:

> For the land to which thou goest, to inherit it, is not like the land of Egypt which ye left—which thou sowest with thy seed and waterest with thy foot like a green garden. The land to which you are passing over, to inherit it, is a land of mountains and valleys that drinketh up its water from the rain of the heavens, a land which the Lord thy God careth for continually. The eyes of the Lord thy God are upon it from the outset of the year until the year's end. (Deuteronomy 11:10–12)

The land of Israel cannot be held simply by a central government's establishing taxation, administration, and irrigation, and so enabling a landowner to open the sluices to his soil, as a garden cultivator in Egypt might kick down the earth ridge between his plot and the common rivulet. This land demands not a bureaucratic hierarchy but a close-knit social fabric built on economic and social justice, integration of all classes, provision against penury and dispossession. Without our strict adherence to the Law, nature will not need to wait for war to uproot us.

Our text does not say that Palestine is lush or needs no cultivation or that Egypt is sere or difficult but only that agriculture in Palestine differs from that of Egypt. The object is not to praise the new land but, as the sequel shows, to warn the Israelites of the marginality of their survival in it: God's favor to the land of Israel extends through the seasons. A favorable flood assured Egypt's crops for an entire year, but the crops of Palestine would not ripen without both the fall and the spring rains. The rainfall is drunk up daily by the soil; little can be channeled or reserved. So the inhabitants must rely on mutual aid and justice.

Is there not still a morally "impure" element in the assumption that one should choose allegiance to God and justice while bearing in mind the potential ruin predicted as a consequence of the failure to do so? The answer, I suspect, is contained in the linkage of obedience to the Law with allegiance to God. If only human laws and conventional institutions were presented, our adherence to them might be dependent on narrowly prudential considerations. But when we are commanded in the same breath to love God with all our being and to keep all his commandments, that seems to place them on a higher plane. To keep the laws because they will benefit us might render our adherence contingent. But to keep them as an expression of our love and fear of God (as Antigonos and the Torah propose) renders our adherence unconditional. Thus, "Justice, justice shalt thou pursue"—justice for the sake of the good it brings and is, and justice again when the paths of justice and expediency *seem* to diverge: justice as fulfillment of the will of God. Not that the positivity of the commandment replaces its rationality. On the contrary, what Moses urges is that only adherence of the sort that expresses our love of God will provide us with the security the Law promises, freeing us in some measure from the vicissitudes of nature by giving us a social system whose stability can withstand and whose values can surmount those vicissitudes. Moses expresses this thought without abstract vocabulary, and with a concision that eclipses what we find necessary in its exposition. Maimonides regarded this combination of supreme concision and the power to conquer the limitations of language as clear evidence of divine inspiration.

NATURAL JUSTICE AND REASON

The Torah does not generally list a reward or punishment next to each commandment. In a law of reason, unlike a purely positive law, the content and consequence, not the sanction, provide the grounds for action, as Plato showed. And the ultimate grounding of the biblical laws is in the unity of goodness and being, which rests finally in the unity of God. Yet certain *mitzvot* are textually associated with reward. The commandment to honor one's father and mother or to spare the mother bird when gathering eggs are linked with long life and well-being (Exodus 20:12, Deuteronomy 5:16, 22:6–7). Elisha ben Abuya, called Aher in the Talmud, is said to have turned apostate after building an Epicurean dilemma out of a boy's fatal fall from a tree he had climbed to get eggs for his father, although he had dismissed the mother bird (Ḥullin 142a). Schooled in Greek philosophy, Elisha read the biblical rewards as inducements to the individual. In the context of the age when they were first spoken, it is clear that the *mitzvot* of honoring parents and sparing mother birds are not magical acts that somehow force God to guarantee longevity or welfare but paradigms of an ethos that will enhance communal survival and well-being. The reward is very compact with desert. Life expectancies will be higher in communities that respect parents and all "rise up before a hoary head." But such mores are of little relevance to the issue of who might slip and fall from a tree.

A grandson of Elisha's felt constrained by the argument to affirm an afterlife as recompense for the unrequited sufferings of innocents. Some of the Sages (*Kiddushin* 39b) voice their approval: If Aḥer had interpreted the reference to well-being in Deuteronomy as an allusion to the hereafter, "in the manner of R. Jacob, his daughter's son, he would not have sinned." Saadiah followed similar reasoning.[41] But the central object of the Torah is not longevity or even "salvation" for the individual but a way of life for the community. Reading the text with an alien bias is a sure route to confusion. It was toward the elimination of such confusion that Gersonides wrote to deny interventionistic providence, quoting *Moed Katan* (28a) in his *Wars of the Lord*: "Length of life, children, and prosperity depend not on merit but on fortune"; God's providence is manifested through the laws of nature and the intelligence of the upright.[42] The latter, as Maimonides argued, is the special providence that protects them—but it works through nature, not in violation of nature's laws. The well-being afforded by the insight of the upright does not somehow make them proof against the forces by which God governs nature at large.

Gersonides can be a naturalist as to providence because God is a naturalist. The philosopher does not regard the laws of nature as foreign to the divine plan because he eschews the egocentricity of the man who complained, "God helps total strangers, why doesn't he help me?" And because Gersonides does not treat the laws of nature as alien to God's wisdom, he does not regard the misfortunes incident upon the operation of those laws as unjust. Maimonides argues to the same effect when he points out (following Saadiah and the rabbis) that the Bible calls Job a righteous man but nowhere states that he was a wise man at the outset of his misfortunes. Had he been wise, the Rambam argues, the source of his misfortunes —not in a divine judgment against him but in the operation of natural causes—would not have been obscure to him, nor would it have been obscure to him that health, progeny, comfort, and prosperity, valuable as they are, are not the ultimate measures of value.[43] To imagine the operations of disease, climate, and natural incident as expressive of divine displeasure is to commit a pathetic fallacy in the truest sense—to make the forces of nature vectors of projected human passions of fear, guilt, jealousy, or zeal. To expect of such forces that they take the same consideration we would expect from ourselves, of merit and desert, rather than following their natural courses, is to rob them of *their* desert as natural forces—hence, as Saadiah teaches us, Job's final revelatory awakening in the message of the voice from the storm wind and its articulation of the entire cosmic panoply. These too are God s work, and their play is as essential in God's plan as is man's pleasure.

But this, of course, does not imply that all that is done in nature is done with moral right, that every victory in nature bears with it moral triumph. The forces of nature operate without moral intent and are therefore morally neutral, not responsible. And all are limited in sway—limited by one another. This limitation is the basis of the natural order and natural justice. Its operation founds the very possibility of there being a moral law for man. Yet even on the most elemental level real power is not to be confused with momentary dominance. Usurpation may appear to be a victory sanctioned by nature, but as the psalmist observed, following the paradigm of Pharaoh and his defeat by his own intransigence, usurpation tends to destroy itself.

GOD'S ACT IN NATURE

Theists face a dilemma about God. If God is a perfect being, as monotheism requires, God would seem to be an ideal. But if God is real and all real beings are finite, the logic of God is violated: God is not a perfect being. We break the dilemma by recognizing that reality itself is a value. We equate being with perfection and argue that what is most perfect is most real. This, I have urged,[44] is the sound core of the ontological argument—not the endeavor to prove God's existence to one who holds it problematic (as a result of adopting pagan notions of the divine, wittingly or unwittingly, picturing God in creaturely terms)—and still less an appeal to tautology as a source of existential import. The argument, rather, is an explication of the logic of perfection, which is grasped through acceptance of the goodness of being (the basis of all religious responsiveness) and the resultant recognition that absolute reality and the fullest perfection coincide. This is the thrust for theism of Plato's recognition that being and goodness, beauty and unity are one. Never what is venal or ignoble but only what is perfect in all ways is worthy of celebration as divine. The same thought, the recognition that the ideal is no mere notional goodness but absolute reality and power, governing history and creation, grounds the Mosaic recognition that God is the fullness of being, Self-existentiating in the fullest sense: I AM THAT I AM.

Being is good, and the goodness of creation is a declension of the absolute goodness which is God's being. We clarify the logic of God not only by recognizing that God is good but by the corresponding recognition that goodness is God. We clarify the concept of goodness not only by recognizing that evil is privation but also by seeing that goodness is real, and that ultimate goodness is the ultimate reality. Through these under-standings not only can we reckon with evil in the world as the price in privations of the authentic existence of finite beings, but we can vault cos-mologically from the recognition of the goodness of being to acknowledg-ment of the absolute Source which it portends—the necessary Reality behind finite beings' contingency, the eternal One behind complexity and temporality, the Perfection behind perfections.

The false dilemma that demands we choose between a vacuous affirmation and a reductive denial, between a notional ideal and a sensuous or empiric god, phenomenon of our senses or projection of our passions or "needs," returns as a demand for resolution of some questions specifically about justice. If the requital of all actions is implicit in their logic and dynamic, as we have argued, how does a world governed justly by God differ from a world not so governed, or from any world at all? If requital arises in the very nature of a being and is manifested in its acts and the working out of their outcomes, wouldn't the justice we profess to find in nature hold in any possible world? Wouldn't its assertion then be trivial, no more than the claim of logic that a thing must be what it is, an act the act it is and none other? If so, it can be argued (just as it was argued that an all-perfect God is a mere ideal) that the operation of justice is not a matter of fact at all but an analytic matter, that the justice we affirm when we uphold intrinsic punishments and rewards is no more than notional, a pallid afterimage of the idea of justice, now limited to some mere corollary of the tautology that asserts a thing to be itself. If God's justice in nature becomes a mere necessity of nature, it can be argued, God's governance becomes imperceptible, not a sign that differentiates a divinely ruled from a neglected or abandoned or merely random world. Creation becomes the mere being of a thing; and providence, its being what it is. The only alter-native, it can be argued, is for God to intervene, forcefully, dramatically and perceptibly in nature. But this we do not observe. For the age of miracles is past.

To this I answer that the endeavor to find empiric highlights of God in nature (as though God were not present also in the lowlights), to discover sensory evidence of God's presence, in effect, or else deny God's presence or action, is simply a recurrence of the pagan telescoping of cause with effect, seeking to explain God by reference to the things God is relied upon to explain and thus making God an (extraordinary) phenomenon rather than the Ground of all being. Miracles would not be God's if they were disruptions of his order. Rather we see the steadiness of God's hand in the constancy of his act, signaling divine authorship with a clarity that no empiric trial or disruption could provide. But constancy is not the same as logical inevitability, and inevitability is not tautology. It is a false dichotomy (generative of a false dilemma) to assume that all necessities stem from logic and that all facts are contingent.

The beginning of an answer to the challenge we confront here, and the beginning of wisdom on the topic of justice, I suspect, is the recognition that the affirmation of a thing's being what it is need not be a mere tautology. God's being, I AM THAT I AM, is His Self-existentiation, a supremely active, never merely static fact. The being of all finite things is their existentiation by God, in which they themselves, by their God-given powers, actively participate. So the givenness of God's being is a consequence of his free act of self-determination. And the givenness of a finite thing is no logically necessary truth: It can be denied without self-contradiction. Such a being as this need not have been. Its givenness is contingent on the creative act of God, traditionally understood as an act of grace;[45] and it is the burden of the natural sciences taken as a whole that the being of each finite thing is contingent upon a universe of causes. Perhaps again these two contingencies express the same idea from differing perspectives. But it is clear that only abstractly is a thing's being what it is an analytic truth. Dynamically, concretely, being is active; and finite beings act in time. For a thing to be what it is is an act expressive of identity, not a mere fact of self-equivalence.

There are matters of fact that involve necessity because they involve the necessities of beings' natures and not the mere formal necessities of abstraction; and there are relations of ideas that imply existence, because such inferences are warranted by the existential givens: as cause by effect, and self-sufficient by contingent. These do not follow from abstract principles of logic, as though dependent from a skyhook, but are the material givens and paradigmatic foci of reflection from which logic itself is derived. Given that a thing exists, its nature and deserts must conform to its mode of being. Given its mode of being, its mode of action and the consequences that its acts engender in their milieu will emerge as well through a dialectic of self-definition in the context of an environment. But neither the being of a thing nor the nature of its actions in a causal milieu are necessities of logic.

There is room, then, for justice (or injustice) on two levels, neither of which is that of analyticity: the metaphysical and the natural. Metaphysical justice is the exact proportioning of being to deserts in which each thing possesses the very nature that allows it to be and act as it does. This we call favor and grace. For, abstracting from the actual givenness of a being, there is no prior entitlement to a specific nature. But the slug and the water beetle, the grub, dragonfly, lion, raven, and asp have the natures they have and the powers to pursue the characters they are given in the perfect economy of providence—that is, their powers proportioned to their métier and locus in the larger scheme, enjoying an existence exactly fitted to their capacity and flourishing in the precise measure and mode that their specific and particular natures allow.

Metaphysical justice acts with the exactitude of logic not because such justice is a matter of synonymy, but because the equilibration of characters to existential givens expresses the logic of being. Nature is the spilling over of that logic into fact. For creation is not an event that ended with the origin of the cosmos. The working out of creation—the existentiation that beings share in—is temporal. It is here that natural justice arises. For actions do have consequences.

It is not true that in all possible worlds beings would have specific natures; nor is it true that in all possible worlds *these* beings would have *these* natures. For *these* beings would not exist in all possible worlds, and in some possible worlds the characters of beings might be at odds with their initial endowment so as to frustrate any conatus at or near the outset. It is not true that in all possible worlds actions would have consequences; nor is it true that in all causal worlds the consequences of actions would be such as to visit the good or ill, wisdom or unwisdom of an act upon the agent. For beings might be insulated so as to be capable of inflicting evils they did not reap, or they might suffer only capriciously or accidentally. Our world, however, renders the actions of all beings (not merely those of moral subjects) constructive or destructive of their natures. This, I have argued, is the sense to be given to the ideas of intrinsic reward and punishment—a system in which we can see God's justice at work.

We do not hold that God exists and acts, governs and judges despite all the evidence—clinging to the claim out of sheer doggedness or brute faith, without experience to give definition or confirmation to give direction to our trust; and we do not hold that God is just in the trivial sense that for God all is right by definition. Our faith is founded in evidence—in our experience and appraisal of the world. What we see when we see God's justice at work is not an empiric datum like a red or blue dot; but it is a factual state of affairs, to which evidence is relevant. And although it operates with a kind of necessity, expressive of the higher, metaphysical necessity of things' being what they are (a necessity readily confused with that of logic, through the *positing* of things' natures as givens), it is not a necessity of logic. For it is not logic that requires a thing to have a given nature; nor is it a necessity of logic that actions have the consequences they do.

My purpose here has not been to try to prove categorically that nature operates justly. Evidence for that thesis (or any alternative to it) would be drawn from a comprehensive and open-ended examination of nature and history, using the analytic eye of a scientist or novelist and the moral and aesthetic insight of a prophet or a poet. The more modest goal of sketching a model of the workings of divine justice in nature and suggesting the types of evidence that would support that model has been all I have attempted here. I do not think that evidence is lacking for our model. Nor do I think that just any conceivable state of affairs is compatible with what might be called the prophetic construction of history and nature. Thus the construction is not irrefutable and vacuous. But neither does it rely for its conception of the work of God upon the idea of arbitrary irruptions into nature. Rather it sees nature as God's work and regards God as working through nature constantly, not sporadically. It counsels neither quietism nor triumphalism but a serious commitment to moral effort based on recognition of all beings' deserts, including one's own.

♦ ♦ ♦ ♦ ♦

CHAPTER FIVE

The Messianic Age

It is easy to misrepresent Jewish messianism. Modern apologists, like commercial chefs, often mask the most distinctive and piquant spices of an original with more familiar or less subtle savors. The messianic age of peace and justice, when poverty, bigotry, famine, war, servitude, and exploitation will be abolished, becomes a generic millennium, more significant for what it aspires to than for how it is achieved—a recasting of ancient arcadian projections and a prototype of modern reformist impulses.[1] But the thought of better times is as natural and universal as that of good or bad times and may carry as many colorations of object and method as there are human ends and means. We do not determine an idea simply by noting its genus or its analogue. And to ignore the question of means is crucially wrong. It does matter, when we talk of goals, both where we think we are heading and how we propose to get there—what sorts of eggs will be broken, and whether breaking eggs can advance us toward our goal at all or will only negate it. For an ideal can be desecrated even before it is approached.

VARIATIONS ON A THEME

The temptation to transmute old ideals into some form of activist or armchair radicalism is well known to modern purveyors of religious and political nostrums and is a chief item in their motivational repertoire. Hopes long transmitted through symbols which are universal in their appeal and particular in their associations are enlisted in behalf of ideologies whose aims are radically at variance with the values whose names and icons they appropriate. Equality, justice, peace, and plenty are among the ideals. The dream of the perfect city, pure land, perfect man, are among the symbols. Surrogate religions like Marxism and Naziism, quasi-religions like EST, and militant religions like Unification Church, which exploits human sociability as a means of mind control, have seized fragments of a larger vision whose humane themes they violate even as they profess to pursue them.

Complementary to the secular reductions that claim universality (and, in the Soviet case, call Jewish hopes parochial abroad while condemning them as cosmopolitan at home) are the ethnic secularizations of those who imagine that they can save a people and its survivable intellectual and cultural modes by cultivating a nostalgia for its tastes—as though ethnicity itself somehow imparted substance to mere styles, food value to flavor principles. But ethnicity for its own sake is as sterile culturally as it is circular intellectually. Just as purely political abstractions omit crucial working elements of the Mosaic ideal, so the ethnic abstractions that mistake particularity for concreteness mislay the universal values and mission which give our polity its claim upon surviving the fortunes and misfortunes of history.

We secularize and vitiate biblical themes when we substitute formal relations of citizenship for the material identity of peoplehood—society for community—or try to substitute negative liberties for positive opportunities. But material particularity, like formal polity, is an abstraction, incapable of grounding norms, let alone guiding them, and incompetent (ironically) even to found a culture. For there is no ethnos without an ethos. Kinship itself is an ideal (although relatively free of material content); and ethnicity, perhaps for that reason, finds it easier to give pretexts to die or kill than grounds to live. That, I think, explains the evanescence of all mere nations, the endurance of cultures, and of nations through their cultures—and the peculiar claim of Israel upon history and of history upon Israel. For the secret of Israel's survival and rebirth must lie within the fact of Israel's mission: Israel exists not merely to exist but to convey and ultimately to realize an idea in this world.

MESSIANISM AND BELIEF

Many thinkers, when they do not ignore the messianic idea, confound it with visions of apocalypse, ancient symbols of its advent. They focus on the extreme, colorful, and vivid. Yet brilliant symbols can become opaque to the meanings they were devised to convey, not by dullness, but by their scintillation, catching imagination's eye and dazzling it.[2] This is as true for skeptics as for the credulous. Skeptics buttress their doubts by heightening the remoteness of the object. The would-be literalist adopts a stance foreign to the many-nuanced play of Israelite prophetic poetry from its outset. For what is idolatry but literalism, and what is the golden calf but an attempt to give a physical sense to the enigmatic words of Moses and doings of his God? Would-be purists set themselves Herculean feats of faith, as though supposing that to believe the possible is easy and greater merit belongs to believing the impossible and absurd. But the familiar notion of faith—merging Plato's *pistis* (which was something less than knowledge) with Stoic willful or heroic affirmation and Cicero's *fides*, loyalty to the civil tradition and its cult—is foreign to the Torah, where the root *a-m-n* refers consistently to trust and trustworthiness and, in the first intension, is not a cognitive term at all.[3] The Tertullian turn on Stoic fidelity becomes a dominant motif in Christian eschatology, where belief in "things unseen" becomes *the* avenue to salvation. But this idea of justification through faith, refined by Augustine, Pascal, and James, undercuts the central concept of Jewish messianism: that historic vindication, salvation in its original sense, the triumph on earth of our yearnings for a day of peace and contentment, must be deserved and can be earned.

In the prophets, belief is a matter of trust—not that there was no sense of an epistemic problem about God,[4] but such problems were resolved by the facts of history, morals, and creation, without resort to the strange mythology of self-warranting beliefs. We trust God, not to overcome a yawning gap between our eyes and what we yearn for but rather to maintain the commitment made in the act of creation and continually confirmed in the constancy of the natural and moral laws. Thus we speak of God as keeping faith even with those who sleep in the dust: God's faith in his covenant. Its fulfillment in nature is the evidence of its validity. The progressive advance of human understanding and compassion is the dimension of its growth. Its ultimate triumph in history is the assurance that even those who lie in the dust bore their segments in a continuity whose meaning and purpose are complete only by reference to its entirety, with no link excluded.

Some seekers of authenticity imagine that the heart of a tradition must lie in its most expressionistic elements. But ancient, even tribal thought need not be primitive, and primitive thought need not be naive[5]—or lurid. Fideists may imagine that they vindicate their spiritual prowess by harboring the figures of mythic imagery in reserved quarters of their imagination. But that displaces the critical thinking which biblical and rabbinic imagery are devised to foster and blocks the avenues of constructive work which messianic images in particular are designed to inspire. Scholars in search of colorful or dramatic pictures to enliven their quiet hours glide readily across the line between the binding force of *halakhah* and the imaginative appeal of *aggadah*, tempted to join the literal minded in representing every piece of symbolism—even where imagery grows drunk on its own excesses—as proclaiming a normative tradition. Descriptive work then displaces analysis. The sterile battles of scholarship between chauvinistic pride and reductionistic hunts for filiations displace the active life which all images of an ideal future seek to inform and guide.

To the skeptically inclined, overcolored and overdrawn images make possible the caricaturing of what is dismissed and relieve those who slight tradition of responsibility for grappling with its intension. How can such ideas as the Leviathan or the four horsemen be taken seriously? The Leviathan, as presented biblically, is probably a natural creature—possibly a crocodile, to judge from the description of its habits and habitat. Behemoth appears to be a hippopotamus. Both are symbols of God's power over nature. For by reference to that power they are mere playthings.[6] The four horsemen, beasts, and kingdoms symbolize the violence of historic judgment. Rabbinically they acquire concrete and topical identities in each changing circumstance,[7] confirming Maimonides' observation that the rabbis freely participate in the prophetic mythopoiesis without taking its images literally. Without poetry the message would go unheard. Yet poetry is unintelligible to those who force imagination out of their souls in fear of departure from the familiar.

Hume understood how things stand between the credulous and the incredulous when he made Demea, the dogmatist, and Philo, the skeptic, unstable allies in his *Dialogues Concerning Natural Religion*. The rationalist task of Cleanthes is much harder than that of either. His mode of exegesis is not that of the positivist; he resorts neither to the legalistic or fideistic positivism of the traditionalist nor to the reductionistic positivism of the skeptic. Rather he must sift and select, adapt and interpret, explain and inquire. His commitment to tradition must emerge in a measured confidence in its propounders, in their veracity and good faith. Not blind acceptance of authority, but that community of values necessary to any joint enterprise is called for: confidence in the generations of bricoleurs, their soundness of intention and grasp of the themes they receive and deepen. To appropriate the achievements of creative figures we must discern the commensurability of their world with our own. A predilection for the bizarre per se canonizes a bias in behalf of incommensurability. That leaves us to sever our connection with the past or assign there a different rule to nature and a different role to reason from the ones we know, persuading ourselves to enter, or abandon, a Yeatsian or Jungian fairyland, where fictiveness is the standard of reality and the world becomes a projection of each imagination, idiom, or fancy. The premise is inconsistent with any serious idea of truth.

A MIDDLE GROUND

On the one hand we have the reductive messianism of the apologist who equates the Jewish project with a love of social justice; on the other, the supernaturalism of apocalyptic literalism, which rivets the imagination of the dogmatist and the skeptic alike. Do these polarities leave no third term beyond allegorizing away the messianic idea and merely adopting or discarding the crudest plaster casts of its iconography? Surely theology is not simply a matter of degree—more or less, left or right, manic or constrained. The question of how radically or violently the pitch of transhistoric judgment should be colored is only one issue—and, at that, more of the pathology of imagination than of the substance of theology. The question of content is far more critical. What I wish to broach in this chapter is a Jewish concept of the messianic age that is neither reducible to a political wish list nor identical with the expectation of a suspension of the laws of nature. The messianic ideal for which I shall argue is at once richer and more practical than its familiar alternatives—more accessible politically and intellectually, yet more worthy of pursuit. It is founded on a distinctive conception of the structure and potentialities of history.

Social justice in Judaism is represented by the Torah. The Talmud expands the logic of the Mosaic system through processes of elaboration already underway within the Torah itself: designation of concrete practices that unfold the ethical thematics of the Law, transforming its ideals into behavioral institutions in much the way that theories are given operational meaning through the elaboration of hypotheses. Corresponding to the elaboration of ordinances, there is a symbolic elaboration that assigns significance to specific acts (rituals) beyond their immediate practical significance.[8] The Torah insists that its law is not transcendent in its demands: "For this commandment, which I command thee this day is not wondrous beyond thy reach, nor is it remote. It is not in heaven that one might say, 'Who shall go up for us to heaven to get it for us, that we may hear it and do it?'; nor is it beyond the sea, that one might say, 'Who shall cross the sea for us and get it that we may hear and do it? Rather the thing is near to thee indeed, in thy mouth, and in thy heart, that thou mightest do it" (Deuteronomy 30:11–14). The Torah does not require superhuman effort for comprehension or effectuation. Access to its norms is not achieved through a privileged class of initiates or caste of interpreters. It is read regularly in public (Exodus 24:7; Deuteronomy 31:9–13) and publicly inscribed (Deuteronomy 27:2–8; *cf.* 17:18, Exodus 34:1, 27), open to all, morally and intellectually. Human justice, then, as conceived in our biblical constitution, does not require excessive searching, let alone re-opening of the gates of heaven, to make its themes intelligible and its obligations appropriable. It does require development of those themes. For the very nature of universal principles prevents their forming a closed and static system. But the ideas that orient our practice of justice, the ideas of holiness and love (Leviticus 19:1–4, 18) are as accessible to us as our own intentions and daily speech. The life of the Torah is a matter of habit and institution; its obligations and the values they serve, a constant image before the mind's eye and signal on the hand and garments, checking hasty action (Deuteronomy 6:8). Accordingly, social justice is not a remote ideal but a present demand, not to be striven for but to be lived up to. The Torah does not presuppose but aims toward the transformation of human nature and institutions, their gradual perfection and ultimate reform—perfecting the soul.[9] The goal does lie beyond all past achievements of humanity. But the means toward it, the laws themselves, rest on the givens of the human condition.

The justice of the messianic age *does* presuppose a transformed human nature and, concomitantly, a transformed social, economic, political nature —outcomes of the fulfillment of the Law. We saw an illustration of this transformation in the story of Katzya and Alexander. The means to it are not left unspecified. They involve exercise of our moral and intellectual capabilities. If human beings can be hardened to the point of making war for slight affronts and petty or illusory gains, we are capable as well of earning a gentler nature and a wiser habit of action. The same capability through which we learn resort to law in place of violence and civility in place of law can teach us to ground our relations in fellowship and respect. Our ideal of universal peace and justice is founded on this possibility and aims at its realization. It is a more concrete prototype of the Kantian universal kingdom of ends—every human subject accorded the dignity due a subject, treated in accordance with his deserts.

The laws of the Torah, as Maimonides showed systematically,[10] are designed not to enforce such recognition but to instill it, to make it part of our ethos. This goal provides the principle of their elaboration and proper dimension of their growth. But clearly we are in a new state when we can act in the assurance that these values have been instilled universally, or nearly so. The messianic age as we envision it, then, is in and of this world, yet it sees the world transformed. The goal is miraculous only in the sense that evolution, learning, and consciousness are miraculous. The Torah is not utopian, because implementation of its standards does not await the messianic age. Rather the messianic age awaits the implementation of the Torah. The Torah's proximate goal is the life well lived, which secular notions of social justice also strive to capture and express. Its higher goal is the messianic age. But that is not its highest goal. Even in initiating the project of reforming human nature, perfecting its potentials and establishing its dignity, the Torah proposes and initiates a larger project, that of universal human perfection. Building on common and accessible human capabilities and readily apprehensible standards, it seeks a goal that far transcends the elements of ordinary experience. For the Torah is not simply a code of law seeking to modulate human action. Its status as a divine law, as Maimonides argues (*Guide* I 46), can be recognized in its higher aims: to transform human nature not only morally but spiritually and intellectually.

It is from the Transcendent that the Torah draws its thrust, and toward the Transcendent that it points. The Torah is not otherworldly, but another world is presupposed in its norms: They are not natural laws serving only natural aims. The worldliness of the Torah lies in its quest to sanctify humanity, not in any willingness to celebrate the ordinariness of the ordinary, the OK-ness of the OK. Thus the Torah is worldly but not secular. Its myths are not fables. Its goal is the opposite of the profane: sanctification, transcendence. The highest level of human transcendence, overcoming the familiar categories of experience, is what mystics speak of, perhaps too familiarly, as *ekstasis*. It is often said to involve escape from time. In my final chapter I shall attempt to say something about this and its relation to life as we live it. But, as Plato urged, to speak of such things circumstantially goes beyond the power of expression. The usual effect is only to diminish the transcendental reference.[11] Yet the Torah clearly projects such a state. It is spoken of by the Sages as *Olam ha-ba*, the world to come.[12]

The Torah speaks the natural language of natural human beings. It shuns abstract notions, particularly higher-order abstractions. But it draws its precepts from the realm of the purely Transcendent, unknown and unknowable in its purity through the categories of finite existence;[13] and it makes demands whose absoluteness is deducible from none of the givens of experience. The same is true in many moral schemes. One cannot deduce the *moral* prohibition against torturing children from any value defined in empiric terms—survival of the race, improved school performance, milk output, petroleum production, or the like. For conditions can always be imagined in which the exigencies so defined would seem to urge violation of the moral demand. But a moral demand is inviolable. There are no exigencies or utilities that justify toleration of torturing children, punishing the innocent, or committing genocide. It is natural to represent the values spoken for by such demands as transcending life and death. And that, in part, is why traditional mythologies associate morality with a hereafter. The transcendent realm provides the counterpart to mundane exigency against which the values of our daily world can be judged and weighed, discarded, or rediscovered.

In seeking graphically to represent the infinitude of God and inviolability of the principles of his law, the rabbis circumvent the difficulty posed by the utter strangeness of the wholly Transcendent by abstracting selectively from finitude. This is the classic method of the *midrash*, emphasizing now one aspect of transcendence, now another, by negating one category or another of finitude while holding the rest constant. As Maimonides explains, it is because the rabbis were confident of the inapplicability of any anthropomorphic projections to God that they could participate so freely and uninhibitedly in the anthropomorphisms of Scripture, elaborating them into a tissue of courtly conceits: "The Sages, of blessed memory, made a general pronouncement rejecting all that is suggested to the imagination by any of the corporeal characteristics mentioned by the Prophets. This statement of theirs shows that this usage never became an object of delusion or confusion for them. That is why throughout the Talmud and the Midrashic literature you will find them still speaking in the literal usage of the Prophets. They knew that this was in no danger whatever of being misunderstood."[14] Thus the rabbis speak of the transcendent realm as pertaining to the future, by way of denying the perfect transcendence or transcendent perfection of present actuality—not by way of denying present actuality to the Transcendent. In fact the Transcendent is actual and present, near and within all beings. We recognize this when we consider the

The Messianic Age

♦

miraculousness of finite existence, the sanctity of human dignity, or the holiness of life and of all being. Isaiah, the most metaphysical of our post-Mosaic prophets, hears this message in the acclamation of the angels: God's supreme transcendence (*kedushah*) is the correlate of the fact that the whole earth is filled with His glory.[15]

The highest goal of the Torah is the fulfillment of our sacred potentialities as spiritual beings. There is a higher project for us than the mere living out of the human given. Where messianism proposes the moral transformation of human nature and history, the idea of *Olam ha-ba* urges the consummation of that perfection in our transfiguration—the perfection of human intelligence to elicit the sacred potential and potential sanctity in all things, reuniting the intellect, and nature through the intellect, with its Source and Author in the Infinite. Social justice, then, is the proximate object of the Torah. *Olam ha-ba* is its highest goal, overcoming the alienation of being in the Unity of God. But intermediate between these two is the messianic age—in which human nature is not transfigured, but morally humankind is transformed.

MESSIANISM AND REALISM

Rabbi Hillel b. Gamaliel in the fourth century argued that Israel can expect no messiah: We had our anointed king in the days of Hezekiah, who ruled in justice and instituted reforms pursuant to the commandments of the Torah. But R. Joseph took issue with Hillel (Sanhedrin 99a). For the moral and political transformations to be expected in a regime of truth and justice were not completed by Hezekiah or by any later regime. This has been the traditional Jewish argument against all who claim that the messiah has already appeared.[16] Even the great Akiba was chastened: "Grass will grow on your cheeks, Akiba, and still the anointed son of David will not come" (Ta'anit 68d). The very idea of a messiah arises as a demand for ethical transformation in this world. To assert that the messiah has come before we witness that transformation is to give up the historic struggle.

Messiahship is a political concept, arising from the idea of political legitimacy and linking it to the social ideals of the Torah. As Cohen writes, "All the prophets, before and after the exile, always understand by the 'end of days,' even if some of them thought it close at hand, only the political future of their own people and of mankind."[17] The amorah Samuel sums up categorically: "There is no difference between this world and the days of the messiah but the subjection of Israel to alien dominion" (Sanhedrin 91b). Individual authorities vary in their images of the political transformation, its prerequisites and consequences, but the veracity of Samuel's reading is borne out in Ezekiel's vision of the dry bones. For the bones are not symbols of resurrection; rather resurrection is made the symbol of national rebirth: "O man, these bones are the whole house of Israel. They say, 'Our bones are dried up, our hope is lost'" (Ezekiel 37; cf. Isaiah 26:16–19). Dead and buried as she may have seemed, Israel is promised renewed life on her soil.

The messianic age is no mysterious phenomenon. Its transformation of human affairs is palpable, without an evangel to announce or exegesis to explain it. The impetus to change is given in the Torah. But the act of ruling by the principles of the Torah or fighting for those principles does not constitute a messianic epoch. Such action or the suffering it entrains may lay a foundation or add definition to our hopes.[18] But love is not complete until consummated, and the messiah has not come until the goal of human history is reached. Thus the messianic age is not just another historic epoch nor yet a sheer apocalyptic act. It is a redemptive phase of history, thought of as a justification of history, and thus represented midrashically (*Pesikta Rabati* 152b) as an a priori condition of the world's existence. Translated into prose, the image of the creation of the messiah with the world means that the world, as an act of God, must bear within it the seeds of the perfection of human relations in accordance with the standards of God's justice. Just as human strivings inform our vision of the messianic future, so the conception of that future gives orientation to those strivings and imparts a meaning to them even when they fail of their proximate goals. If messianism is the regulative idea that orients us toward the transformation of human nature, then messianism is latent in the Torah as tragedy is latent in Homer.[19]

DEMYTHOLOGIZING THE MESSIAH

The epic is not tragedy; but epic celebration of the heroic leads to tragedy as surely as the poetic elaboration of heroic virtues leads to dramatization of their clash. Biblically there is no epic. There are champions, of course, *gibborim*, and again *shoftim*, but no focus on the man, the woman—no hero worship. We are given no description of the person or personality of Deborah, no details of the upbringing of Samuel or Samson, no *Bildungsroman*, no cinematic visualization of the battles of David or Saul. The focus is always at a plane just beyond that where fictive personalities are resolved, a plane of moral virtuality by whose normative appeal *real* personalities and societies emerge. This is the reason, I suspect, that a cult of personal messiahship never did succeed among Israelites —still less any belief in avatars or *ḥulûlî* imâms. Messiahship is a function, not a personality, and at bottom Jews always knew this—hence the radical insistence of the Passover *Hagaddah* on the immediacy of God's act in Egypt: "Not by the hands of an angel, not by the hands of a seraph, not by the hands of an emissary. . . ." Rashi argues that R. Hillel's denial of a messiah for Israel serves only to underscore the dependence of our redemption upon God alone.

There was no divine kingship in ancient Israel. The first hints at the idea of monarchy voice its radical critique; its acceptance is *faute de mieux*. The identities, appetites, and weaknesses of even the most celebrated monarchs, David and Solomon, are never confounded with the work for whose sake such kings (but never their failings) are tolerated or admired. And, as Mendelssohn explained, the very act that established a monarchy in ancient Israel, by creating a state distinguishable from the Law of God, whose standards it was to uphold, but whose standards did not alone determine its existence or dictate its form, drove a deep wedge, ultimately not removable, between the idea of God's will and the demands of any merely human government.[20]

In Jeremiah (33:14–15) we read God's promise that the restored scion of David will "execute justice and right in the land." This is the task of legitimate government and the criterion of its recognition. The longing for a Davidic restoration, then, is the longing to regain national autonomy and self-respect, restoration of Israel to Zion and of Zion to itself—less to its past than to its potential. The achievement of that goal cannot be identified with the advent of any single individual or mechanism of administration. The foundation of a messianism that does not quail at the facts of history or place responsibility for enhancing human destiny outside the realm of humanly acquired deserts is in the recognition that the righting of the world (*tikkun 'olam*) depends not on a literal Davidic restoration but on the rule of justice established through the changing of human hearts.

WHO IS THE MESSIAH?

It has been argued that the secular messianism of the founders of modern Zionism expresses a revulsion against the cult of personality, a reaction to the trauma of Shabtai Zvi. But the case can be generalized.[21] The early Zionists, like the rest of the world, were in reaction against Napoleon; the later ones, against Hitler. Jewish messianism was never a personalistic concept; its modern forms do not depart from but continue the ancient conception of messiahship as a role rather than an identity. The secularism of the Zionist leaders was a reaction specifically against the use of religion as a surrogate for action—against the passivity of awaiting the messiah. But Judah Halevi, whose poetry attuned him to the yearnings of his people, expressed in their sacred songs, reacted equally strongly—not with secular sentiments but with activist intentions, long before. What stirred him was not the thought of a man but the vision of a life. Even with Shabtai Zvi, the Jews like Glückel's father-in-law who sold their goods and packed provisions for imminent removal to the land of Israel[22] were awaiting historical redemption, not a particular personality. The question in their minds was one of time—would redemption come now, next week, next year? They were confident of what redemption meant, regardless of its vehicle. Shabtai's personality was of consequence only to the close circuit of his devotees and sponsors—until his political and then his moral failure ruined his cause and made clear the vanity of the hopes that had been pinned to him.[23] Then all but the most committed of his adherents discarded him and put their hopes once more in abeyance.

In recognizing the criteria of messiahship we must confront a question of temporal scale. If the messianic ideal of society, of history and the world, can be the achievement only of a generation or of a lengthy series of generations progressively working out their destiny and defining that destiny as they work, then the tasks of the messiah can never be achieved by a single pair of hands.[24] Thus Rabbi Tarfon: "It is not your responsibility to complete the work, but you are not free to desist from it" (*Avot* 2:21). If we ask the question of the prophets who or what the messiah is, we discover that the messiah, properly called the hope of Israel, is not a person at all. The function of governance vested in a king is the natural paradigm and symbol of an epoch. The generations and their age must be the object to which the symbol points. The messiah is a person in the poetry of political imagination, the paradigm of an age.

A similar personification in the ancient Confucian texts is instructive. Shun, we read, a sage king of antiquity, ruled if any monarch did, by indirection; he had only to take his place reverently facing due south, and all things were done as was proper (*Analects* XV 5). As Confucius said, "He who rules by moral force is like the pole star, which remains in place while all the lesser stars pay it obeisance" (II 1). The anointed king of the canonical Jewish sources is not, of course, a figurehead, a symbol representing nothing but the image of authority. He is seen as a ruler; indeed, the founder of a regime. His role is dynamic. There is much to be built and accomplished before his reign as such can begin. As a symbol he represents the causal agency by which what must be done shall be done to set right the world and to maintain and augment its peace and justice even after they are established. Still, the messiah does not invent but only implements and reforms the Law; and even the Law does not fulfill its own requirements. Only its subjects can do that. Just as Shun's rule was typified by the propriety internalized in the minds of all his courtiers and administrators so that none so much as required a command, messianic rule is typified by the internalization in human hearts of all the obligations of love of God and regard for one another which are the central objects of the Torah's legislation.[25] The messianic rule is one of moral force; and the order the messiah ushers in is not the project of his fiat but the outcome of our reformation. As Ibn Verga argued a century before Hobbes published the *Leviathan*: "The king in essence is the people."[26]

Nowhere is conscious personification more evident in imaging the theme of historic redemption than in the book of Isaiah: "How lovely on the mountains — the feet of the messenger who bringeth the news of peace, good news, of victory, telling Zion, 'Thy God is King.' The voice of thy lookouts! They raise up their voices together, joyously, as each eye seeth the return of God to Zion." Our transformation will be decisive as the news of a battle won and a war ended, visible on all sides — "Look how my servant shall prosper. He shall be lifted up, exalted, raised most high. Just as many were appalled at thee — so marred was his appearance, unlike that of a man, his form beyond the human semblance — so shall many nations be astounded at him and kings shut their mouths. For they shall see what has not been told them and recognize for themselves what they have never heard tell of" (Isaiah 52:7–8, 13–15; cf. Rashi and Ibn Ezra ad loc.).

The prophet's slipping into the second person — "appalled at *thee*" — reveals the identity of the servant. It is Israel, explicitly identified (in 49:25–26), whose historic revival is at once the vindication of her faithfulness and the proof of God's faithfulness to her.[27] The gaping kings admit their fault (53:5). Israel, so lately shunned and despised, seeming mad in clutching her ideals with no apparent purchase on reality (53:1–3) triumphs, like a gnarled, all-but-dead root in the desert that bursts forth as a sapling with the first rain. The servant is not a person but a nation of people who refuse to relinquish the vital insight embodied in their covenant: that justice rewards and evil destroys itself. The coming of the messiah confirms that truth, by the redemption of humanity in rightful

living; its means is neither force nor fraud but the example of Israel living
by her law (42:1−4, 49:6−7).

THE MESSIANIC ROLE

Maimonides resolves into prose the hopes that the prophets entrusted
to imagery and recaptures conceptually the tinctures their images leave in
rabbinic homily—their yearning and sense of immediacy, the contingency
of the world's destiny upon the intimate turn of our moral choices. His
summary has a value beyond the sway of his name, because it is conceptual.
No mere figment of imagination joined to hope, alternating naturally with
despair, could win a comparable authority. I divide his statement from the
final pages of his *Code* into its theses:

> The King Messiah will arise and restore the kingdom of David to its
> former state and original autonomy. (*Hilkhot Melakhim* 11.1)

The criterion of messiahship, then, as the ancient rabbis held, is functional, critically political. As Samuel's distillation requires, it means recon-
stituting Israel as an autonomous state governed under the principles of
the Torah.

In a restored Israel, Maimonides argues, prophecy will be recovered.
For prophecy is philosophic insight given wings by imagination, and so
translated into norms and symbols—the beliefs and practices by which we
may live and visualize our place in nature and history. Self-confidence is the
only requisite of prophecy lacking to a subjugated or exiled Israel, so prophecy will return with the restoration of Israel to sovereignty in her
homeland.[28] In such circumstances the insights will not be lacking to restore and reform the ancient practices of Israel. Even if the cult of animal
sacrifices has been outgrown,[29] prophetic authority will be at hand to
adjust our worship to the spiritual modes of the matured nation, just
as the ancient worship was adjusted to the conditions of our spiritual
infancy:

> He will rebuild the sanctuary and gather the dispersed of Israel. All the
> ancient laws will be reinstituted in his days. Sacrifices will be offered once
> again [even if not the very animal sacrifices of antiquity, whose details
> Maimonides sees as restrictions on the time, place, manner, and object of
> sacrifice so as to perfect the ethos and spirituality of the people]. The Sab-
> batical and Jubilee years will be observed as commanded in the Torah.
> (*Hilkhot Melakhim* 11.1)

The restoration of Zion will mean an ingathering, an end to unnatural and unhealthful dispersion. The laws will be amplified, as in ancient times, by interpretation grounded in the insights of the prophets and sustained by a populace who derive guidance from the symbolisms of the ancestral religion and the governance of its principles—not only in personal and family matters but in agriculture, industry, stewardship of nature—as in the practices of *yovel* and *shemittah*. Central here is the moral thematic. For it is not mere performance of the laws unelaborated or elaborated only as rituals that constitutes the messianic fulfillment of history, but their moral implementation—the establishment of a society founded on their principles.

> He who does not believe in a restoration or expect the coming of the messiah denies not only the teachings of the Prophets but also those of the Law and of Moses our teacher. For the text affirms the rehabilitation of Israel: "Then the lord thy God will reverse thy captivity and have pity on thee and return and gather thee. . . . Even if you are scattered to the furthest reaches of the heavens . . . the Lord thy God will bring thee into the land which thy fathers possessed. . . ." (Deuteronomy 30:3–5). These words explicit in the Torah comprehend all that the Prophets said on the subject. (*Hilkhot Melakhim* 11.1)

Sandwiched between the seeming severity of a dogma and the authority of his proof-text, the Rambam makes two radical but textually anchored claims here: (*1*) The messianic idea is embedded in the Mosaic Torah, since, as he argues a few lines further on, no commandment was given without a view to its fulfillment. This means that the Torah is given with a view to instituting the entire socio-legal system it projects. (*2*) Nothing more is intended by our messianism than is implied in the biblical expectation of a world reformed through the fulfillment of the Law. Symbolic and projective visions of a supernatural end to history are mere surrogates of the moral changes by which alone the transhistoric goal is brought about and made lasting. Without moral transformation, cosmic cataclysms would be mere pyrotechnics.

The Rambam expresses his thesis negatively, as though excoriating incredulity—for much the same reasons, I suspect, that Plato couches his radical reconstitution of the idea of divinity in an excoriation of "the poets" for suggesting that the divine is venal: The blow falls not on the poets but on the vulgar notion that the venal can be divine. Similarly, when Maimonides defends belief in the messiah, his target is not an audience who have no taste for messianism but rather one inclined to believe too well, or to interpret such beliefs in primitive terms, as a prelude to bracketing them. He muffles the radicalism of his view, sidestepping his adversaries who reject the very idea that a divine law might address human needs and purposes and who prefer to regard each commandment (even in isolation from the system that gives them life) as though it were an end in itself rather than a means to God's end, the perfection of humanity through the commandments.[30] Yet Maimonides' radicalism is of a piece with prophetic and rabbinic radicalism. Messianism is not merely a bundle of isolated promises but a central premise of the Law, made explicit in the proof-text (as so many Mosaic principles are in Deuteronomy), but implicit, as we have argued, in the very fabric of the Mosaic legislation. That was my first point.

As for the proof-text itself, my second point emerges from the comprehensiveness and exclusivity of Maimonides' reading of it. Beyond the expectation of Israel's return to live as God's people under God's law, there is no further content to our messianism. Anything more is poetical expansion or spurious, possibly unwholesome invention. Maimonides argues that the themes found in the prophets of Israel are broached in the prophecy of Balaam—a momentous remark, since Balaam's prophecy and its exigency insist that Israel's ultimate vindication, like her general well-being, rest upon allegiance to the precepts of the Law. What rendered Balaam incapable of cursing Israel was that she was already blessed; and what made her blessed was her way of life—its order and goodliness, outcomes of the moral and social appropriation of justice and tact, inspired by the commands of Perfection. The duality of Balaam's vision suggested in the words "I see him but not now; I behold him but not nigh" (Numbers 24:17), is glossed by Maimonides as alluding to two historic phrases: the monarchy of David and the ultimate national restoration, with its attendant international order. Both are outcomes of Israel's allegiance to her laws. Supernatural readings[31] miss the force of the inference from the peace and order Balaam beholds, first to the immediate future—in his blessing—and then to the remote future (where the observed tendencies are consummated)—in his prophecy.

The civil and even military work of the Davidic monarchy, Maimonides argues, remains uncompleted—paradigmatically, the building of new cities of refuge and the overcoming of new enemies who endanger the future messianic state. But such work is typical of the constructive and protective work of governments in rebuilding a society.[32] Maimonides vigorously opposes the externalization of redemption as a matter of astrology, arguing that if there was uncertainty about the date of the redemption from Egypt —"the term of which was fixed"—how much more so about our future redemption,[33] which depends upon our choices. Thus he assigns no occult significance to Daniel's kingdoms or to Balaam's Moab, Edom, Seth, and Seir, and no cosmic consequences to battles with them, as was the stock and staple of medieval apocalyptic speculation. In his Letter to Yemen, Maimonides does find figural counterparts to the great kingdoms of his day—as Scripture seems to invite one to do. But he apologizes in the same document for Saadiah's excursions into messianic calculations, pleading the depression and frustration of Saadiah's day. The long-term effect of such prognostications, he argues, is heightened frustration, when the hopes they arouse are disappointed. Projections of a *deus ex machina* messiah are symptoms of despair, not elements of faith: "the hardships of our people's exile are the cause of these extravagances—for a drowning man catches at a straw."[34] The identifications, then, are tokens of the times—not cosmic signals of the end of history but ad hoc applications of a scriptural typology. They were preceded by other identifications and will likely be followed by more political analogies of no less relevance or pertinence. The fulfillment of the messianic function does not require any supernatural interventions or displays:

> Do not think that the King Messiah must perform signs and wonders, bring anything new into being, revive the dead, or do similar things. It is not so. Rabbi Akiba was a great sage, a teacher of the Mishnah. Yet he was an armor bearer of Ben Kosiba [leader of the revolt against Rome (132–35), whose *nom de guerre*, Bar Kokhba, 'son of the star,' alludes to Balaam's prophecy]. Rabbi Akiba affirmed that Ben Kosiba was the King Messiah. He shared this view with the sages of his generation until Ben Kosiba was slain in his own sin and it was manifest that he was not. Yet the Rabbis had not asked him for a sign or token. (*Hilkhot Melakhim* 11.3)

The messianic hopes attached to Bar Kokhba were laid to rest by his defeat and execution, but they were not refuted or even questioned for the absence of miracles. In the Letter to Yemen, Maimonides tells of a number of messianic pretenders—some pious, some mad, some seemingly fraudulent —who performed wonders, healing the sick, and the like, yet whose claims were discredited. They expressed a premature urgency, like the precocious eroticism mentioned in the Song of Songs: seeking to arouse love—to restore and redeem Israel—before the proper time.[35] Politics is relevant to morals, but messianism rests on morals, not on politics:

> The fundamental principle is this Law of ours. It is everlasting and not to be added to or subtracted from. (*Hilkhot Melakhim* 11.3)

The words look almost like a non sequitur. But what they say is that the Torah affords the sole criterion of messiahship. Our fulfillment by the means proposed in the Torah is the real mission of the messiah. Nahmanides underscores the point by adapting an ancient skeptical argument: If the messiah *were* to come to a stultified Israel, they would fail to recognize him.[36]

> If there arises a king from the house of David who meditates on the Torah and practices the commandments [making them his principle in thought and action], as did David his ancestor, follows the precepts laid down in the Written and Oral Law [not, like the Karaites, rejecting the Talmud and so subverting the ongoing development of the Law in continuity with tradition], who prevails upon Israel to walk in the way of the Torah and repair its breaches [restoring disused practices and reenlivening biblical principles], fights the battles of the Lord [waging war only for sacred principle], he may be assumed to be the messiah. If he succeeds in these things, rebuilds the sanctuary on its site, and gathers the dispersed of Israel, then beyond all doubt he is the messiah. . . .[37] [Figures like Jesus and Muhammad serve to] prepare the world as a whole to serve the Lord with one accord, as it is written: "For then will I restore to the peoples a pure language, that they may all call upon the name of the Lord and serve Him with one consent" [Zephaniah 3:9]. (*Hilkhot Melakhim* 11.4)

Maimonides' expectations[38] are formidable—all the more so when one considers the peace and justice, political and economic stability needed in the world to allow the security of Israel and safe ingathering of exiles. But Maimonides does not delight in difficulties for their own sake, so he does not dilate upon them. He dismisses some of the favorite rabbinical conundrums about the genealogy of the messiah, Priests and Levites, with the remark that there will be time to settle such matters when the issue becomes a practical one. At that time doubtful cases can be settled with the aid of the Holy Spirit (a natural inspiration in the Rambam's prophetology)[39] and a certain measure of arbitrary dispatch. Maimonides' care about the Davidic house reflects the ancient legitimist concern with usurpers, puppets, and pretenders, but it does not displace the functional criteria of messiahship.

Messianism is not ritualism, but our liberation is not to be understood in antinomian terms: "He will come neither to declare the clean unclean nor the unclean clean." There will be no inversion of values; our symbols will retain their polar division, between holy and unholy, good and evil. Yet the messiah will not declare some families baseborn or slaves. Once mingled in the common stream, no lineage shall be diminished. Rather, the task is "to bring peace to the world, as it is said, 'And he shall reconcile the hearts of the fathers to the children'" (Malachi 3:24).

> Let no one think that in the days of the messiah any laws of nature will be set aside or any innovation introduced into creation. The world will follow its normal course.[40] The words of Isaiah: "The wolf shall dwell with the lamb, and the leopard lie down with the kid" (11:6) are to be taken figuratively, meaning that Israel will live securely among wicked heathens, who are likened to wolves and leopards, as it is written, "A wolf of the deserts doth spoil them, a leopard watcheth over their cities" [Jeremiah 5:6—for a literal wolf or leopard does not take spoil or lay siege to cities]. They will all accept the true religion, and neither plunder nor destroy but along with Israel will honestly earn a comfortable sustenance, as it is written: "And the lion shall eat straw like the ox" (Isaiah 11:7). (*Hilkhot Melakhim* 12.1)[41]

Any comparable images whose meanings are not clear now, Maimonides announces, cutting off what he takes to be idle debate, will be clear when the time comes. As to the return of Elijah and the great wars and portents of the future, "No one [not even a prophet] can know the particulars of this and similar events until they take place. They are not stated explicitly by the prophets, and the Rabbis have no tradition [no reliable received authority] about these matters. They base themselves simply on what scripture seems to imply. Hence the divergence of opinion." Since such particulars are not authoritatively understood, to embroider upon them is a waste of time or worse. To "calculate the end" rather than pursuing it through fulfillment of the Torah, to attempt to second-guess or manipulate it, is a grievous affront (*Hilkhot Melakhim* 12.2, citing Sanhedrin 97b).

THE MESSIANIC AGE AND THE NATIONS OF THE WORLD

Israel's messianic hope emerges from the transcendent expectation of divine, saving aid in struggles informed with integrity and justice—a recurrent theme of the Psalms. The transhistoric dimensions of value naturally attach most readily to the mission of the nation: Assyrian destruction,

Egyptian alliance, Babylonian captivity, and Persian liberation are all seen through a historical vision that regards faithfulness to Israel's covenant with God as the key to vindication and restoration. A remnant of the people will endure and return to the land of their hopes (Amos 3:12, Jeremiah 31:6), stirred by the memory, which exile only intensifies, of the promised life. Exile is the fruit of faithlessness; return and restoration show the possibility of forgiveness. But the life of exile (Jeremiah 29:1–14) is not to become a mere waiting for return. It must be full, reflecting and still projecting the values that gave substance to life in the land: "Build houses and settle, plant gardens and eat their fruit, take wives and raise sons and daughters, and take wives for your sons and give your daughters to husbands, and let them bear sons and daughters, that ye may increase there and not diminish." Dejection must not suppress the progress of life and pursuit of its simple goods. The life of an integrated community remains an orienting norm, and sedition is no substitute for redemption. Rather, God commends active pursuit of the commonweal: "Seek the wellbeing of the city to which I have exiled you and offer prayers in its behalf to God, for through its welfare will your welfare come about." False prophets and false dreams foster the illusion that Israel's restoration might be achieved by violence or by magical incantations against the ruling power. But the order of nature gives incantations as little purchase as dreams. The simple expedients of living hopefully and fruitfully in a land whose welfare is linked with our own will render our return inevitable.

The idea of redemption fuses here with the ancient biblical theme of divine providence working through rather than despite nature. And we see through Jeremiah's eyes the parallel between violence and magic—the one attacking the social, the other the natural order. The message is Mosaic: that God's will is achieved in and through the good life, not through sabotage or the futile and frustrate expressionism of the professional mutterers of imprecations (*kosmeikhem*, 29:8). For the sterile anger and alienation of terrorism join hands with superstition in substituting symbols for effective acts. Even our union with God, the aim beyond garden fruits and fruitful families, is achieved not in fanaticism but in a studious quest by the whole resource of our moral and intellectual being (*tidreshuni bekhol levavchem*). That quest demands a milieu of peaceful material and moral fulfillment, which we must create even in exile.

The message remains relevant long after it was delivered. Israel still dwells apart—among the nations, but never wholly of them, learning from other cultures, but not parasitically dependent on them, dying only insofar as a timeless message is subordinated to temporality, deathless insofar as what is learned is rendered universal and the mission is maintained of capturing and rediffusing life-giving ideals. Israel's mission is achieved, Jeremiah argues, not by any *coup de main* but by the subtler means of culture—living well, which is, to be sure, no real strategy for revenge, but clearly the highest form of teaching. God's plan for Israel, as in the Mosaic tableaux, is blessing and life. In time the oppressors shall come to be oppressed (30:16), and the yoke shall be stricken off Israel's neck (30:8). Self-rule shall be restored (30:21), maidens will emerge adorned in the dancing throng of merrymakers, vineyards shall be planted once again in the hill country of Samaria. The paradigms of the covenantal life are now symbols of redemption: "they shall come in exultant song on the heights of Zion, thrilling in God's bounty—the wheat and wine and oil, sheep and cattle—their souls like a watered garden. And they shall grieve no longer" (31:12). The joys of shared goods in plenty (31:14) are linked with moral and spiritual fulfillment. The soul becomes a watered garden, mirroring the watered garden of the land, in which good fellowship and shared labor foster the highest human potentialities and serve the most fundamental human needs.

The time shall come, Jeremiah urges, when it will no longer be said, "The fathers ate sour grapes and the children's teeth are set on edge." Sins of the fathers will no longer be visited on their offspring, but the Mosaic norm of individual responsibility will be fulfilled (31:29–30); cf. Ezekiel 18. How does this occur? Surely not by dissolution of the bonds of interdependence but by the deep internalization of the ideal: "Behold, the days are coming, saith the Lord, when I shall make a new covenant with the House of Israel and the House of Judah, unlike the covenant I made with their fathers on the day I held them by the hand to bring them out of the land of Egypt, which covenant of mine they broke, although I was their husband. But this is the covenant I shall make with them after those days, saith the Lord: I shall put my Law within them, in their hearts will I write it, and I shall be their God, and they shall be my people. No longer will one man teach his fellow or one man teach his brother: 'Know the Lord.' For all shall know me from the small to the great, saith the Lord" (31:31–34).

It will no longer be necessary for the will of God, the ideal of goodness, to be transmitted verbally, since all will know it individually. Individuals will not limit but foster one another's perfection, through an inward understanding. Plainly, norms will always be transmitted culturally. But when they are embedded in the practical structure of society they are no longer taught as abstract formulae. As patterns in the fabric of habit and custom they are appropriated directly into the moral and intellectual core of our being, the heart.

The messianic age, then, is achieved in the fulfillment of the Law as a commitment of conscience. It is not an external eruption of some numinous horror into the workings of human living but the fulfillment of our living through the principles by which life itself is made possible. Davidic restoration, dynastic legitimism, is a motif of national self-expression, a focal point of historical identity and direction (Jeremiah 17:25; cf. 33:17, Ezekiel 37:24–25). But the image resolved at that focal point is always that of justice, eclipsing personal and dynastic concerns: "Behold the days are coming, saith the Lord, when I shall raise up a true offshoot of David. As king he shall reign—and ably—do justice and right in the land. In his days Judah shall be saved and Israel shall dwell secure. And this is the name he shall be called: 'The Lord upholdeth our righteousness.'" (Jeremiah 23:5–6; cf. 33:14–16). The true offshoot of the Davidic line is a way of life and governance, not a party or a lineage any more than it is a personality.

Jeremiah's vision provides the background for understanding the prophecy of Isaiah: "A bough shall emerge of the stock of Jesse, a branch from his roots shall bear fruit. Upon him shall rest the spirit of God, spirit of wisdom and understanding, spirit of counsel and courage, spirit of insight and reverence for God." Again the figure is identified by his virtues and functions, not by idiosyncrasies or personal marks. "His sense shall be reverence for God"—that is, he will be guided by love of the Good—"and he shall not judge by what his eyes see nor admonish by what his ears hear. He shall judge the weak justly and reprove forthrightly in behalf of the poor of the land. He shall strike the land with the rod of his utterance and with the breath of his lips shall he slay the wicked"—ruling, that is, by ideas and words, not violence or terror. Thus his power rests upon his righteousness—"Justice will be the girdle of his loins and faithfulness the girdle of his reins. The wolf shall dwell with the lamb, the leopard lie down with the kid. The calf, the young lion, the fatling together—a little lad shall lead them. Cow and bear will graze, and their young lie down together. The lion shall eat straw like cattle. The nursling shall play on the asp's hole, and the weanling place his hand on the adder's den. None shall harm or destroy in all My holy mountain, for all the earth shall be filled with knowledge of the Lord as the waters fill the sea" (Isaiah 11:1–9).

The lion, the asp, the child, kid, and calf are figural, as Maimonides taught. If they were literally animals, universal knowledge of God would be no explanation of the change. Knowledge—not abstract theology, but a practical knowledge of God as the ultimate Source and Referent of the principles of goodness and justice—disperses the fear of the strong by the weak. The sight of justice realized, as Plato hoped, will suffice to establish the sovereignty of the Principle by which it was achieved in all the nations of the world, to which the prophet's image of the waters of the sea naturally turns attention (Isaiah 11:10–16). The redemption of Israel, as Maimonides explains, is won by the respect Israel earns in the world for her achievement in integrating the idea of the Absolute into the fabric of communal life. It is through their respect for that ideal, not through adherence to the symbols or assimilation to the ethnicity of Israel, that the nations are redeemed. Ezekiel's prediction (34:23–25) that evil beasts shall cease, that it will be possible to sleep safely in the woods, follows the same lines. Literal beasts are not evil, although they may be dangerous. But the beasts here are nations. The Israelites are the sheep, tended by David, the shepherd king. Nations, too, are not evil literally. It is their ethos that must be cultivated—tamed in a very special sense—for the tasks of peace. The real source of the world's security in the age foretold is God's "covenant of peace," a more concrete image for what Isaiah calls knowledge—for Ezekiel habitually gives more concrete expression to the same ideals as Isaiah. The Davidic ruler (Isaiah 9:1–6) is the magistrate of that peace (*sar shalom*).

The revival pictured in Ezekiel's vision in the valley of the dry bones (37:1–14) engages us in the messianic project, since we are the dry bones spoken of. The idea that salvation is an external event worked upon passive recipients is on a par with the idea that creation is the mere mobilization of inert bodies. On the contrary, just as creation imparts a life and being that allow all creatures to enact their own existence, so redemption imparts the opportunity of self-revival, overcoming passivity and inertia. Ezekiel chidingly echoes the woe-filled judgment of the Israelites that they are dead and done for (*nigzarnu*); he challenges them to recognize their restoration (which can be achieved only by their own deed and choices) as an act of God, since it is—by their own confession—tantamount to revival of the dead from the grave, like God's first imparting of his spirit to Adam's inanimate earth. But the transformations of the messianic age are symbolized not merely as the fleshing out of bones but as the substitution of a heart of flesh for a heart of stone—a moral and ultimately spiritual revitalization. The meaning of the symbolism is not left in doubt but specified within the prophecy: It is the imparting of inward guidance through an understanding of God, expressed as adherence to God's commands (Ezekiel 36:26–27).

All prophecies of Israel's hegemony (such as Isaiah 43:3, 44:5, 45:14) must be read in the light of the same vision. Insight into God's perfection becomes the actuating principle of communal relations, establishing the rule of justice and allowing Israel to be the little child that leads the ponderous and powerful creatures, not by force of domination, since that is impossible, but by power of example: "He shall come to Zion to save them, to those in Jacob who renounce wrong, saith the Lord. And—this is my covenant with them, saith the Lord—my spirit [insight into God's transcendent perfection] which is upon thee, and my words [the imperatives derived from that understanding], which I have put into thy mouth, will not disappear from thy mouth and the mouth of thy children and thy children's children—God hath said it—henceforth and forever" (Isaiah 59:20–21). The divine idea, it is promised, will not be lost (cf. Jeremiah 31:35–37). And through the idea of God justice will be kept alive and imparted not only from generation to generation but from nation to nation: "In place of thy being neglected, despised and shunned, I shall make thee the wonder of the world, a joy for generations. . . . I shall make thy officers peace and thy bailiffs, righteousness"—thus the image of the magistrate of peace is resolved as a metaphor expressive of the power of peace and justice themselves, when these are internalized and appropriated as our motives—"No longer will lawless strife be heard in thy land, waste and destruction within your borders, but thou shalt call thy wall salvation and thy gates praise"—that is, the recognition due to God (praise) and the resulting practice of justice (salvation, divine aid) will be acknowledged as the bastions of society and the sources of its strength, more powerful in ensuring its security than any literal guards, walls, or gates—"Thy people shall all be righteous forever" (Isaiah 60:15–21). As a result the nations will be drawn, as by a light, to follow the lead of the nation whose ethos is built on an understanding of the proper foundations of a life of justice and peace (Isaiah 60:1–14). The whole is accomplished not by divine interference in the processes of nature but by God's bringing those processes to fruition: "Just as the earth brings forth her shoot or as a garden sprouts her seed, so will the Lord God cause justice and praise to spring forth before all the nations" (61:11).

Even the conundrum of universality versus particularity, which Israel's detractors even now hold up as a reproach, calling every universal hope of Israel overbearing and every particular dream chauvinistic, is dissolved here, through the recognition that a moral transformation can become historic. Thus, in the vision as recaptured conceptually by the Rambam:

> The sages and prophets yearned for the days of the messiah not so that Israel might exercise dominion over the world or rule over the heathens, or be exalted by other nations, or that she might eat, drink and be merry. Their aspiration was that Israel be free to devote herself to the Law and its wisdom, with none to oppress or disturb them and so be worthy of the life of the world to come (*Hilkhot Melakhim* 12.4)

Israel's contemplation and practice of the Law can be perfected only in a world at peace, and that peace is perfected by the prosperity that flows from justice—itself the work of changed human hearts. Thus the stability of the messianic world rests on the same powerful dynamics as those which generate the present world's instability. The key to the reversal by which the familiar forces of social and economic nature are set to the service of justice and peace is intellectual (not mechanical), and Israel has a crucial role as a teacher and exemplar at the juncture between the theory and praxis of the good life:

> In that era there will be neither famine nor war, neither jealousy nor strife. Blessings will be abundant; comforts, within the reach of all. The one concern of the whole world will be to know the Lord [grasp the idea of Perfection morally and spiritually]. So Israelites will be very wise. They will know things that are now unknown and will attain an understanding of their Creator to the utmost capacity of the human mind, as it is written: "For the earth shall be filled with knowledge of the Lord as the waters fill the sea (Isaiah 11:9)." (*Hilkhot Melakhim* 12.5)

Israel's much decried visions of hegemony, then, when articulated conceptually as a vision of the world transformed by moral means, resolve to a moral leadership by example. And Israel's spiritual wisdom becomes the world's wisdom, neither automatically nor by imposition, but through the natural spread of understanding, classically expressed in the Plotinian image—that a light is not diminished but increased when shared.

ACCESSIBLE MESSIANISM

Much has been made of a supposed disagreement between two of the rabbinic sages as to the coming of the messianic era. The story is told of Rabbis Ḥiyya and Simeon ben Ḥalafta walking in the Valley of Arbela at early morning, watching the sun rise. Rabbi Ḥiyya said: "Just so is Israel's redemption. At first it will be only barely visible, then it will glint forth more brightly, and only in the end will it break forth in all its glory" (Song of Songs *Rabbah* VI 10). But to Joshua ben Levi the prophet Elijah himself was said to have made known the sudden and unexpected coming of the messianic age: "If Israel were to repent," we read (Y. Ta'anit 64a, Sanhedrin 98a), "even for a single day, they would be instantly redeemed and the son of David would come, for it is said (Psalm 95:7): 'Today if ye will hearken to His voice.'"

THE MESSIANIC AGE AS A MORAL REVOLUTION

Once we have recognized the moral nature of the messianic transformation, it becomes clear that the two conceptions are not genuinely opposed. The idea of the suddenness of redemption refers to the immediacy of its possibility, since the radical transformation of history which the messianic idea portends rests wholly upon a universal change of heart possible in principle for all. The idea that progress toward that goal will be gradual refers to the inertia of our individual and social nature, the extreme unlikelihood of an instantaneous universal change of heart within the framework of history as we know it. It is in just these terms that the apparent biblical antinomies regarding the messianic age are interpreted rabbinically. Thus "I the Lord will hasten it in its time" (Isaiah 60:22) in the refracting prism of talmudic exegesis is differentiated into a moral disjunction: "If you are worthy, I will hasten it; if you are not worthy, it will transpire in its time" (Sanhedrin 98a). But when is that time? Once again talmudic authority elucidates in moral terms: Only repentance speeds redemption (Yoma 86b). Does a fatal destiny grant it otherwise, or can it be withheld indefinitely as humanity asymptotically approaches a vast array of goals irrelevant to or incongruent with the realization of our human moral and intellectual natures?

In no case, the rabbis inform us, does the messianic epoch simply arrive with the passage of the years. Moral conversion (*teshuvah*) is its absolute prerequisite. Yet it will not be indefinitely withheld. When two disciples of Yoḥanan ben Zakkai, R. Eliezer ben Hyrcanus and R. Joshua ben Ḥananiah, disputed about the epoch of the messiah, the underlying necessity of moral transformation was denied by neither, and its ultimate occurrence was also denied by neither. Rabbi Joshua predicted the coming of the messiah in Nissan, the beginning of the vernal year, suggesting that the messianic era would come in the course of nature with the inevitable revolutions of cosmic history—as the original redemption of the exodus from

Egypt had come in Nissan. Rabbi Eliezer predicted that the messianic epoch would begin in Tishrei, the beginning of the moral and spiritual year. He even suggested that the historic redemption from Egypt had begun in Tishrei—with the turning of human hearts—and was only completed in Nissan, at the time of Passover, when God's response to the inward transformation became manifest. But Rabbi Joshua himself did not negate the necessity of repentance. If the time woven into the cosmic fabric in the very act of creation arrived before Israel was ready, God would force repentance by imposing a ruler of the type of Haman (Sanhedrin 97b). Destiny would be inviolate, but so would the requirement of desert.

The idea that redemption rests upon desert was axiomatic, and for good reason. For the very concept of a covenant, from which the idea of redemption is extrapolated, responds to questions of desert. To say that humanity will be redeemed when morally unready was thus an absurdity even for one who wished to emphasize that God's promises are categorical; a fortiori, for one whose homiletic thrust was the contingency of redemption upon moral choice. It is in the same spirit that the Talmud admonishes against passive, mantic calculations and theurgic manipulations: "All the 'ends' have passed; it depends on repentance and good deeds" (Sanhedrin 97b). The admonition is timely, since our penchant for "calculating the end" persists, both in secular apocalyptic visions that calculate the catastrophic exhaustion of the earth's resources[42] or the cataclysmic depletion of the nuclear forbearance of nations and in triumphalist fantasies of "rapture" or alienated projections of cosmic holocaust and millennial judgment. The "ends" always pass, because their projection is founded in emotive dissociation and sanctimonious wish fulfillment rather than factual or moral necessity.

If the analysis of my earlier chapters is correct, fatal judgment will befall humankind only if we exhaust our place or desert in nature. What the premature projectors of humanity's demise actually express is their impatience—pettishness like Jonah's over the sparing of Nineveh. The generosity of scale in God's plan and the latitude of freedoms that divine grace allows become objects of choler for the projectors of apocalypse—as they are in other choleric forms of popular expression, the murder mystery and the disaster film. The same extravagance of imagery and perversity of judgment occur medievally in the work of Hieronymus Bosch and the preaching of the Crusades. Saadiah, with his characteristic psychological insight, remarked on the bitter and misanthropic tendency of anchorites who make abstemiousness their all-consuming goal.[43] Rabbinic thought turns cynicism in a more hopeful, yet more realistic direction: The observance of two Sabbaths in succession (*Shabbat* 118b) or even a single Sabbath (*Taʿanit* 64a) would bring history's denouement. But consider what would be involved spiritually, morally, psychologically, internationally, for all Israel to observe a perfect Sabbath, for all things in that sense to be done properly.

I think it can be seen now why the messianic concept must be situated in a middle ground between the natural and the transcendent. The idea involves no violation of the cosmic laws governing the motion of matter and the behavior of the elements. Yet it does involve the universal realization of our moral perfectibility, hardly an ordinary occurrence, although no charismatic figure can achieve this goal of history *for* us. Only homely, inward self-transformation can accomplish it. This moral theme is not a rabbinic invention. It lies at the heart of Ezekiel's, Isaiah's, and Jeremiah's visions of their people's future and rests in turn on the moral vision of the Mosaic law and the clear articulation of that vision in Deuteronomy.[44]

IS JEWISH MESSIANISM ROMANTIC?

In a famous essay,[45] Gershom Scholem treats Maimonides' restatement of the prophetic messianic promises as the "grandest" expression of a line of thinking that is hostile and suspicious toward what Scholem sees as the major trend in Jewish messianism: its fundamentally apocalyptic character, its potential as a seedbed of revolutionist ideas—leading even to the radical critique and rejection of the Torah itself—its latent antinomianism, expressed when the yearning for the messiah "bursts out" into historic expressions. The powerful dictum of Rabbi Samuel, "The only difference between this age and the days of the messiah is the subjection of Israel to alien dominion," is taken not as counter-evidence to Scholem's claim that "When the messianic idea appears as a living force in the world of Judaism . . . it always occurs in the closest connection with apocalypticism." Nor does Scholem take R. Samuel's dictum as confirmation of the Maimonidean position, but as an expression of "repulsion" for apocalypticism and fear of the imaginative excess which, Scholem argues, is the authentic popular content of Jewish messianism. Maimonides' work and that of Saadiah before him and Naḥmanides and Crescas after him are treated as contretemps, "counter-tendencies" to the apocalypticism that was "both a content of religious faith as such and also living, acute anticipation."[46]

Scholem's project is not that of a Maimonides or a Saadiah. As a historian it is not his role to reconcile idea with idea or fathers with sons. What he seeks to render comprehensible is the background of longings that make possible such phenomena as the Sabbatian movement, Hasidism, and the Kabbalah. He does not take it as his task to render intelligible the central themes of Jewish prophetic and rabbinic insight in their full conceptual coherency, their extreme self-discipline, responsibility, and comprehensibility. As a historian he is concerned not with the credible and universal but with the plausible and particular. His writing and even his choice of subject matter are tinged with historicism and positivism.[47] The larger life of Jewish thought, beyond the imaginative flights, transitory movements, fantasies, nightmares of diaspora and persecution, may seem abstract from the plane of the history of myths and legends. But it is real.

Scholem rightly campaigned to restore intellectual attention to the spiritual underworld and demi-world created by a frustrated but never impoverished poetic imagination. He offers respect and not mere cognizance to themes that historically expressed (and still express) pent longings and denied desires that earlier historians like Graetz did not much care to take account of as authentic manifestations of "the" Jewish spirit. But since his was a campaign and one focused on imaginative excesses, Scholem inclined not merely to pursue the mythic but also to regard as most significant its most *outré* expressions, relying on their actual or putative popular appeal. His methodic tends to ignore or diminish the more conceptually chaste expressions of ideas, flattening their significance artificially by slighting the intellectual dimension that gives them depth and rigor. Philosophically and normatively, however, we have criteria of authenticity beyond those of vividness: the dual controls of conceptual coherency and thematic continuity by which our tradition has continually checked and verified the appropriability of every notion that comes within its purview.[48]

Scholem's method grants an authority to constitute our conception of what the Jewish tradition will have been no less to the vaguest dreamer, the most vulgar, irresponsible schemer, than to the prophetic writers, the talmudic sages, or the great medieval codifiers and philosophers, the rational and intuitive exponents of the tradition, whose commitment and results were tested repeatedly in theory and in history. Graetz erred in looking askance at the elements of tradition whose rationality he could not accept. But there is an opposite error to avoid: that of assuming that all that is intelligible and coherent is therefore inauthentic. Scholem teaches us of the hidden needs that grow out of the deprivations of a nightmare past. But Jewish experience also includes waking thought and coordinated action. These too must have their place. Indeed, there are grounds for giving them precedence over the nocturnal—the grounds of coherency, whole-someness—the absence of a need to bracket, cage or contain a mode within the phial of its historicity, the capability daylight has of continuing to guide our lives. For a nation cannot be nourished morally or intellectually on the tailings of its archaeology.

Conservatism, utopia, and restoration are central values in rabbinic Judaism, Scholem writes. But his analysis of Jewish messianism seizes upon restoration and utopia—opposite sides, he recognizes, of the same coin: "the conservative tendencies, great and even crucial as their role and their significance were for the existence of the religious community of Judaism, have no part in the development of messianism within this community."[49] The gradualism of R. Ḥiyya and the widespread rabbinic opposition to "pressing for the end" thus become unaccountable. So does the Torah's program of transforming our daily acts and choices. For our messianic idea is nothing but a vision of the goals of the Torah realized in history. Imagination, with its penchant for polarities and perversities, may please itself by picturing that the Torah is to be fulfilled through its supersession or, in the phrase keenly studied by Scholem, by "redemption through sin." But the Mosaic nexus between ethical endeavor and the messianic future was no more obscure to the Israelite many than it was to their teachers throughout our history, since the message of the Torah was never without an audience in Israel. Given the ethical and spiritual content of our messianic concepts, especially when these can be disentangled from their most vivid symbolizations and sometimes fervid anticipations, we find that conservatism (which is not reaction, irredentism, or nostalgia for a lost —because ideal—golden age) has a crucial role in Jewish messianism, a role which Buber articulates with sensitivity in *For the Sake of Heaven*:[50] that of restraining impatience. Jewish messianism is not an indefinitely prolonged expectation of immediate alteration, as some forms of apocalypticism may become. It is a sustained (hence conservative) hope and struggle for far-reaching historic change based on appropriation by Israel of the ideals of the Law.

The naturalism we encounter in the Rambam's schematization of the prophetic messianic vision, then, is not merely a reaction against traditional apocalypticism or a counterblast to the free play of symbolism, not merely a cold breath of reason seeking to douse or dampen the hot flame of passion which may color messianic expectation with tinges of violence against the social and international or even the natural order. Rather it is an expression of the authentic and normative Jewish conceptions of the messianic age which run back to the rabbinic roots and prophetic origins of the idea. It is not the case that more fevered—even Christological—conceptions must be accepted as normatively Jewish simply because they are articulated in a Jewish context.[51]

In the Midrash on Song of Songs Rabbi Ḥelbo interprets "I adjure you, daughters of Jerusalem, by the gazelles and the hinds of the field, do not stir up love until it is ready" as an admonition against political revolution in the face of the gentile powers, against "pressing for the end," against revealing Israel's secret to the nations, and against mass movements of exodus "coming up like a wall" out of exile.[52] What does this mean? Political revolution, to begin with, cannot fulfill our messianic hopes because they depend on the perfection of human character and cannot be imposed by external authority. Likewise magic and theurgy are like stirring up sexual ardor before maturity—the gestures and intentions may be present or partly present, but neither the body nor the spirit is prepared. So the symbols remain empty gestures, the actions sterile. This does not mean that revolutions are never justified. Tyranny demands revolution. But revolutions fought for utopia with the tactics of apocalypse are founded on lies and doomed to fail: They promise to achieve by violence what requires the inner revolution of human hearts.

The same must be said of crusades to perfect the world through economic or political manipulation. They are externalizations, substituting phrases, notions, and names for facts, as Communism substitutes words about peace and justice for the practical respect of human worth and dignity. It is because the Sages see that our proper goal is the culmination of an ethical process, not a magical act, that they can insist that efforts to calculate or manipulate "the End" rest on a delusion. Scholem writes that "in the Biblical texts which served as the basis for the crystallization of the Messianic idea, it is nowhere made dependent upon human activity."[53] He takes R. Ḥelbo's advice against impatience as creating a scriptural imperative of quietism. But all this is alien to rabbinic and prophetic discourse. Scholem seems to be responding to the discontents of modern neoorthodox movements whose pleas are more reactions against secular Zionism than they are rejections of activism. The word *activity* is often used as a euphemism for revolution, or here as a placeholder for Zionism. But tactical counsel against revolutionary action is not the same as quietism, and the adjuration not to try to force reform is not a prohibition against the very social program that the Torah mandates.

What is Israel's secret that is not to be revealed? In essence, I think, it rests on the investment of our ethnicity with our ethos. There is a crucial sense in which an ethos cannot be taught without being vitiated and cannot be shared without being destroyed. That is the sense in which people, including our people, speak of the God of their fathers, and the intimate sense in which children partake of the ethos of their parents—not because it is a precept they have been taught to speak but because it becomes a value of their own. Elie Kedourie wisely sees that Toynbee's demand that we "give up the national form of the Jewish community's distinctive identity in order to become, without reservations, the missionaries of a universal church" is only the last "somersault" of the same genocidal urge that earlier led Toynbee to denounce Judaism as a "fossil" outcropping of the ancient Syriac civilization and allowed him to cheer Israel's enemies and to equate Zionists with Nazis. As Kedourie rightly argues, "There is no reason to believe that sharing a 'great spiritual treasure' requires its possessors to divest themselves of their identity."[54] Indeed there is every reason to expect that the reduction of Israel to its mission is a sure form of self-euthanasia, for the means by which the message has been kept alive, not merely on the written page, but as the ethos of a culture, will then be lost. As Kedourie patiently explains, the teachings of Isaiah, "Deutero-Isaiah," which Toynbee professes to hold so dear, were not promulgated as rhetorical slogans; indeed, "the prophet's strictures and exhortations were addressed not to abstract individuals but to a community bound, as such, to God by a covenant."

Burke says that history is a pact between the present and the past and generations yet unborn. If there is a secret to Israel's survival that other nations did not know long ago in R. Ḥelbo's time, it is in the way in which we reappropriate our past through critical rediscovery in each generation, not to glorify but to recapture what is appropriable. We seek what is ours not because it is ours but selectively, reviving what is good in the values and thinking of our forebears and projecting those values further, in forms appropriable by our posterity, guided by the idea of God's absolute perfection and the impossibility of accepting any lesser principle as absolute. Yet a crucial term in all of this is "ours," just as a crucial subtext in all the blessings by which we pray is "our," when we say "Blessed art Thou, O Lord, our God." The first-person plural pronoun is not the focus of the blessing, yet the blessing cannot be pronounced without it, and in blessing God we become blessed by God. There is no critical appropriation and the propagation of any culture without the *we*, and the *we* of Israel is empty without its reference to the Highest.

Thus it is not the particularity of our ideals that we value, nor is the universality of our values a mere abstraction. Our mission to the nations is not to try to make them share in our particularity but to invite them to strive for perfectibility in themselves. We adopt what is appropriable from the ideas and ideals of others—Midianites, Greeks, Syrians, Europeans, Americans—as we expect them to learn from us. We discard what is not appropriable, even if it has been our own. History has taught us and the clear themes emerging from our tradition and refined of dross by our philosophers have confirmed that not every value leads to survival and growth, not every law is a law of life. But this lesson is not one that can be taught by words alone, any more than the formulations of Sophists or other professional teachers of success can capture the idea of the good life in wise sayings or clever nostrums. Wisdom must be morally appropriated to be of real value, and Israel's proper teaching is by example, living so that the nations spontaneously say, Blessed is the people whose God is that person's God, who leads that people to their way of life. Only such responses fulfill the prophecy of universal blessing made to Abraham. Mass migration to the land of Israel, then, is not enough. *Aliyah* fulfills a *mitzvah* and a need, but our destiny is not fulfilled when Israel is collected in her land. That is just another magic substitution of part for whole and symbol for reality. It answers to a dream of restoration and can be achieved on a wide scale, as can other elements of the messianic dream. But it is not historic redemption.

The function of messianic conservatism in Judaism, then, is not to combat messianic yearnings but to remind us, constantly, of the full meaning of our aspirations for personal, national, transhistoric fulfillment—a meaning that is ethical, spiritual. It is also political in impact, but not wholly political in basis, and certainly not magical, not revolutionary in the sense of seeking to subvert the processes of history or tyrannize over the transformation of human nature. We cannot simply engineer changes that require penetrating and comprehensive moral perception. Rituals and education can foster but cannot determine a change of heart. As Maimonides argues, the *mitzvot* of the Torah are sufficient to its aim. An excess of such means is an overdose, destructive, not productive.[55] No surrogate will achieve the same end. For just this reason, the apocalyptic, in imagination or in praxis, is largely counterproductive. It does not yield our desired goal because it seeks action through violations of the natural and human covenants, for whose sake that goal is sought.

Rabbi Samuel, author of the famous ruling that the edicts of the Imperium are law (*dina d'malkhuta dina*) was not a great supporter of political rebellion against Rome. He accepted the ruling power (Gittin 10b) and urged that clothes should not be rent in mourning for those who fell in the struggle against the Empire. So it is not surprising that he argued for the anti-apocalyptic thesis that the only difference between the life we know and the days of the messiah is the subjection of Israel. In rejecting apocalypticism he rejected the projection upon the cosmos of the revolutionary frustrations of his countrymen; turning the world upside down would not bring to fruition the hopes embedded in the biblical ideals. Yet Samuel held to the idea of a messianic age and insisted that such an age could not be achieved while Israel was subject to alien power but only through Israel's autonomous pursuit of her prophetically envisioned destiny and mission—the fulfillment of her law and attainment of its promises at home and the dissemination of its ideals abroad—as biblically laid forth.

TODAY, IF . . .

Just as no icon, archetype, or surrogate brings about the messianic age for us, so no mechanical transformation of social relations or transfer of title to property can effectuate the necessary changes. That too would be a magic substitution of names and notions for realities, declaring that this father figure rules the state or that class owns the means of production, when what is needed is an opening of human hearts to one another as fellow subjects whose ends are worthy of respect. The point is not that changes are unneeded but that the most real and lasting changes come from within. Even the Torah, as a document, symbol, or ritual form, cannot substitute for moral change. The transformation of character is not equivalent with adherence to the Law. Rather it is the practical aim toward which the whole Law drives. The immediacy suggested in the talmudic reading of the psalms is the immediacy of moral choice to each of us at every moment.

But here we confront a problem. If the transformation of the messianic age is moral, how can it be lasting or universal? For morally each of us is free. The messianic age is not a robotic utopia. But the radical contingency of moral choice entails the moral necessity for each of us to define an individual moral vision. It thus entails radical contingency as to the future; and moral perfection, even if reached and agreed, would remain contingent.

Our answer is that the messianic age does not homogenize humanity or even a single nation, nor does it neutralize or supervene upon the moral necessity of choice and self-construction. What it does do, as the method of the Torah makes clear, is place the institutions of society in the service of our moral and intellectual growth, enhancing our capabilities for freedom and judgment and promoting the social integration that in turn strengthens humanity, not only materially but morally and intellectually. Justice is made stable and dynamic by the progressive strengthening of an ethos of respect for deserts. This is the virtuous circle I cited in arguing that our Law is not utopian. The stability of the messianic age rests not on ever more repressive sanctions against individuality but on the support provided for a thoughtful ethos through the fulfillment of the commandments of the Law, and on what that ethos in turn creates to raise the sights of our humanity still higher.

Neusner's comprehensive studies show that Judah the Prince did not include the messianic idea in the Mishnah (although Sotah 49b has it in a *baraita*).[56] As a code of law, the Mishnah needs no direct reliance on this concept. Its purpose is to determine how we ought to live, not to project (as in the prophetic idiom) what we shall become by following the Torah's precepts. But this difference of focus, say from that of prophecy or liturgy, reflects a return to the perspective of the Torah itself. The Mishnah focuses on life—not as an alternative to soteriology, but as a vigorous answer to the questions of soteriology. The messiah is not a magical or revolutionary figure who intervenes to save Israel from her historic fate but rather is the means to the fruition of her destiny and that of the world.

The figure of the messiah emerges in the Talmud, Neusner observes, in the apodosis of a series of conditionals, all moral, all bound up with our fulfillment of the Law. The conception openly contradicts the vulgar notion that God will simply send an external savior to redeem Israel from subjection. But it reaffirms what the prophets had always said, that redemption depends on adherence to the covenant and return to the Law. It was the teachers of the Mishnah themselves who gave the messianic idea this now familiar moral structure. But the Mishnah transformed that idea not from an active to a quietistic mode but from a militant to a moral tack. Allowing for the shift from the scriptural to the rabbinic idiom, we can say that they returned it to the moral basis that its origins in prophetic thought required.

R. Yohanan b Zakkai said: "If you have a plant in your hand and they tell you the messiah has come, first plant it and then go out and welcome him." The remark does not express rejection of the idea of the messiah or distaste for messianism. Nor does it propose passive waiting for redemption. It sets messianic expectation in a rather realistic framework, as an event that might actually occur and must be reckoned with in pragmatic terms: Life must go on, food must be grown. The counsel of the "young" to rebuild the Temple leads only to a camouflaging (*s'tirah*) of the true historic situation. The counsel of the old, to bury the Temple, is the constructive one. Only so do we get on with the life and growth that provide the context for "salvation." As Neusner explains, Ben Zakkai overcame his self-doubts when he recognized that his role was not to confront Vespasian and save the country as Hezekiah had done with Senacherib at the gates. Rather the academy at Yavneh was Ben Zakkai's sapling.[57] What Ben Zakkai planted in reformulating the moral and spiritual life of Israel in terms of the rabbinic ideal was the deeply buried root from which Isaiah's sapling would spring. For rabbinic teaching made a way for the moral and spiritual life of Israel to continue without the concrescence of the Temple. The most effective action is not always of the kind that most satisfies romantic imagination. Quiet pursuit of the purposes of the Law allows the dynamic of the Law to fulfill itself, through the evolution of its concepts in thought and practice, and through the working of the ethos of the Law upon the character of individuals and the nation.

The quest for moral and intellectual perfection is not mere waiting, nor is it a quest that becomes irrelevant once the rebuilding of Zion is underway. On the contrary, that rebuilding provides it with a critical context. Clearly it is wrong to expect redemption as a result of passivity. As the rabbis put it, Israel can expect no messiah solely by virtue of past desert; the merit of our forebears ran out in the days of Hezekiah. Some authorities, to be sure, argued that God would redeem Israel for his name's sake.[58] But God can hardly be said to act for his name's sake in redeeming those who are positively undeserving or unready.

R. Joshua b. Levi explicated the twenty-six *hodu*'s or acknowledgments of Psalm 136 as expressing thanks for the twenty-six generations sustained by grace until the giving of the Torah. Thereafter merit became the basis of judgment. Even so, R. Joshua seems to have urged that Israel's suffering is sufficient grounds for her redemption. In the aftermath of holocaust, exile, and destruction, many have echoed his sense. It is enough for the bereaved to observe the laws of mourning; no new initiative is demanded.[59] But this leaves us with two questions: (*a*) Does God's judgment of Israel bear no relation to his judgment of the world? The notion is frequently contradicted in both prophetic and rabbinic texts. (*b*) Do Israel's deserts, conceded to be relevant to her redemption when her sufferings are cited, have no relation to her activity? That notion is repugnant to the entire Mosaic scheme and symptomatic only of the exhaustion of spirit that results from persecution and exile themselves.

To Israel, stricken with grief for the destruction of the Temple, the exile, and worse, the reassurance that the messiah is yet to come is neither a deception nor a counsel of passivity. Scripture speaks of all events as acts of God. But that does not obviate the imperative to act. The commandment "six days shalt thou do thy work" remains in force, even though we say that "all is in the hands of Heaven save the fear of Heaven." When Micah promises that God will redeem us from exile (4:6) he is not urging passivity and does not undermine his own activist summation of what God expects of Israel (6:8). The consistent message of all the prophets was and remains that Israel's destiny rests on her moral choices. Thus Amos (5:18) warns his countrymen against their eagerness for the day of the Lord and cautions them that it will be a day of darkness, not of light: God's day is not simply a new creation, apocalyptic destruction, or "renewal" but a judgment that calls due the accrued deserts of humanity. Amos knows his people are unready for such judgment. His message is not the imminence but the logic of judgment. Creation will endure; so will God's rule and law. Judgment lies in the consequences of our acts. It is these that we must heed, not the distracting notion of an external cataclysm.

Yet even in the words "It is sufficient for a mourner to observe the laws of mourning" we can discern, through the exhaustion of spirit, a glimmer of the messianic vision. The words find their echo and in a sense their answer in the thought of Emil Fackenheim, when he argues that some act of Jewish consciousness is the obligatory response to the holocaust, if we are not to give a posthumous victory to the Nazi scheme.[60] Even on so slender a rhetorical thread as this it is possible to recrystallize the full richness of our messianic idea. For the notion of performing some Jewish act takes meaning only in the context of the larger historic aspirations of the entire people of Israel, whose regulative goal is the messianic age. The spiritual exhaustion which seems to breathe the language of quietism thus translates itself into minimalism; and that minimalism, dressed out (like Malamud's Fixer) in the ancient garb which alone can give authenticity to its content, proves tantamount to an undiminished prophetic hope of the world's transformation through Israel's perfection of her own moral life. The most basic law of mourning is the imperative that life must go on and morally must go forward.

To become an obligation a goal must be compassable as well as worthwhile. What can we say of the relevance of messianism in such terms? The material blessings held forth by the Rambam seem far more accessible now than they could possibly have seemed to the contemporaries he addressed with his confident predictions. The moral transformation seems, if anything, more remote. But the intellectual revolution, still taking place, which has vastly improved the material human condition through invention, theory, and the spread of education, as well as through improved techniques of hygiene, communication, production, and distribution, shows the possibility of radical and unexpected change which can affect the entire human population. Is a moral transformation on such a scale impossible?

Improved standards of civility, like enhanced prosperity, indeed may become factors in the promotion of such a change, as Maimonides suggests and recent political experience confirms. There is no iron law, of course, that requires they must. Decadence, anomie, and violence are as likely manifestations of an affluent life as are peace, love, and justice. The radical contingency of choice remains—and morals remain relevant. But there are some heartening signs. One cannot say after the experience of the present century that humanity has become more humane. The tools of violence, like those of peace, have been raised to more efficient forms. But we may be, as a race, we humans, somewhat less tolerant of violence than in earlier ages. And that may be a sign for hope—unless our intolerance of violence itself takes violent forms.

The problem of channeling our responses to violence and our other impulses into creative tasks is one in which the best culturally borne, intellectually elaborated, and symbolically articulated traditions of Israel can continue to make their contribution. Whether it will flow forth as richly as it once did, making its new forms, in close articulation to the old, a cynosure of the world's moral growth, is very much dependent on our continued intellectual vigor and communal resolve. But the task is not impossible. To paraphrase Rabbi Tarfon, it is not up to any one of us alone to complete it, but we are not free to desist.

What then is the coherent and rationally comprehensible pattern of Jewish messianic thinking? To sketch it in summary: The Torah projects a system of norms. These may seem to be contradicted by the passivity of Israel's experience among the nations, first as a small, disunited community, then as a tiny nation beset by adversaries, dependent on alliances, then as a tributary land, then as a metic people in diaspora, then as an international scapegoat and victim of repeated attempts at genocide, now as a small nation, again beset by adversaries, still in part in diaspora, still in part within vassalage to a triumphalist empire on the verge of dissolution, and still vulnerable to exploitation as the scapegoat of the nations. Through all, the realization of the biblical ideals is to be confidently awaited, expected, and striven for, as it was awaited with breaking heart even in the Nazi death camps: not the norms without the promises nor the promises without the norms but the *mitzvot* as a means to the fulfillment of the promises, and the fulfillment of the promises as a means to the fulfillment of the *mitzvot*.

Apocalypse is only the outward symbol of the inner transformations that can and must occur. What is awaited is not the supernatural transmutation of nature but the natural transmutation of humanity—of Israel by the Torah and of the nations by the teaching and example of Israel. The two processes of redemption are interdependent. Israel is redeemed when she is given respite and employs it in the practical and intellectual fulfillment of the Law. Her perfection in accordance with the principles of that Law is the means by which she becomes a light to the nations, by which they all are blessed. She becomes the little child that leads them, not by coercion but by discovery, fulfilling through her own consciously chosen national and communal fulfillment the words of the prophecy: that the earth shall be filled with knowledge of the Lord, that out of Zion the Law shall issue forth, the word of God from Jerusalem.

◆ ◆ ◆ ◆ ◆

CHAPTER SIX

Whereafter?

The Torah knows no afterlife. The notion that individuals outlive their finitude as subjects is foreign to the Mosaic outlook, which is predicated in large part upon rejection of Egyptian thanatology and on a vigorous love of this life and its joys and possibilities.[1] In biblical thought what is strictly deathless is unbounded and absolute;[2] the mortal (*enosh*; rabbinically, *basar va-dam*) is finite and contingent. Genesis bespeaks the connectedness of finitude and contingency. Finite beings are counterparts but not rivals to the Infinite or pretenders to its limitlessness—any more than the Infinite pretends to finitude. If humanity partakes of transcendence—as experience argues that we do—it will not be by attaining ontic self-sufficiency.

The ritual laws of Leviticus 18 are all specifications of a single sentence. Just as the priestly laws of chapters 16 and 17 are specifications of a reform to the sacerdotal function, and the moral and ritual laws of 19 are specifications of the command "Ye shall be holy, for I the Lord your God am holy," so the laws of chapter 18 articulate the rejection of the ethos of Egypt and that of Canaan. The chapters are related. For the reform of the priestly function responds to the offering of "strange fire," a descent into the symbolisms of pagan religiosity. The confinement of sacrifice to the official cult (Leviticus 17) is an endeavor, ultimately successful, to contain the horror of the act of slaughter—to eliminate private sacrificial worship (as Maimonides explains[3]) because of its pagan colorations, which the Torah fixes as the colorations of violence. Correspondingly, the universal ideal of holiness, by which the holy nation of chapter 19 is made possible, is formed by the moralization of the idea of the numinous:[4]

> God spoke to Moses saying, "Speak to the Israelites and say to them: 'I am the Lord your God. You shall not imitate the practices of the land of Egypt in which you dwelt, and you shall not imitate the practices of the land of Canaan, to which I bring you, and you shall not follow their institutions. You shall practice my laws and observe my institutions, and follow them. I am the Lord. You shall observe my laws and my institutions, which a human being shall observe and thereby live. I am the Lord.'" (Leviticus 18:1–5)

The two assertions of God's Identity frame a rejection of idolatry—not in general terms, but aimed specifically at the death cult of Egypt and the orgiastic blood cult of Canaan. In the verses that follow, the ritual incest of Egypt, which seeks to hem in and hold the forces of life, and the human sacrifice, homosexuality, and bestialism of Canaan—again expressive of an eagerness to seize life's energies—are identified as abominations.[5] No promise of immortality is offered in their place. Such a promise would amount to an admission of absoluteness to the terror of death. Rather the Torah sets forth a simple, open, lusty love of life. The new laws—framed in the wilderness between a civilization left behind that was founded in the vision of death and the symbolism of the blood-drenched world to be displaced, a world whose sacred symbols discover vitality most vividly only in its violation—are laws of life by which we live in the full vitality of wholesome families, stable communities, prosperous cities, and a countryside blessed by the bonds of fellowship and the thought of God. This is the highest and fairest prospect the Torah has to offer.

SCRIPTURE AND IMMORTALITY

In an epic poem or mythic cycle a descent into Hades, crossing the terrain that separates our world from the dead, is expected, almost demanded.[6] The Torah offers no such episode. Rather, those wishing to find an afterlife there must themselves descend into vague conjectures about "the beliefs of the Hebrews," founded on few and random poetic uses of words like *sheol*—as though the Bible were written to reflect "the beliefs of the Hebrews." The excursions fail because the Hebrew Bible is manifestly a life-oriented rather than a death-oriented canon. The searchers weakly admit their lack of evidence by arguing that Israel would be unique in the ancient world if its people did not expect an afterlife. But ancient Israel was unique in many ways. King David was not startled to hear the "wise woman" say, "For all of us will surely die, like water spilled on the ground that cannot be gathered up" (2 Samuel 14:14). For that is the human condition, the mortality defined in Genesis by man's being taken from the earth, getting his bread from it, and returning to it in the end (Genesis 3:19). In his proudest moment the king himself could claim no more: "Thine are the greatness, the might, the splendor, the triumph, and the majesty—everything in heaven and earth. . . . All is from Thee and is Thy gift. . . . For we are but sojourners with Thee, mere transients, like all our fathers. Our days on earth are like a shadow, with nothing in prospect" (1 Chronicles 29:10–15).

The Torah, which guides rather than merely recording popular beliefs, does have a different value system from those of the surrounding nations. Its mythology is the reflex of theirs more in its contrasts than in its echoes. Even an alien observer who had hoped to focus spite upon the nation was compelled to acknowledge: "They are a people that stands apart, not to be counted among the nations" (Numbers 23:9). And Balaam sees Israel's blessedness not just in general righteousness (23:21, 24:5) but specifically in freedom from superstition: "There is no enchantment in Jacob, no divining in Israel" (23:23)—naming the very arts that Deuteronomy (18:10–15) links with the child sacrifices of Moloch. The death of Israelites is enviable, not because they outmagic mortality but because they die in righteousness. Theirs is a subtler yet surer way of besting mortality than is a putative life reached only through the gateway of the grave.

THE SEARCH FOR A BIBLICAL AFTERWORLD

Egypt's culture was shadowed by the idea of death. Israelites knew by the aches in their backs and the calluses of their hands the monumental scope of the Egyptian cult of death and afterdeath. They could joke bitterly with Moses: "Weren't there any graves in Egypt, that you had to take us to the wilderness to die" (Exodus 14:11). Their labor had built the royal tomb cities of Pithom and Ramses. But the law of Moses would not center on death and its aftermath. It rejects a landed priesthood, scarification, permanent debt slavery, and, of course, polytheism and idolatry; it declares unclean the sacred animals of Egypt and records the Egyptian abomination of sheep—Israel's ancient patrimony and sacrificial paradigm. It demands a *shabbat*—a stoppage of all labors like those that in Egypt had engrossed human hopes and thoughts in ceaseless industry and

Whereafter?

♦

service of the symbolism of death—dedicating one day in seven, even for bondmen, to freedom, leisure, joy, and contemplation. And it shuns elaborate funerary customs, Moses himself keeping his burial site unknown. The mummification of Jacob and Joseph reflects earlier, happier relations with Egyptian culture; but even that was for the sake of the return to the ancestral soil (Genesis 47:29–31, 50:2–14, 24–26; Exodus 13:19). In the law unfolded from the biblical foundation, the dead are buried promptly, without extensive ceremony or elaborate monument. There are no biblical rites for the dead and no role for them in biblical cosmology.

To call the Torah primitive because it does not reflect familiar ancient views of death is arbitrary and pretentious. To call it unspiritual because it has no complex system of afterworldly judgments is to miss the central nexus between biblical naturalism and monotheism, the dovetailing of divine justice and the natural order that has been a central theme of ours. The preoccupation with death that leads many to deem an afterlife the central concern of religion may find exotic a culture or religion unpreoccupied with death as the great looming fact of life. Yet death is rather unimportant to the Torah, and Spinoza is a true child of the Torah when he writes: "The free man thinks of nothing less than death, and his wisdom is a contemplation not of death but of life" (*Ethica* IV, Prop. 67).

For the psalmist the traditional notion of *sheol* is sufficient shorthand for the idea of death. Little is said of it that is not negative. Typically, it is argued votively that the dead are silent and darkened; God should therefore spare one to life and the pleasant duty of praising and thanking him in song.[7] So the emphasis, when death is contemplated, is turned back to life. The poet has reason to live. His theme is the joy of survival, the bounty of creation, the more than merely neutral fact of being. It is awkward to say that the dead are not; more natural to say that they are gone down to silence and the grave. But it is not proposed, paradoxically, that the dead live.

Jacob speaks, still bitter with the loss of Joseph, "I shall go down mourning to my son, to *sheol*" (Genesis 37:35), not expressing but implicitly denying any hope of meeting him there. The rebels swallowed up alive by the earth (Numbers 16:30–33) clearly do not reach these lower depths alive. *Sheol* is figured as the place to which the dead depart (Deuteronomy 32:22), without at all detracting from the fact that they are dead. Thus Saadiah, drawing comprehensively on the diction of the canon, translates by a cognate of the words *terra* and *tellus*, the Arabic *tharâ*:[8] Abraham, in being "gathered to his people," is merely said to die; he joins his ancestors in that he too is dead.[9] There is no metaphysics behind the metaphor—on the contrary, it tends to exclude eschatological elaboration. Any cosmic meaning is pinned to the idiom, not deducible from it.

The prohibition of necromancy (Deuteronomy 18:11) marks the intent of the Law to free life from the grip of the idea of death. That Saul consulted a necromancer and experienced an apparition (1 Samuel 28) shows only that the king went outside the law and his own edict to satisfy an obsessive quest. The act reveals the king's state of mind. So does his recognizing Samuel in the apparition, repeating what Saul had heard from the living Samuel and what he had dreaded hearing, that the kingdom was rent from his hand. The message might have come in other ways. The witch perhaps is needed only so that Saul may assure himself that it is not his madness that speaks. The story no more endorses the reality of ghosts or efficacy of witches than the first scene of Macbeth reveals Shakespeare's opinions about witchcraft.

Normatively, it is the Law that speaks. A later prophet can only exclaim at the absurdity of seeking counsel "for the living from the dead!" How can the dead, who are nothing, direct decisions of the living? "When they tell you to inquire of familiars and wizards that gibber and mutter—should not a nation inquire of its God!" (Isaiah 8:19). The guidance we need, Isaiah argues, is found in the Torah and our own experience (*te'udah*). Any contrary source "has no light" (8:20). A desperate and disquieted monarch might seek aid from ghosts and witches,[10] but there is no place for them in the daylight world of the Torah. The God of the universe is a God of life, and only vulgar superstition links his name with a spirit world whose denizens are the residues of human guilt, appetite, and fear.

If ritual incest and orgiastic frenzy evince a transfixed fascination with the fact of death, banishment of such symbolisms fostered banishment of afterworlds as well, along with the ethos those symbols sustained. The urgent quest for an afterlife is calmed by a life-centered outlook, rooted in an integrated and well-individuated rather than isolated and alienated personhood. Since guilt and fear are linked, overcoming the fear of death depends on overcoming anxiety and its symbolisms. Thus the Torah's images of the pleasantness of pleasant ways—the ways of life.

The rewards promised by the Torah are all, as we have seen, consequences and constituents of adherence to its Law, achieved in this life as we live it. They are bound up with its simple goods and opportunities for our fulfillment. Their fruit is the realization, through the generations, of projects beyond the powers of a single individual or generation—but which integrated individuals can readily appropriate as their own. The natural punishments of the Torah, too, as we have seen, lie in the limitation of our degrees of freedom. So there is no biblical need to supplement this life with another that is different in its categories or more definitive in its sentences. On the contrary, the faith of the psalms in the working of justice in this life is sustained throughout the Bible. Even in the Book of Job, where that faith is stringently tested in a dramatic thought experiment devised to reflect the human condition at its most severe, an afterlife is not reckoned among the proposed solutions—except by discontented glossators.

The Book of Job *should* ignore the possibility of an afterlife: Restitution does not justify Job's suffering, and an afterlife would not undo his losses or those of his loved ones. The frame tale's conclusion with Job's restoration reminds us that horrors have an end. It softens but does not warrant the sufferings or teach us their meanings. Neither would an afterlife give greater value to life than life holds intrinsically. For even to justify life as an anteroom to the hereafter is to say that the value of this life must be intrinsic; otherwise, it would be impossible to exclude the argument that our recompense should have come without the trials. If life is not worthwhile in itself, there would be no justice in making endurance of its trials the price of admission to an afterlife. Thus Saadiah, who upholds transtemporal recompense, rightly insists that the purpose of the hereafter is not simply to grant pleasure but to requite desert. Only through authentic existence, with all that it demands, can God's purpose be realized. The Torah places being above nothingness and life above death. That is the real issue, and nothing extrinsic is relevant; the sufficient and appropriate justification of life is that good is possible in it, that survival is not only possible but more likely than its alternative, that growth and joy occur at all.

Job is eloquent in his recognition of finitude: "Thou liftest me up to the wind and makest me ride upon it and dissolvest me—for I know Thou wilt return me to death, the abode appointed for all that live" (30:22–23). "Recall that like clay Thou didst fashion me and to dust Thou wilt return me—Didst Thou not pour me out like milk and curdle me like cheese? In skin and flesh dost Thou clothe me, and with bone and sinew dost Thou knit me up. . . . Lo my days are few and feeble. Leave off with me that I may take respite, before I go, not to return, to a land of dark and gloom, a land murky as dark itself . . " (10:9–11, 20–22). Death is the object of the metaphor. To reject Job's premise of its emptiness and irreversibility is to trivialize his questioning. Our personhood commands the body but is existentiated through and sustained by that body and so made vulnerable through it: "Remember that my life is but wind; my eye shall not see good again. . . . A cloud dissolves and is gone, so one who goes down to *sheol* will not rise up" (7:7–9). Job can think of death as surcease (3:17) but not as recompense; and there is no reason why he should. The only positive character death has is its perfect definiteness, removal from the contingencies of hope and fear. Hence David's abandonment of self-mortification when he learns that his child is dead (2 Samuel 12:13–23). Death is a leveler; this Job knows.[11] But his knowledge, prior to his enlightenment by God, is not yet complemented by the deeper understanding of the price at which life is acquired.

Mortality is the price of personhood. This is what Job initially does not see. Yet the elements of his answer are contained in the matter of his complaint: "For a tree there is hope. Even if cut down, it may sprout again. Its shoots will not fail, if its root is old in the earth. Though its trunk be dead in the dust, at the scent of water it will bud and branch like a sapling. But a man dies and he is helpless; a person perishes, and where is he then?" The very ambitiousness of the human project, our claim to individuality, assures the irreversibility of our death. Job does not yet compass the implication, but he clearly confronts the consequence. "Water faileth from the sea, a river is ruined and parched. And when a man lieth down and doth not get up, then until the heavens are no more he shall not awake and shall not be roused from sleep" (Job 14:7–12). It is on these terms, clearly, on these terms only, that Job will be reconciled with life.

For Job there is no solacing thought of an afterlife: "Comfort me, comfort me, my comrades, for the hand of God hath touched me. Why do you pursue me like a god, insatiable for my flesh! Would that somewhere my words were written down, would they were set in a book—with an iron pen graven in lead upon a rock forever. I know that my redeemer liveth, and at the end He will testify on earth, after my skin and all this is destroyed, when my flesh is gone. But I would behold God while still in my flesh—I myself, with my own eyes, and not a stranger's, when my kidneys have rotted in my breast" (19:21–27). This is the passage that Origen, Jerome, and others would make into a triumphant affirmation of Job's faith in an afterlife. Jerome renders it: "I know that my Redeemer liveth, and I shall be raised up from the earth on the latest day and be enclosed again in my own skin and see my God with my own eyes. . . ." If Job said that, why does Zofar answer him (20) with continued comforts as to the judgment of the wicked in this life, and why does Job brand his comforts as empty (21:34) and accuse his comrade of mocking rather than comforting him (21:3)? On the contrary, Job finds tragic irony in the fact that God has the power to vindicate him and yet does not spare him. Bildad's "consolation" (Job 18) amounts to an admonition to believe in divine providence. But Job replies that he has never doubted providence. That is just the difficulty. For it is providence that torments him, as is the consistent burden of his outcries. He does not doubt that when he is dead and his body is decayed God will manifest himself; his wrongs will be requited or avenged and his innocence made clear. But like the victim of a homicide whose death is requited or avenged by a redeemer (*goel*), he is spared not at all by posthumous vindication.[12]

Job's view of death remains constant: "When the tally of my years is spent, I shall travel the road by which I shall not return" (Job 16:22; cf. 6:11–12, 7:6–7, 10:20–21, 30:21–23). And his plight is universal: "Man, born of woman, brief of days and full of trouble—blooms like a flower, then withers; he flees like a shadow that abideth not. And dost Thou consider such a one and bring me to judgment with Thee? . . . Thou has appointed the bounds he cannot pass. So give over from him and let him have respite that he may like a hireling live out his day" (Job 14:1–6). If there is an answer to this plaint, it does not come in the promise of another life that could not compensate for the many undoings of this one and would not be exempt by any guarantee from what Job sees as God's ironies. If suffering makes this life intolerable, neither more of the same nor any radically new state would justify what has gone before. Suffering is justified only if it is a condition of this life and this life is good. It is not justified as a condition of another life. For in that case one must ask why it was made such a condition and why this life itself was made incapable of justification. *The demand for an afterlife is a rejection of the intrinsic worth of the life we have. It flies in the face of biblical theology, morals, and cosmology because it clashes with the recognition of the goodness of being, which is the basis of that cosmology.* We can understand suffering as the condition of finitude, but not as the price of everlasting duration.

IMMORTALITY VERSUS AFTERLIFE

The horrors of exile, the ancient destruction of settled life and of the Temple at its symbolic core, the memory of the auto-da-fé and the immediacy of the holocaust prompt expectations of reversal and release. The long delay in the fulfillment of such hopes prompts sublimation: Our expectations shall be answered, if not in time then beyond it, if not in life then beyond death. The certitude and positivity of death make it a ready receptacle for displaced hopes. Its emptiness cooperates. Only an absoluteness of some affirmative sort seems capable of answering and filling up the absolute emptiness of death. The hope for an afterlife, accordingly, arises as the reflex of a human hatred of annihilation. We project our temporal experience beyond the limits whose very recognition seems to human passions and appetites to demand their negation. Yet neither hope nor fear provides firm grounds for expectation; and Scripture, the literary source of the values and ideas on which our notions of life after death are founded, promises no such denouement.

Conventionally the threat or promise of an afterlife has been presented as of crucial relevance to morals. Enlightenment *philosophes* in particular, who needed to defend their moral earnestness before a dubious, partly clerical public, showed alacrity to adopt the afterworldliness which once recommended itself to the world-fatigued philosophers of late antiquity, but which ill assorts with modern worldliness. The deists, urged on by Hobbesian or Rousseauvian notions of a civil credo, argued outspokenly that the hope of transcendent futurity was the mainstay of morals—a line of argument that Plato (in the *Euthyphro*) had rejected as corrupting to religion and that Epicurus had refuted with equal rigor as destructive of morality. In Kant, where the issue of heteronomy should have excluded any effort to found morality on the expectation of transcendent rewards, the idea that an afterlife is critical to morality is not discarded but rationalized and resublimated into the notion that immortality is a necessary precondition of moral choice. Kant thus echoes in elegant philosophic tones the more vulgar claims of men less eloquent than Rousseau, that a man who does not believe in afterliving is simply not to be trusted.

Epicurus had argued to just the opposite conclusion from premises remarkably similar to those of Kant, uncovering a fundamental heteronomy in the predication of moral judgments upon afterworldly expectations of any sort. Extending the logic of Epicurus' position and translating its thrust for our context, where we recognize the problem of heteronomy as a problem of appropriability, we can say that no act dictated by considerations of otherworldly expediency could at the same time be performed for its own sake, in recognition of its intrinsic merit or the intrinsic value of its goal. Only an act done for its own sake can be said to be done "for the sake of Heaven." In hewing to the logic of autonomy or moral candor which is a vital feature of every thoughtful moral system, Epicurus remained a faithful student of Plato and disciple of Socratic moral earnestness. Plato had rightly set aside all questions of immortality in the *Republic* as long as he was considering the intrinsic worth of justice and its component virtues. It is an expression of his earnestness that when he does return to immortality, he seeks to derive it from the nature of justice (as the virtue that integrates identity) rather than proceeding in the opposite and all too familiar direction of trying to found justice upon an extrinsic requital.

To us it seems clear that thoughts of an afterlife are less likely to purify morality than to muddy its judgments. So the claim that morality requires immortality is a red herring. It becomes unnecessary for us to seek apologies for the Kantian (and later Nietzschean) notion that ontology must postulate whatever morality is thought to demand. The proximity of moral, religious, even political concerns remains insufficient to warp the geometry of judgment to our "needs"; and we can be thankful that it is, when we observe the bizarre extremes that human passions may present as "needs" with Jamesian or existential pretension. Whatever claims are to be aroused in behalf of human deathlessness must state their arguments and confront the sorry evidence and the disconfirming case made by our embodiment. For we do know that our body grounds our personhood, and the impact of that fact must be confronted like any other: the full weight of the congruity between our mental and our physical natures. The so-called moral argument, then—like the argument from nostalgia used at funerals—is of value only for the light it sheds on motives, not for providing any grounds.

The only passage of the canonical Hebrew Scriptures that clearly expects judgment of individuals after death is in the Book of Daniel. Speaking of the apocalyptic future it states: "At that time Michael will arise, the great prince, who protecteth thy people. It shall be a time of trouble like none since nations came to be. But at that time thy people shall be saved, all who are written in the book. And many who sleep in the dust will awaken, some to life eternal, some to disgrace and eternal shame. The wise shall shine with the splendor of the firmament and those who lead the many to justice, as the stars, forever and ay." The passage closes with two similes and is followed by enigmatic symbols whose meanings are not disclosed even to the prophet (12:5–9) in whose poesy they were formed —although modern scholars can discern references to the events of Daniel's era. It cannot mean anything literally to say that someone will shine like the firmament or glow like a star. What, then, is the figurative glowing? How will those who have slept in the dust be vindicated? Plainly the splendor of the wise is the counterpart of the shame and disgrace (not torment)

visited on their adversaries. The glowing, then, evokes the ancient metaphor of shame as darkening the face and honor as lightening and brighten-
ing. The righteous are in honor and glory, eternally; the wicked are discredited. The reference, then, in the first instance, is to the messianic age,
with its exposure of false values and expectations. But what of the "life
eternal"? The awakening of those who sleep in the dust extends the contrast of honor and shame, the absoluteness and permanence of the vindication of the righteous: There will be no Reich of a thousand years. The
culmination of history will see the vindication of right. The temporary
triumph of injustice gives it no permanence. It is the psalmist's fire of
thorns. But beyond that, the seeming defeat of innocence is specious
—illusory where it is not temporary. Death is not temporary, and those
who sleep in the dust are dead. But the text demands that we find a sense in
which even the dead are not defeated absolutely. And once that suggestion
is made numerous senses are readily seen. To be humbled by history is not
to be dishonored. Even in death there remains not only the possibility of
historic vindication but also the fact—the absolute fact—of righteousness. This ultimacy gives meaning to sufferings undergone, not by righting
or avenging wrongs but by transcending them.

The subtle and subtly enunciated idea of transcendence here takes its
place alongside the idea of historic vindication. The certitude of that vindication indeed becomes the vehicle expressing the subtler notion. Temporally evil may seem strong; and temporarily, wickedness may triumph. But
the day will come, the passage states, when a reevaluation will be required
—made necessary by manifest facts of history. The roles and relative success or failure of many who are now dead will be reappraised. In the
triumphalist language of Israel's enemies, even glory and humiliation will
be reversed, unalterably—by the clarity of the case, the manifest superiority of the enlightened who imparted justice. Glory will belong to some
who "lie in the dust," and shame to the unjust. But beyond these are the
realities to which they make reference. Behind honor duly paid lies the
character whose goodness is indestructible; and behind shame duly accorded lies veritable shamefulness, again a fact not ever to be erased.

The prophecy gains its point and poignancy from the recognition that
death is not a real absolute, despite its actuality and the absoluteness of its
emptiness. Vindication is possible and transcendence can be real even for
those who are really dead. When Isaiah calls upon the dead to awake and
sing (26:19), it is because they have *not* "won victory on earth" (v. 18).
Daniel promises that victory will yet be theirs. To read such promises as

offers of another life is merely to shift the subject, as though the novelty or subtlety of the suggestion of transcendence were something uncomfortable, to be exchanged at the earliest opportunity for a less demanding idea. Transcendence of death is naturally expressed in the language of immortality. But immortality is a far more important notion than the paradoxical image of surviving death can possibly convey.

The apocryphal 2 Maccabees (12:38–46) mentions a sin offering by Judah Maccabee in behalf of fallen troops of his, with whose bodies evidence of pagan worship had been found. The text urges that Judah must therefore have believed in resurrection: "For had he not hoped that the fallen would rise, it would seem superfluous and vain to pray for the dead" (2 Maccabees 12:44). But Judah made only a sin offering, commemorating the fallen without condoning their lapse. As religious militants, the Hasmoneans were called upon repeatedly to make religious innovations — as in their rulings about warfare on the Sabbath, and in purifying and rededicating the desecrated Temple. But obsequies for the war dead give slender evidence of belief in resurrection. Better texts are available to attest to scriptural ideas of immortality, and the themes they open up are of greater interest.

The same source (2 Maccabees 7) tells the famous story of the seven martyred sons, placing in their mouths, as they died of tortures, expressions of faith in eternal life. To take such statements as literal affirmations of the unreality of death is to trivialize the sacrifice martyrs make while in no way strengthening the case for personal immortality. For martyrs give up nothing if they do not really die. And if the seven sons, like many others, believed in an afterlife, or if the narrator of their story endorsed or stood in awe of such a belief, the fact would have little consequence for later readers apart from the meaning that might be found in such transcendent faith. What all martyrs affirm by the testimony of their deaths is not the unreality of death but its lack of ultimacy. Death is not a god and cannot be the ultimate value ordering our choices or framing our epistemology. *Here* we *can* learn through the referential translucency of others' beliefs. For they can call attention, through the acts they inspire, to dimensions of value that command departure from the seemingly unquestionable dictates of nature's general deontic structure favoring survival, pleasure, repute, and all speciously self-sufficing goods. This outcome is hinted at in Plato's meditations written soon after the martyrdom of Socrates, when Socrates is made in the *Laches* (199) to define courage as a kind of knowledge that evaluates wisely what risks are worth taking and what losses are worth bearing. Plainly what martyrs bear witness to, in virtue of which they are said in our tradition to die (or live) for the sanctification of God's name, is the reality of transcendence.

On this reading a choice made by martyrs testifies to an insight about what is truly better or worse. An ancient text conveys the confidence of a simple woman and her children that even for survival some options must not be chosen. Their earnestness naturally adopts the language of resurrection—just as its counterpart is transposed into myth by Plato when he seeks to interpret the death of Socrates and resorts to Pythagorean and Orphic images and tales of transmigration to express the subtle nexus between timelessness and individuation. But the moral reality behind the symbol, which the martyr's sacrifice expresses authentically, is the recognition that survival is not the ultimate claim upon us. Dignity, integrity, uprightness, truth itself, and justice may transcend it.

ETERNAL PUNISHMENT?

In circles where an afterlife is most vigorously upheld, the belief is not confined to affirmations of eternal bliss but rather takes a disjunct form —the familiar yoking of unending bliss for some with unending torment for others. Structurally hell seems almost a necessary counterweight to heaven, as though by some perverse logic the sufferings in one paid for the pleasures in the other. Such bipolar visions betray like a signature their origins in projective imagination. It is not right or logic but spite and bias that organize heaven and hell in concentric circles around ego's significant others. We readily make out the earthly implements of torture, projected and enlarged in the fervid visualizations of the afterworld, and clearly discern the boundaries of affiliation preserved there: political, confessional, factional. How curious that the transnatural should mirror our communities, that pleasures and pains which no theist can take as absolute measures of value should be the coin God uses to pay out the wages of merit and sin—and in so doing exact from his victims and visit upon his favorites the dreams of those who tell the tale.

Greater confidence might be inspired in claims about God's intentions toward the blessed and the damned if the periodic revelations of those intentions were focused less parochially. It was hard to believe that the long war of 1980–88 in which children were called upon to die as martyrs for Iran and Iraq was veritably a holy war, when the fulminations of its authors so frequently reverted to a sense of personal grievance. And greater confidence would be inspired by soteriology were it less prone to direction by the elements of drama. Deathbed conversions, for example, are the stuff of storytellers' art; doctrines of their potency or ironic defeat make God a sentimentalist. Such stories, hardened into dogmas, pervert the idea of residual deserts and redeemability. Insights like those of Dostoevsky, transmogrified into doctrine, become stagy and problematic bits of melodrama.

The marks of projection mar the idea of permanent damnation too. That death is permanent seems unproblematic, given the finitude of our powers—and our deserts. But that suffering should be permanent does seem problematic. *Cui bono?* At whose behest are the natural limits set to all things human now removed? Some crimes cannot be expiated—not because bigger potatoes need more baking, but because expiation can be impertinent. The notion of infinite tortures suggests that fact, but misleadingly. Consummate evil is not a power that grows and must be balanced by a counter-power: Evil festers, flares, and gutters out. Its ill effects are not undone by punishment. Penitence and purgation may expiate wrongs—if they are expiable. But if they are not, extending chastisement into new reaches of pseudo-temporality will add nothing.

If we are to think of punishment in terms of immortality, then, it must be not through the spurious notion of eternal suffering, as though evil could sustain itself limitlessly to bear sufferings without end, but rather by way of self-alienation from the transcendent within us. Thus Maimonides states: "The greatest retribution is for the soul to be 'cut off' and fail to attain That Life, as it is written, 'That soul shall be cut off utterly, through its own fault' (Numbers 15:31). That is the annihilation which the prophets symbolically call 'the pit,' 'ruin,' 'destruction,' 'Tofet,' 'the worm' and all the other terms whose theme is that of destruction—inasmuch as this loss is irrecoverable and irreparable."[13]

Even if sins were purged in sufferings beyond the grave, endured by beings no longer capable of sin, the idea of eternal punishment would remain internally incoherent and incompatible with monotheism. It is internally incoherent because even the transcendent wrongs of finite beings are finite. So infinite punishment would violate the proportion required in retribution. It is inconsistent with monotheism because it undercuts the conception of God's absolute goodness and ultimate power and fails to take account of the identity of the two. Origen, who held steadfastly to the logic of expiation and was unwilling simply to transform the God of Abraham into a theatrical bestower of destinies and plights, argued that in cosmic time all evil ultimately will be assuaged; Satan himself will be reconciled.[14] We need not hold to Origen's image of the winnowing of souls to recognize the integrity in his account. Like any sound philosopher he balks and stops dead at inconsistency: There is no motive in the God who is good absolutely to leave evil unresolved. For God to fail in reconciling evil would be a lapse either of his will or of his power. So even if acts and sufferings in a life after this *could* erase wrongs done here, a consistent monotheism holds no room for unending punishment. The admission of an eternal hell would be an admission of God's finitude and the absoluteness of evil—the very point the prophets sought to exclude when they voiced the promise (Isaiah 25:8) that death too shall die.

WHAT ARE WE TO EXPECT?

The wish for immortality and the fear of it have no bearing on the truth or falsity of judgments about it. What is relevant is the tension between the claims all living beings make to boundlessness and the limitation of those claims by one another and by the inherent boundedness of finite subjects. Pascal and later James seized upon justification by faith to suggest that if we want immortality badly enough, we have but to will ourselves to believe in its reality.[15] But the groundwork that makes possible such an inference is an anthropomorphism in which emotions of divine pleasure and displeasure are crucial and human feats of faith are more significant for requital than, say, moral, mystical, or ritual virtues.

The ritual quest for immortality is trivial, and Pascal rightly set it aside: "masses and holy water" are at best avenues to faith. Pascal knew that faith can be trained, since it is a discipline, and a virtue less of the intellectual than of the moral self. But he also knew that ritual is no substitute for commitment, since symbols do not replace what they represent. Yet mystical and moral claims to immortality are harder to dismiss. Mystics pursue immortality through gnosis, seeking to touch the boundlessness of the divine. Phenomenalists are curiously reticent about such claims. A Sartre can argue for the reality of nothingness from the experience of loss or disappointment; a Kantian can argue for the confinement of experience to the sensory from the phenomenal ineluctibility of temporality. But when temporality vanishes—as in ecstasy or dreamless sleep, or even in the timeless aspects of rational understanding—we are not accordingly assured in phenomenalist quarters that new categories have come into play. More regularly we are informed that reveries do not constitute "experience"—as though they were unreal—and that thoughts cannot intend more than the sensory matter they are made of, there being no rational (or timeless) intuitions.

It seems evident to me that thoughts as much as words can and do intend far more than they arise from. It is thus that they can be conceptual. Thoughts must attain the rational, if not through pure intuitions then constructively, if they are to operate categorically, universally, or necessarily—as they do in mathematics and in science. Hence the force of Plato's remark (*Republic*, 522) that leaders must study mathematics if they are to escape confinement in the world of becoming. Abstractions and signs allow us to reason about what we can never simply imagine, sense, or hold in memory. And in this way, obliquely, we do intend what we cannot engulf or encompass. What many mystics intend is the wholeness of being. There is no consistent way for a phenomenalist to gainsay them, but non-phenomenalists must allow that mystics too might apprehend more than they can directly intuit—that their sense of boundlessness might portend what they cannot truthfully lay claim to. Perhaps a mystic reaches too far when he imagines that he has *taken in* the unboundedness of the Infinite. But intellectually, to intend is to apprehend, just as linguistically to refer is to signify. The Torah alludes to our propensities toward infinity when it refers to our creation in God's image, and our philosophers signal the nature of the relation when they specify the human mind as the bearer of the affinity.[16]

Focusing on the moral avenue, we see again the disproportion between our finitude and what it seeks in boundlessness. Plato argued courageously that what integrates the soul makes for its indestructibility. The argument is fittingly placed in the *Republic*, since it is there that Plato shows, at its fullest and most glorious, the truth of the identity of strength and goodness, the dynamic by which both social and psychic stability rest on virtue in its public and inward forms. But integration is not immortality; to hold together a state or a personality is not to make it deathless. The perspective of Genesis instantly makes clear why this is so. Temporality does bespeak eternity, but not its own. The Socratic swan song of the *Phaedo*, the argument that the mind will be immortal to the extent that it is kin to the Ideas, fails when the analogy fails between consciousness and its eternal objects; for the mind is not the pure idea it may intend. In the same way the moral argument of the *Republic* in behalf of deathlessness fails. For what is integrated is composite and, by Plato's own reasoning, subject to temporality, change, and dissolution. Plato's discovery (in variance, conflict, tension, and dialectic) of the basis of temporality undermines his expectation of immortality and underscores the fact of finitude. Whatever we are, we are not gods.

Plato wisely sought our moral history's reward constitutively in the logic of our character and actions, but he did not fully confront the fact that if we had the power to integrate the self beyond survival of the changes which our virtues can breast, we would not be the sort of being that needs virtues. So convinced was he of the divinity of our essence that he glossed over the fact that the same arguments which show the divine to be immune to vices render the divine transcendent of virtues as well. Our moral virtues accordingly impart no deathlessness from within. Is deathlessness, then, given from without? Clearly not on Pascal's grounds. If there can be no passions in God, the mythic eschatology that rewards faith with immortality is impossible. If natural theology achieves its maturity in the recognition that God's justice operates through nature rather than despite it, an afterworldly eschatology is contrary to the naturalism of natural theology as well.

RECOMPENSE FOR FINITUDE?

The idea of an afterlife, traditionally, is a moral demand addressed to the human condition at large, demanding negation of the conditions that deny us access to our goals—hereafter, surely, if not here, must be a world more to our liking. But our frustration lacks the power that imagination has to erect a compensatory universe conforming to our wishes. It is curious that our discontent often regards justice as being served only by another helping of the same pudding—like the prisoners who complained that prison food was bad, and in such small portions. Maimonides writes: "Do not think so lightly of the reward of the commandments and of a man's living the perfect life in truth and integrity as to suppose that it consists of eating and drinking well, espousing fair forms, wearing fine linen and brocade, dwelling in ivory pavilions, using silver and gold utensils, and the like, such as these foolish, thoughtless and dissolute Arabs imagine. The wise and thoughtful know that all such things are worthless nonsense and seem great goods to us in this world only because we have bodies which demand such things"—and make us vulnerable to suffering.[17]

An afterlife, of course, is not intended to be quite as bad (for those who are rewarded) as the present life has been for them—or quite as pleasant for the wicked. Yet even in a beatified existence or an inferno, the familiar categories of experience tend to be maintained—not just because they are familiar, I suspect, but because of the function afterworlds are called upon to serve. Requital would be meaningless without moral continuity and some liability to joy or suffering. But these are the very conditions that make us vulnerable to pain or susceptible to pleasures distinct from what we merit. The more an afterlife resembles this life, the less adequate it will appear to those who are disappointed with this existence and its frustrations. An immortality that exempted us from vulnerability would demand transcendence not only of death but of time, change, individuality. But that would leave no moral being to be requited. To offer surcease, immortality must involve transcendence of particularity. To offer requital it must preserve that very particularity as a foundation of moral continuity.

One may complain that what one wanted is not more bad food but more and better, a second go on terms that commend themselves more highly. But such a claim is founded on a misunderstanding of the terms we have complained against. Our capacity to abstract has played us false: We imagine that *this* might have been different without a change in *that*. Specifically, that individuation, memory, and the rest might last while temporal finitude, liability to change, and disruption—materiality, in short —are abolished. But our ability to imagine disembodied finitude, or at least verbally to propose it, in no way establishes its possibility. Without temporality, memory, enjoyment, and suffering would be contradictory. The immortal soul that enjoys or suffers a post-mortal history and experience is a projection to which a specious materiality and temporality have been assigned. Recognizing that individuation depends upon the same categories that necessitate potential victimhood shows us the ontic futility in the idea of life after death. The inevitable vulnerability of the "in itself" cannot fail to affect the "for itself." As an insect Gregor comes to enjoy insect pleasures and postures and loathe human ones, ultimately even to accept his insect death with the same sense of fittingness as his sister finds in the new vitality of her youthful limbs.[18] The human object grounds the personhood of the human subject. Any transcendence we may enjoy arises from that point; any that does not is not ours.

Quite apart from the incoherency of the demand for individuation without contingency, our hankering after a fantasy realm of accountability without vulnerability is based on a moral illusion. Specifically, it overlooks the fundamental fact about desert which I have sought to explicate, that the desert of finite beings is coextensive with the claims they can viably support. Death is the exhaustion of those claims. We may deserve more from one another than we receive, but no finite being deserves more or less "from life." Existence itself is a boon, a miracle in which the All triumphs over nothingness in many ways. No being receives less in this regard than it deserves, for this would assume that it might have been other than the thing it is. But it might have been nothing at all. Avoiding that abstraction and looking at beings as already constituted, we see the precise equilibration of their powers to their métier and the capability of marginally enhancing their mode of being—two further existential boons, by which all beings have the limited power actively to be and dynamically to forward what they are. Only a specious essentialism would expect such powers to be realized equally in every case. Only a spiritless diffidence would deny that it is ever realized at all.

In nature, I have argued, no good goes unrewarded; good, to the extent that it is such, tends to consolidate the claims each being makes by uniting virtue with virtue, strength with strength. For the same reason, no evil goes unpunished. Evil tends to undermine its chooser. That is its character, regardless of its disguises in trappings of power, honor, pleasure, or reward. Singling out moral evil, we may feel dissatisfied with the speed or the completeness with which malefactors are brought to book. But assuredly they are brought to book, in and through the logic and dynamic of their own actions, their self-isolation, and ultimate self-destruction. Their potential victims are protected to the extent of their strength and adequacies as individuals and members of well-integrated communities. They are protected further by the inviolability of their innocence; and that, I shall argue, speaks to the nature of transcendence in a far richer and more coherent sense than does the equation of immortality with an afterlife.

Nature, this life, is an elaborate system of homeostases, a constant adjustment of balances. The subtlety of the process may elude our imaginative grasp, but the continuous equilibration remains. There is no zeroing out of a final balance, no closing of the books. As at Las Vegas, this door remains open at all times; the game is always open for play. That is the promise of the rainbow, the covenant of God with nature and with humanity through the stability of nature. Unlike Las Vegas, the odds are stacked in favor of the players and in favor of their strength, insight, skill, and catholicity of concern. But that does not mean there will never be a gain by one lacking in moral concern or a loss of life by one whose perfection was nearly complete in one regard or several. There can hardly be complaint of such an outcome when the stakes themselves—even the perfection that consolidates itself as merit—were contributed by the House.

MULTIPLE LIVES?

For some of us the very idea of immortality is wrapped tightly in the myth of reincarnation, souls transposed from body to body across the bounds of life and death, or even species. Accompanying these souls is their *karma*, reflecting their good and evil tendencies and bearing their destiny. Justice rests in the promotion or demotion of souls according to their merits, cosmically conceived. Or perhaps one attains fulfillment in disengaging from the eternal cycle by renunciation of all desiring. Sometimes transmigration is rationalized by reference to an oversoul, where we are perfect and at one with the divine. In our individuated forms we are so compromised with mutability that we may not recognize our former selves. But the barrier to such knowledge is not absolute: We find traces of our former selves in dreams, *déjà vu*, hypnosis, and trance.

At my university, some time back, we were honored with a visit by an eminent figure from an Eastern sect, accompanied by his youthful acolyte. Preparations of course had been made. My colleagues in the neighboring host department had been instructed to prepare a dais, lest anyone be seated above the spiritual dignitaries. Announcements went out detailing the background and experience of the visitors. The high-ranking personage had clearly earned his accolades in years of training, discipline, scholarly pursuits, meditations, travels, and leadership. But his disciple was heralded as the more distinguished visitor. Although a mere lad by comparison, he had been recognized by his mentor as a famous saint of the eighteenth century.

What does it mean to say that the same person has recurred without the usual spatio-temporal contiguity for external observers, continuity of consciousness and memory for the subject? If there were two persons living in different places, the contents of whose consciousness and memory were distinct, we should hardly be inclined to regard them as simultaneous appearances of the same individual.[19] If occasionally such a subject had a powerful impression that he was identical with the other, many explanations would do far less violence to our knowledge than does the supposition that the two were one person.

Morally, too, there is a difficulty. Rinpoche *A* bears a kind of credit balance for the achievements (and charisma) of Rinpoche *B*, who died two hundred years ago. Yet he does not share the other's skills, does not recall the books his former self has studied or profit on a conscious level from the experiences Rinpoche *B* learned from. *A* does not appropriate *B*'s choices, although he suffers for *B*'s faults. The two are quite distinct on a conscious level but fused indissolubly below the surface. Agency is neatly severed, accountability and responsibility falling like two halves of an orange into sundered centuries so that as *A* I reap what *B* has sown. But then, of course, there is the claim that I am he.

He is not then someone else but is myself. Yet many of his characteristics are not mine. He may speak a different language, love a different wife, father different children. Whose genes do they bear? The lure of the exotic may tempt the hypothesis that I am he. But what meaning can the claim have? Does it express a desire for catholicity of experience? Is my alterego a person or a mere abstraction? My second self may be of a different sex, a different race, or a different religion. Rarely is he of a wholly different order of being. Prior selves do not seem to come from realms of which we have no notion. Indeed they are not of different categories of being, even when those categories are familiar. They are not qualities or times or places; still less are they selected among those hybrids which ontological relativity may have taught philosophers to handle gingerly. They are not fusions of bandannas with the color of last night's sunset, or of yesterday with my daughter's score in jacks at the sixth game played on her seventh birthday. Imagination demands that they be things—not even parts of things like your dog's left ear. They have a function to perform, and their nature is limited by that function, even though—or rather, because—that function lies in the psyche of the beholder.

Dreams are called to witness in behalf of transmigration, and dreams are full of category shifts. But dreams too have work to do. No one, I would venture, except perhaps for Lewis Carroll, has ever dreamed of being a category error. If we take as second selves those exotic persons who emerge now frequently from UFOs, equipped to communicate in our language, they are creatures capable of entering our imagination—our often quite conventional imagination—and doing work there. They took a different form in an age that thought little of exobiology, but then too their form was pertinent to the urgencies of the moment.[20] If they are to serve our yearnings or our other needs, prior selves must be describable in familiar terms. Yet they would hardly be of value as exotics if identical qualitatively with what they professedly replicate; and so they rarely are.

If prior selves are distinguishable from their doubles, what does it mean to find that the two are identical? Can what is distinguishable be identical? If Rinpoche *A* lives today and *B* was born and died in the eighteenth century, in what sense are they the same person? The likeness is supposed to be arithmetic. How does this work? I lived in part of 1944, in all of

1956 and 1963; I lived when delivering the Littman Lectures, and I live now as I make my final revisions to this text. Many of my characteristics are not constant through all of those times. Yet that does not diminish my claim to arithmetic unity. No one on the basis of the differences in my characteristics in those different times would deny that I am the same person I was then in the same sense that he would affirm because of the differences between us that I am not the same person as you.

The discontinuity among my states at different times, evidently, is deceptive. If I trace the time interval from my birth to the present, I find that for every moment t there is a state of my being at that moment, which has most of its characteristics in common with those of my immediately preceding and succeeding states—far more, as long as my identity is preserved, than it has in common with the characteristics of any other being. It is in virtue of the preservation of the bulk of my characteristics from moment to moment that identity is said to be maintained. Part of this continuity is the maintenance of matter—the bulk of my matter from moment to moment. Part of it is a continuity of spatial and temporal positions. Each position I occupy is very close to the last and the next. Each moment I live lies cheek by jowl with the one before and the one behind it, and each process I undergo is closely related in intimate but explicable ways to specific related processes that closely precede or follow it. All this is a consequence of the fact of my embodiment.

Material and geometrical continuities are critical to the maintenance of arithmetic identity because they underlie the continuity of qualities by which identity is maintained, not only in the eye of a beholder but also inwardly, for a being considered as a subject. Continuity of qualities includes that continuity of experience by which consciousness establishes itself as a coherent, integrated personality. Skilled writers of fiction know this, for they do not expect sympathy from their audience toward characters to whom no background has been given. They can generally expect some concern for characters (even unsavory ones) to the extent that the audience has participated in the criminal's experience—not shared it, literally, but followed the contours of continuity that give substance to its objects and identity to its subjects. Without continuity, objectively or subjectively, identity may well be lost.[21] Through continuity identity is established and preserved. And continuity is missing (*ex hypothesi*) between present and prior selves.

Michiyo Takeyama's poignant novel *Harp of Burma*[22] exploits to telling effect the ambiguity left open by reincarnationism as a mode of thought. A few days after the war in the Pacific has ended, the protagonist, Mizushima, a popular and lovable captain who often led his company in part singing, is apparently killed in a heroic attempt to convince a diehard body of Japanese comrades to lay down their arms rather than die in expressionistic futility according to the ancient samurai ideal of *bushido*. But just as there may be an ambiguity about the ontic standing of a song (Mizushima's troops are saved from an ambush because the encircling British hear them humming "There's No Place like Home"—which the Japanese soldiers assume to be a Japanese song), so also is there an ambiguity about the identity of persons. On a naturalistic level, it seems that Mizushima has improbably escaped the cross fire between the British troops and his besieged compatriots and has been nursed back to health. A changed man, he vows to stay in Burma and devote his days to burying his country's dead. He discards his uniform for a monk's robes and tells his homeward-bound comrades that they must transform their minds and hearts to the ways of peace.

Accumulating bits of evidence tell a different story. Still on a naturalistic plane, Mizushima has died. He has been replaced by another man of another race and culture, a man whose outlook complements his own in a line that guides the way to a transition from the fidelity of a warlike ideology to another fidelity more suited to the virtues of peace and understanding. Here the story departs from naturalism, drawing upon the Japanese tradition of "tales of rain and moonlight" and the corresponding Western traditions of Gothic romance. The evidence grows increasingly clear and finally explicit that Mizushima and the Burmese monk are one and the same person. Ambiguity is transformed into a fact that does not answer to the categoreal continuities of natural experience.

The unnatural or supernatural character of this fact bears the thrust of Takeyama's theme. It may be impossible for certain observers to determine whether Mizushima has died and been reincarnated, whether he has been "replaced," or whether he has survived miraculously, but transformed. On one level it makes no difference, and this is the level to which the ambiguities of the tale call attention, creating continuities where the natural facts of life and death deny them. The ambiguity of Mizushima's identity—whether he has died and been reborn or survived and been transformed—becomes a haunting symbol of the author's theme, the need for Japan to bury her dead, to retune her harp to the strains of peace, to accept life and friendship with other nations. The naturalistically irresolvable puzzle of Mizushima's fate—whether he has in fact died or survived, whether the strange and quiet monk is really the music-loving soldier—bespeaks the comforting message that the old virtues will not die completely (as militarist romantics may fear) when they have been transposed into a softer and more pliant key.

It is to convey such themes as this, I suspect, that poetry creates the idea of reincarnation, just as it continually creates and re-creates the oedipal myth, in part to express the opposite idea, of discontinuity in change. But to adopt as literal truth the symbols which carry a poet's theme is to turn insight into confusion and stultification. Takeyama wants to accentuate the presence of certain continuities in national consciousness which can survive and overcome the natural discontinuities occasioned by the deaths of individuals and defeats of nations or of particular cultural movements. A nation can be reborn, can rearrange the fragments of its consciousness over several generations. Vital continuities can overcome the disruptions of spiritual or moral consciousness—as in the transformation of the code of *bushido*, or of the Temple cult of Jerusalem. There can be transfiguration for individuals without death; and, for peoples, there can be national, cultural, spiritual rebirths. Nations must undergo such reawakenings as a condition of the spiritual growth which the continuance of life for a culture requires.

But an individual's consciousness cannot be fragmented any more than his body can be pressed beyond its limits if he is to remain an individual. I am not you. I am only myself. And, to the extent that I am a person at all, I am a single, self-identical person, the contents of whose consciousness (and subconsciousness, too, if the evidence about it can be trusted) are as distinct from those of others as the contents of my skin. What founds the molecularity of my identity is its existentiation in experience—through my proprioception and dynamic interaction with other identities. Without that distinctive, dynamic character of a single self capable of consciousness, there would be no identity to be equated or compared with that of others. Reincarnation, then, is unintelligible as a metaphysical hypothesis and irrelevant as a moral postulate. For it claims an identity between individuals whom it assumes to be different and assigns the deserts of one person to the lot of another—explains my fate not by the causal impact of others' acts and choices and the moral impact of my own but in terms of my accountability for the acts and choices of others, other selves, which it treats as my own, although I exercised no control over them.

Whereafter?

◆

Just as the poets and prophets of other nations may—indeed, must
—mean many things beyond the literal when they speak of reincarnation,
so the prophets and poets of Israel cannot be taken to speak literally when
they address the human virtuality by speaking of the future. The
literalization of prophecy and poetry is as deadening to spirit as the routin-
ization of charisma; and intellectually it is far more deadening. Reenliv-
ening our sensitivity to scriptural poetics is not the contrary of demythologizing. Rather, the two tasks go hand in hand. For we cannot take seriously
what we read as simple fable. We only dull its significance by assigning its
conception and gullible acceptance to a stereotypic audience invented for
the occasion. We thus allow a rather supercilious prejudice in the name of a
spurious historicism to flatten into insignificance the claims of the canon,
leaving any who still assume that prophets are creative or face a critical and
questioning audience to wonder how anyone could ever have taken their
words seriously—let alone held them to be inspired. The proper premise,
I would argue, in reading any poetry, especially prophetic poetry, is the
assumption that prophets, like other poets, use symbols, metaphors, and
other displacements to express concretely what cannot be said directly.
They speak of knowledge and understanding in terms of light, blessedness in terms of joy, peace in terms of rest, guilt and wrong in terms
of stumbling, moral accountability and spiritual reward in terms of
futurity.

The "after days," the *aharit ha-yamim* of the prophets, are not an ending
of time but a future transformation of history.[23] The prophets speak of
God's day as one of doom, judgment, the calling in of God's due bills.
Humanity is fulfilled in humaneness. Cruelty and unconcern bear their
own harvest, with mothers devouring their offspring in terrible sieges as a
corrupt ethos is brought to book.[24] Since the after days are within history,
they are not confined forever within the future. Some have already
occurred. Some are occurring presently. We are living in the after days of
our ancient forebears. The hereafter is now. When I speak of the present as
the hereafter, I am addressing community over time. All our projects in the
larger sense are left unfinished, to be carried forward by ensuing generations. Worthy projects carried on through generations may lead toward the
perfection of the human condition materially, morally, intellectually, and
spiritually. Alternatively, vicious cycles of frustration and confusion perpetuated through the generations and unrelieved by human energy and in-

sight become obstacles to civilizational growth and movement. What has all this to do with immortality?

In the *Kuzari* Judah Halevi seeks to explain the slight attention given to the afterlife in Jewish prayers.[25] Halevi does believe that the human soul will be united with God's logos when somehow disengaged from the body. But he anchors that belief in the possibility of such a union in this life: "One whose soul is in communion with the divine word while still taken up with the accidents and sufferings of the body is all the more apt and suited for that communion once free of this base vehicle." The point is underscored in a parable. An intimate of the king, so close to the royal presence that even in disfavor he is but entreated to return to his former ways, is criticized by his fellows for not beseeching the king's protection when about to undertake a dangerous journey. The others have spent their lives petitioning for such protection. He replies: "Madmen! Is not one who relied on him in time of safety more entitled to expect his aid in time of danger, even without voicing his request? . . . All my doings have been at his command and instruction, while you have honored him according to your own estimate and conjecture—yet he fails you not. How then will he abandon me on my journey, since I did not speak out as you did, but trusted to his justice."

The fable, Halevi explains, addresses those who do not accept the glosses of the Sages that find allusions to an afterlife throughout the Hebrew scriptures. Like the Ikhwân al-Ṣafâ', who criticized the kind of piety that turns to God only when all else has failed,[26] Halevi prefers a spirituality that rests in divine support continually and sees God's aid, grace, and justice in every moment of life rather than seeking it frantically only as death approaches. The common notion of immortality is only a reflex of our fear of death. Real immortality lies closer at hand. "What I would have objected to," the Khazar king remarks, "the infrequent mention of the hereafter in your prayers, you have already explained by demonstrating that one who prays for attachment to the Divine Light, during his life, who prays to see it with his own eyes and at the level of prophetic awareness—than which there is no closer approach to God for man—has necessarily prayed for more than the hereafter. And if he achieves this, he achieves the hereafter." This intimacy is the goal alluded to by poetic talk of deathlessness and underlying the calmer and more resolute pursuit of immortality. Spinoza captures it when he dissociates the incoherent idea of invulnerable duration from the sound idea of the eternity of the soul in its self-awareness as an aspect of God's thought.[27]

IMMORTALITY WITHIN THE WORLD

The Torah has its own idioms for the hopes that human longings for immortality can harbor. Abraham is promised offspring as numerous as the stars in the heavens or the sand on the shores of the sea (Genesis 22:17–18; see also 17:4, 20; 12:2–3). That certainly speaks to the values of a patriarchal age. Yet the numbers are transcendental rather than exhaustive, and the thrust is made qualitative by the further promise "through thy seed shall all the peoples of the earth be blessed." It is characteristic of the Torah that the focus of its promises, even as they grow more spiritual, remains in this world—a world not abandoned by holiness. Isaiah (64:3) speaks directly to the transcendental character of God's highest promise: "Never have they heard or harkened, eye hath not seen, beside Thee, what God worketh with those who wait for Him." Quoted in 1 Corinthians 2:9 and in the rabbinic and Islamic sources, these words become emblematic of a life that replaces this life. In Hellenistic and post-Hellenistic contexts alienation from this world is often taken as tantamount to attachment to the Highest Good—in much the same way that the upturned eyes of late ancient portraits instantly signal spirituality by portending otherworldliness. But in their ancient Hebrew context, where worldly justice is a cardinal means to transcendental holiness, Isaiah's words promise fulfillment of God's design *on earth*. The natural powers of brushfire and even the fire that sets water aboil are paradigms of God's act; the mountains quake at God's descent (64:1–2). The unseen wonders are an epiphany; they *will* be seen on earth by those who hope and wait for them. Stirred by the events of his time, Isaiah foretold the manifestation of God in history. But he drew his theme from the cosmic perspective of the Pentateuch, where God's act is seen in the law of nature and heard in the law for humankind. His words refer to this world and the undreamed potentials it holds for our self-transcendence.

WHEREAFTER

We have already discovered the dimension in which human history answers to its fullest potential and we gain more adequate moral dispositions to overcome the dialectic of warfare, hatred, and fear, which are its accustomed pivots. This is the dimension referred to as the messianic age. But our more comprehensive self-transcendence is called *olam ha-ba*. I do not think the rabbis were wrong to discover intimations of such transcendence in our sacred texts. But the suggestion of its futurity is somewhat misleading. When Maimonides refers to the proximity of redemption, urging that immortality is near enough right now that we can reach out and pluck it like an apple from a tree, he refers not to the temporal proximity of apocalypse but to the moral immediacy of choice. Immortality could have belonged to Adam—might belong to any of us now, if we reached out our hand and plucked it.[28] The key to understanding this is in recognizing that our immortality is not prolonged duration. Extended survival is no radical answer to the reality of death. As long as there are individuals there will be finitude. Even when the familiar causes of death are pushed back indefinitely to a minute fraction of their present prominence, or banished altogether, there will remain finitude of knowledge, trust, and capability. Immortality contrasts not merely with death but with any of these limits. It involves timelessness but also selflessness, catholicity of spirit, encompassing understanding, and that awakening of awareness which places us in touch with the harmony and comprehensibility of the universe that Halevi called God's word. We attain some measure of immortality, I argue, insofar as we attain transcendence of any of the categories of our boundedness and impermanence. It is not something to be sought solely by extending the confines of normal human life, but rather by enlargement of those boundaries. Our immortality is reached not after or in spite of death but in life and through it. Again the words of Maimonides: "The Sages called it the 'World to Come' not because it does not exist now and will come only when this world is gone—not at all. Rather it is real and exists now, as it is said, 'which Thou hast treasured up . . . which Thou hast made . . ? (Psalm 31:20). But it is called 'the world to come' because this higher life comes to a man after his living the life of this world, in which we subsist by body and soul, as all men must start out."[29]

The message we find in the Torah and the prophets is that immortality is to be sought not *after* life as its recompense, but *in* life as its fullness. It is not that Scripture has not heard of an afterlife or has never considered the human desire for extended survival. But the Torah does not consider survival, for which it sets so many wheels in motion, to be the highest value. The quest for persistence beyond the grave is misguided. Immortality is found in the practical and speculative dimensions of human existence—I would say, of ordinary human existence, but this dimension, naturally achieved by a kind of self-transcendence of nature, makes human existence extraordinary. The just human being, who unites the practical and speculative virtues (thus serving his own and all deserts) knows that mere survival is not the ultimate value and so can be confident even in confronting death

(Proverbs 14:32)—not because death is imagined to be the mere turning of a page; on that basis confidence would involve no courage but only faith that death is not death. Rather, he knows that integrity and insight are achievements *sub specie aeternitatis*, which even the fact of death, real death, from which there is no return, cannot touch. This is what Proverbs (12:28) suggests by the words "In sustained justice is life, and adhering to that path is immortality." Immortality, assayed by its power to stare down death, is all around us. The last place to look for it is after death.

We can judge the values of the Torah by what it sets against death, precisely because it does not imagine death to be unreal. Wealth and honor, even the dynastic illusion, are not proof against the corrosion of time (Psalm 49). Only the integrated life of the good person withstands that test. That is, only life itself and the values that support it can be ranged successfully against death—as the Torah proposes: "Behold I lay before you this day a blessing and a curse—the blessing of hearkening to the commandments of the Lord, which I command you this day. And the curse, if you do not hearken to the commandments of the Lord your God but depart from the road which I command you this day" (Deuteronomy 11:26–28). The blessing is life—the good and full life, whose acts and thoughts are not to be undone by time: "I call heaven and earth to witness as to you this day: Life and death have I laid before thee, the blessing and the curse. Choose life, that thou mayest live, thou and thy seed, loving the Lord thy God, hearkening to His voice and cleaving to Him. For this is thy life and thy length of days: to dwell on the soil which the Lord swore to give thy fathers Abraham, Isaac and Jacob" (Deuteronomy 30:19–20). Hearkening to God refers, of course, to the moral life. Cleaving to him refers to the intellectual and spiritual quest whose fulfillment, as Halevi and Spinoza saw, brings us to the closest intimacy with God.

The Torah, then, does not offer a substitute for life, some fictive construct represented as better than life in favor of which life is to be rejected as wanting. It offers life itself as the only real alternative to death. Immortality, in biblical terms, must be found within life, the only locus where a dispassionate philosophy would have deemed it possible but the last place where a disquieted philosophy would have thought to look. In this regard, we can say that Plato was right to associate immortality with justice. Indeed, Plato's theory of justice as the virtue that presides over and gives their due to all our other virtues, integrating individuals and societies and thus giving them stability and power, taught Aristotle how we can integrate the moral and intellectual virtues and so attain the good life, in which reason governs our acts and opens the way to the highest intellectual and spiritual attainments. Such an integration, as Maimonides showed at length, is the object which the Torah consummately lays out.[30] In many texts, the promise of immortality is voiced in the language of mystic experience, but its means are those of justice: "As for me, through justice shall I see Thy face; I shall be sated when I awake, with the vision of thy Presence" (Psalm 17:15). So it is not the mystic alone who "sees God." Anyone who fulfills the goal of the Law in living by the moral and intellectual virtues lives "in the presence of God"—seeing God not just in rarefied glimpses but as an abiding reality in life, sated with his presence from the moment of waking, as husband and wife are continually sated and delighted with one another's presence and not subjected to the frustrating trysts of furtive lovers or the excesses of sensual gourmands.

The curious kinship between mystic and sensuous excess is not surprising, since they share a common source and end point. One type of mysticism is called drunken, hinting at its irresponsibility, its penchant for antinomianism, pantheism, loss of balance. It was to this category (and not to authentic piety) that Novalis unfairly alluded in calling Spinoza a God-intoxicated man. Mystic excess, whether sought through drugs or through other surrogates, such as deep, hypnotic meditation, involves not a fulfillment but a loss of self which the wiser mystics acknowledge must be transcended. Thus Sufis argue that beyond a mystic's dying unto self (*fanâ'*) lies the true immortality (*baqâ'*) which is the object of the mystic's quest, a dying unto dying (*fanâ' 'an al-fanâ'*). Zen masters teach in much the same sense (although in a different idiom) that liberation occurs through the discovery of the extraordinary within the seemingly banal, not in mere escape from the quotidian. Like sexual excess, mystic excess begins in a misguided pursuit of immortality. It seeks to lose the human self, because it confuses the self with the conditions of its limitation. It ends by reaching what it sought—not transcendence, but loss of self. By sexual excess I mean promiscuity, sado-masochism, "ambisexuality" as classically described by Masters and Johnson and earlier (as Don Juanism) by Camus, who saw the nihilism inherent in what he called "the dandies' rebellion."[31] Mystic excess begins in the same misguided groping after immortality and ends in the same sensuous overload.

Drunkenness brings loss of balance and control, loss of the conscious self in which we are existentiated, through pursuit of an illusory larger self, a grandiose godlike self that cannot act and is tragically or ludicrously denied or travestied in the eyes of all who do not share the drunkard's stupor. Plato preserved balance when he defined our task as to become as like to God as humanly possible. Our task is the perfection of our humanity, its transcendence, to be sure, but transcendence as humans, not as gods—lest we suffer the fate of the monkey in Sandburg's poem, who, reaching for the nuts that had slipped from his grasp, lost those and more, and snatching for those in turn, lost all. To enlarge the consciousness is not to dissolve but to sharpen the focus by which alone consciousness is made possible. To transcend the ego is not to sink consciousness into primal incoherency, pseudo-infantile delusion, merging with the elements or the blurred and echoed voices of the race. It is to learn kindness and concern, to spread and cast the net of identity, not to ravel it.[32] Here, in the self-discipline of spirituality, which is the nerve of every religious handbook of mystic training and initiation, we discern again the reason why immortality can be attained only while the soul remains within the flesh, mastering and inspiring it, imparting an identity which can be made transcendent if it is not lost. For without that identity, grounded in the flesh, there is nothing to transcend, no ground to reach up from and perhaps beyond. With it there is a life to be made holy—beauty to discover, truths to be known, acts of kindness to perform.

The full of awareness of God's presence in one's daily acts (and nightly counsel with oneself) imparts a sense of well-being by which all the doings of life acquire the joy and certitude that mystics habitually ascribe to ecstasy. All things are done in the presence of God; and, as it were, at God's behest. Transcendence is everywhere: "I bless the Lord who counsels me —even for the nights when my kidneys school me. I set the Lord before me constantly. With Him at my side I will not falter. So my heart is glad and my liver rejoiceth—even my flesh lieth down secure. For Thou dost not leave my soul to the pit, nor give Thy favored to corruption. Thou showest me the path of life: To live in Thy presence is the fullness of joy. To be guided by Thy right hand is blessedness eternal" (Psalm 16:7–11). The point is not that the psalmist's organs escape corruption but that (even though his consciousness is seated in those organs) there is more to what he is and does that can be corrupted with his body, if he lives in the sight of God. The sense of life well lived founds the sense of immortality the psalm expresses. Every moment of joyful contemplation and integrity of action becomes a fragment of the beatific vision.

ETERNITY—ITS IMMEDIACY AND ITS EXCLUSION

A hint of the presentness of the hereafter is contained in the talmudic usage *yesh lo ḥelek ba-olam ha-ba*, 'He has a portion in the world-to-come.' Note the use of the present tense: One who enjoys the fruits of his own labor (Berakhot 8a, citing Psalm 128:2) has a portion in *olam ha-ba*. One who adds the blessing "hast redeemed Israel" immediately after the Eighteen Benedictions of the *Amidah*, without interjecting personal petitionary prayers, enjoys a portion in this transcendence (Berakhot 4b), appreciating the blessings he has rather than suspending himself in purgatorial yearning after ever more elusive goals. The sense of fulfillment is voiced in the use of the perfect tense—*hast* redeemed Israel. Whoever recites Psalm 145 three times each day *has* a portion in *olam ha-ba*. For in the poetry of that psalm he sees transcendence as a present reality: "Thou openest Thy hand and satisfiest every living thing" (Berakhot 4b, citing Psalm 145:16). The study of Torah, rearing a child in its study, even walking a few steps in the land of Israel, practice of humility and diffidence to seeking credit for oneself—all touch the Transcendent. So does the experience of uttering the grace after meals over a full wine cup; and the awareness that this is so helps to make it so. For the lengthy and poetic grace we sing keeps the *mitzvah* of enjoying and appreciating the blessings we are given—experiencing them *as* blessings. The Talmud finds a paradigmatically transcendent character in all these experiences (Berakhot 51a, Pesaḥim 113a, Ketubot 111a, Megillah 28b, Sanhedrin 88b). As Jaspers writes, "The real truth in doctrines of eternal life is not that we shall go on existing temporally but that there are values and decisions which are not merely temporal, because they incorporate an indestructible significance. We should not be concerned with some illusory future existence but with the spiritual struggle whereby the moment can unite the temporal and the eternal."[33]

But the naturalness and even the arduousness of our access to the transcendent does not imply the ordinariness, secularity, or even omnipresence of transcendence. God is omnipresent, but our access to God is in the measure of our pursuit of justice and all the intellectual and moral virtues it comprises. It is not to be awaited passively or to be pursued narrowly by closing down the mind to experience at large. Our contact with God is not a separate and isolable phenomenon (to deem it such would be a species of idolatry), not a particular flavor distinct from all those that can be tasted; it is no flavor at all but rather the dimension of transcendence that might attach to any experience entered into with integrity—a dimension which is lost when pursued sensuously, like a "high." When we deny that God has an image we deny as well that God has a color or a scent, an ethnicity or a gender. Idolatry is any notion that God might be "experienced."

Despite God's omnipresence and the ubiquitous accessibility of the transcendent, it is not difficult to exclude the transcendent from one's life. Paradigmatically, one who crosses a stream behind a woman has no share in *olam ha-ba* (Berakhot 61a). Taken as a threat that lewd eyes are damning, the assertion that great joys reserved for after death will all be canceled if a man is tempted to look up a woman's dress seems a rather empty pronouncement. Taken as stated, it contains a subtle truth: that a man who spends his time in calculating how to see a woman's thighs robs his experience systematically of its transcendent dimension. His mind will be on other things. A child might cry so hard for a piece of candy that he ignores the jewel clutched in his hand.

One who shames another publicly forfeits transcendence (*Baba Metzia* 59a)—not only because of the moral wrong but because the frison of broken tact blocks the way to the transcendent. A similar masking is an occupational hazard for scribes, teachers, physicians, magistrates, enchanters, butchers, and synagogue beadles (*Avot d'Rabbi Nathan* XXXVI 5). All of these handle holy things in a manner likely to profane, by familiarity or by a psyche-guarding irreverence that leathers over the sensibilities. We might add undertakers, coroners, and police beat officers to the list. A child-abuse worker, to apply R. Nathan's thesis in a contemporary context, may see too much incest, rape, and abuse to retain that freshness through which the transcendent, Halevi's logos of God, is manifested in the small wonders of daily life. Likewise the combat veteran and the prostitute. Even a teacher (to revert to R. Nathan's list) engages in a dialectic over trivia which can in some measure deaden the heart to the miracle of growth and learning.

It is tempting to assume that the rabbis polemically barred adversaries from *olam ha-ba*—hence its denial to those who reject resurrection as a biblical doctrine (the Sadducees), those who reject the divine revelation of the Torah and the talmudic "*apikoros*." But there is a somewhat deeper reading. For what motivates the polemic? All these "heresies" in some measure deny the reality of the transcendent *in this world*—in conquering death, inspiring humanity, or governing nature and our lives. To the Epicurean any assertion of divine concern with the world is the height of superstition and impiety. But for those who take it as the goal of life to incorporate the transcendent in the mundane, the immediacy and elusiveness of the Divine look very different. Even one who pronounces the Tetragrammaton, we read, deprives himself of a portion in *olam ha-ba*. This is not a mere polemical stricture. For the ineffability of the Tetragrammaton symbolizes God's transcendence. To seek to pronounce it is, as it were, to relativize what is absolute—rendering God a thing delimitable in language, an archetype on all fours with others in the genus of pagan gods and promptings. The Bible critics who write out the letters meant to spell the name of Israel's God, as though they were the proper name of some tribal deity, are succumbing to an occupational hazard like that of magistrates and surgeons whose work inures them to manhandling the holy—to the point that it becomes impossible or difficult for them to entertain the transcendence suggested by that name. Bible scholars often remythologize reductionistically when they most intend to demythologize, transforming the conceptual pointers of scriptural language, deracinated, into fables, carefully catalogued in files of now pointless motifs. Like beadles and butchers they might wish to preserve something of the awe that first spurred on their studies or watched over their work. But use militates against it, as the clinical ethos can against the very reverence for life that medicine should serve. Plato recognized dialectic as the midwife of higher awareness, and the analogy was carefully chosen. A midwife does not bring the seed necessary to conception; dialectic operates but does not think, and exegesis is empty without inspiration. We can understand the wisdom of the Torah in not suffering most priests to witness the dismembering of the Sanctuary —"lest they die" (Numbers 4:15–20)—lest their sensibilities be hardened and they lose the portion in immortality that their work is meant to open up to others.

Forfeiture of *olam ha-ba*, although expressed talmudically in categoric terms, is plainly not absolute. Otherwise there would be no system to the talmudic utterances, and none would need to be taken seriously: All would reduce to mere expressions of pleasure or displeasure. But in fact there is a hierarchy among these pronouncements. The most general rule is that all Israel and the righteous of all nations "have a share in *olam ha-ba*" (Sanhedrin X 1, *Tosefta* XIII 2)—regardless of the flaws which may limit that share in any given case. The doctrine dovetails with our interpretation, that *olam ha-ba* is not a deferred reward of infinite life after this life but a brush with the Absolute in the here and now, which may enlighten a moment or a life.

TO CULTIVATE OUR IMMORTALITY

Three areas of activity pursue the transcendental, not to control but to foster it: art, science, and sports. Wit is one synthesis of the three. Morals is another. For in wit we artfully integrate our knowledge into playful pattern. In morals we give practical expression to the apprehension of deserts whose recognition we have practiced—as if in sport—in our moral growth and training. Religion (sometimes thought humorless or even joyless by advocates as well as critics) is another endeavor to channel our experiences toward transcendence. In monotheism we find an avenue toward the One God in all values whose authenticity as values we acknowledge. Moral values are expressions of Transcendence; the possibility of extending and receiving moral regard is a miracle expressive of divine grace. But so too is the creativity of the artist, which realizes and celebrates the values given in experience. So is the creative work of the scientist, which captures the transcendent dimensions of reality in another way, synthesizing an understanding that overcomes mere positivity of data and demonstrates in the intelligibility of nature the miraculous wisdom of its order. Even when individual artists or scientists or moral agents do not interpret their acts as apprehensions of the sacred they may have that character. They lose it only by a profanation which violates rather than realizing the sanctity latent in the given.

Art discovers eternity in the instant when the creative artist apprehends those values in nature which transcend mere positivity—the formal values, for example, of truth and authenticity, of pattern, beauty, rhythm, symmetry, or complex order; or such material values as texture, timbre, tone, color, even scent and savor.[34] The material aesthetic values proper are clearly dependent on time and space; and the formal, intellectual ones are dependent in turn on the material ones. Yet when any of these is captured in consciousness, articulated or reapprehended through communication, the boundedness of time and space is in some measure overcome. So also with the apprehension or invention of higher-order patterns—harmony and counterpoint, for example, where rhythms, timbres, tones, and colors are combined sagaciously, or the novelist's or dramatist's discovery of patterns of interaction which resolve the nuances of motive and character.

I make these comments not to justify or glorify the arts or even to attempt to explain what they accomplish for their practitioners and recipients. To develop a theory of the arts would be the work of another book. But I point to the arts as an avenue of immortality, not in the cheap sense of fame or recognition, which can be by-products of artistic achievement, but in the sense that every creative act is a self-transcendence and thus a triumph of life over finitude, an immediate, natural and inalienable snatching of a portion in immortality. Creative work is neither the production of novelty nor the display of the bizarre; it is the apprehension, elicitation, elaboration of patterns of order as yet unseen or too easily lost sight of. Each one of those patterns (and there are, within our natural world, infinities of infinitudes of them, even within a single human glance or complex of emotions or drop of water or bouquet of wildflowers) has a deathless or, less anthropopathically, a time-transcending system of dimensions which the artist can pursue and indeed enlarge for himself and others. To do so is to partake of eternity in a far more real and far more valuable sense than any atavistic notion of the survival of the dead can provide.

Science too pursues such finite and manageable dimensions of infinitude —the timeless truths of laws and patterns; the elegance, comprehensiveness, and economy of universal theories; the practical and speculative satisfaction of explanatory hypotheses, which accord control not only in a technical but also in an intellectual sense. Again, as in art, there is the elicitation of pattern. And in science as in art there is the free selection of formal values to be weighted in accordance with one's always answerable sense of the proprieties emergent from (but never simply dictated by) the initial given.[35] The eliciting or devising or mimetic abstracting of pattern, in nature or history, is as much the province of the scientist or scholar as it is that of the artist. But where artists can maximize creative freedom by determining for themselves exactly what weightings to assign to each of the formal and material values they accord recognition, scientists are subject to the further discipline that the external values to be imposed on their constructs must maximally respect the material given. The successful theory or scientific construct (as distinguished from the successful work or act of artistic apprehension and expression) must accord with a set of data, as wide and as elegantly construed as possible, taken from those findings which are to be held as facts or as the factual implications of other constructs —in much the same way that a mathematician acquires a maximal commitment to coherence by abstracting away from other values. It is in this sense that while an artist may be said to construct a world, the scientist endeavors intellectually to reconstruct *the* world. But the artist too is responsible to truth, for the focus of the artist on specific issues and values does not only abstract from other dimensions of reality but heightens the requirement of responsibility to the values and realities drawn to the fore.

The prominence of measurement and the demand for formal rigor in scientific reasonings are expressions of scientific earnestness. Since the world on which scientific constructs are to be projected is no virtual world but nature itself, all constructs to be accepted must fit together, both with one another (since they have a common reference) and with that reality whose dimensionalities they seek to name, coordinate, and describe. The artist can afford to consider only *aspects* of nature or experience. The scientist— or community of scientists—considers one aspect at a time but pursues a goal of comprehensiveness to be achieved only at the price of deep abstraction. In eliciting the patterns where a passive or inattentive observer might have detected only "noise," the scientist, like the artist, is transcending the limitations of the given—his own finitude and the subjective irrationality or incomprehensibility of nature and experience—making contact (to use the favorite medieval image) with nature's transcendent intelligibility, in which the perfection of God is manifested on the plane of finitude. This again is the attainment of "a portion in immortality"—a portion which befits our finitude without confining us to that finitude in every respect.

In athletic sports the triumph is more physical and moral than intellectual. As in art or science, or even religion, the real triumph may be masked by the accompanying pomp and ritual, *éclat*, invidious aggression, sensation, bruit, lightshow, and parasitic decadence. But sports, like art, seek to recapitulate—in a setting controlled in the case of sports by rules, records, and measures, and heightened by competition, discipline, and training —certain unique moments of human self-transcendence. Athletic sports seek these moments not through mimesis, as in the arts, but through performances in a challenged yet in some measure standardized environment. The object is not only to minimize the risks likely in the pursuit of physical extremes while maximizing certain dimensions of challenge but also to strip away extraneous and confounding accompaniments, to isolate the moments of achievement—much as a scientist seeks to isolate a particular effect or cause, or as a novelist or dramatist seeks to isolate a specific or particular complex of motives, emotions, actions, and responses. Sports, then, pursue virtue for virtue's sake. Strength, power, speed, agility, control, strategic cunning, endurance, cooperation, coordination, and numerous other physical, moral, social, and intellectual virtues are deployed to no immediate pragmatic end. Their very isolation from praxis or techne imparts to their development, execution, and exhibition an aesthetic, celebrative quality that the pragmatic exploitation of sports activities for military, valetudinarian, spectacular, or other extraneous purposes can only partly mask.

Unlike scientists or writers, athletes do not achieve the isolation of particular values by intellectual abstraction. Their variables are not symbols in the first instance, and their terms are not fictions or constructs but movements and performances. Yet athletes work in a realm of virtualities nonetheless. Their goals are token goals and possibilities, and the extremes they pursue are given definition (as in art) not solely by experience but by ideals and by structured, focused endeavor. Although athletic virtues are developed and deployed outside the workaday or extraordinary contexts of human struggles for survival where such virtues normally arise,[36] they remain powerfully referential to those contexts. Again there is answerability to nature and the constraints of the human condition; again there is creativity, a virtue demanded by our limitation, and again there is self-transcendence—not merely rejection of limitations or violation of bounds but departure in a direction defined by values already given, yet toward goals which exceed the given in broadly prescribed respects but sometimes by newly discovered means. The nisus of the performance signals the dimension of unboundedness.

Art, science, athletics, and the other disciplines through which we reach for immortality have themselves (as is too little understood) no particular affinity to transcendence. The transcendence we seek is a dimension of reality, and in grasping it we make it a dimension of our lives. The disciplines are means of regularizing (but we hope not routinizing) contact with aspects of reality which might otherwise remain diffuse; they are not substitutes for experience or superior surrogates for life, avenues to "higher consciousness," but ways of organizing experience to elicit what it holds for us. Pure unboundedness remains a state that finite beings can never attain. Yet we can make contact with it, in a suitably human fashion, in the very act of reaching for it. That is the general goal of prayer, in its diverse forms. By naming the goal beyond our strivings, prayer can give them a fullness of meaning which they lack in isolation. But prayer itself, like the rituals that surround it, rarely achieves what it sets out for. There is no reason to expect assured success from any human striving. But what prayer seeks is some aspect of the Unbounded. Access is assured by the ubiquity of the Infinite, the theme with which we should close this work.

As finite, conscious beings we grope for immortality. As moral beings we naturally apply our notions of fairness and unfairness to the universe and (promiscuously, as though it were the same thing) back to ourselves.

So we sometimes celebrate the richness of our lot and at other times mourn its terrors. There are, we are told, black holes in the cosmos, gravitational fields so dense that light cannot escape them; whole stars are sucked into their midst, to be crushed into unrecognizability. It would be inhuman to feel no emotion at such a thought. Yet the terrible thought that the universe ignores us exaggerates our importance and simultaneously overlooks the extent to which the cosmos does answer to our needs: It is made for the stars and the black holes, and for us. The miracle of creation is that it affords room to all these things, ourselves included. Immortality is all around us, and we do not need to survive death to attain it—only to conquer death, by discovering any truth or beauty or goodness that will redeem our moment. Death is conquered whenever one human being helps another smile or makes another laugh with joy. Even martyrs conquer death, as all ancient sages intimate. Every act of purity and goodness endures forever *sub specie aeternitatis*. Even those who did not knowingly choose death but died through their persistence in principle or adherence to humble virtues and a gentle way of life lived *'al kiddush ha-shem*, in sanctification of God's name. Their death consummates that act of sanctification and witness which was their life. They have a portion in immortality, and death does not entirely overwhelm them. But what triumphs in them is not their death or some ghost persistent after it, projective of the significance to others of the fact of that death. Rather, what is immortal is their life: In the measure of their joy they are not to be eroded or effaced.

The immediacy of eternity is readily overlooked but not easily denied. Eternity is transcendence not just of change but of the limits of particularity. It can never be ours in absolute terms, and those romantics who pursue its sensory surrogates in trancelike euphorias, in social submersion in an egoless mass, or in nothingness are pursuing a contradiction as well as an illusion. We can never transcend the I in absolute terms. It is always present to itself. But partial, relative transcendence is accessible to us at every moment. Recognizing that value must reside in the particular, since there is nowhere but being where value can reside, brings us to the fringes of it. This argument, which I used in setting out the equation of the being of a thing with its power and deserts, is related to our present concern with the locus of immortality. For the value in things (or the value of them, the value which they are) is their finite window upon Infinity. It is through that window in all things that we glimpse Divinity when we argue that nature bespeaks a divine Creator and Sustainer, and it is through that window in ourselves that we glimpse the Infinite in ourselves, which is not (qua Infinite) identical with ourselves nor (qua particular) identical with the Infinite and yet must fill our being if we are to exist at all.

Plato argued similarly when he maintained that the possibility of relative truth or value of any sort (unity, beauty, existence) bespeaks a Truth, Beauty, and Goodness which are absolute. The givenness of our being, I argue, bespeaks an absoluteness of being which is God. The significance of our being bears a value beyond its facticity. And that relative value in our finitude bespeaks a higher value which is absolute, yet accessible by the very logic that gives us knowledge of its reality as our source. Human immortality is finite immortality, the finite possibility of self-transcendence that is open in some measure to all particulars in a world of self-creative change. We attain to immortality—a measure of immortality, to echo the usage of the Sages—when we transcend the facticity of the given: in procreation, in education, in creative work, in overcoming any of the limits that bind and confine the fullness of our being as moral actors, spiritual and intellectual beholders of the universe, ourselves, and one another.

Death cannot diminish the value of a life well lived, even in simple industry, fidelity, and hope. The plainest of lives has a transcendent dimension and is worthy of being made exemplary. Our disciplines merely define more vividly, extend, elaborate, and articulate more clearly the simple but immortal virtues of our mortality. The arts and sciences, even the athletic sports, can be means of regularizing self-transcendence, affording us the occasions, the challenges to our present standing, the symbolic language and dialectic of growth, through which self-overcoming and discovery can be fostered. Even spectatorship of artistic, intellectual, moral, or spiritual achievement can lead us in the same direction, if the spectatorship is not merely passive but participatory and if the values recapitulated through mimetic symbolization, athletic recapitulation, moral exemplification, or scientific demonstration are those which show us in some measure a way beyond what we have been and toward what we can become.

NOTES

PREFACE

1. Alasdair MacIntyre, *Whose Justice? Which Rationality?* (Notre Dame: University of Notre Dame Press, 1988), 7.

1. TOWARD A THEORY OF JUSTICE

1. Maimonides, *Guide to the Perplexed* III 53; cf. Aristotle, *Nicomachaean Ethics* V 9, 1136a 25–28. Returning a pledge is a positive duty, not supererogatory. Yet it enhances our character and so serves an end beyond the immediate act.

2. Cicero, *Philippics* 2.5, ed. D. R. Shackleton Bailey (Chapel Hill: University of North Carolina Press, 1986) 34; cf. 2.59–60, p. 68.

3. See Bronislaw Malinowski, *Crime and Custom in Savage Society* (Totowa, N.J.: Littlefield Adams, 1976; 1926), 18–32; Cora Lee Gilliland, *The Stone Money of Yap* (Washington, D.C.: Smithsonian Institution Press, 1975).

4. See L. A. Sagan in W. T. Reich, ed., *Encyclopedia of Bioethics,* **3.**1348; Georg K. Sturup, "Sex Offenders in Denmark," in Ian T. Ramsay and Ruth Porter, eds., *Personality and Science* (Edinburgh, 1971), 25–40; "Castration: The Total Treatment," in H. L. P. Resnick and M. E. Wolfgang, eds., *Sexual Behaviors: Social, Clinical, and Legal Aspects* (Boston: Little Brown, 1972). The response is couched therapeutically, but the context is penal. Cf. Manfred Guttmacher, *Sex Offenses* (New York: Norton, 1951), 105–09. In 1984 Roger Gauntlett of Kalamazoo, an heir to the Upjohn Pharmaceuticals fortune, was sentenced for sexual offenses to "castration by chemical" for five years, using the controversial drug Depo-Provera, manufactured by Upjohn. See Immanuel Kant, *The Metaphysical Elements of Justice (Metaphysic of Morals* I), trans. John Ladd (Indianapolis: Bobbs Merrill, 1965),

131–32: "The mere Idea of a political constitution among men involves the concept of penal justice. . . . The only question is whether the particular kind of punishment is a matter of indifference to the legislator as long as it serves as a means of suppressing crime . . . or whether the respect due the humanity in the person of the miscreant (that is, due the human species) should also still be taken into account simply on grounds of justice. I have contended that the *jus talionis* is the only principle of penal Law that accords with the form stipulated *a priori* by the Idea. . . . But how can this principle be applied to punishments that do not allow reciprocation because they are either impossible in themselves or would themselves be punishable crimes against humanity in general? Rape, pederasty, and bestiality are examples of the latter. For rape and pederasty: castration, after the manner of either a white or black eunuch in the sultan's seraglio, and for bestiality . . . the criminal . . . is unworthy of remaining in human society. *Per quod quis peccat, per idem punitur et idem.*" The "miscreant" is punished through that by which he sinned.

5. See Michel Foucault, *Discipline and Punish: The Birth of the Prison*, trans. A. Sheridan (London: Allen Lane, 1977), 3–16.

6. Cf. Plato, *Republic* VIII 564–68; M. Djilas, *The New Class* (New York: Praeger, 1957), 37–69, 199–214; *The Unperfect Society* (New York: Harcourt Brace and World, 1969), 133–49.

7. Adam Schaff, *A Philosophy of Man* (New York, 1963), 130–31; cf. 33–35, 43–45, 55, 76, 95–97, 118–21.

8. See my "Equality and Human Rights: The Lockean and the Judaic View," *Judaism* 25 (1976): 357–62; "Maimonides' Philosophy of Law," *Jewish Law Annual* 1 (1978): 72–107; for *reʿut*, 358 and 90 respectively; Ernst Simon, "The Neighbor (*Reʿa*) Whom We Shall Love," in Marvin Fox, ed., *Modern Jewish Ethics* (Columbus: Ohio State University Press, 1975), 29–56.

9. See Hermann Cohen, *Religion of Reason out of the Sources of Judaism*, trans. S. Kaplan (New York: Ungar, 1972; first published in German, 1919), chap. 8; *Jüdische Schriften*, ed. B. Strauss (Berlin, 1924), 1.148–50; cf. David Novak, "Universal Moral Law in the Theology of Hermann Cohen," *Modern Judaism* 1 (1981): 101–17. Some talmudists press the notion that the biblical *ger* is (rather anachronistically), a proselyte, not (historically) a metic. But this narrow reading ill consorts with the usually concomitant strict insistence on a narrow reading of *reʿa*. If the familiar abstract sense of *reʿa* is simply ignored, and *reʿut* in its full strength is understood to refer to the bond of fellowship among Israelites, then the assumption that the *ger* is a proselyte makes it defeatingly redundant for the Torah to admonish us explicitly to love the *ger*, and Maimonides' inference that we must love "the stranger who comes to take refuge under the wings of the Shechinah," i.e., the proselyte, *because* he is a stranger, "and the Torah said, 'Thou shalt love the stranger,'" is reduced to a miserable tautology.

10. Jersualem Talmud *Baba Metzia* 8c; cf. Abû Hâmid al-Ghazâlî, *Nasîhat*

al-Mulûk, trans. F. R. C. Bagley as Ghazali's *Book of Counsel for Kings* (London: Oxford University Press, 1964), 61.

11. *Chronicle of Higher Education*, 5 March 1979; *New York Times*, 8 April 1990.

12. Cf. Robert Goodin, *Protecting the Vulnerable: A Reanalysis of Our Social Responsibilities* (Chicago: University of Chicago Press, 1985).

13. Cf. Maimonides, *Guide* III 42; and my "Unjust Enrichment and Regulation," *Jewish Law Annual* 3 (1978): 98–111. Leo Strauss in *Natural Right and History* (Chicago: University of Chicago Press, 1953), 202–51, and "Locke's Doctrine of Natural Law," *American Political Science Review* 52 (1958): 490–501, and C. B. Macpherson, *The Political Theory of Possessive Individualism: Hobbes to Locke* (Oxford: Oxford University Press, 1962), have taken Locke to task—for defending property more rigorously than personhood. John Dunn, *The Political Thought of John Locke* (Cambridge: Cambridge University Press, 1969), shows how Locke's religious and communal ideas mitigate the resultant asperities. But Dunn, the most learned and sensitive defender of the texture of Locke's thought, rightly sees a low point when Locke writes in his notebooks, under "*Venditio*," that the just price of a good, at which one ought to sell, is "the market price at the place where he sells." See Dunn's "Justice and the Interpretation of Locke's Political Theory," *Political Studies* 16 (1968): 72, 84; cf. S. Herbert Frankel, *Money and Liberty* (Washington, D.C.: American Enterprise Institute, 1980), 29–39.

14. Leviticus 25:8–55, Deuteronomy 24:6 15. See Neal Soss, "Old Testament Law and Economic Society," *Journal of the History of Ideas* 34 (1973): 323–44; Jacob Neusner, "Why Does Judaism Have an Economics?" Reinfeld Lecture (New London: Connecticut College, 1988). See also Roger Brooks, *Support for the Poor in the Mishnaic Law of Agriculture: Tractate Peah* (Chico, Calif.: Scholars Press, 1983).

15. Alexander Bickel, *The Morality of Consent* (New Haven: Yale University Press, 1975), 8. Cf. Gordon Freeman, *The Heavenly Kingdom* (Lanham, Md.: University Press of America, 1986).

16. Cf. David Gauthier, *Morals by Agreement* (Oxford: Clarendon Press, 1986), and the important critique by Allen Buchanan, "Justice as Reciprocity versus Subject-Centered Justice," *Philosophy and Public Affairs* 19 (1990): 227–52.

17. Contrast Plato, *Republic* II 359b, 369b.

18. Baruch Spinoza, *Tractatus Politicus* II 12, ed. C. Gebhardt (Heidelberg: Winter, 1925), 280; cf. A. G. Wernham, *Benedict de Spinoza, The Political Works* (Oxford: Clarendon Press, 1958).

19. See A. E. Taylor, "Some Incoherencies in Spinozism II," *Mind* 46 (1937), repr. in S. P. Kashap, ed., *Studies in Spinoza* (Berkeley: University of California Press, 1974), 289–309.

20. Moses Mendelssohn, *Jerusalem: Or on Religious Power and Judaism*, trans. A. Arkush (Hanover, N.H.: University Press of New England/Brandeis, 1983),

36–37; cf. Gottfried Wilhelm Leibniz, *New Essays on Human Understanding* IV iii, 18, ed. P. Remnant and J. Bennett (Cambridge: Cambridge University Press, 1981), 384.

21. See Sanhedrin 56a. Cf. David Novak, on the relation of civility to morality: "by seeing the rule of law as a universal social requirement, [law] becomes a necessary condition but never [society's] sufficient ground." *The Image of the Non-Jew in Judaism* (Toronto: Mellen, 1983), 73. See also Novak's well-argued defense of the natural law tradition, "Natural Law, *Halakhah* and the Covenant," *Jewish Law Annual* 7 (1988): 43–67, and his Goldman Lecture, "Law and Ethics in Maimonides' Theology."

22. For morality as "facing facts," see A. C. Graham, *Reason and Spontaneity* (London: Curzon, 1985).

23. As Steven Schwarzschild explains, in the Jewish sources "the commonplace dichotomy between individual and collective responsibility . . . is transcended in the recognition of the dialectical interrelationship between the two"; see "Justice," *Encyclopedia Judaica* 10.476–77.

24. In his trenchant critique of Plato's organicism, Aristotle argues that the life of the state is in diversity, plurality, and individuality (*Politics* II 2, 1261a 14–31).

25. John Rawls, *A Theory of Justice* (Cambridge: Harvard University Press, 1971).

26. Rex Martin argues that Rawls' model makes insufficient allowance for those whose contributions (and voice) are unequal to their needs; see his "Poverty and Welfare in Rawls' Theory of Justice: On the Just Response to Needs," in Kenneth Kipnis and Diana T. Meyers, eds., *Economic Justice: Private Rights and Public Responsibilities* (Totowa, N.J.: Rowman and Allenheld, 1985), 161–75. Norman Daniels argues that special allowances beyond what Rawls' model affords must be made for those with health challenges, since such challenges themselves limit the opportunities that Rawls' model professes to leave open. See his *Just Health Care* (Cambridge: Cambridge University Press, 1985); "Fair Equality of Opportunity and Decent Minimums: A Reply to Buchanan," *Philosophy and Public Affairs* 14 (1985): 106–110; "A Reply to Some Stern Criticisms," *Journal of Medicine and Philosophy* 8 (1983): 363–72; and "Justice and Health Care," in D. Van De Veer, ed., *Health Care Ethics* (Philadelphia: Temple University Press, 1987), 290–325.

27. Contrast F. A. Hayek's more genuinely synthetic discovery of the nexus between economic and political liberties, *The Road to Serfdom* (Chicago: University of Chicago Press, 1944). Hayek generalizes and further substantiates his thesis in arguing on Burkean and ultimately Platonic lines for the evolution of political institutions out of their social substrate. See his *Law, Legislation and Liberty* (London: Routledge, 1973–79), 3 volumes.

28. See Alasdair MacIntyre, *Whose Justice? Which Rationality?* (Notre Dame:

Notre Dame University Press, 1988); cf. S. Schwarzschild, "An Agenda for Jewish Philosophy in the 1980s," in N. Samuelson, ed., *Studies in Jewish Philosophy* (Lanham, Maryland: University Press of America, 1987), 65; Kenneth Seeskin, *Jewish Philosophy in a Secular Age* (Albany: State University of New York Press, 1990), 155.

29. See Richard Wasserstrom, *Today's Moral Problems* (New York: Macmillan, 1979), 78.

30. Alex Michalos argues against Kenneth Arrow's *Social Choice and Individual Values* (New York: Wiley, 1951) that it is impossible to assign "an ordinal measure of acceptability" without a general assignment of values; see "The Impossibility of an Ordinal Measure of Acceptability," *The Philosophical Forum* 2 (1970): 103–06. Discussions of this issue in terms of scientific hypotheses are readily transposed to general decision making, where we also require standards for weighing purported benefits and costs.

31. See Francis Galton, *Inquiries into Human Faculty and Its Development* (London, 1883) 200–19; M. J. Goodman and L. E. Goodman, *The Sexes in the Human Population* (Los Angeles: Gee Tee Bee, 1984), 149–63; 177–78.

32. Garrett Hardin, *Promethian Ethics* (Seattle: University of Washington Press, 1980).

33. See *A Theory of Justice*, 256.

34. Seeskin argues that Rawls' intent is to flesh out the Kantian idea of autonomy, but the formal skeleton may bear or reject varieties of flesh; compare the liberalism of Rawls or of Kant himself with the idea of respecting persons that Harry van der Linden outlines in his suggestive application to the Kantian framework of a form of humanistic socialism developed from the teachings of Hermann Cohen and Steven Schwarzschild: *Kantian Ethics and Socialism* (Indianapolis: Hackett, 1988). Seeskin sees that Rawls edges away from the Lockean contractualism that was the starting point of his argumentative appeal, toward an avowed Kantian, even Platonic moral realism: "What is wrong with arguing that rationality is normative, i.e., that it has a should built into it? This is perfectly in keeping with the Platonic / Kantian tradition of which Rawls is a part." But the difficulty is not with rationality per se but with the abstractness of the rational as narrowly construed. What is missing is the idea of the human person, not as an abstract subject but as a personality, and indeed a creature, and a social, cultural creature at that, with needs, limits, capabilities, quirks, sensibilities, and sensitivities. Reason here must draw its content from the study of nature—above all, human nature. See my "Crosspollinations: Philosophically Fruitful Exchanges between Jewish and Islamic Thought," in J. Lassner, ed., *The Judaeo-Islamic Tradition* (Detroit: Wayne State University Press, 1992).

35. Plato, *Republic* 557a; cf. VI 488; at *Laws* VI 759, priesthood is by lot, but with strict prerequisites.

36. Cf. Michael Bayles, *Procedural Justice: Allocating to Individuals* (Norwell,

Mass.: Kluwer 1990). See also John Plamenatz, "Equality of Opportunity," in L. Bryson et al., eds., *Aspects of Human Equality* (New York: Harper and Row, 1956), 79–107.

37. See Karl Marx, "Alienated Labor," in T. B. Bottomore, ed., *Karl Marx: Early Writings* (London: Watts, 1963), 120–34.

38. Marx regularly blue-penciled moral language in workers' manifestos, changing normative judgments to predictions; denunciations, to pronouncements of historical necessity.

39. "The source of coming-to-be for existing things is that into which destruction too happens, 'according to necessity; for they pay penalty and retribution to each other for their injustice according to the assessment of Time,'" Simplicius *Physica* 24.17, trans. after Kirk and Raven, *The Presocratic Philosophers* (Cambridge: Cambridge University Press, 1985), 117.

40. Cf. Kant, *The Metaphysic of Morals* II: *The Metaphysical Principles of Virtue* (1797, 435–36), trans. James Ellington (Indianapolis: Bobbs Merrill, 1964), 97–99.

41. See Bentham's *Theory of Fictions*, ed. C. K. Ogden (Patterson, N.J.: Littlefield Adams, 1959), 118–25.

42. See my *Case of the Animals versus Man* (Boston: Twayne, 1978), 12–25.

43. Cf. Tibor Machan, *Commerce and Morality* (Totowa, N.J.: Rowman and Littlefield, 1988).

44. Jeremy Bentham, *Outline of Pauper Management Improved*, ed. J. Bowring 8.389 (first published in Young's *Annals of Agriculture*, 1797).

45. See Jeremy Bentham, *Principles of Morals and Legislation*, chap. 2, 1789.

46. See my essay in *Journal of the American Oriental Society* 92 (1972): 250–70.

47. Maimonides, "Eight Chapters," 4; cf. *Guide* III 13, ed. Munk (Paris, 1856–66) 3.25, lines 11 ff.

48. This does not imply that Jewish law countenances complacency. Schwarzschild argues rightly that the call to imitate God makes demands beyond "middlingness." See his "Moral Radicalism and 'Middlingness' in the Ethics of Maimonides," *Studies in Medieval Culture* 11.65–94; cf. Daniel Frank, "Humility as a Virtue: A Maimonidean Critique of Aristotle's Ethics," *Studies in Philosophy and the History of Philosophy* 19.89–99. Beyond Maimonides' commitment to extremes in humility and avoidance of anger, or his prescription of deviating toward an extreme to reach the mean, the Aristotelian mean itself is an extreme, not mere moderation but an optimum located *as such*, not by its situation between extremes. The Maimonidean synthesis of Aristotelian virtue with biblical command ethics and the Platonic / Mosaic ideal of *homoiosis theoi* rests on the recognition (*a*) that we become like God not in acquiring divine perfection but in perfecting our humanity, through the human virtues, and (*b*) that the commandments are not promulgated for their own sake but as means to our perfection; cf. Herbert Da-

vidson, "The Middle Way in Maimonides' Ethics," *Proceedings of the American Academy for Jewish Research* 54 (1987): 31–72. The ground for Maimonides' synthesis of command ethics with virtue ethics was prepared by his Muslim predecessors Miskawayh and al-Ghazâlî; see my "Islamic Ethics and Social Philosophy," in the *Encyclopedia of Asian Philosophy*, forthcoming. The point remains that the Torah's "radicalism" lies in its efforts to reform human character through the reform of social institutions. The object is not to promote mere expressionistic iconoclasm but to build the ethos that can ground the good society. Thus Jakob Petuchowski amply documents his claim that "even the principles of *lifnim mishurat ha-din* [we go beyond the ruling of the law] and *middat hasidut* [the ethos of piety] have their halakhic limits" ("The Limits of Self-Sacrifice," in M. Fox, ed., *Modern Jewish Ethics*, 103–18). As Maimonides puts it, "One of the things you must realize is that the Law is not directed toward the singular, and legislation will not be oriented in terms of the exceptional. Rather, all that it seeks to accomplish in the realm of belief, ethos (*khalq*), or beneficial action is directed solely to the preponderant sorts of situation, not to the rare event, nor to the detriment that its rules and rulings might occasion to a particular individual" (*Guide* III 34; cf. "Eight Chapters," 4).

49. See Sebastian de Grazia, *The Political Community: A Study of Anomie* (Chicago: University of Chicago Press, 1963; 1948), and Zevedi Barbu, *Democracy and Dictatorship: Their Psychology and Patterns of Life* (New York: Grove Press, 1956).

50. See Deuteronomy 11:13–21 and chap. 4 below.

51. Spinoza, Ethics IV 18, scholium, ed. Gebhardt 2.223 lines 4–18; cf. lines 19–24; Cicero, *De Officiis* III 5, trans. John Higginbotham as *Cicero on Moral Obligation* (London: Faber, 1967), 143–44.

52. See my introduction to Ikhwân al-Ṣafâ', *The Case of the Animals versus Man* (Boston: Twayne, 1978), 16. Cf. my essay "The Biblical Laws of Diet and Sex," *Jewish Law Association Studies 2* (1986): 17–57; John Passmore, *Man's Responsibility for Nature: Ecological Problems and Western Traditions*, chaps. 1, 2; C. D. Stone, *Should Trees Have Standing: Toward Legal Rights for Natural Objects* (Los Altos, California: W. Kaufmann, 1974).

53. See Lenore Weitzman, "Legal Recognition of Marriage," *California Law Review* 62 (1974): 1169, esp. appendix.

54. I survey the biblical and rabbinic norms in "The Individual and the Community in the Normative Traditions of Judaism," in D. Frank, ed., *Proceedings of the 1989 Meeting of the Academy for Jewish Philosophy*.

2. PUNISHMENT

1. Hermann Cohen, *Religion of Reason* (New York: Ungar, 1972), 431.

2. Cf. Mishnah *Ketubot* 3.7: "Fines are the same for all."

3. Thus rape was punished halakhically not to protect a husband's or a guardian's property interests. For the *Mishnah* (Sanhedrin 8.7) demands that we prevent rape even at the cost of the assailant's life—to save the *assailant* from sin. The parallels are with other affronts to human life or dignity (murder and pederasty), not with property crimes or even desecration of the Sabbath.

4. The discipline of children conceded to families except in very extreme cases is not univocal with punishment as applied to criminals. Child abusers often confound the two, using rigid and excessive standards and disproportionate severity. See David Gil, *Violence against Children* (Cambridge: Harvard University Press, 1973). Normal discipline, as distinguished from abuse, seeks to evoke moral development, not to inflict pain or harm per se.

5. See my "Equality and Human Rights," *Judaism* 25 (1976): 357; *Monotheism*, 101–03.

6. R. Judah b. Pazzi urges that Moses and the Elders would have placed Phineas under a ban had not the Holy Spirit intervened. See E. E. Urbach in *Violence and Defense in the Jewish Experience*, ed. S. W. Baron, G. S. Wise, and L. E. Goodman (Philadelphia: Jewish Publication Society, 1977), 104–05. The same *amorah* glossed the biblical allusions to a divine retinue as hints of a heavenly tribunal: "Even the Holy One, blessed be He, does not judge alone, as it is said, 'And all the host of heaven standing by Him on His right and on His left'—these arguing in favor and those against." See Urbach's *The Sages* (Jerusalem: Magnes Press, 1975) 179. Ben Pazzi champions proceduralism, but his gloss of the Phineas episode is not pure invention; it rests on the Torah's need to produce an apologia for Phineas from the mouth of God himself (Numbers 25:7–11). Phineas received a "covenant of peace" because his act stayed the plague in which twenty-four thousand human beings had died (25:9, 12–13). Ben Pazzi bars the founding of a precedent on the act.

7. Kant, *The Metaphysic of Morals* I, *The Metaphysical Elements of Justice*, 331, trans. after John Ladd (Indianapolis: Bobbs Merrill, 1965), 100. Kant is, of course, quite mistaken about the Pharisaic law, which refuses to give up a single soul, even to save the group. See Jerusalem Talmud, Terumot, 46b; Maimonides, *Code, Hilkhot Yesodei ha-Torah* 5.5; Elijah J. Schochet, *A Responsum of Surrender* (Los Angeles: University of Judaism Press, 1973).

8. Under crimes of desperation we must include not just the romantically salient ones but also child abuse (see Gil, 110–14) and many "victimless" crimes (i.e., crimes against the self) such as prostitution, suicide, and drug abuse.

9. John Rawls, "Two Concepts of Rules," *Philosophical Review* 64 (1955): 3–32.

10. See Garrett Hardin, *Promethean Ethics* (Seattle: University of Washington Press, 1980), v. The preface lionizes Hardin as an ethicist, one of the "truly great scholars and thinkers of the world."

11. John Stuart Mill, *Utilitarianism*, ed. H. B. Acton (London: Everyman, 1983; first ed., 1861), 58.

12. See Herbert Morris, *On Guilt and Innocence* (Berkeley: University of California Press, 1976), 31–58.

13. As Kant puts it, "judicial punishment is entirely distinct from natural punishment. In natural punishment vice punishes itself, and this fact is not taken into consideration by the legislator" (*The Metaphysical Elements of Justice*, 100). Further on I shall argue that in a sense it is *exactly* the natural element of punishment that judicial penalties do take account of, but what they respond to is not the haphazard outfalls of criminal intent but the inevitable impacts of criminal actions upon character and desert.

14. Cicero, *De Officiis* III 5, 6, 8, 13.57 ad fin., 20, trans. Higginbotham (London: Faber, 1967), 143, 145–46, 148, 156, 163; cf. II 12, 13, citing Xenophon, *Memorabilia Socratis* II 6, 39.

15. Cf. *Qur'ân* 3:184; Ibn Ṭufayl, *Ḥayy Ibn Yaqẓân*, trans. L. E. Goodman (Boston: Twayne, 1972; repr., Los Angeles, 1983), 163.

16. Plato, *Republic* 335, 591, *Gorgias* 504–05, 516; cf. 472–80; *Crito* 49; *Laws* 862–63; *Protagoras* 324.

17. Philo, *On the Sacrifices of Cain and Abel* IV xxxviii, 128–29, trans. Colson, 2.186–87.

18. Cf. the John Courtney Murray Jesuit Writing Group (Donald Gelpi, Stephen Rowntree, Drew Christiansen, Frank Oppenheim, John Staudenmaier, Carl Starkloff, and John Stacer), *Beyond Individualism: Toward a Retrieval of Moral Discourse in America* (Notre Dame: University of Notre Dame Press, 1989).

19. See Kant, *Metaphysic of Morals II, The Metaphysical Principles of Virtue*, trans. James Ellington (Indianapolis: Bobbs Merrill, 1964; first ed., 1797), 90–93.

20. Kant, *Groundwork of the Metaphysic of Morals*, trans. H. J. Paton (New York: Harper, 1964; first ed., 1785) 90.

21. Cf. Tom Sorell, *Moral Theory and Capital Punishment* (Oxford: Blackwell, 1988).

22. Maimonides, *Guide* I 51–53, 57.

23. See Maimonides, *Guide* I 47, on *Avot* 2:1.

24. Ibn Ṭufayl, *Ḥayy Ibn Yaqẓân*, 153.

25. Cf. my *Monotheism* (Totowa, N.J.: Allenheld Osmun, 1981) 92–108 and Cohen, *Religion of Reason*, 127.

26. *Ethica*, Definitions of the Emotions, 38; Gebhardt, 2.201.

3. RECOMPENSE

1. Florence Goodman, in *Four Lyric Poets* (Los Angeles: Westwood, 1967), no. 90.

2. See Antony Flew's recasting of John Wisdom's fable in *New Essays in Philosophical Theology* (New York: Macmillan, 1964), 96–99, and Wisdom's "Gods," in *Philosophy and Psychoanalysis*, (London: Blackwell, 1964; first ed., 1944), 154–56.

3. John Stuart Mill, *Utilitarianism*, ed. H. B. Acton (London: Everyman, 1983; first ed., 1861), 4.

4. Contrast Philippa Foot, "Morality as a System of Hypothetical Imperatives," *Analysis* 35 (1975): 305–16; cf. my *Monotheism*, 62–68.

5. Cf. Robert Gordis, *Koheleth—The Man and his World: A Study of Ecclesiastes* (New York: Schocken, 1968; 1951), 96, 116–32.

6. Kant, *Groundwork of the Metaphysic of Morals*, trans. H. J. Paton, (New York: Harper, 1956; Riga, 1785–86), 109–10; 90–91/442.

7. Kant, *Groundwork*, trans. Paton, 99–100; Riga 71–74/431–33.

8. Mill disclaims psychological hedonism when he argues that Utilitarianism is not a descriptive but a prescriptive system: "ninety-nine hundredths of all our actions are done from other motives" than the disinterested pursuit of universal happiness (*Utilitarianism* II, 17). But he takes back the admission when he argues that "the sole evidence it is possible to produce that anything is desirable, is that people do actually desire it" (IV, 32).

9. See Jack Bilmes, *Discourse and Behavior* (New York: Plenum, 1986).

10. See Cicero, *De Finibus* I ix 30, *De Rerum Natura* I 10–25. Cf. Dewey's reliance on adaptation and adaptability, and the quest for evolutionary precursors of altruism and egoism in sociobiology: Edward Wilson, *Sociobiology* (Cambridge: Harvard University Press, 1975), and Richard Dawkins, *The Selfish Gene* (New York: Oxford University Press, 1976).

11. Epicurus, *Kyriae Doxae* 9, Vatican Fragments 33.

12. See Philip Rieff, "George Orwell and the Post-Liberal Imagination," in Irving Howe, ed., *Nineteen Eight-Four: Text, Sources, Criticism* (New York: Harcourt Brace, 1963), 229–30.

13. See *De Rerum Natura* V 783–924, II 700–729; cf. Empedocles *ap.* Aristotle *Physics* II 8, 198b 29, Aetius V 19.5; Diels B57, 61, A72.

14. For a lucid exposition of the (Darwinian) values pursued and preserved through sexual reproduction, see Graham Bell, *The Masterpiece of Nature: The Evolution and Genetics of Sexuality* (Berkeley: University of California Press, 1982). The "generation of genotypic diversity" is "the leading characteristic of sexuality" (58); and the genetic mixis of sexual reproduction is the source of the population in a genetic sense. For "sexual reproduction thus knits together the population into a single entity" (45–46). The concomitance of individuality with community at this primal level is emblematic and foundational of their interdependence in higher senses as well. For the ethnic and familial community are the prototypes and molecular constituents of the social and cultural community, and it is the ethnic and familial tie that first binds the fate of one individual to the next, even as the individual first emerges to a distinctive identity.

15. Hence the playful gloss of Genesis Rabbah IX 5 that takes God's judgment that the world was *tov me'od*, very good (Genesis 1:31), as hinting that death

is good (*tov mavet*). For without death there is no indivuality and without individuality there is no excellence.

16. Cf. Jacques Monod's remarkably static notion of the goal of evolution: invariance, an endpoint which clearly does not need the miraculous devices and systems of biochemical genetics and evolutionary advance—for there is invariance of a high degree, as Monod points out, in crystals; *Chance and Necessity* (New York: Knopf, 1971).

17. Cicero, *De Finibus* III vi; "*Quod est bonum omne laudabile est; quod autem laudabile est omne est honestum; bonum igitur quod est honestum est,*" III viii 27.

18. See Cicero, *De Finibus* III v–vii.

19. Cf. Arabic *ikhlâs* and *safâ'*. See my "Bahyâ on the Antinomy of Free Will and Predestination," *Journal of the History of Ideas* 44 (1983): 116–30.

20. See Isaiah Berlin, "Two Concepts of Liberty: Inaugural Lecture," (Oxford: Clarendon Press, 1958).

21. Immanuel Kant, *Critique of Pure Reason*, trans. N. Kemp Smith (New York: St. Martin's, 1965; A = 1781; B = 1787) A5/B9.

22. For the endeavor to "tether" deontic axiology to forestall its dismissal as idealism, see Kant's, "On the Old Saw: That May Be Right in Theory, But It Won't Work in Practice," trans. E. B. Ashton (Philadelphia: University of Pennsylvania Press, 1974); for Kant's Christian concessions, the discussion of original sin in *Religion within the Limits of Reason Alone* I, trans. T. M. Greene and H. H. Hudson (New York: Harper and Row, 1960; German original, 1792), 15–39. For resistance to the dissolving of ethics into pragmatic vacuity, see the supremely practical discourses of Epictetus. But the disparity between the example and the sublimated rhetoric of Seneca warn of the danger. Seneca's life and art are charged with the tragic tension between praxis and principle resulting from even partial concession of the irrelevance of the ideal. This tension, I suspect, rather than any merely clinical condition, excites that morbidity of which Moses Hadas found "a kind of excrescence" not only in the tragedies but also in the philosophic writings; *A History of Latin Literature* (New York: Columbia University Press, 1952), 245–46.

23. Epicurus advises making friends where one can, avoiding entanglements where one cannot (*Kyriae Doxae* 39). Seeking to reconcile men to oneself or one another is folly. Seeking to bring them into conformity with some ideal of human nature is worse—it is meddlesomeness—the primary defect from which blessedness and immortality exempt the gods (*K.D.* 1). It is also religion, understood as the organized fear of death. Such fear, as Lucretius presents it, is the basis of all vice. The Epicurean caricature of religion as intolerance is perpetuated in the satires of Voltaire. Lucretius, *De Rerum Natura* I 80–100 is the *locus classicus* for the equation of religious motives with those of fanatic zeal and hence profound impiety.

24. Deuteronomy 30:12–14; Aristotle, *Nicomachaean Ethics* I 7, 1097a 20–23, cf. 1096b 33–4; and see Plato, *Laws* 631; cf. Plato, *Gorgias* 468b, *Philebus* 62, *Laws* 705d.

25. What the Kingdom-of-ends adds to the End-in-itself formulation of the categorical imperative is a commitment to the progress of mutuality which will widen the effective recognition of human dignity to humanity at large. The same commitment becomes lyrical in Robert Burns' 1795 "For a' that and a' that."

26. See my essay "Context," *Philosophy East and West* 38 (1988): 307–23.

27. *De Finibus* IV xx 56.

28. See Voltaire, "Poeme sur le désastre de Lisbonne," 1775; David Hume, *Dialogues Concerning Natural Religion* X.

29. Kant, *Critique of Pure Reason* A811/B839, trans. after Kemp-Smith 1929 (1965), 639.

30. Lewis White Beck, *A Commentary on Kant's Critique of Practical Reason* (Chicago: University of Chicago Press, 1960), 213–15, citing A812–13/B840–41.

31. For Mendelssohn's gift of the *Phaedon* and Kant's first response to it, see Alexander Altmann, *Moses Mendelssohn* (Philadelphia: Jewish Publication Society, 1973), 148, 179.

32. Kant, *Critique of Practical Reason*, trans. L. W. Beck (Indianapolis: Bobbs Merrill, 1956) 126–27, 129.

33. See Kant, *Lectures on Ethics*, trans. Louis Infield (New York: Harper, 1963) 252.

34. See, for example, Saadiah, *Kitâb al-Mukhtâr fî 'l-âmanât wa 'l-I'tiqâdât = Sefer ha-Nivḥar ba-Emunot ve-De'ot* (Book of Critically Chosen Beliefs and Convictions) VII–IX, trans. S. Rosenblatt as *The Book of Beliefs and Opinions* (New Haven: Yale University Press, 1948); and my "Saadiah Gaon on the Human Condition," *Jewish Quarterly Review* N.S. 67 (1976): 23–29.

35. Cf. Cicero, *De Natura Deorum* I ix 23, xliii 121–22; Mill, *Theism* (Indianapolis: Bobbs Merrill, 1957; first ed., 1874), 36, 86.

36. Philo, *On the Sacrifices of Cain and Abel,* 28. *Avot de-Rabbi Natan* 5 holds two disciples of Antigonos responsible for denying any afterlife and founding the Sadducee and Boethusian sects. But the denial is not an implication of Antigonos' view (and is not represented as such by R. Nathan). Antigonos speaks only to the question of the proper motive and intention of our actions. See *The Fathers according to Rabbi Nathan*, trans. Judah Goldin (New Haven: Yale University Press, 1955), 39.

37. Bahyâ Ibn Paquda, *Kitâb al-Hidâya ilâ Farâ'id al-Qulûb = Hovot ha-Levavot* V 5.

38. H. Zeitlin, *R. Nahman Bratslaver* (New York: Matones, 1952) 137; cf. Shneor Zalman, *Likutei Torah, Deuteronomy* (1851, 1928) 25a; R. Pedat in *Avodah Zarah* 19a: "Happy is he that delights in His commandments—'In His com-

mandments,' not in their reward"; and again, commenting on Proverbs 31:26, at Sukkah 49b: "Only a law fulfilled for its own sake is 'A Torah of Love.'" Elijah, the Gaon of Vilna, is quoted: "Elijah can serve God even without a world to come" (Brainin, *Mi-Mizraḥ Umi-Ma'arav*, 1899).

39. Hedonism is morally transparent: It leaves open the question what will count as pleasure. The *Sonnenkinder*, in articulate antipathy to natural and socially given modes of self-expression, seized the role of an aesthetic elite and redefined pleasure, fun, style (or beauty), and other values for themselves and many followers, palpably revealing the discontinuity between naturalism and hedonism. See Martin Green, *The Children of the Sun* (New York: Basic Books, 1976). Râzî even urged an ascetic life on hedonic grounds, a line of argument initiated by Epicurus himself. See my "The Epicurean Ethic of Muḥammad ibn Zakariya' ar-Râzî," *Studia Islamica* 34 (1971): 5–26.

40. Kant, *Groundwork*, Paton 109–10; Riga 90–92/442–43.

41. Kant, *Groundwork*, Paton 110; Riga 91/442–43.

42. Spinoza exonerates true religiosity and pinions its counterfeit by distinguishing ambition, which desires others to be like oneself, from humanity (true piety), which desires to serve others for their own sakes. See *Ethica* III Schol., Prop. 29, Gebhardt, 2.162, lines 28–31, Schol., Prop. 56, 185, lines 21–28, V Schol. Prop. 4, 283, lines 21–25, IV Schol. Prop. 73, 265, lines 17–21; cf. Prop. 51, 248, lines 18–22.

43. See Saadiah, *The Book of Theodicy*, trans. L. E. Goodman (New Haven: Yale University Press, 1988), 359–60.

44. See my *Monotheism*, 89–91.

45. See Kant's "On a Supposed Right to Lie from Benevolent Motives," and W. Matson, "Kant as Casuist," *Journal of Philosophy* 51 (1954): 855–60, repr. in R. P. Wolff, ed., *Kant: A Collection of Critical Essays* (Garden City, New York: Doubleday), 331–36.

46. See my "Maimonides' Philosophy of Law," *Jewish Law Annual* 1 (1978): 83–91, and "Crosspollinations," forthcoming.

47. Erich Auerbach, *Mimesis* (Princeton: Princeton University Press, 1953), 3–23.

48. Deuteronomy 8:10. I fondly recall learning this gloss from R. Emanuel Rackman; similarly when we are commanded to rejoice (Leviticus 23:40; Deuteronomy 12:7, 12, 18; 14:26, 16:11, 14; 26:11, 27:7), the duty and its reward are identical.

49. See my "The Biblical Laws of Diet and Sex," *Jewish Law Association Studies* 2; "The Individual and the Community in the Norms of Judaism," *Studies in Judaism*, forthcoming.

50. See *Monotheism* III. *Bereshit Rabbah* XLIV 1 asks, "What difference does it make to the Holy One, Blessed be He, whether one slaughters animals by cutting their throats or chopping off their heads? One must say the *mitzvot* were given

only to purify humanity." The passage, often taken as a bastion of legal positivism, specifies not an arbitrary but a *purifying* discipline, aimed at perfecting our humanity. Cf. Maimonides, *Guide* III 26.

51. See Yoma 84ab, Shabbat 151b.

52. Ahad Ha-Am, *Ha-Shiloah* III 6, 1898; *Al Parshat Derakhim* III 79.

53. Commenting on the liturgy in *The Authorised Daily Prayer Book* (New York: Bloch, 1957; London, 1948), 341.

54. Even in the days of the Messiah, we are still bound to provide for the needs of the less fortunate, so there is no contradiction between the Torah's caution that the poor will never cease (Deuteronomy 15:11), which regards our obligations, and its allied provisions for the progressive elimination of destitution. See Berakhot 34b.

55. See Neal Soss, "Old Testament Law and Economic Society," *Journal of the History of Ideas* 34 (1973): 323–44.

56. Deuteronomy 7:13, 11:21; cf. Genesis 27:28, Micah 4:4, Isaiah 36:16.

57. Cf. Maimonides, *Guide* II 40; see my RAMBAM (New York: Viking, 1976), 378–403.

58. *Mekhilta*, Shirta, 3 to Exodus 15:2, ed. Lauterbach (Philadelphia: Jewish Publication Society, 1933), 2.24, lines 29–31.

59. Exodus 20:7, Deuteronomy 5:11; cf. *Monotheism*, 12–16, 110–16. The Fourth Commandment—"the Lord will not clear one who applies His name to ill"—voices the enormity of assigning divinity to any but the highest Reality, or ascribing to God's will any but the highest and truest course. The idea that God will not clear one who is guilty of a merely verbal infraction in the use of His name is inadmissable. The verse must be interpreted in light of the Maimonidean canon that divine wrath denotes logical hostility between Perfection and any surrogate. See *Moreh* I 36: "If you scrutinize the entire Torah and all the prophetic writings you will observe that the expressions 'kindling of wrath,' 'anger,' 'jealousy' are applied exclusively with reference to idolatry; only an idolater is called God's enemy or adversary, hated of God." For *shav'* see Deuteronomy 5:20, Psalms 24:4, 26:4, 89:48, 139:20, 119:37, Job 11:11, 15:31, 31:15, Isaiah 1:13, Hosea 12:12. Cf. Eric Voegelin, *Order and History* (Baton Rouge: Louisiana State University Press, 1956–), vol. 1, *Israel and Revelation*, 425–26.

60. Deuteronomy 16:20 and *Monotheism*, 91.

61. See my "Saadiah's Ethical Pluralism," *Journal of the American Oriental Society* 100 (1980): 407–19, for an analysis of one mode of integrating the diverse goods of the Torah. Maimonides' scheme, using the Aristotelian means-ends relationship, achieves a higher-order integration; see my "Maimonides' Philosophy of Law," *Jewish Law Annual* 1 (1978): 72–107.

62. See Peter Brown, *Augustine of Hippo* (London: Faber, 1967), 63; cf. *Monotheism*, 6–7.

63. See Exodus 21:10 with *Mekhilta*, Lauterbach, 3.27–29; *Ketubot* 62b; Maimonides' *Code, Ishut* 14.2; and *Shuihan Arukh, Even ha-'Ezer* 76.5; cf. David

248

Feldman, *Marital Relations, Birth Control and Abortion in Jewish Law* (New York: Schocken, 1975) 60–71, 94–103.

64. See *Monotheism*, 107–10.

65. See 1 Chronicles 29:10–13; *ED* X 8; Maimonides, "Eight Chapters," 5; cf. Proverbs 22:4.

66. Cf. Saadiah, *Emunot ve-De'ot* X 4. In "Eight Chapters," 4, Maimonides approves the rabbinic explanation (*Nazir* 19a, 22a, *Taanit* 11a, etc.) that a *nazir* must offer a sin offering on grounds that his vow constitutes a sin against the self.

67. Cf. Maimonides, *Guide* II 6, 10, 12. Maimonides argues elegantly and emphatically for the intrinsic value of fulfilling the commandments. Commenting on Ben Azzai's dictum in *Avot* 4:2, he cites a Talmudic gloss (Makkot 10a on Deuteronomy 4:41) arguing that if Moses was eager to fulfill even "half a commandment" by setting aside three cities of refuge across the Jordan, before the conquest of the Land made possible the full implementation of the divine command to establish *six* cities of refuge (Numbers 35:13), "how much more so should those whose souls are in an advanced and confirmed state of leprosy!" One might read the gloss as a qualification to Maimonides' general assertion that all God's commandments serve a purpose. The claim would be that intrinsic as well as extrinsic benefits are irrelevant to our obligations, since Moses did not await the time when the full benefits of the complete system of cities of refuge would be accrued before hastening to fulfill even part of God's command. But that line of reasoning breaks down. Extrinsic rewards are what can be presumed to await complete fulfillment of the commandment as made, whereas intrinsic and consequential benefits could flow from even partial fulfillment of the scheme. The impact of Maimonides' argument is that it is only because Moses saw the fulfillment of the commandment as a good in itself, for its constitutive and consequential benefits, that he could assume that half a commandment was better than none and hasten to accomplish half of what was mandated before achievement of the other half was possible.

4. DO BEINGS RECEIVE WHAT THEY DESERVE?

1. Cf. Pierre Teilhard de Chardin, *The Phenomenon of Man* (London: Collins, 1959).

2. Such statements, like "Vanity of vanities," evoke the metaphysical melancholy (midrashically associated with middle age) that Kohelet addresses in his inner dialogue with despondency. See Chapter 3, note 5 above.

3. *Eleh Ezkerah*, Musaf of Yom Kippur, stanzas 6–7; cf. Menahot 29b.

4. Saadiah, *Emunot ve-De'ot* IV, Exordium, Rosenblatt, 180; cf. Maimonides, *Guide* I 2, III 13, 25.

5. Cf. my introductory essay in *The Case of the Animals versus Man* of the Ikhwân al-Ṣafâ' 3–14; "Ibn Khaldûn and Thucydides," *Journal of the American Oriental Society* 92 (1972): 250–70.

6. *Mekhilta, Shirta,* 8, ed. Judah Goldin (New Haven: Yale University Press, 1971), 198.

7. Saadiah, *The Book of Theodicy,* trans. L. E. Goodman (New Haven: Yale University Press, 1988), 123–24, 127, citing Psalm 145:9.

8. See M. J. Goodman and L. E. Goodman, *The Sexes in the Human Population* (Los Angeles: Gee Tee Bee, 1984), 92–123.

9. *Baba Metzia* 83b; cf. Bernard Jackson, *Theft in Early Jewish Law* (Oxford: Oxford University Press, 1972), 255.

10. See John Wisdom, "Gods," in *Philosophy and Psychoanalysis* (Oxford: Blackwell, 1964; repr. from the Proceedings of the Aristotelian Society, 1944), 164; Antony Flew, in A. MacIntyre and A. Flew, *New Essays in Philosophical Theology* (New York: Macmillan, 1964), 96.

11. See N. Glueck, *Ḥesed in the Bible,* trans. A. Gottschalk (Cincinnati: Hebrew Union College Press, 1967). Favor regards an established relation; here, of Creator to creature.

12. See my "Matter and Form as Attributes of God in the Philosophy of Maimonides," in *Essays in Honor of Arthur Hyman* (Washington: Catholic University of America Press, 1988).

13. See J. A. Wheeler, "The Universe as a Home for Man," *American Scientist* 62 (1974): 683–91.

14. Baḥyâ Ibn Paquda, *Kitâb al-Hidâya ilâ Farâ'iḍ al-Qulûb,* trans. M. Mansoor (London: Routledge, 1973) 295 *ad fin.*

15. Exodus 34:7. For the loss of freedom, ₃ee Maimonides, "Eight Chapters," 8. Christians emphasize the *dialectic* more than the *dynamic* of character; see William James, *Varieties of Religious Experience* (New Hyde Park, N.Y.: University Books, 1963; first ed., 1902), 245: "the more literally lost you are, the more literally you are the very being whom Christ's sacrifice has already saved"— paraphrasing Luther on Galatians 3:19 and 2:20.

16. See my "Determinism and Freedom in Spinoza, Maimonides and Aristotle," in F. Schoeman, ed., *Responsibility, Character, and the Emotions* (Cambridge: Cambridge University Press, 1987), 107–64.

17. Spinoza, *Ethics* I, Definitions 2, 5, and Prop. 26.

18. *Cf. Guide* III 16–25; my RAMBAM (New York: Viking, 1976), 296 ff.

19. Psalms 5:11, 7:12, 9:5–16, 10:15, 11:5–7, 32:10, 34:15–21, 37:17–28, 58:10–11, 72:5–7, 73, 75:9, 94, 97:11, 112:10, 119:119, 140:12, 145:17–20, 146:8–9, 147:6.

20. Cf. B. K. Matilal, "Karma," in T. M. P. Mahadevan and Grace Cairns, eds., *Contemporary Indian Philosophies of History* (Calcutta: World Press, 1977): "The karma doctrine . . . may be rendered simply as our moral responsibility for whatever we do . . . it means that our destiny is our own making. The present comes out of the past and the shape of the future depends upon what we do in the present. . . . To Artabhaga's question as to what happens after death, Yajnavalkya

chose to discuss it in private with Artabhaga . . . what they discussed was karma alone, what they praised was karma alone, viz., that a man becomes good by good works and evil by evil works." Matilal continues, "I would like to make an unorthodox suggestion. The *karma* theory should not only be related to individuals. It should be extended also to cases of human societies, to nations and to countries, to collections of human beings. Individual moral responsibility should be extended, in modern contexts, to make room for collective moral responsibility."

21. Exodus 34:7; cf. 20:5, Deuteronomy 5:9.

22. See Deuteronomy 24:16, Ezekiel 18:4, 20; cf. Leviticus 5:17–19, 17:16, 24:15, Numbers 5:31.

23. Saadiah follows Sanhedrin 27b in glossing Leviticus 26:39 at Job 21:19; cf. the same gemara on Leviticus 26:37; and Targum Exodus 20:5, where Ibn Ezra and the Ramban emphasize "of those that hate me": those who persist in the offense. We read idolatry as viciousness of ideals, promoting vicious mores.

24. Proverbs 2:6, 3:13, 19; 4:5–7, 8:1–14; 10:13, 21, 31; 13:10, 15:33, 16:16; 19:8; 24:3; cf. Psalms 37:30, 51:8, 106:24, 111:10, 136:5. Cohen writes: "*the psalms grow out of prophecy.* . . . Though the psalm becomes *epigrammatic* poetry, it does not contract and ossify into prose; Kohelet soars up to the Song of Songs, and the Proverbs deepen into Job." *Religion of Reason*, 25–26. The insights of the Psalms are spelled out in Proverbs, in epigrammatic prose.

25. Pentateuchal wisdom is artistic—hence practical; see Exodus 28:3, 31:3, 6, 35:21, 31.

26. Richard Adamiak, *Justice and History in the Old Testament: The Evolution of Divine Retribution in the Historiographies of the Wilderness Generation* (Cleveland: Zubal, 1982), finds the theme of retribution, fused with that of grace, in all the passages he studies; grace and law, mercy and judgment are counterparts pervading the Mosaic scheme.

27. See my parallel discussion in "An Historic Misunderstanding of the 'Keriyat Shema,'" *Conservative Judaism* 22 (1979): 36–49. While differing in diction and tone the 1976 Jewish Publication Society version does not differ materially, nor does the King James differ appreciably from the old JPS, which often follows its style. The Revised Standard Version changes the pronouns from "I" to "he," since Moses is the speaker. The New English Bible simplifies the rhetoric somewhat but imparts no new meaning.

28. Berakhot 55a; cf. Taanit 2ab. Rosh Ha-Shanah 17b naturalizes the moral model when it regards rain as determined annually by God in keeping with the doings of Israel. Any notion that cult rather than morality was the determinant, as Moshe Weinfeld suggests in *Deuteronomy and the Deuteronomic School* (Oxford, 1972), 294, was clearly rejected by the rabbis and would be inconsistent with the biblical tendency to merge ritual and moral concerns. For Hertz's comments, see his edition of the Pentateuch, 769, 792.

29. Thus Rashi on Deuteronomy 11:14 follows *Sifre*: "You do your part; I

[God] will do mine." Nahmanides naturalizes the fate of the individual but expects miraculous intervention in the oversight of the community.

30. Bribery and threat might seem more salient in Leviticus 26:3–46 or Deuteronomy 32; but these passages bear a naturalistic interpretation, and others, such as Deuteronomy 27:9–28:69, which seem to offer sanctions distinct from the natural consequences of good and evil choices, plainly embody oathing symbolism that incorporates a ritual wish for misfortune in the event of default. Hence the response *amen*, as in Numbers 5:22. The force of the ritual, as I have argued, is the acknowledgment of the ruinousness of injustice and wrong.

31. For the Aramaic term *pras* see the entry in M. Jastrow, *Dictionary of the Talmud* (New York: Traditional Press, repr. n.d.).

32. *Sayings of the Fathers*, ed. J. H. Hertz (New York: Behrman, 1945), 15.

33. Philo, *De Specialibus Legibus* I 303–04, trans. F. H. Colson (London: Heinemann, 1939), 7.274–77.

34. Philo, *De Praemiis it Poenis* 101, Colson, **8**.372–73.

35. *De Praemiis it Poenis* 98–100, Colson, **8**.372–73.

36. Maimonides, *Guide* III 30; my RAMBAM, 415–16.

37. Maimonides, *Guide* III 32.

38. Spinoza, *Tractatus Theologico-Politicus*, chap. 13; cf. 2, 5, 6, 7.

39. In a personal communication to me, David Novak compares Genesis 28:20, Jacob's vow, with Nahmanides (and on Deuteronomy 29:18; and Maimonides, *Hilkhot Teshuvah* 9). Jacob's allegiance is not conditioned on God's material aid, but its expression is made possible *by* that aid.

40. For the modern commentaries, see my "An Historic Misunderstanding of the 'Keriyat Shema.'"

41. See my "Saadiah on the Human Condition," *Jewish Quarterly Review* N.S. 67 (1976): 23–29; and Saadiah's *Book of Theodicy*.

42. Gersonides, *Milḥamot Ha-Shem* IV 6, J. D. Bleich, trans., *Providence in the Philosophy of Gersonides [Milḥamot IV]* (New York: Yeshiva University Press, 1973), 91.

43. Maimonides, *Guide* III 17.5, II 48; III 22–24; cf. Saadiah, *Book of Theodicy*.

44. See my *Monotheism*, 65–69.

45. See my "Three Meanings of the Idea of Creation," in D. Burrell and B. McGinn, eds., *God and Creation: An Ecumenical Symposium* (Notre Dame: University of Notre Dame Press, 1990), 85–113. For the contingency of being, see my *Avicenna: A Philosophical Appreciation*, forthcoming.

5. THE MESSIANIC AGE

1. See H. Gressman (1913) *et al.* in Leo Landman, ed., *Messianism in the Talmudic Era* (New York: KTAV, 1979); John Passmore, *The Perfectibility of Man*

(London: Duckworth, 1970); Robert Gordis, *Root and Branch* (Chicago: University of Chicago Press, 1962); Eugene Kamenka, *The Ethical Foundations of Marxism* (London: Routledge, Kegan Paul, 1972); J. L. Talmon, *The Origins of Totalitarian Messianism* (London: Secker and Warburg, 1952) and *Political Messianism* (New York: Praeger, 1968).

2. See Ibn Ṭufayl's *Ḥayy Ibn Yaqzân*, trans. Goodman (Boston: Twayne, 1972; repr., Los Angeles, 1983), 161.

3. See 1 Samuel 25:28, 2 Samuel 7:16, Psalm 78:8, 37; 93:5, Jeremiah 15:18; Isaiah 22:23, Deuteronomy 28:59, 1 Kings 8:26, 1 Chronicles 17:23–24, Genesis 42:20, Exodus 17:12, Deuteronomy 32:4, Psalm 37:3. The *hiphil* form does refer to belief, though not with the later connotations of the concept of faith. But we can return any epistemic emphasis imputed in the notion of faith to the moral emphasis on trust by asking the very practical question: What do the faithful believe God will do? That is, what do they trust God to do? Surely always more than simply to exist.

4. It is anomalous to argue that faith in the modern (Christian) sense is a prophetic notion while holding that the rule of God was unproblematic for the prophets. For such faith is a response to epistemic quandaries and does not arise where such quandaries are not felt.

5. See Claude Lévi-Strauss, *The Savage Mind* (Chicago: University of Chicago Press, 1966; Paris, 1962); Paul Radin, *Primitive Man as Philosopher* (New York: Dover, 1957; 1927).

6. J. Feliks, *The Animal World of the Bible* (Tel Aviv: Sinai, 1962), 24, 95. Saadiah interpreted the Leviathan and Behemoth naturalistically over a thousand years ago without doing violence to the textual or contextual catena; on Job 40:15–41:26.

7. See Joseph Sarachek, *The Doctrine of the Messiah in Medieval Jewish Literature* (New York: Jewish Theological Seminary, 1932), 118–20, 136–39, 175, 248, 257–59, 280–81.

8. For a paradigm case, see my "The Biblical Laws of Diet and Sex," *Jewish Law Association Studies* II (Atlanta: Scholars Press, 1986).

9. Maimonides, "Eight Chapters," 4, on Psalm 19:8–9. In *Guide* II 39 Maimonides explains that it is because the Torah is balanced in its requirements, verging neither to excess nor to deficiency, that its laws can perfect the human spirit.

10. See my "Maimonides' Philosophy of Law," *Jewish Law Annual* 1 (1978): 72–107.

11. Plato, Seventh Letter, 341–44, trans. Glenn R. Morrow, *Plato's Epistles* (Indianapolis: Bobbs Merrill, 1962), 237–42. Cf. Saadiah, *Emunot ve-De'ot* I, Exordium, trans. Rosenblatt, 38–39.

12. For the sharp distinction of the messianic age from *Olam ha-ba*, see Sanhedrin 99a, 113b, Berakhot 34b; David Novak, *Journal of Religious Studies* 9 (1982): 44.

13. Cf. K. Seeskin, *Jewish Philosophy in a Secular Age* (Albany: State University of New York Press, 1990), 164.

14. Maimonides, *Guide* I 46.

15. Ibn Ezra shows that *melo kol ha-aretz kevodo*, "the fill of all the earth is His glory," means, "the whole earth is full of his glory"; on Isaiah 6:3 and Numbers 22:18.

16. If R. Hillel was responding to Christological exegeses, perhaps by Origen (see *Jewish Encyclopedia* 6.401), R. Joseph's sharp rejoinder, that the messiah's work remained undone even while the Second Temple stood (witness Zechariah 9:9), speaks to the *same* effect. The uncensored text of Maimonides' *Code* argues: "If he does not succeed or is killed, obviously he is not the Messiah promised in the Torah but is to be regarded like all the other sincere and worthy kings of the House of David who died, who were raised up by God to assay the multitude, as it is said, 'And some of the insightful shall stumble, to refine them, and purify, and whiten, until the time of the end; for the time appointed is not yet come.'" See Maimonides' *Code, Hilkhot Melakhim* 11, end, in the uncensored edition of Rabinowitz (Jerusalem, 1962); the Rome, 1480 text; Nahmanides' sermon, *Torah Temimah*; the Oxford and Cambridge MSS of the *Code*; and Kafaḥ's Yemenite MS represented in *Rambam la-'Am* (Jerusalem: Mosad ha-Rav Kuk, 1962); cf. *ED* VIII 8, esp. Rosenblatt 318. See also and the discussion in David Novak, *Jewish-Christian Dialogue: A Jewish Justification* (New York: Oxford University Press, 1989), 63.

17. Hermann Cohen, *Religion of Reason* (New York: Ungar, 1972; 1919), 289.

18. This is what Maimonides understood by "testing, purifying and whitening."

19. See my *Monotheism* I.

20. 1 Samuel 8:11–14, 18; Deuteronomy 17:14 ff., with Abarbanel; cf. 3 Maccabees 3:19; Testament of Job 7; 1 Kings 10:9, Zechariah 9:9. Ibn Gabirol, *Mivhar ha-Penimim* nos. 366, 370; Eric Voegelin, *Israel and Revelation*, 242–48; cf. 397. Mendelssohn, *Jerusalem*, trans. A. Arkush (Hanover, N.H.: University Press of New England/Brandeis, 1983; Berlin, 1783), 132.

21. For the tensions between personal and political messianism, see Talmon, 2.272–78.

22. *The Memoirs of Glückel of Hameln* III 2, trans. M. Lowenthal, (New York: Schocken, 1977; 1932), 45–47.

23. Gershom Scholem, *Sabbatai Sevi, The Mystical Messiah*, trans. R. J. Zwi Werblowsky (Princeton: Princeton University Press, 1973), 203–325.

24. Cf. Gustave Gottheil in *Judaism at the World's Parliament of Religions* (Cincinnati: Union of American Hebrew Congregations, 1894), 32: "as one of the Talmudists distinctly taught, 'Messiah's days are from Adam until now.'"

25. See Jeremiah 4:4, 24:8; Deuteronomy 30:6; cf. Joseph Sarachek, *The Doctrine of the Messiah in Medieval Jewish Literature* (New York: Jewish Theological Seminary, 1932), 37–39, 67.

26. Ibn Verga, *Shevet Yehudah* (1550), ed. M. Wiener (Hanover, 1855), no. 7, p. 21.

27. Cf. Ezekiel 28:25, 37:25; Isaiah 41:8, 9, 42:1, 8.

28. Maimonides, *Guide* II 36; "Eight Chapters," 7.

29. Maimonides, *Guide* III 32.

30. Maimonides, *Guide* III 31.

31. Cf. Ibn Ezra; Sarachek, 169.

32. Cf. Maimonides' *Code, Hilkhot Melakhim* 4.10 and 7.15, quoting Deuteronomy 20:3 and Jeremiah 48:10. Cf. David Novak, "Non-Jews in a Jewish Polity: Subject or Sovereign," in Jacob Neusner, Ernest Frerichs, and Nahum Sarna, eds., *From Ancient Israel to Modern Judaism: Intellect in Quest of Understanding—Essays in Honor of Marvin Fox* (Atlanta: Scholars Press, 1989), 23. Reflecting on the military and civil obligations of the Maimonidean king, Novak glosses sagely: "Maimonides correlates the dignity of human beings with the honour of God. . . . Without this ever present consideration in sight, the human concern for the furtherance of religious goals degenerates into bloody fanaticism. In fact, without this emphasis on human dignity, the honour of God is not enhanced but, rather, disgraced. As Maimonides noted [*Hilkhot Shabbat* 2.2], the *Torah* was not given to be 'vengeance in the world but as mercy, kindness and peace in the world.'" See "Maimonides and the Science of the Law," *Jewish Law Association Studies* 4 (1990): 130–31. We should not, of course, be overly apologetic about the fact that a military role is assigned to the messiah. In some wars it is criminal not to fight. It was criminal of the United States to fail to wage war against Hitler until attacked by his ally; even more so of Stalin to sign a pact with him.

33. Trans. Boaz Cohen, in A. Halkin, ed., "The Letter to Yemen" (New York: American Academy for Jewish Research, 1952), repr. in *Crisis and Leadership: Epistles of Maimonides* (Philadelphia: Jewish Publication Society, 1985), 115.

34. Letter to Yemen, in Halkin, repr., 120; cf. R. Samuel b. R. Naḥmani, Sanhedrin 97b.

35. Maimonides, "Letter to Yemen," Halkin repr., 123–30.

36. See Sarachek, 174.

37. Here follows the passage cited above in note 16.

38. Cf. Naḥmanides, *Disputation* no. 78, trans. Chavel (New York: Shilo, 1978), 2.685.

39. Maimonides, *Guide* II 45.

40. Maimonides glosses miracles like the ready baked bread of the messianic age as emblems of prosperity; on Mishnah Sanhedrin X.

41. Cf. Nahmanides *Disputation* 73, Chavel, 2.684.

42. Cf. M. J. Goodman and L. E. Goodman, *The Sexes in the Human Population* (Los Angeles: Gee Tee Bee, 1984), 92–118.

43. Saadiah, *Emunot ve-De'ot* X 4.1: and my "Saadiah's Ethical Pluralism," *Journal of the American Oriental Society* 100 (1980): 409.

44. Cf. Cohen, *Religion of Reason*, 280, citing Ezekiel 11:15–17, 19.

45. Gershom Scholem, *The Messianic Idea in Judaism and Other Essays on Jewish Spirituality* (New York: Schocken, 1971), 1–36.

46. Philosophic messianism like that of Maimonides "can claim no value as a truthful representation of the historical reality of Judaism. For this denial of apocalypticism set out to suppress exceedingly vital elements in the realm of Judaism, elements filled with historical dynamism even if they combined destructive with constructive forces" (Scholem, 9, cf. 204, 209, 293).

47. Scholem's vision of history and historiography is a mirror image of the authoritarian vision of Toynbee: Rather than celebrate the races and civilizations that organized human labor to construct great feats of engineering and administration, Scholem follows the yearnings of an oppressed race, those who built the pyramids, not those who ordered them. History becomes the story of the overthrow of oppression rather than of its triumph. But in the course of valorizing his popular focus, Scholem overlooks Voegelin's subtler alternative to Toynbee's oppressive triumphalism: the awakening of history to the constructive work of the spirit, rather than of arms and bodies, the creation of a moral rather than a geometric order. The lasting achievement of civilization is not the monument of stone, as Voegelin showed exhaustively in *Order and History*, but the order worked by ideas. And the most enduring order of ideas is that which can withstand the test of criticism and the test cases of long and culturally varied historical experience. Here, in philosophy, we find an authenticity beyond the merely symptomatic authenticity of suffering and "the defenses of the imagination."

Scholem's monumental study of Shabtai Zvi and the Sabbatian movement is in one sense a chapter in the protohistory of Zionism, and all of Scholem's landmark work on Jewish mysticism is a prelude to that study, asking how the inner passivity against which Zionists rebelled was transformed to action. Scholem's answer, if we dare reduce it to a word, is that between the idea and the act falls the dream. Perhaps it was with reference to this precept that Cynthia Ozick called Scholem the ocean on which Freud's thoughts are whitecaps: Scholem becomes an interpreter of dreams—not to seek their realization, like Joseph, nor to exorcise them, like Freud, but to find within their memory the seeds of a recognizable present. His historiography, with all its *wissenschaftlich* apparatus, is a science of dream interpretation; and it is in part for this reason, I suspect, that the central personages of his narrative appear to be somnambulists, acting out a role not of their own devising: Shabtai Zvi, his prophet Nathan, his wife, and many of his followers are figures who try to live out a dream. Having understood that, we can perceive their contrast with the Zionists as clearly as we can (with Scholem's aid) perceive their affinity. For Zionism is a daylight movement, public, exuberant, alive, and active, not on a theurgical but on a more patient and practical plane. When we say of the modern state of Israel that it is the "first budding of our redemption," we are not only renouncing the cult of personalities, which confuses the figures of myth with what they represent, but also renouncing dream substitutions of all kinds for active subjecthood in which we take responsibility intellectually and morally on the stage of history. For (as Jeremiah showed us) revolutionism as much as theurgy, even when it arrogates to itself the name of praxis, is a substitution of symbols for acts.

48. For the power of conceptual thematics to orient exegesis where traditionalism may fail, see my commentary to Saadiah's *Book of Theodicy*. Maimonides argues (*Guide* I 63) that criticism of any claim to prophetic knowledge should be expected. Bahya, whose spiritualism can be misread as anti-rationalism, shows that critical thought is a religious obligation: *Duties of the Heart*, trans. M. Mansoor (London: Routledge, 1973), 85–105.

49. See Scholem, 3.

50. Martin Buber, *For the Sake of Heaven*, trans. L. Lewisohn (New York: Meridian, 1958; Hebrew, *Gog and Magog*, 1943). The date speaks eloquently to the concerns of historical messianism, theodicy, and "pressing for the end" which provide the work's problematic.

51. See Scholem's *Sabbatai Ṣevi* (Princeton: Princeton University Press, 1973), 283–87, on "the Christian character of Nathan's religious terminology" as prophet of Shabtai Zvi: "There is no way of telling a priori what beliefs are possible or impossible within the framework of Judaism. Certainly no serious historian would accept the specious argument that the criteria of 'Jewish' belief were clear and evident until the kabbalah beclouded and confused the minds. The 'Jewishness' in the religiosity of any particular period is not measured by dogmatic criteria that are unrelated to actual historical circumstances, but solely by what sincere Jews do, in fact, believe, or—at least—consider to be legitimate possibilities" (283). All this is based on the lack of evidence of an "immediate rabbinic outcry" against Nathan's resort to Christian notions as early as 1666. Yet Scholem himself reports (286) that Jacob Sasportas responded to Nathan's Christianizing tendencies in the most violent language. Scholem's methodological standards are unexceptionable if they are to be taken, as he uses them, "as a guideline in the inquiry" in the study of Judaism as an object of natural history. The history of Baalism, the membership of the Hare Krishna movement, or the Supreme Soviet are equally proper topics in the history or sociology of Judaism and the Jewish people. But if Judaism is a conceptual system creating and requiring standards of continuity by which it may be identified (and without which its relations to other movements cannot even be discussed), one needs criteria that allow distinctions between Judaism and its aberrations or alternatives. Where historiography or sociology at times cannot afford to pass normative judgments, philosophy, at times, cannot afford to avoid them.

52. Song of Songs *Rabbah* II 7; cf. Ketubot 110a. If the "adjuration" applies to ʿ*aliyah*, R. Abraham of Sochaczew, ruled it not a *halakhic* oath. For, unlike the Covenant, it did not receive Israel's assent; see Ephraim E. Urbach, *The Sages* (Jerusalem: Magnes Press, 1975), 2.1002, n. 11.

53. Scholem, 14.

54. Elie Kedourie, "Arnold Toynbee and His Nonsense Book,'" *The New Criterion* 8:7 (March, 1990): 28–29, quoting Toynbee's *Reconsiderations* (1961).

55. Maimonides, "Eight Chapters," 4.

56. See Jacob Neusner, *Messiah in Context: Israel's History and Destiny in Formative Judaism* (Philadelphia: Fortress Press, 1984), 3, 20, 76, 92, 96, 163, 177, 184–86, 201–03, 211. Besides Sotah 9.15, see Berakhot 1.5. The messianic idea is not foreign to the Mishnah text.

57. Jacob Neusner, *A Life of R. Yohanan ben Zakkai*, 2d ed. (Leiden: Brill, 1970), 228–29.

58. Leo Landman, *Messianism in the Talmudic Era*, xxvi–xxvii.

59. *Tanḥuma Vaʾera* 6. Cf. Sanhedrin 97b.

60. Emil Fackenheim, *God's Presence in History* (New York: Harper and Row, 1972), 84–98.

6. WHEREAFTER?

1. Cf. Eric Voegelin, *Order and History* (Baton Rouge: Louisiana State University Press, 1956–), 1 *Israel and Revelation*, 57–58, 75, 99–100.

2. Cf. Erwin Rohde, *Psyche*, trans. W. B. Hillis (New York: Harper and Row, 1966; Heidelberg, 1893), for the nexus between immortality and divinity.

3. Maimonides, *Guide* III 32.

4. Holiness in Leviticus 19 and the Torah at large is not Otto's numinous or *mysterium tremendum*. It specifies and objectifies itself in laws that fuse it with morality and purge from its realm whatever will not cohere with human dignity and divine goodness—the values whose congruence was established in Genesis, where the relative perfections of humans are made a mirror of God's absolute perfection.

5. See my "The Biblical Laws of Diet and Sex," *Jewish Law Association Studies* 2 (Atlanta: Scholars Press, 1986).

6. See Northrop Frye, *The Secular Scripture* (Cambridge: Harvard University Press, 1976), 30, 43, 53, 57–58, 97–126.

7. Psalms 88:10–12, 6:5, 30:9, 115:17, 118:17; cf. Ecclesiastes 9:4–10.

8. See Saadiah, *The Book of Theodicy*, trans. L. E. Goodman (New Haven: Yale University Press, 1988), 242, 248, 325. The normal sense he gives the word is clearly naturalistic.

9. Genesis 25:8; cf. 15:15; 25:7; 35:29; 49:29, 33; Numbers 20:24, 26; 27:13; 31:2; Deuteronomy 32:50.

10. The Ikhwân al-Ṣafâ' note the dependence of tyrants on superstition; *The Case of the Animals versus Man*, trans. Goodman (Boston: Twayne, 1978), 175–76. The dependency exposes the insecurity of tyrannical minds whose fears and guilts people the darkness with unseen foes.

11. Job 3:19; cf. Psalms 49; 89:49; Ecclesiastes 2:14, 9:2; *Baba Kamma* 60a, *Sifre* 339 to Deuteronomy 32:50, ed. Friedman, 141a.

12. Job knows that his righteousness will be vindicated in the end by God but wants to see it for himself, while living, not after his kidneys—seat of the passions—have rotted away. Christian glossators seek attestation of a life after this life here, but as early as Chrysostom this approach was refuted as inconsistent with 14:12, etc.; cf. Marvin Pope, Anchor Bible, *Job*, 157; Solomon Freehof, *Book of Job: A Commentary* (New York: Union of American Hebrew Congregations, 1958), 147–48. As Edmund Sutcliffe observes, it is hard to derive Jerome's rendering from the Hebrew. Rather we must note "the admission made by St. Jerome that where the meaning of the prophecies has become plainer through their fulfillment, as in the case of the Messianic prophecies, he has made the prophecies themselves correspondingly plain. Towards the close of the preface to his translation of the Pentateuch he states explicitly that he translates Messianic passages in a more definite and clear sense than the Septuagint: 'They translated before the coming of Christ and put forth what they were ignorant of in ambiguous sentences, but we after His Passion and resurrection are writing a history rather than prophecy; what is heard is narrated in one way, what is seen in another. Where our understanding is better so is our exposition.' In principle, no doubt, this is correct. What is better understood can be better translated. But the condition of accuracy is that nothing be read into the Hebrew text which is not there, and this condition St. Jerome in his zeal for the correct understanding of Messianic prophecies sometimes disregarded . . . other examples justify the remark which Father Vaccari, S.J., makes about St. Jerome: '*Non raro textum plus aequo sollicitat, praesertim in locis Messianicis.*' . . . 'Not infrequently he worries a text more than is right, especially in Messianic texts.'" *The Old Testament and the Future Life* (London: Burns Oates, 1946) 131–33, citing *Institutiones Biblicae* (Rome, 1925) 1.202.

13. *Code* I, *Hilkhot Teshuvah* VIII 5; cf. Ibn Ṭufayl, Goodman, 153–54; and 163–64; "What weariness is heavier, what misery more overburdening,"; "the torture pavilion already encircled them, and the shadows of the veil already enshrouded them. . . ."

14. *De Principiis* III vi 6, ed. Koetschau, trans. G. W. Butterworth as *Origen on First Principles* (New York: Harper and Row, 1966; London, 1936), 251–52.

15. "The Will to Believe" began as a talk for the philosophy clubs of Yale and Brown, reflecting on Pascal's wager. Generalizing the argument, James opened truth to the claims of our psychic "needs" and interests. For the wager, see Ian Hacking, "The Logic of Pascal's Wager," *American Philosophical Quarterly* 9 (1972): 186–92.

16. See Maimonides, *Guide*, I 1, 36; cf. "Eight Chapters," 5.

17. *Code* I, *Hilkhot Teshuvah* VIII 6; cf. 7: What the imagination thinks of a pleasure is merely the counterpart of physical suffering or depletion, and it is for that reason that we cannot imagine and the prophets cannot represent to the imagination the conditions of a truly transcendent mode of being. Maimonides is aided to this thought by Râzî's analysis of pleasure. See my "Râzî's Psychology," *Philosophical Forum* 4 (1972): 26–48.

18. See Franz Kafka, "The Metamorphosis," trans. W. and E. Muir, in *The Complete Stories*, ed. N. Glatzer (New York: Schocken, 1971), 89–139.

19. See Gottfried Wilhelm Leibniz, *Discourse on Metaphysics* 34, in L. Loemker, *Leibniz: Philosophical Papers and Letters* (Dordrecht: Reidel, 1969), 325–26.

20. See E. R. Dodds, *The Greeks and the Irrational* (Berkeley: University of California Press, 1964), 102–15; cf. 193–95.

21. See John Locke, *An Essay Concerning Human Understanding*, II xxvii, 9–10, ed. Peter Niddich (Oxford: Clarendon Press, 1979; 1689), 335–36, for the requirement of continuous or at least continued memory if life after death is to have moral relevance; cf. Spinoza on the Spanish poet afflicted with amnesia, *Ethics* IV 39 scholium.

22. M. Takeyama, *Harp of Burma* (Rutland, Vt.: Tuttle, 1975; Tokyo, 1946).

23. Cf. Maimonides, *Code* I, *Hilkhot Teshuvah* 8.7: "For all the goods that the Prophets prophesied to Israel refer to corporeal things that Israel will enjoy in the days of the annointed king, when sovereignty returns to Israel. But the bliss of the life of *Olam ha-ba* has no comparison or image."

24. Leviticus 26:14–45, Deuteronomy 28:15–67; cf. 32:1–47.

25. Judah Halevi, *Kitâb al-Radd wa-'l-Dalîl fi '-Dîn al-Dhalîl* (The Book of Rebuttal and Evidence in Behalf of the Despised Religion, known as *The Kuzari* 3.20), ed. David Baneth (Jerusalem: Magnes Press, 1977), 110–12; trans. H. Hirschfeld as *An Argument for the Faith of Israel: The Kuzari* (New York: Schocken, 1964), 159–60; cf. my "Baḥyâ on the Antinomy of Free Will and Predestination, *Journal of the History of Ideas* 44 (1983) 128–30.

26. Ikhwân al-Ṣafâ', *The Case of the Animals versus Man*, trans. Goodman, 180.

27. For Spinoza, as Genevieve Lloyd writes, "the eternal intellect of God is more appropriately seen as the totality of all that is ever true, than as a totality of omnitemporal truths," "Spinoza's Version of the Eternity of the Mind," in M. Grene and D. Nails, eds., *Spinoza and the Sciences* (Dordrecht: Reidel, 1986), 211–31.

28. "Eight Chapters," 8, RAMBAM, 247, 259–61.

29. Maimonides, *Hilkhot Teshuvah* 8.8. This means that the idea of futurity in the rabbinic concept of *ʿolam ha-ba* pertains to the necessity of our embodiment, as a prerequisite. We are individuals through the temporality and the history that our embodiment bestows, and it is meaningless to speak of transcending embodi-

ment except in the case of what has been embodied. Here Maimonides dissolves one of the great conundrums bedeviling the idea of immortality from Plato to Averroes, the question of how *individuals* can enjoy immortality if the soul is immortal only insofar as it is intellectual, i.e., at one with the universal. Maimonides is aided by Avicenna and al-Ghazâlî's recognition that history sustains individuality on a spiritual level and by Saadiah's insistence that life in this world, with all the vulnerabilities that embodiment entrains, is the necessary precondition of any transtemporal reward.

30. This thesis is stated in Maimonides' "Eight Chapters," 5, where all our powers are enlisted in behalf of the knowledge of God, which will in turn inform our practical lives. It is demonstrated by the entire corpus of Maimonides' legal writings: the *Code, The Book of the Commandments*, and the *Commentary on the Mishnah*. Their aim, of discovering the rational principle of the *mitzvot*, is voiced in the motto of the *Code*: "Then shall I be unabashed to scrutinize all thy commandments" (Psalm 119:6). Cf. M. Kellner, *Maimonides on Human Perfection* (Atlanta: Scholars Press, 1990).

31. Albert Camus, *The Rebel*, trans. A. Bower (New York: Vintage, 1956; Paris, 1951); Masters and Johnson, *Homosexuality in Perspective* (Boston, 1979), 222–23; Goodman and Goodman, *Sex Differences in the Human Life Cycle*, 290–91.

32. Part of the beauty of Spinoza's idea of immortality is that it does not accept the Neoplatonic universalizing distaste for individuality but rides the Renaissance tide of nominalism and humanism to a reaffirmation of the moral and spiritual individual, who was the cynosure of biblical and rabbinic concern. Spinoza thus escapes drowning in the Romantic flood of "oceanic consciousness," which is all too widely equated with the whole of mysticism. See Genevieve Lloyd, "Spinoza's Version" and my "Determinism and Freedom in Spinoza, Maimonides, and Aristotle" in F. Schoeman, ed., *Responsibility, Character and the Emotions* (Cambridge: Cambridge University Press, 1987), 107–64.

33. Quoted in David Roberts, *Existentialism and Religious Belief* (New York, 1957), 247–48.

34. I list truth among the formal values because it mirrors the structure of reality in a symmetry, and its formal coherence reflects the formal order of reality.

35. See my essay, "Why Machines Cannot Do Science," in D. DeLuca, ed., *Essays on Creativity and Science* (Honolulu: Hawaii Council of Teachers of English, 1986).

36. See S. Rowe, "Athletic Sport as an Experience of Survival," Ph.D. diss., University of Hawaii, 1982.

INDEX OF PASSAGES

SCRIPTURAL

Index of Passages

♦

Plato

Crito

49	243 n. 16
50e	4, 16

Euthyphro, 99

Gorgias

468b	246 n. 24
475	111
504–05, 516,	
472–80	243 n. 16

Laches

199	206

Laws

631, 705d	246 n. 24
759	239 n. 35
862–63	243 n. 16

Phaedo, 210

Philebus

62	246 n. 24

Protagoras

324	243 n. 16

Republic, 104, 204, 210

335, 591	59
359b–369b	35, 237 n. 17
422	9
488	239 n. 35
522	210
557a	239 n. 35
564–68	236 n. 6

Seventh Letter

341–44	253 n. 11

Rashi

on Deuteronomy

11:14	251 n. 29
on Isaiah 52	168
on Sanhedrin 99a	166

Rawls, John

A Theory of Justice, 238 n. 25

256	239 n. 33

"Two Concepts
of Rules" 242 n. 9

Saadiah

Book of Theodicy, 252 n. 41, 43;
257 n. 48

242, 248, 325	258 n. 8
359–60	247 n. 43

Sefer ha-Nivhar ba-Emunot ve-De'ot

I	253 n. 11
IV	122
VII–IX	246 n. 34
VIII 8	254 n. 16
X 4	249 n. 66
X 4.1	256 n. 43
X 8	115

Shneor Zalman of Liadi
Likutei Torah,
on Deuteronomy

25a	246 n. 38

Spinoza, Baruch
Ethica, 116

I, Defs. 2, 5,	
Prop. 26	135
III Prop. 29,	
Schol.	103
III Prop. 56,	
Schol.	247 n. 42
IV Prop. 18	38

Arrow, Kenneth, 239n30
Art, 27, 40, 133, 229
Asceticism, 89, 115, 182
Athletics, 11, 229, 231–32
Auerbach, Erich, 106, 247n47
Augustine, 56, 115, 158
Authenticity, 93, 98, 158–60,
    183–85, 192, 229
Autonomy: moral, 78–79, 87–88,
    99–103, 203–04; political, 19, 34,
    166, 169, 176
Avarice, 2–3, 9, 107
Avicenna (Ibn Sînâ), 252n45, 261n29

Baal Shem Tov, Israel, 99
Bad faith, false consciousness, 98,
    135, 191
Baḥya Ibn Paquda 99, 133, 257n.48
Balaam, 171–72, 197
Bar Kokhba, 172
Barbu, Zevedi, 241n49
Bayles, Michael, 239n36
Beasts: deserts of, 8, 31, 40; figural,
    159, 177–78
Beauty, 229, 234
Beck, Lewis White, 96
Being: dynamic of, 71, 124–25,
    131–33, 151–54, 200, 213, 218;
    sanctity of, 29, 40, 54, 68, 164;
    wholeness of, 210
Bell, Graham, 244n14
Ben Azzai, Simeon, 116
Beneficium latronum, 2
Bentham, Jeremy: on punishment,
    49–50; on rewards, 93; on rights,
    31; on utopia, 34–35
Berlin, Isaiah, 245n20
Bergson, Henri, 86
Bestialism, 196, 236n4
Bias, 44–45, 79, 82, 89, 207
Bickel, Alexander, 13
Bilmes, Jack, 244n9

Biology, 83–85; succession, 123. *See
    also* Evolution; Ecosystems; Sexual
    reproduction
Blessing, 100, 106–07, 113–16, 130,
    137, 144, 176–80, 187–88, 194,
    200, 219–25
Bodies, 132, 201–04, 211, 218–20,
    225
Bosch, Hieronymus, 182
Boundlessness, 58, 120, 125, 208–10,
    232
Brooks, Roger, 237n14
Brown, Peter, 248n62
Buber, Martin: *For the Sake of Heaven*,
    185
Buchanan, Allen, 237n16, 238n26
Burke, Edmund, 100, 187
Burns, Robert: "A man's a man for a'
    that," 91

Camus, Albert, 224
Canaan, 111, 195
Castration, 67, 235n4
Categories: explanatory, 88; shifts of,
    211–12, 215; of understanding, 132
Causality, 69, 74, 79, 88, 122,
    150–54, 168
Cephalus, 104
Character, 29, 134, 137, 211; change
    of, 35, 69, 181. *See also* Ethos
Chelm, 75
Chimneying, 103
Choice, 21, 87, 189; of life, 100, 107,
    137
Christianity, 58, 90, 186
Cicero, 2, 57, 93, 158
Circle: virtuous, 190; vicious, 14–15,
    42, 79, 102, 111
Cities of Refuge, 43, 61, 107, 171,
    249n67
Civility, 42, 45, 64–66, 72–73, 105,
    161, 193

Good, 16, 32, 55, 77–78, 102, 110,
137, 150, 174–77, 233–34; and
being, 27, 141, 149, 151; doable,
90; life and 76, 81, 94, 103–16,
162, 175, 180, 188, 202, 210–13,
223
Goodin, Robert, 237n12
Gordis, Robert, 244n5, 253n1
Gottheil, Gustave, 254n24
Government, 17–19, 28, 34, 45–47,
66, 73, 104, 166, 176. *See also* State
Grace, 75, 125–31, 134, 153–54,
182, 220, 233
Graetz, Heinrich, 184
Graham, A. C., 238n22
Gratitude, 107, 226, 252n39
Grazia, Sebastian de, 241n49
Green, Martin, 247n39
Gregor Samsa, 212
Gressman, H., 252n1
Growth, 83, 87, 108, 111, 121, 125,
190, 200, 218, 227
Guarantee, 121, 128, 133, 142, 145,
149, 202
Guilt, 56, 150, 199; presumed, 127
Guttmacher, Manfred, 235n4

Habit, 9, 161, 177
Hadas, Moses, 245n22
Halevi, Judah, 167, 220, 260n25
Haman, 182
Hamas, 42, 114
Happiness, 77–78, 86, 97, 100,
110–11, 118; in Aristotle, 104; in
Kant, 81–82, 96; and the Law,
105–06
Hardin, Garrett, 20, 53
Harm, 28, 65, 83
Hasidism, 184
Hasmoneans, 206
Hayek, F. A., 238n27
Health, 5, 72, 238n26

Heaven, for the sake of, 99, 143, 203
Hedonism, 82–84, 95, 115; in after-
worlds, 207; transparency, 84, 247
n. 39
Helbo, R., 186–87
Hell, 207–09
Hen, 129
Herakles, 36
Hertz, J. H., 109, 143, 252n32
Heschel, A. J., 109
Hesed, 114, 129
Heteronomy, 82, 89, 98–103, 143,
203–04
Hezekiah, 164, 191
Hillel ben Gamaliel, R., 164, 166
Hillel the Elder, 6, 37
History, 41, 108, 112, 157–60, 165,
170, 174, 201–05; historicism,
184–85, 219
Hitler, Adolf, 72, 133, 166, 255n32
Hiyya, R., 180, 185
Hobbes, Thomas, 14, 31, 168, 203
Holism, 93, 136
Holocaust, 182, 191–92, 202
Holy, the, 104, 110–13, 138, 161,
174, 195, 221, 258n4; inurement
to, 227–28; and martyrdom, 117;
only upgraded, 114
Homeostasis, 213, 245n16
Homer, 165
Honor, 19, 29, 38, 52, 81, 100, 116,
205, 223; of parents, 149
Hope, 234; of Israel, 165–67
Humanity, 90–91; frailty of, 129,
195; image and sensibility of, 67, 73
Hume, David, 90, 159
Humility, 226
Hunger, 38, 89; imposition of, 53,
72, 134

I AM THAT I AM, 151, 153
I am the Lord, 8

220, 223–24; on obedience, 145; on power, 27; on utopia, 35

State, 34, 104, 166; prosecutor, 45–47, 66, 73; organic model of, 17

Stoics: on affirmation, 158; on duty, 91; on externals, 77–78, 87–88, 93, 99, the ideal in, 89

Stone, C. D., 241n52

Strauss, Leo, 237n13

Sturup, Georg K. 235n4

Subjecthood, 27, 40–41, 58, 63, 105, 108, 128; rational, 90; virtual, 40; and objecthood, 141, 212, 216

Success, 84, 94; biological or historical, 123

Suffering, 73, 84, 131, 138, 150, 191, 202, 211, 219

Suicide, 38, 77

Supererogation, 36, 143, 235n2

Supernatural, 75, 171

Superstition, 131, 172, 175, 197–99; and UFOs, 215

Sutcliffe, Edmund, 259n12

Suttee, 20

Symbols, 48, 117, 156–59, 167–69, 174–76, 185–88, 194, 209, 218–19, 234

Takeyama, Michiyo: *Harp of Burma*, 216–18

Talmon, J. L., 253n1, 254n21

Taoism, 91

Tarfon, R., 167, 193

Taylor, A. E., 237n19

Teaching, 176, 188, 194

Teilhard de Chardin, Pierre, 103, 129, 249n1

Teleology, 77–118; reductionist 86–90, 94, 99

Terrorism, 49, 56, 64, 72, 77, 105, 134, 175; state 45, 67

Tertullian, 158

Teshuvah, 53, 181

Tharâ, 198

Theology, 160, 211

Thieves, 66, 69, 126–27; forfeit trust, 57

Thoreau, Henry David, 130

Time, 122, 125–26, 132–34, 136–37, 154, 162, 167, 203, 209–10

Torah, 6, 29, 34–36, 39, 41, 45, 76, 90, 100, 105–112, 116, 121, 137, 141–50, 160, 162, 165, 173–74, 185, 188–93, 196–99, 221–23

Torture, 41, 50, 53, 67, 163, 206, 207–08

Toynbee, Arnold, 187, 256n47

Tradition, 137, 159, 187

Tragedy, 42, 59, 112

Transcendence, 32, 77, 101, 117, 162–64, 205–07, 212, 221–34

Transformation, moral and political, 114, 162, 165–70, 180–82, 186–89, 193, 215

Trial, 16, 26, 28, 43–45, 242n6

Trust, 16, 25, 29, 37–38, 57, 65–66, 72, 158

Truth, 80–81, 92, 130, 153, 230, 233–34; telling, 25, 64, 104–05

Tyranny, 9, 45, 52–53, 90, 135, 176, 186

Uniqueness, 40–41

Urbach, Ephraim. E., 242n6, 258n52

Utilitarianism, 49–54, 82, 94

Utopia, 9, 34–39, 161–62, 185–86, 189

Values, 27, 32, 150, 174; aesthetic, 229–30; and infinity, 233–34 integration of, 18–23, 33, 48, 82, 86,